Read Think Write

TRUE INTEGRATION THROUGH ACADEMIC CONTENT

REVEL™

BREAK THROUGH
To learning reimagined

Educational technology designed for the way today's students
read, **think**, and **learn**

When students are engaged deeply, they learn more effectively and perform better in their courses. This simple fact inspired the creation of REVEL: an immersive learning experience designed for the way today's students read, think, and learn. Built in collaboration with educators and students nationwide, REVEL is the newest, fully digital way to deliver respected Pearson content.

REVEL for Read Think Write enlivens course content with media interactives and assessments—integrated directly within the authors' narrative—that provide opportunities for students to read about and practice course material in tandem. This immersive educational technology boosts student engagement, which leads to better understanding of concepts and improved performance throughout the course.

An exceptional value, REVEL is more affordable than comparable print and digital options, and long-term access for students is part of the deal. Learn more about REVEL's pricing options at **www.pearsonhighered.com/REVEL**.

To order printed REVEL access code cards for your students, use the following ISBN: 0-13-409664-9.

Read Think Write

TRUE INTEGRATION THROUGH ACADEMIC CONTENT

David Rothman
Queensborough Community College

Jilani Warsi
Queensborough Community College

PEARSON

Boston   Columbus   Indianapolis   New York   San Francisco
Amsterdam   Cape Town   Dubai   London   Madrid   Milan   Munich   Paris   Montreal   Toronto
Delhi   Mexico City   São Paulo   Sydney   Hong Kong   Seoul   Singapore   Taipei   Tokyo

Executive Editor: Matthew Wright
Program Manager: Eric Jorgensen
Executive Development Editor: Gillian Cook
Product Marketing Manager:
Jennifer Edwards
Digital Editor: Kara Noonan
Media Producer: Alex Brown
Content Specialist: Annette Fantasia
Project Manager: Shannon Kobran

**Project Coordination, Text Design, and
Electronic Page Makeup:** Lumina Datamatics
Program Design Lead: Heather Scott
Cover Art: Zadorozhnyi Viktor/Shutterstock
Senior Manufacturing Buyer: Roy L.
Pickering, Jr.
Printer/Binder: R. R. Donnelley/Willard
Cover Printer: Lehigh-Phoenix Color/
Hagerstown

Acknowledgments of third-party content appear below appear on the appropriate page within text or on pages 473–476.

Pearson, Always Learning, Revel, and MySkillsLab are exclusive trademarks owned by Pearson Education, Inc. or its affiliates in the United States and/or other countries.

Unless otherwise indicated herein, any third-party trademarks that may appear in this work are the property of their respective owners and any references to third-party trademarks, logos, or other trade dress are for demonstrative or descriptive purposes only. Such references are not intended to imply any sponsorship, endorsement, authorization, or promotion of Pearson's products by the owners of such marks, or any relationship between the owner and Pearson Education, Inc., or its affiliates, authors, licensees, or distributors.

The Library of Congress Cataloging-in-Publication Data is available at the Library of Congress.

1 2 3 4 5 6 7 8 9 10—RRD—19 18 17 16

www.pearsonhighered.com

Student ISBN 10: 0-13-409664-9
Student ISBN 13: 978-0-13-409664-3
A la Carte ISBN 10: 0-13-411462-0
A la Carte ISBN 13: 978-0-13-411462-0

Brief Contents

Detailed Contents

Chapter 6 Education   210

Preface

The Philosophy of *Read Think Write*

Read Think Write is an integrated reading-writing text that offers a meaningful, content-driven experience for students. This is a text that does not simply throw together some key features of traditional writing and reading texts, but rather celebrates the reciprocal, response relationship of reading and writing. Clearly, reading is the food for writing, and writing is enriched by exposure to vast amounts of reading. It is no surprise that most prolific writers also tend to be compulsive readers. For our purposes, the integrated approach ensures that students are given the opportunity to follow the organic path from reading, reflecting on what they have read, to exploring their thoughts in writing. In addition, integration does not stop after students write their first draft. In fact, integration is further extended as students think about what they have written, revise their preliminary draft, and read more for reference and cite other works. So, our book is about *Read Think Write* and *Write Think Read*.

Each chapter of *Read Think Write* focuses on an academic discipline (e.g., psychology, business, health) and weaves a narrative rich in reading, reflection on ideas, and written responses. Our goal with the chapter narratives is to take students on a journey that resembles the journey they will take when they encounter their 100-level content class curricula. The integration of reading and writing plays out organically. Students have the opportunity to discuss preview questions to build their interest in a number of issues raised in each academic area. They then share their reactions to some of these provocative questions in writing on a blog feature aptly named The Wall. Students interact with discipline-specific terminology to build their academic vocabulary. They are given a chapter essay question to think about and delve into the chapter readings with the understanding that they will need to integrate some ideas from these readings into their chapter essay. Moreover, the chapter readings are further utilized to illustrate such key reading skills as making inferences, identifying the topic and main idea, and recognizing key patterns of organization within a text.

The chapter journey continues with a free-writing activity in response to a thought-provoking quote related to the academic discipline. Later on, students are asked to write a summary of a chapter reading of their choice and to find a video clip related to the chapter theme; both activities serve to deepen their understanding of the chapter content. Finally, after interacting with a variety of input (readings and video), and some output (short writing activities), students are better equipped to compose their chapter essay. The figure below illustrates the integrated journey students will take in each chapter.

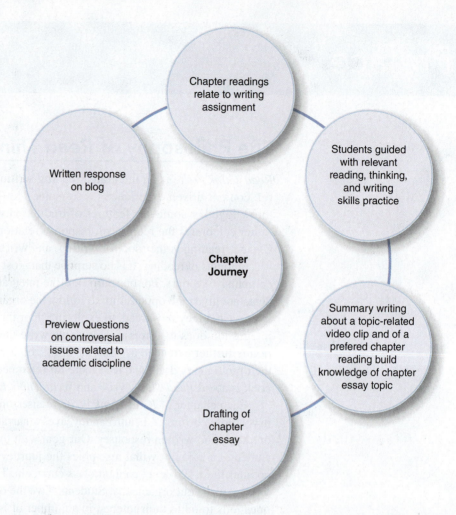

This is true integration in action! Foundational reading and writing skills are woven into the students' journey and serve as important tools to guide their understanding and smoothen their paths as they make their way through the reading and writing process. If you examine the Table of Contents, you will see how reading and writing skills are aligned and build on each other from chapter to chapter. So, in Chapter 3, for example, while the reading focus is on determining topic and main idea, the writing focus is on creating a thesis statement (an essay's main point). In Chapter 4, the reading-writing focus is on recognizing and writing topic sentences. In Chapter 8, the reading-writing focus is on recognizing patterns of organization and choosing appropriate patterns to match a given writing assignment.

Four Critical Goals of *Read Think Write*

Read Think Write was conceived from the idea that four critical goals for an integrated reading-writing text could be realized within a thematic, content-based approach. At the forefront of our vision is the understanding that developmental readers and writers must be fully engaged in stimulating content as they acquire the college reading and writing skills that are key to their academic success. This multifaceted approach motivates students to become active readers and more comfortable with the task of reacting to text in written form. It also prepares them for reading and writing across the academic disciplines, builds their academic vocabulary through heavy reading exposure and writing usage, and last, but certainly not least, cultivates their critical-thinking skills by giving them multiple opportunities to reflect on provocative, contemporary issues.

Here is a brief description of the four primary goals of *Read Think Write*:

- **To encourage active reading and writing in response to text.** *Read Think Write* strives to motivate students to become active readers and active writers by fostering intellectual inquiry through the exploration of contemporary themes related to the most popular academic disciplines. If students' curiosity is sparked, there is no stopping them! Working with this text, students will have ample opportunity to read stimulating articles on controversial topics and to integrate some of what they have understood from these readings into their chapter essays. They will also have significant opportunities to respond to text, whether it be in the form of reacting to classmates' postings on The Wall blog, summarizing a theme-related video clip they have chosen online, summarizing one of the chapter readings, or developing their chapter essay, which draws from the themes of the chapter readings.

- **To prepare students for reading and writing across academic disciplines.** *Read Think Write* helps prepare students for the challenges of the 100-level survey courses that lie just around the corner. The text chapters cover a wide array of academic disciplines (psychology, sociology, business, health, literature, criminal justice, and more). This exposure to a variety of readings, involvement in discussions of contemporary topics in each academic field, practice with discipline-specific terminology, online research on famous people in each field, and opportunities to debate and share written responses on these themes gives students a valuable edge in their academic preparation. Moreover, many students in the developmental stage of their college careers have not decided on their majors, and reading and writing across the curriculum introduces them to the most popular academic disciplines and gives them a chance to explore potential areas of academic interest.

- **To build academic vocabulary through reading exposure and writing usage.** In *Read Think Write*, students build their academic vocabulary through exposure to thematic readings and discipline-specific terminology. Vocabulary terms included in the discipline-specific word bank, which students practice with at the beginning of the chapter, are highlighted in green the first time they appear in chapter readings, and other key terms emphasized in specific readings are highlighted in bold.

Vocabulary development is reinforced through active usage of new words in written form. Students are encouraged to work with new vocabulary terms as they blog with other students on academic content, write summaries of chapter readings, and develop their chapter essays. This heavy emphasis on vocabulary building makes it unnecessary for students to work with an additional vocabulary text.

- **To cultivate critical thinking skills through reflection on provocative, contemporary issues.** It is our belief that college students most effectively develop their reading and writing skills when they are given the chance to express themselves, to bounce ideas off each other and to weigh in on relevant contemporary issues. For instance, in Chapter 2 on psychology, students are asked to consider if human behavior can be changed; in Chapter 3 on criminal justice, they are left to ponder whether the police fulfill their promise to "protect and serve" their communities; and in Chapter 9 on business, students reflect on the question of whether business and ethics can truly coexist.

  When students' interest and curiosity are piqued, they do more focused reading and invest more in developing their written responses. Students are given guidelines and practice with such critical-thinking skills as evaluating the relevance of Web sites, asking pertinent questions as they read, assessing the validity of an author's argument, and considering the strength of their own arguments.

Content Overview

Read Think Write is organized into ten chapters. The first chapter serves as an introduction to the reading, thinking and writing processes and offers a detailed discussion of the features of the text. The nine chapters that follow each focus on a different academic discipline, from psychology in Chapter 2 to sociology in Chapter 10, and each culminates with an essay assignment that asks students to integrate ideas from the chapter readings.

Special Chapter Features of *Read Think Write*

- **Introduction to the Field:** Includes an introduction to the academic discipline and a brief account of the selections students will be reading.

- **Previewing Questions:** Students are asked to discuss four to five provocative questions related to the given academic discipline. This is a way for students to share what they already know about each academic field.

- **Writing on The Wall:** The Wall is an interactive platform where students can post written responses and read and respond to the ideas of their classmates.

- **Discipline-specific Word Bank:** This section contains ten discipline-specific terms culled from the chapter reading selections. Students are asked to interact with this vocabulary through synonym-antonym work and integration of key terms in their chapter essay.

- **Success in Reading:** This feature focuses on a specific reading strategy to enable students to become more fluent readers.

- **Chapter Reading Selections:** Each chapter contains three highly engaging readings, which relate to the theme of the chapter. Each reading includes both pre-reading and post-reading activities.

- **Writing Without Boundaries: There Are No Checkpoints!** Students are given ten minutes to respond in writing to a famous person's quote related to the chapter's discipline.

- **Reading Skill Focus:** A new college reading skill is introduced briefly in each chapter along with practice exercises. Chapter readings serve as instructional content for each of these reading skills. Throughout the text, reading skills are aligned with related writing skills.

- **Think to Write:** In this feature, students are asked to consider which of the three chapter readings is most interesting to them. Their task is to write a paragraph response about their chosen reading and to post it to The Wall.

- **It's Showtime!** Students are asked to find a video link that ties into one of the chapter readings, and to write a half-page summary of the video's key points.

- **Writing Skill Focus:** This section introduces students to a key writing skill in each chapter. There is a strong focus on the writing process, and these skills often intersect with the chapter's reading skill focus.

- **Trouble Spot in Writing:** This feature focuses on a different writing/ grammar trouble spot in each chapter.

- **Then and Now:** In this section, students are asked to do Internet research to gather information about two experts in the chapter's given discipline: one from the past and another contemporary.

- **Virtual Scavengers:** This feature provides students with the opportunity to do Internet research on a milestone document in the discipline.

- **Chapter Essay Assignment:** Each chapter concludes with the Chapter Essay assignment. Students are alerted to the topic of each chapter's essay early on, so that they can organize their essay plan as they make their way through the chapter. The chapter essay topic directly relates to the themes covered in the chapter readings. In fact, students are required to source at least one of the chapter readings in their essay.

- **Focus on Form:** This feature offers students additional grammar-focused practice with an editing exercise reemphasizing the writing/grammar trouble spot highlighted earlier in the chapter. The students are then asked to apply their editing skills to the chapter essay they have just written.

- **Chapter Debate Option:** Each chapter concludes with a debate option related to the chapter essay assignment. These collaborative activities give students the opportunity to put the some of the ideas they have been reading and writing about into action!

Book-Specific Ancillary Materials

Annotated Instructor's Edition for *Read Think Write: True Integration Through Academic Content*, 1/e

ISBN: 0134127390

The Annotated Instructor's Edition (AIE) is a replica of the students' text that includes answers to the activities and exercises.

Instructor's Resource Manual (Download Only) for *Read Think Write: True Integration Through Academic Content*, 1/e

ISBN: 0134127412 / 9780134127415

The material in the IRM is designed to save instructors time and provide them with effective options for teaching their integrated reading and writing classes. It provides lots of extra practice and quizzes for students who need it and offers sample syllabai for various course settings. This valuable resource is exceptionally useful for adjuncts who might need advice in setting up their initial classes or who might be teaching a variety of classes with too many students and not enough time.

PowerPoint Presentation (Download only) for *Read Think Write: True Integration Through Academic Content*, 1/e

ISBN: 0134127366 / 9780134127361

PowerPoint presentations to accompany each chapter consist of classroom-ready lecture outline slides, lecture tips and classroom activities, and review questions. Available for download from the Instructor Resource Center.

Answer Key (Download only) for *Read Think Write: True Integration Through Academic Content*, 1/e

ISBN: 0134127374 / 9780134127378

The Answer Key contains the solutions to the exercises in the student edition of the text. Available for download from the Instructor Resource Center.

Test Bank (Download only) for *Read Think Write: True Integration Through Academic Content*, 1/e

ISBN: 0134127382 / 9780134127385

This resource contains lots of questions for each chapter in the book.

Revel for *Read Think Write* by Rothman/Warsi

REVEL is Pearson's newest way of delivering our highly respected content to students. Fully digital and highly engaging, REVEL offers an immersive learning experience designed for the way today's students read, think, and learn. Enlivening course content with media interactives and assessments, REVEL empowers educators to increase engagement with the course like never before.

Video and Rich Multimedia Content

Videos, audio recordings, animations, and multimedia instruction provide context that enables students to engage with the text in a more meaningful way.

Interactive Readings, Exercises and Effective Activities

Integrated within the textbook content, interactive multimedia elements and videos empower students to engage with concepts and take an active role in learning. REVEL's unique presentation of media as an intrinsic part of course content brings concepts to life and enlivens instructional material. REVEL's media interactives have been designed to be completed quickly, and its videos are brief, so students stay focused and on task.

Just-in-Time Context

Just-in-time context—encompassing brief quizzing, scroll-over key terms, reading comprehension, and open ended questions—is incorporated throughout, giving students an opportunity to meaningfully interact with the content and understand what they read.

Integrated Writing Assignments

Minimal-stakes, low-stakes, and high-stakes writing tasks allow students multiple opportunities to complete reading and writing assignments, leading to better class preparation and participation.

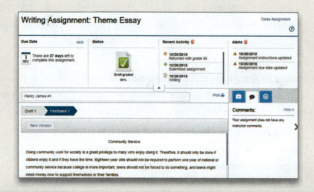

MySkillsLab®: Improve Basic Reading and Writing Skills Through Personalized Learning

In an ideal world, an instructor could sit with each student to discuss reading and writing skills and give individual direction. Without that luxury, MySkillsLab can provide students with personalized and adaptive instruction, with integrated learning aids that foster student understanding of skills and ideas.

Flexible and Personalized Learning

MySkillsLab can be set up to fit your specific course needs, whether you seek reading and writing support to complement what you do in class, a way to administer many sections easily, or a self-paced environment for independent study.

Learning in Context

In addition to distinct pre-loaded learning paths for reading/writing skills practice and reading level practice, MySkillsLab incorporates numerous activities for practice and readings from the accompanying textbook.

Quantifiable Student Performance

The online gradebook in MySkillsLab allows you to see a full range of performance data from individual students to an entire course. Instructors can also identify common mistakes in student work and tailor their teaching accordingly.

NEW! Learning Tools for Student Engagement

Create an Engaging Classroom

Learning Catalytics is an interactive, student-response tool in MySkillsLab that uses students' smartphones, tablets, or laptops, allowing instructors to generate class discussion easily, guide lectures, and promote peer-to-peer learning with real-time analytics.

Build Multimedia Assignments

MediaShare allows students to post multimodal assignments easily for peer review and instructor feedback. In both face-to-face and online courses, MediaShare enriches the student learning experience by enabling contextual feedback to be provided quickly and easily.

Direct Access to MyLab

Users can link from any Learning Management System (LMS) to Pearson's MySkillsLab. Access MyLab assignments, rosters and resources, and synchronize MyLab grades with the LMS gradebook.

Visit www.myskillslab.com for more information.

Acknowledgements

Many dedicated individuals have contributed to *Read Think Write* and it would have been impossible for us to complete the book without their guidance and much-needed support. First and foremost, we wish to thank our reviewers, who offered their valuable suggestions for improvement during the course of writing our book:

Amy Boltrushek, *Richland College*

Susan E. Bowling, *University of Arkansas at Little Rock*

Deborah Davis, *Richland College*

Leah Deasy, *SUNY Jefferson*

Supriya Draviam, *Cuyahoga Community College*

Genevieve Dibua, *Baltimore City Community College*

Barbara S. Doyle, *Arkansas State University*

Kelly Edmondson, *Cincinnati State Technical and Community College*

Jennifer Ferguson, *Cazenovia College*

Adam Floridia, *Middlesex Community College*

Terese Francis, *Doane College*

Laura B. Girtman, *Tallahassee Community College*

Cynthia M. Gomez, *Hodges University*

Karen W. Hackley, *Houston Community College, Spring Branch*

Barbara Hampton, *Rend Lake College*

Annaliese Hausler-Akpovi, *Modesto Junior College*

We owe special thanks to Matthew Wright, our acquisitions editor, for his vision, support and encouragement. We are incredibly thankful to Gill Cook, our development editor, and sorceress in disguise, for working her magic time after time to make our work shine. We also would like to thank our production team of Eric Jorgensen and Shannon Kobran at Pearson and Cathy Castle at Lumina. Last but not least, Jilani Warsi would like to thank Shabana, his life partner, for her patience, understanding, and constant support throughout the writing of this book. David Rothman would like to thank Zlati, Sophia, and Miro for putting up with him during the writing process. We are greatly indebted to all of these individuals who made *Read Think Write* a reality.

Sincerely,

David Rothman and Jilani Warsi

1 Introduction to *Read Think Write*

IN THIS CHAPTER, YOU WILL LEARN TO . . .

1 Understand the philosophy guiding this textbook

2 Recognize the interrelationship among reading, thinking, and writing

3 Read actively and effectively

4 Think critically about what you read

5 Use the writing process to communicate clearly

6 Use the chapter features in this text to learn and develop new skills

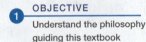
OBJECTIVE
Understand the philosophy
guiding this textbook

The Philosophy of *Read Think Write*

Welcome to the integrated world of three siblings without rivalry: reading, thinking, and writing! We often overlook the simple fact that everything we read was thought about and written by someone. If you reflect on it, reading and writing are mirror images that complement each other and both require critical thinking. However, it is also important to consider that reading and writing involve somewhat different processes.

Examine the two photos below and answer the questions that follow:

1. What similarities do you see between the two processes illustrated?

   _____

   _____

   _____

2. What differences do you see between the two processes?

   _____

   _____

   _____

3. How are these two processes interrelated?

   _____

   _____

   _____

   _____

EXERCISE 1.1   Reading, Thinking, Writing Survey

Directions: Explore the universe of reading, thinking, and writing by conducting the following survey with three of your new classmates. Be sure to record their responses to each of the survey questions.

Question	Respondent 1	Respondent 2	Respondent 3
1. Which activity do you prefer, reading or writing, and why?			
2. What types of reading do you enjoy?			
3. Beyond the written word, what forms of media inform your world (music/video/movies/TV/Internet)? Explain.			
4. Which process (reading or writing) involves a higher level of critical thinking? Explain.			
5. What do you find most difficult about composing an essay?			
6. What are the characteristics of a good reader and good writer?			
7. In what ways do reading, thinking, and writing influence each other?			

Note: Save the results of your reading/writing survey. You will be asked to compare your classmates' responses for a short writing assignment in Chapter 3.

How *Read Think Write* Works

Let's cut to the chase! Life is short, and you want to reach your academic goals as smoothly and as efficiently as possible. Rather than have chapters that are named after specific reading and writing skills (such as main idea, making inferences, post-writing revision, thesis statement, and so on), *Read Think Write* is thematically organized so that each chapter focuses on a popular academic discipline such as Psychology, Business, Criminal Justice, and Nursing. This approach is based on the logic that reading, thinking, and writing are not discrete skills, but rather evolve from their interplay. In other words, the act of reading leads to the act of thinking, and writing is a way to express your thoughts on what you have read.

Each chapter will take you on an academic journey and challenge you with activities rich in reading, self-expression and written response. You will discuss provocative questions related to each particular academic discipline and share your ideas with your classmates on a blog (you will think about ideas/write responses/and read and respond to your peers' postings). There will be a strong focus on building your academic vocabulary through exposure to reading and practice exercises. You will be given an interesting chapter essay question to think about and will begin reading the discipline-focused chapter readings with the understanding that you will need to integrate some ideas from these readings into your chapter essay (again *reading* to *thinking* to *writing*!). Key reading and writing skills are integrated into your journey and will help guide your understanding of the reading and writing process.

You will also journey deeper into each academic area; searching online for a video clip related to a chapter reading topic, free-writing in response to a thought-provoking quote related to the academic area and writing a summary of your favorite reading in the chapter. As you near the end of each chapter, you will be able to put your knowledge into action and compose your chapter essay. This is a true integration of Reading, Thinking, and Writing!

EXERCISE 1.2   Getting Your Feet Wet: Focus on Academic Disciplines

Directions: Take a glance at the nine disciplines listed in the table below that provide the content for the chapters in this book. Work with a partner to determine each discipline's focus and its application in the real world, and then jot down your main ideas. The first one is completed for you as an example.

Discipline	Focus	Application	Preference 1 to 9
Psychology	How the mind works, Human nature	Psychiatry, Counseling, Social work, Therapy	
Criminal Justice			
Environmental Science			
Literature			
Education			
Health/Nutrition			
Nursing			
Business			
Sociology			

If you are a careful reader and pay attention to detail, you may have noticed the fourth column on the right side of the table. Consider which disciplines most pique your interest, and rate them on a scale of 1 to 9 in the right column. When you are finished, discuss your preferences with your classmates.

Visual Road Map of *Read Think Write:* *A True Integration of Skills*

Carefully examine Figure 1.1: A Visual Road Map of *Read Think Write* with a classmate.

FIGURE 1.1 A Visual Road Map of *Read Think Write*

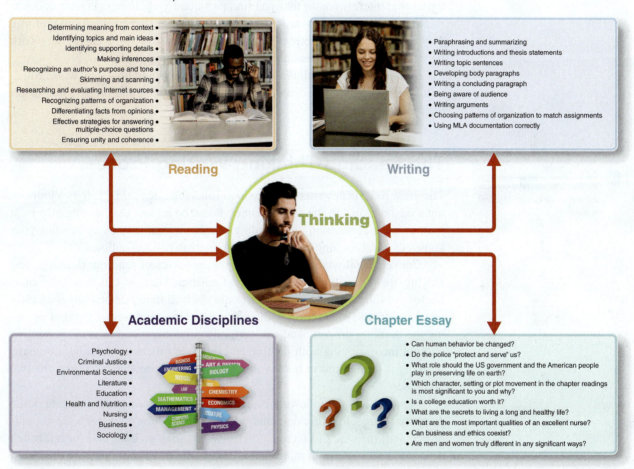

Reading

- Determining meaning from context
- Identifying topics and main ideas
- Identifying supporting details
- Making inferences
- Recognizing an author's purpose and tone
- Skimming and scanning
- Researching and evaluating Internet sources
- Recognizing patterns of organization
- Differentiating facts from opinions
- Effective strategies for answering multiple-choice questions
- Ensuring unity and coherence

Writing

- Paraphrasing and summarizing
- Writing introductions and thesis statements
- Writing topic sentences
- Developing body paragraphs
- Writing a concluding paragraph
- Being aware of audience
- Writing arguments
- Choosing patterns of organization to match assignments
- Using MLA documentation correctly

Thinking

Academic Disciplines

- Psychology
- Criminal Justice
- Environmental Science
- Literature
- Education
- Health and Nutrition
- Nursing
- Business
- Sociology

Chapter Essay

- Can human behavior be changed?
- Do the police "protect and serve" us?
- What role should the US government and the American people play in preserving life on earth?
- Which character, setting or plot movement in the chapter readings is most significant to you and why?
- Is a college education worth it?
- What are the secrets to living a long and healthy life?
- What are the most important qualities of an excellent nurse?
- Can business and ethics coexist?
- Are men and women truly different in any significant ways?

EXERCISE 1.3 Summation of Visual Road Map

Directions: Based on your examination of the Visual Road Map and the information you have just read about how the chapters work, try to explain the flow of *Read Think Write* in sentence form. Imagine you are trying to market this text to a college professor.

When you are done writing, discuss what you have written with a classmate.

_____

_____

_____

_____

How Chapter 1 of *Read Think Write* Works

As well as introducing the philosophy of the text, this chapter includes a brief overview of the reading, thinking, and writing processes to give you the tools to hit the ground running in Chapter 2 and beyond. Page references are provided so that you can access the more detailed instruction on each topic that appears in later chapters. You may want to jump ahead and read more about topics that interest you or that you find particularly challenging (such as determining an author's purpose, writing a summary, or using transitions), or you may use the chapter to refresh your memory or to give you a basic framework on which to build your reading, thinking, and writing skills.

Chapter 1 also lists all the main chapter features and how they work, which will help familiarize you with the structure of the book and prepare you to get the most out of it.

OBJECTIVE

Explore the interrelationships among reading, thinking, and writing

The Reading-Thinking-Writing Process

The great American writer Ralph Waldo Emerson once said, "Life is a journey, not a destination." In the same manner, it can be argued that writing also is "a journey, not a destination," and reading enlightens your journey by building your knowledge and opening doors to a world of creative imagination.

Conventional wisdom has it that the processes of reading, thinking, and writing are sequential and independent entities. Clearly, this is not the case. On the contrary, these three processes are cyclical in nature and are constantly overlapping and interacting with each other. One cannot read without applying the thinking process, and one certainly cannot respond to a text in writing without incorporating both reading and thinking processes. Last but not least, thinking is paramount to both reading and writing because it triggers the two processes.

Figure 1.2 on the following page illustrates the interdependent nature of the processes of reading, thinking, and writing. Notice how the arrows are not unidirectional; they are bidirectional because one may go back and forth through these processes. Keep in mind that although the three processes are presented separately here for the purpose of explication, they are not to be followed sequentially.

After reviewing Figure 1.2 and completing Exercise 1.4, take time to carefully review Figure 1.3: Steps in the Reading Process, Figure 1.4: Steps in the Writing Process, and Figure 1.5: Steps in the Writing Process to obtain a more detailed picture of the steps involved in order to be successful in applying each process to reading and writing.

FIGURE 1.2

The Interdependent
Nature of Reading,
Thinking, and Writing

EXERCISE 1.4 **Thinking About Reading, Thinking, and Writing**

Directions: Consider Figure 1.2 above. Think about ways in which you move back and forth between reading, thinking, and writing in school, work, and your personal life. Write down a few examples of where you use all three processes to achieve a goal. It can be as simple as writing a shopping list to working on a proposal in a work situation.

_____

_____

_____

FIGURE 1.3

Steps in the Reading Process

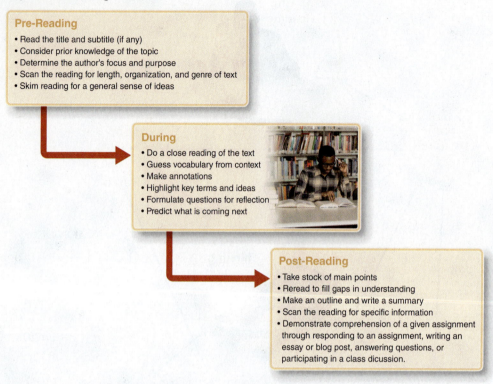

Pre-Reading
- Read the title and subtitle (if any)
- Consider prior knowledge of the topic
- Determine the author's focus and purpose
- Scan the reading for length, organization, and genre of text
- Skim reading for a general sense of ideas

During
- Do a close reading of the text
- Guess vocabulary from context
- Make annotations
- Highlight key terms and ideas
- Formulate questions for reflection
- Predict what is coming next

Post-Reading
- Take stock of main points
- Reread to fill gaps in understanding
- Make an outline and write a summary
- Scan the reading for specific information
- Demonstrate comprehension of a given assignment through responding to an assignment, writing an essay or blog post, answering questions, or participating in a class dicussion.

FIGURE 1.4

Steps in the Writing Process

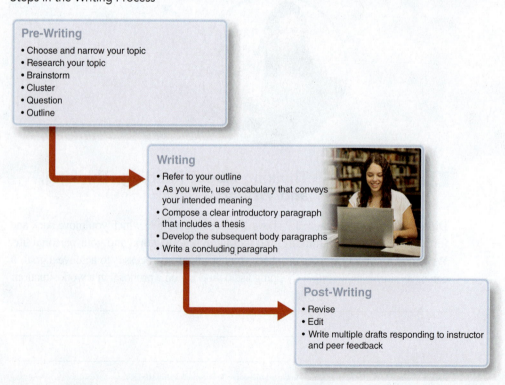

Pre-Writing
- Choose and narrow your topic
- Research your topic
- Brainstorm
- Cluster
- Question
- Outline

Writing
- Refer to your outline
- As you write, use vocabulary that conveys your intended meaning
- Compose a clear introductory paragraph that includes a thesis
- Develop the subsequent body paragraphs
- Write a concluding paragraph

Post-Writing
- Revise
- Edit
- Write multiple drafts responding to instructor and peer feedback

FIGURE 1.5

Steps in the Thinking Process

Observation

- Who wrote the text? What is their position, if mentioned?
- What is the main point of the text, namely the author's thesis?
- What evidence does the author give to support the main point/thesis?

Evaluation

- Is the evidence convincing? Why or why not?
- Does the evidence match the conclusions? If not, what might explain the mismatch?
- What other conclusions might be drawn?
- What other evidence might be offered to better support the claim, if any?
- Why might the author have left out evidence that could potentially change the meaning of the text?
- Is there anything in the language of the text, which indicates beliefs, feelings, and/or values, which help us understand why the author drew the particular conclusion(s)?
- What conclusions might we draw concerning the author's personal, political, and social positions?

Critical Response

- What is it about this text that interests me?
- Did I agree or disagree strongly with the author at any time during the course of reading the text? What specific parts of the text, if any, did I disagree with?
- Does the idea under consideration relate in any way to my own life or the lives of people I know? How so?
- Is there something I might gain or lose by agreeing with the conclusion of the author? What is the gain or loss?
- Do I share the values and beliefs of the author? If not, is this mismatch responsible for my judgment of the idea?

EXERCISE 1.5 **Comparing the Reading, Thinking, and Writing Processes**

Directions: Examine Figures 1.3, 1.4, and 1.5, and make a list of the similarities among the steps involved in the three processes.

Similarities: _____

_____

_____

EXERCISE 1.6   Contrasting the Reading, Thinking, and Writing Processes

Directions: Examine Figures 1.3, 1.4, and 1.5 and make a list of the differences among the steps involved in the three processes.

Differences: _____

_____

_____

_____

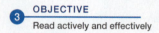
OBJECTIVE
③ Read actively and effectively

The Reading Process

The **reading process** consists of applying a variety of strategies before, during, and after reading that will increase your connection to and understanding of the content.

Pre-Reading

Before jumping head first into a reading, it is useful to get the lay of the land in terms of the topic covered in the reading, the author's focus and purpose, and how the text is organized. The following steps can be useful in preparing for a reading assignment.

Read the Title and Subtitle (If Any)

Many students rush into a college reading without paying attention to its title. The truth is that the title often says a lot about the direction of a given reading. Good readers can often predict the author's main idea by simply reading the title. For example, if the title of a sports article is "This Time It's a She Who Is Champion," most fluent readers can surmise that the championship was traditionally won by a male, but in this case it has been won by a female. In a similar manner, when you are wearing the hat of a writer, an important consideration is how your title reflects and indicates the content of your writing.

EXERCISE 1.7   Predicting a Reading's Main Idea from the Title

Directions: Read the following title with a partner and try to make some predictions about the main idea of the reading to which it belongs.

Title: There Is No Thanksgiving for the Native Americans

Your predictions:

1. _____

2. _____

3. _____

Consider Your Prior Knowledge of the Topic

Continuing with the previous example, once you understand from the title that the reading is about Native Americans, it is a natural step to consider how much you know about this topic. In other words, prior knowledge of a topic can help you grasp new information on the subject in focus. Fluent readers develop a knowledge base that enables them to better understand a given reading. Clearly, the more you read, the better reader you will become.

EXERCISE 1.8   Building on Prior Knowledge of a Topic

Directions: Working with the title you just examined, "There Is No Thanksgiving for the Native Americans," explore your prior knowledge of Native Americans and jot down a few notes on what you know about their culture.

1. _____

   _____

2. _____

3. _____

Determine the Author's Purpose

As you enter a reading, consider why the author wrote this particular piece. Some authors write to simply inform readers about a topic area. Some have the goal of persuading readers to agree with their point of view through argumentation, and others simply want to entertain readers with an amusing or dramatic narrative. Understanding an author's purpose will help you gain a general sense of the direction a reading is going. (Refer to Chapter 6, p. 233 for more information on the author's purpose and tone.)

Skim the Reading for Length, Organization, and Genre

Another strategy you can employ to effectively approach a new reading is to glance over the text before you read it in depth, paying attention to length, how information is organized, and the genre. For example, a poem may be divided into three stanzas and still be only half a page, whereas an excerpt from a textbook may run several pages and be organized by subtopics. (For information on different types of genre, see Chapter 8, page 300.)

Skim the Reading to Gain a General Sense of the Ideas It Contains

Before doing a close reading of a given text, skim through it to get the gist of the whole piece: what it is about, the author's main points, and so on. As with the previous strategy, skimming is effective for familiarizing yourself with the reading to come and helps you connect the new information to what you already know, which will increase your understanding and memory of what you read.

During Reading

Reading should be a pleasure, not a curse. If you make a conscious effort to focus on the task at hand, you may discover that reading can be an enjoyable experience. It may be counterproductive to discount a given reading simply because you have a preconceived notion that the subject matter is boring. You may be pleasantly surprised to find that the reading is engaging and builds on your knowledge base.

Do a Close Reading of the Text

Once you have taken a bird's-eye view of a reading passage, you are better prepared to read it. At this point, your goal is to obtain a deeper understanding of the full text. While many people assume that reading is a passive activity, the following active reading strategies will keep you engaged as you make your way through the text.

- **Guess vocabulary from context.** As you read, it is not realistic to look up every unfamiliar word in a dictionary. A more effective technique is to guess the meaning of new vocabulary items from the given context. Keep in mind that many words have multiple meanings, so pay attention to how a word is used in a sentence to zero in on the intended meaning. (For a detailed lesson on vocabulary in context, refer to Chapter 2, p. 51.)

- **Make annotations.** Active readers annotate a text for various reasons: sometimes they jot down the author's main points in the margin, and other times they simply make note of difficult terms and concepts. A good reader's book is usually quite marked up by the end of the semester! (For more on annotating, see Chapter 6, p. 217.)

- **Highlight key terms and ideas.** In addition to annotating, highlighting key ideas and terms is another effective reading strategy. As with annotating, a key advantage of highlighting is that it sets you up well to revisit the text at a later point, perhaps during a test review. You cannot expect to simply memorize where the key points were in a given reading and that is where highlighting comes into play. Make sure to choose bright highlighters and remember that highlighting can be used in conjunction with annotation. (For more on highlighting, see Chapter 6, p. 216.)

- **Formulate questions for reflection.** As you make your way through a reading, frame pertinent questions in the back of your mind for further reflection. Try not to be swayed too easily by the author's arguments. Instead, ask questions that test whether the claims an author makes are valid and if there are holes in his or her arguments.

- **Predict what is coming next.** Engaged readers make predictions about the direction an author is going based on what they have already read. As you digest ideas and information, it is natural that you will wonder what is coming next. For example, if you are reading a persuasive essay about why people should quit eating meat, you may predict some of the reasons after reading just the introductory paragraph. (In each of the following chapters, you will be asked to complete a predictive activity with one of the readings.)

EXERCISE **1.9**   **Making Predictions as You Read**

Directions: Read the first paragraph of "'Identical Strangers' Explore Nature versus Nurture," from Chapter 2, that follows. Working with a partner, make two or three predictions about what the author might say next.

> What is it that makes us who we really are: our life experiences or our DNA? Paula Bernstein and Elyse Schein were both born in New York City. Both women were adopted as infants and **raised** by loving families. They met for the first time when they were 35 years old and found they were "identical strangers."

1. _____

2. _____

3. _____

Now read the entire reading on page 40, and revisit your predictions to see if they were right or wrong.

Post-Reading

Many students believe that once their eyes have glanced over the last paragraph of a reading, they have completed their reading assignment and fully grasped the important points. Clearly, this is a misconception. Just as with the writing process, the reading process also involves thinking and the clarification of ideas. After you have read a passage, take the following steps to enhance your reading comprehension.

- **Take stock of the main points.** Before you respond to a reading either in writing or through answering reading comprehension questions, reflect on what you have just read and consider the author's main points. If you have highlighted and annotated the text, it would be a wise idea to review your work now.

- **Reread to fill in any gaps in your understanding.** Even though you have completed a reading, it is possible that you may have misunderstood certain sections of the text. This is where rereading helps fill any gaps in your understanding. You will be surprised to discover how much better you grasp a text after reading it a second time. (For coverage of rereading, see Chapter 5, p. 164.)

- **Make an outline and write a summary.** You may also prepare an outline of the reading by making a list of the author's thesis and supporting details. Once you have the outline ready, you can write a brief summary of the reading, including the thesis and details that support it. For a detailed discussion of summarizing, see Chapter 2, p. 64.)

- **Scan the reading for specific information.** As compared with skimming, where the reader aims to get a general sense of the text, scanning involves catching particular bits and pieces of information. The goal is to zero in on content related to a given task. If a reading assignment requires you to answer multiple-choice questions, to write a brief response, or to discuss open-ended questions, scanning the text is a pertinent step toward accomplishing these tasks. (For a detailed discussion of scanning, refer to Chapter 7, p. 260.)

- **Demonstrate comprehension of a given assignment.** Throughout this text, you will be asked to complete a variety of assignments related to the chapter readings. Whether you are responding to a text in essay or blog form, answering multiple-choice questions, or having a brief discussion about the topics covered in a reading, you will need to rely on your reading comprehension to carry out these activities successfully. After all, the journey of reading can be an enriching experience, but only if you fully go along for the ride. Keep your comprehension helmet on!

The Thinking Process

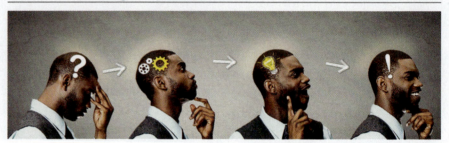

As a college student, you will be required to do a lot of academic reading and be expected to think critically about the ideas, claims, and arguments you encounter. It is important to your academic success to build the habit of *never* accepting things at their face value and *always* questioning the basic premise of any assertions made. This is called **critical thinking**, a process of thinking about an idea or ideas in a methodical way and from a variety of angles.

Critical thinking involves three key stages of asking pertinent questions about a text. What follows is a discussion of each of these stages, some concrete examples, and an opportunity for you to apply each of these concepts:

- **Observation:** Questions that help you observe a text.
- **Evaluation:** Questions that help you evaluate a text.
- **Critical Response:** Questions that help you respond to a text critically.

Observation

Here are some observation-based questions to ask and answer that will help you identify the source of information you read, the author's line of reasoning, and the evidence he or she offers to support it:

1. Who wrote the text? What is their position, if mentioned?
2. What is the main point of the text, namely the author's thesis?
3. What evidence does the author give to support the main point or thesis?

Let's practice the process of observation by interacting with the following passage.

EXERCISE **1.10**   Observing a Text

Directions: Read the following passage and answer the questions with a partner.

In Japan, You Don't Need Love: Married Couples Do Fine Without It

by John Campbell

Director of American Marriage Counseling Society

Many psychologists believe that if you love someone, you must articulate your romantic feelings by saying the three magic words to your partner, "I love you." In American society, it is commonplace for couples to share these amorous words quite frequently. However, in Japanese society it is not customary for married couples to follow this widely accepted Western practice. The Japanese find alternative ways to express their romantic feelings without being so direct. It is a shame that these magical words are rarely ever heard in the land of the cherry blossoms. To better appreciate love, the Japanese should learn from their American counterparts.

1. Who wrote the text? What is his or her position in relation to the topic discussed?

   _____

2. What is the main point of the text, namely the author's thesis?

   _____

   _____

3. What evidence does the author give to support the main point/thesis?

   _____

Evaluation

Let's turn to the second stage of questioning: evaluating the text. Here are some questions you can ask and answer to evaluate and analyze what you read:

1. Is the evidence convincing? Why or why not?

2. Does the evidence match the conclusions? If not, what might explain the mismatch?

3. What other conclusions might be drawn?

4. What other evidence might be offered to better support the claim, if any?

5. Why might the author have left out evidence that could potentially change the meaning of the text?

6. Is there anything in the language of the text that indicates beliefs, feelings, and/or values that help the reader understand why the author drew the particular conclusion(s) he or she did?

7. What conclusions might the reader draw concerning the author's personal, political, and social positions regarding the topic being discussed?

EXERCISE **1.11**   **Evaluating the Text**

Directions: Reread the passage by John Campbell, and answer the evaluation questions below with a classmate.

1. Is the evidence convincing? Why, or why not?

    _____

    _____

    _____

2. Does the evidence match the conclusions? If not, what might explain the mismatch?

    _____

    _____

    _____

    _____

3. What other conclusions might be drawn?

    _____

    _____

4. What other evidence might be offered to better support the claim, if any?

    _____

    _____

5. Why might the author have left out evidence that could potentially change the meaning of the text?

    _____

    _____

6. Is there anything in the language of the text that indicates beliefs, feelings, and/or values that help the reader understand why the author drew the particular conclusion(s) he or she did?

    _____

    _____

7. What conclusions might the reader draw concerning the author's personal, political, and social positions regarding the topic being discussed?

    _____

    _____

Critical Response

To gain a deeper understanding of the ideas in a text, a critical thinker will usually include him or herself in some way as part of the context, using critical response questions. Certainly, we judge an idea's worth to us as we study it. If we take logic and evidence-based thinking seriously, we hold off on our conclusions until we have applied observation and evaluation questions to the text. The following response questions lead to a critical understanding of the reader's relationship to a text.

1. What is it about this text that interests me?
2. Did I agree or disagree strongly with the author at any time during the course of reading the text? What specific parts of the text, if any, did I disagree with?
3. Does the idea under consideration relate in any way to my own life or the lives of people I know? How so?
4. Is there something I might gain or lose by agreeing with the conclusion of the author? What is the gain or loss?
5. Do I share the values and beliefs of the author? If not, is this mismatch responsible for my judgment of the idea?

EXERCISE 1.12 Responding to a Text

Directions: Read the passage by John Campbell a third time. Write a paragraph incorporating your response to some or all of the above questions. Before jumping into this task, review your answers to the observation and evaluation questions. When you have finished writing, compare your paragraph response with that of a partner.

As you can see, the response and application questions, like the evaluation questions, are *why* questions. They enable you to think critically, examine claims by looking for concrete evidence, and consider how ideas are shaped. Taken together, they are the foundation of critical thinking and the art of argumentation.

The Writing Process

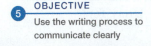

OBJECTIVE
5
Use the writing process to communicate clearly

You will be given the opportunity to practice a number of different types of writing as you make your way through the chapters of this textbook. Summary writing is very much in focus throughout. You also will be asked to share your opinions in response to controversial questions on a blog (Writing on the Wall). You will respond to your peers' ideas, and you will be asked to do Internet research and share your findings in written form. Finally, each chapter will include an essay assignment that asks you to write a response to a controversial question related to the academic discipline in focus.

While some of the stages in the writing process outlined below apply to these different forms of written expression, this discussion of the writing process focuses on the composition of a traditional essay.

Pre-Writing

Before you begin to write your essay, you need to choose a specific topic, do research on it, organize your thoughts, and get some ideas on paper as a point of departure. What follows are some effective ways to prepare yourself for a writing assignment.

Choosing and Narrowing Your Topic

Most of the time, your instructor may ask you to write an essay on a given topic. However, sometimes you will have to choose your own topic for a writing assignment. Once you choose a topic, you will need to narrow it down so that you can write an essay about it. Consider the funnel diagram below, which shows how to choose and narrow a topic for an essay assignment.

Theme: Health

Topic: Obesity

Subtopic: Obesity in the United States

Narrow topic: Obesity among children in the United States

Essay Topic: What factors cause child obesity in the United States?

Notice how the general topic of obesity is chosen from the discipline of health and is further narrowed down to the essay topic, which is to examine what causes obesity among children in the United States.

EXERCISE 1.13   Narrowing Topics

Directions: In the table that follows, choose a topic for each of the listed disciplines from this book. Then narrow each one down sufficiently that you could write an essay about it with an introduction, body paragraphs, and a conclusion.

Discipline	General topic	Subtopic	Essay Topic
Psychology			
Criminal Justice			
Environmental Science			

Researching a Topic and Evaluating Sources

Most college writing assignments involve responding to topics based on class readings within a specific discipline. For example, you might be asked in an economics course to write an essay tracing the roots of inflation, while in a business course your instructor may assign an essay on "the professional qualities of a successful entrepreneur." Although you may know a lot about these topics, you cannot depend entirely on your own knowledge base and imagination. You will need to utilize relevant assigned readings, library resources, the Internet, and other sources of information.

Some students tend to believe that anything they read in print or on a screen must be credible. However, it is important to carefully evaluate the sources of your work by questioning the veracity—truthfulness—of claims and statements made by any given author to ensure the information you are using is accurate.

Imagine that you have just found an interesting article on the Internet that is pertinent to your writing assignment. What types of critical questions might you ask to decide whether this particular source is relevant and reliable? Examine Figure 1.6: Critical Questions to Ask When Assessing Sources on page 20.

Brainstorming

The purpose of **brainstorming** is to make a list of words, phrases, and ideas related to the topic you are planning to write about, either one that has been assigned or one you have chosen after researching. Your goal is to relax and get some ideas on paper. Do not worry about grammar and spelling errors at this point.

EXERCISE 1.14   Brainstorming for Ideas

Directions: Imagine you are writing an essay on how to be a successful college student. Work with a partner and brainstorm a list of the qualities that define a good student. This is a timed activity, and you are allowed only five minutes to brainstorm. One example is provided.

• Manage your time effectively.

• _____

• _____

• _____

• _____

• _____

FIGURE 1.6

Critical Questions to Ask When Assessing Sources

Critical Questions	Paths to the Answer
1. Has the author established her or himself as an expert in the field?	• Look for the writer's credentials, which often are listed just before or after the article. • Consider how the author's work title may influence the position she or he takes. For example, if the author works for a large cigarette company, would you be surprised if he or she argued against a ban on cigarettes?
2. Has the author offered cogent (clear and convincing) arguments to support the claim?	• Review the author's words carefully. Is the claim backed up logically with relevant evidence?
3. Are there any obvious flaws or logical gaps in the argument?	• You may notice that an author's claim has an obvious flaw. For example, if an author argues that all college students have the legal right to drink alcohol, how can this be true if the drinking age is 21 and most students begin college at age 18 or 19? • Do not accept everything that you read just because you see it in print!
4. Is the article published on a reputable Web site or in a respected news source?	• When evaluating Web sources, consider the following: Read the Web address, and look for a tilde sign (˜) followed by a personal name. This indicates a personal Web site. If it is a personal Website, check to see if the person lists credentials that suggest he or she is qualified to write on the subject. • If the domain of the URL is *.com*, it is a commercial site, and you will need to consider the company's credentials and their particular bias on the topic at hand. • If the domain of the URL is *.gov*, it is a U.S. government site, and if it is *.edu,* then it is a college or school site, which means the information is probably accurate and trustworthy. • Finally, if the domain of the URL is *.org*, you are on a nonprofit site, which is probably accurate, but you should do further research to determine the purpose of the site and whether its coverage of a topic is well balanced (many nonprofits exist to advocate for specific causes). • Consider the purpose of the Web site. Is it trying to sell you something or convince you to join a political cause, or is the goal to supply information? • Make sure the Web site information is up to date. It is important to have current information when doing research on most topics.
5. Is the author giving a one-sided viewpoint on an issue?	• Consider whether you are getting a balanced viewpoint on the subject matter. • Are differing views on the topic presented? • Are credible arguments supporting an opposing viewpoint being ignored? • If the author represents an organization that advocates a particular position on an issue, is the writer simply playing the role of a spokesperson for this position?

Clustering

Clustering is a process of drawing thematically connected ideas. This activity can help you visually organize your thoughts and arguments related to a topic area. To begin, draw a circle in the middle of a page and write the main topic inside it. Then draw more circles around the central circle, connect them, and write related ideas within them.

EXERCISE 1.15 Clustering to Find Ideas

Directions: In the cluster below, the topic—how to live a long and healthy life—is provided in the central circle and only a few related ideas are provided. Draw more circles, and write ideas that are related to the topic. Keep doing this until you have generated enough ideas to write about the topic.

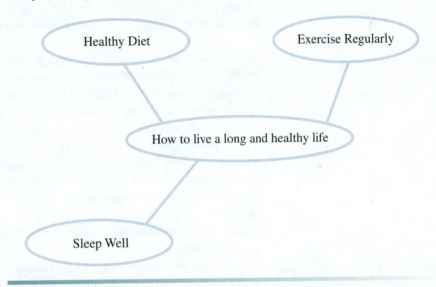

Questioning

Another useful pre-writing tool is to make a list of questions about the topic that you may want to address in your essay. Keep in mind that your reader will expect you to touch upon certain issues related to the essay topic. Generating questions about your topic will better prepare you to cover significant issues that you may otherwise overlook. In developing your list of questions, work with the following question types: *Who? What? When? Why? Where?* and *How?*

EXERCISE 1.16 Asking Questions about a Topic

Directions: Working with a partner, come up with a list of relevant questions revolving around the following essay topic: *Are vegetarians healthier than meat-eaters?* One example question is provided for your reference on the next page.

Question List

1. What are the advantages/disadvantages of eating meat?

2. _____

3. _____

4. _____

5. _____

Outlining

Once you have some ideas about your essay topic on paper, you need to get a sense of how you will structure all the relevant information into a cohesive essay. There are many ways to outline an essay; some are more formal and detailed, while others are briefer and more flexible.

As you brainstorm ideas for the first draft of your essay assignment, keep in mind that your introductory paragraph should include a narrow **thesis statement**, the central idea of an academic essay. (Refer to Chapter 3, p. 105 for a lesson on writing an introduction with a circumscribed thesis statement.)

An effective outline will include clear **topic sentences**, which introduce the topic and state the controlling idea of each body paragraph. By definition, a **controlling idea** expresses the writer's opinion about the topic. (See Chapter 4, p. 138 for a focus on the topic sentence and the controlling idea.) It may not be necessary to include **supporting details**—which include facts, statistics, reasons, personal experience, professional opinions, and specific examples that elaborate on the controlling idea—in your outline because they will organically evolve when you write the first draft. (See Chapter 4, p. 141 for a lesson on supporting details.)

Last but not least, your outline should include a concluding statement, which summarizes the main points of the essay. (See Chapter 5, p. 199 for information on writing a conclusion.)

Examine the outline below that a student created in preparation for writing an essay on "Reasons Couples Divorce."

I. **Introduction**

   Thesis Statement: Divorce is often caused by issues concerning communication, sexuality, and finances (central idea).

II. **Topic Sentence:** Lack of communication is one of the leading causes (controlling idea) of marital breakups (topic).

III. **Topic Sentence:** Infidelity can weaken the fabric (controlling idea) of a marriage (topic).

IV. **Topic Sentence:** Financial instability often takes a toll (controlling idea) on a marriage (topic).

V. **Conclusion:** Poor communication, disloyalty, and economic concerns can lead a marriage falling apart.

Writing a First Draft

As you begin to write the essays assigned in the following chapters, use outlines as springboards for composing your first drafts. It is important to keep in mind that as you put your ideas together, you will need sufficient supporting details to write well-developed paragraphs. Think of an outline as a skeleton, and your job is to add lots of meat to the bone (apologies to the vegetarians out there).

Writing Unified and Coherent Paragraphs

When you are composing your essay, you want your writing to flow smoothly forward in a manner that will make it easy for your readers to follow. You do not want your readers to keep stopping every few sentences with confused looks on their faces.

The act of writing is fundamentally different from the act of speaking in that when you speak, you have the opportunity to constantly make clarification checks, but when you write, you will not be there to explain your meaning to your reader if you have not expressed yourself clearly and logically. Examine the transcript of a phone conversation below. A woman is speaking with her boyfriend.

> **Woman:** *"But ... I know, but it's just ... I really don't have time to speak. Okay? But, really what I wanted to say. I mean, what I kind of need to say is. This event next weekend. Well... "*
>
> **Boyfriend:** *Why can't you speak now? Don't you want to go? If you don't want to go, why don't you just come out and say it?*
>
> **Woman:** *Yeah, that is kind of what I'm trying to say.*

Here the boyfriend can ask questions to clarify his girlfriend's somewhat incoherent communication. In contrast, when someone reads your writing, you will not be there to help if he or she cannot follow your line of thought.

When composing a formal essay, you cannot write in a conversational speech style. Your paragraphs should be well thought out and logically constructed; they should be *unified*. As new ideas come to you as you write, you cannot just throw them into your essay. You must first consider where these concepts and examples logically fit within your essay outline. Each of your paragraphs must show internal unity as well. As you review a given paragraph, you must ask yourself whether all the sentences effectively relate back to the topic sentence. If you stray from the idea your topic sentence conveys, the reader will wonder why you chose to include an unrelated example or discussion point in this particular paragraph.

Here are a few guidelines for writing in a more coherent and cohesive manner.

Keys to Unified and Coherent Writing

1. **Transitions:** Use transitional words and phrases effectively to ensure that your ideas are connected smoothly. (See Chapter 6, p. 247 for more on working with transitions.)

2. **Paragraph links:** To guide the reader from one idea to the next, or from paragraph to paragraph, try integrating *paragraph links*. The process of paragraph linking involves referring to the main idea of the previous paragraph in the topic sentence of your new paragraph. Let's examine an example of paragraph linking below. Notice how the topic sentence of Body Paragraph 2 connects back to the focus of Body Paragraph 1:

> **Body Paragraph 1:** Many partners live busy lives and do not spend much time together.
>
> **Body Paragraph 2:** Because partners do not spend much time together, they often feel rushed or stressed when they do meet face to face.

3. **Outline:** As stated earlier, it is helpful to make an outline before you begin writing so that you can plan how each piece of your essay fits together (arguments/major details/examples). However, an outline is not set in stone; you may find as you write that you have new ideas and insights that will lead to reorganizing your paragraphs and the order in which they appear.

4. **Read your draft carefully:** When you have completed a first draft of an essay, read it over carefully and look for issues in unity and coherence:
   - Have you repeated the same point more than once?
   - Is every piece of your essay in the right place?
   - Are ideas and examples grouped together logically?
   - Have you used appropriate transitional words and phrases to connect one idea to the next?
   - Are the main ideas outlined in the introduction, stated in the body, and summarized in the conclusion?

EXERCISE 1.17   Writing a Short Essay

Directions: Write a well-developed, short essay response to the following question:

What future goals do you have for your life after college?

Because this is your first draft, focus on your ideas, and do not worry about grammar, spelling, and punctuation errors. You will have the opportunity to revisit your first draft, revise it, and edit it carefully.

Post-Writing

You have written a preliminary draft, but your short essay is not ready to be turned in yet. Your professor should not be the first person to read your writing. You must carefully review your essay yourself before handing it in. You will need to spend some time both revising and editing your first draft to make it worth your professor's time. Most professors will provide feedback on your first draft and will expect you to incorporate their constructive criticism into subsequent drafts. Keep in mind that suggestions for improvement may also come from your classmates.

> **POP QUESTION! (Answer with a classmate)** What is the difference between revising and editing?

Revising

As you revise the first draft of your "What future goals do you have for your life after college?" short essay, it is important for you to keep your audience in mind. After all, the burden of clarity is on the writer, not the reader. The following questions will help you make the necessary revisions so that the reader can follow the progression of your thoughts with relative ease. Remember this mantra for the purpose of clarity: *Say what you mean!*

Questions to Guide Revision

1. Have I said what I meant to say? In other words, are there gaps between my intended meaning and what I have written?
2. Have I given enough examples to develop the main idea of the essay?
3. Is my introduction inviting? Have I started with a good hook to grab the reader's attention?
4. Is my thesis statement circumscribed, or narrow, enough to be developed further in the essay?
5. Do my body paragraphs begin with a topic sentence that contains a clear controlling idea?
6. Is the controlling idea in each paragraph developed by sufficient supporting details? In other words, are my body paragraphs well developed?
7. Do all of the controlling ideas explain or illustrate the thesis statement?
8. Have I used transition words to make my sentences flow smoothly?
9. Does my conclusion summarize the main points of the essay?
10. Does it restate the thesis statement?
11. Does it leave a lasting impression on the reader?

EXERCISE 1.18 Revise Your Writing

Directions: Revisit the first draft of your essay and use the above revision questions to make the necessary changes. Be as objective as possible as you do the revisions. Pretend that you are reviewing someone else's paper and read it with a critical eye.

Editing

Once you are satisfied that your paper says what you want it to, it is time to do some editing and find grammar, vocabulary, spelling, and punctuation errors. Remember that when used inappropriately, a word can change the meaning of an entire sentence or a paragraph. Refer to the following questions to edit your first draft.

Questions to Guide Editing

1. Have I written a variety of sentences such as simple, complex, and compound? (See Appendix 1, p. 435 for sentence variety.)

2. Do my pronouns agree with their nouns?

3. Do my verbs agree with their subjects? In other words, have I made many subject–verb agreement errors? (See Chapter 3, p. 109 for subject–verb agreement errors.)

4. Have I spelled the words correctly?

5. Have I used a word incorrectly?

6. Are my verb tenses appropriate? (See Chapter 5, p. 201 for a focus on controlling verb tense.)

7. Are there instances of fragments and run-on sentences? (See Chapter 6, p. 244 for fragments and run-ons.)

8. Are there instances of comma splices?

9. Have I used commas and semicolons appropriately? (See Chapter 9, p. 378 for a focus on punctuation.)

10. Have I eliminated all instances of contractions such as *won't* and *don't*?

EXERCISE 1.19 **Editing Your Short Essay**

Directions: Edit the first draft you just revised, using the Questions to Guide Editing. This time, focus on the mechanical aspects of writing, such as grammar and punctuation errors. As an editor, pay attention to the finer points of grammar and correct spelling and punctuation errors. After making the editorial changes, ask one of your classmates to review your second draft, or submit it to your instructor for feedback.

Revision Is a Recursive Process

You may think that since you have revised your first draft thoroughly and edited it meticulously, you have completed your essay assignment. The truth is that your instructor still may not be satisfied with your revisions and may ask you to further revise your second draft. In some cases, you may have to write multiple drafts incorporating your instructor's and peers' feedback. It is important that you swallow your pride and accept the feedback with an open mind. You may not have to make all the changes your instructor and peers suggest, but it will probably be worth your while to incorporate most of the important revision suggestions.

EXERCISE 1.20   Final Review of Your Essay

Directions: Answer these questions before you submit the final draft of your essay to your instructor.

The First Draft

1. What did your instructor/classmates/tutors suggest?

2. What revisions did you make to incorporate the suggestions?

The Second Draft

3. What revisions did your instructor/classmates/tutors suggest?

4. What changes did you make to improve the second draft?

The Final Draft

5. What further revisions did your instructor/classmates/tutors suggest?

6. Do you think your final draft is a significant improvement on the first two drafts? What makes this draft better than the previous ones?

Plagiarism

The word *plagiarism* is derived from the Latin word *plagiarius*, which means "kidnapper, seducer, plunderer, one who kidnaps the child or slave of another" (http://dictionary.reference.com/browse/plagiarism).

Plagiarism is stealing ideas from another author and presenting them as one's own work. North American educational institutions consider this act an academic crime, and a student can be expelled from college or university for plagiarizing. If you wish to succeed as a college student, it is imperative that you use your own words to write short and long papers for your instructor.

EXERCISE 1.21   Understanding Plagiarism

Directions: Examine the cartoon below and answer the questions that follow. You can discuss the cartoon with a classmate before answering the questions.

Calvin and Hobbes: Explain Newton's First Law of Motion in Your Own Words

1. What loophole did Calvin find in the writing instructions?

2. How is this cartoon related to plagiarism?

Oral versus Written Communication

In oral communication, also called "connected speech," people connect words, drop their endings, and sometimes use slang and idiomatic expressions. They also use contractions frequently when they speak. It is important for you to know that contractions such as *can't*, *don't*, and *won't* are not acceptable in academic writing. In addition, many phrasal verbs such as *run into* and *bring up*, which are common in spoken English, are not appropriate for written communication. When you write academic essays, remind yourself to adhere to the linguistic conventions of North American academic written discourse and impress upon the reader the fact that you have a good command of the English language.

EXERCISE 1.22   Avoiding Informal Language

Directions: Read the following sentences carefully and write a more formal alternative for the bolded words in each.

1. Obesity in the United States is **brought on** by gluttony and a lack of exercise.

   _____

2. Researchers are **checking out** effective ways to combat the Ebola virus.

   _____

3. Students are trying to **figure out** how to do the writing assignment. _____

4. Environmentalists have **come up with** a perfect solution to reduce global warming. _____

5. The union has been able to **keep up** the number of their members for ten years. _____

6. U.S. consumption of corn has **gone up** to 76 million tons per year. _____

7. The college has begun to **get rid of** many problems related to cell phone use in the classroom. _____

8. The number of students passing the standardized reading and writing tests has **gone down** considerably this semester. _____

9. The university **looks over** about 2,500 job applications every semester.

   _____

10. Meat and potatoes **make up** a major part of the diet of the American people.

   _____

Previewing the Features of *Read Think Write*

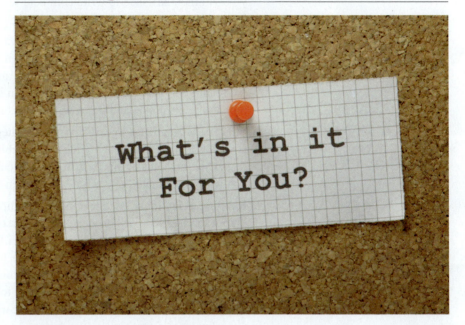

Interacting with the many features in this textbook will help you learn, practice, and apply the reading, thinking, and writing skills critical to your academic success.

1. **Learning Objectives:** Every chapter in this book begins with a list of specific learning objectives that outline what you are expected to learn from reading the chapter. Read through this list carefully before you begin each chapter, make the objectives into questions, and look for answers as you read.

2. **Introduction to the Field:** This feature introduces the chapter discipline and includes a brief account of the selections you will be reading.

3. **Chapter Essay Question:** Chapters 2–10 begin with an essay question related to the chapter discipline. It is critical that you keep the chapter essay question in mind as you make your way through the chapter readings. You might keep a "chapter essay notes page" to prepare yourself for the end-of-chapter essay assignment.

4. **Previewing Questions:** Four to five questions at the beginning of each chapter ask you to think about what you already know about the field. Read them carefully, and discuss them with your classmates at length. You will be asked to write brief responses to two out of the five questions on "The Wall" (see below).

5. **Writing on The Wall:** "The Wall" is an interactive platform where you can post written responses and read and respond to the ideas of your classmates. It is a platform that allows you to articulate your thoughts in a civil manner, to take other perspectives into consideration, and to keep an open mind as you learn. Remember to make The Wall your romping ground!

6. **Brainstorming Vocabulary:** Working with a classmate, you are asked to think of at least five words that related to the chapter discipline.

To demonstrate your understanding of your brainstormed vocabulary terms, you will then be asked to write complete sentences using these words. This is a creative way to build vocabulary through practice with associated terms.

7. **Key Terms in the Discipline:** In this section you start by brainstorming and working with discipline-specific words you are already familiar with, and then practice finding synonyms and antonyms for ten key words taken from the readings. This gives you a head start on learning and using terms common to the discipline and will help you understand the readings more fully.

8. **Success in Reading:** Specific reading strategies (such as skimming, scanning, highlighting, and annotating) that enable you to become a more fluent reader are the focus of this feature. As you learn and employ these strategies, you will notice that your reading comprehension significantly improves.

9. **Reading Selections:** Each reading is accompanied by questions and vocabulary exercises that will deepen your understanding of its content and build your vocabulary, reading, and thinking skills. In reading selection 2, you are asked to stop at the halfway point to reflect on what you have read and to predict the contents of the second part of the reading. Making predictions about reading content is a solid way to integrate reading and critical thinking skills. Reading selection 3 is excerpted from a 100-level college discipline-specific textbook. It is designed to get you in the habit of reading authentic text and learning academic vocabulary.

10. **Writing Without Boundaries: There Are No Checkpoints!** In each of Chapters 2–10, you are asked to write for ten minutes in response to a famous person's quote related to the chapter's discipline. This is an exercise in focusing on ideas and not getting hung up on word choice and form.

11. **Reading Skill Focus:** A new college reading skill is introduced briefly in each chapter along with a few practice exercises. Each chapter builds on the reading skills that were the focus of the previous ones. Mastery of these key reading skills is critical to your success as an academic reader.

12. **Think to Write:** You are asked to write a response to *two of the three chapter readings in a response journal.* You are given observation, analysis, and critical response questions to assist you in writing the journal. Keep in mind that you will be required to include at least six discipline-specific words in the journal. You also will be asked to post one journal entry for each chapter on a The Wall blog and respond to at least two of your classmates' postings. This feature gives you the invaluable experience of responding to the ideas in a text and to the ideas of your peers.

13. **It's Showtime!** Your task is to find a video link that ties into one of the chapter readings and to write a half-page summary of the video's key points. You also will have the opportunity to post your personal reaction on The Wall. This feature provides you with an opportunity to explore a chapter topic of interest and gain more experience in summary writing, a key academic skill.

14. **Writing Skill Focus:** A new college writing skill is introduced in each chapter (such as paraphrasing, summarizing, writing a circumscribed thesis statement, and many others). You will have the opportunity to peer-edit and revise your preliminary drafts. In addition, you will be encouraged to read

your classmates' first drafts and provide constructive criticism on improving purpose and clarity.

15. **Trouble Spots in Writing:** Each chapter offers a focus on a writing/grammar trouble spot, which will enhance your ability to avoid it and write with relative ease and success.

16. **Then and Now:** This section asks you to do Internet research to gather information about two experts in the chapter's discipline, one from the past and another contemporary, and compare and contrast them in an essay. This feature offers you practice both in doing Internet research and in compare/contrast writing.

17. **Virtual Scavengers:** To guide you toward a deeper understanding of the chapter essay question, you are asked to do Internet research on a milestone document in the discipline and answer two to three questions about the content.

18. **Chapter Essay Assignment:** Chapters 3-10 conclude with you handing in the "Chapter Essay" assignment (in Chapter 2, you are asked to complete a chapter paragraph assignment). Peer review of essay assignments is essential, so you will have the opportunity to review your classmates' drafts and offer constructive criticism. In Chapter 2, you have the option of writing a summary of one of the readings, but for each of the subsequent chapters, you will be required to write a full essay.

19. **Focus on Form:** This grammar-focused feature reinforces the mechanical aspects of writing you learn about in the Trouble Spots in Writing section of each chapter. You will have the opportunity to review your essay with a particular grammar area in mind. Before setting your *editing* eyes on your own writing, you will first practice grammar editing with a sample essay paragraph.

20. **(Optional) Debate Project/Panel Discussion:** Each chapter concludes with either a debate or a panel discussion. For debates, you will explore a controversial issue related to the chapter discipline. For panel discussions, you will have the opportunity to role-play and think critically about a given issue within the field.

These features and activities form core part of this academically oriented, integrated text. As you can see, this text is designed to mirror a university-level content course, and your active participation in it will not only improve your reading and writing skills but also increase your familiarity with the North American higher education system.

EXERCISE 1.23 A 60-Second Paper

Write a brief response to the following questions in 60 seconds and submit your paper to your instructor. Your answers will help the instructor plan lessons according to your needs.

1. What did you learn from this chapter?

2. What did you find difficult to understand?

2 Psychology

Learning Objectives

IN THIS CHAPTER, YOU WILL LEARN TO . . .

1 Read in the field of psychology

2 Understand and use key terms in psychology

3 Focus your attention as you read

4 Determine word meanings from context

5 Accurately restate the ideas of others by paraphrasing

6 Write concise, accurate summaries

7 Use reporting verbs appropriately in summary writing

8 Read, think, plan, and write a paragraph in response to the chapter essay assignment

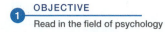
OBJECTIVE
Read in the field of psychology

Introduction to the Field of Psychology

Psychology is formally defined as the scientific study of the behavior of individuals and their mental processes. Many psychologists seek answers to such fundamental questions as *What is human nature?* and *Why do we behave the way we do?* They study such phenomena as cognition, perception, emotion, personality, and interpersonal relationships. Why is psychology relevant to our daily lives? Psychological research focuses on our physical and mental health, our personal growth, and our ability to understand one another, all topics that regularly impact us.

There are many subdivisions within the field of psychology. For example, clinical psychologists focus on understanding, preventing, and relieving psychologically based distress or dysfunction; cognitive psychologists focus on perception, memory, judgment, and reasoning; and school psychologists focus on students' behavior in educational settings. Each area of psychology offers the opportunity to undertake research and apply research-based findings in a real-world setting.

This chapter focuses primarily on issues related to the "nature versus nurture" debate, which frames many research questions in the field of psychology. Some people believe that human behavior is largely determined by our genetic makeup, while others claim that we are the products of our environment. How similar are identical twins who were separated at birth? Why is it so difficult to follow through on our New Year's resolutions? How much of our behavior is genetically determined? These are some of the topics that are explored in the chapter reading selections.

Chapter Essay Question

As the title of the textbook suggests, you will be playing an active role in the learning process by *reading* interesting, thematic articles and essays, *thinking* critically about issues pertinent to the theme of the chapter, and *writing* relevant responses to what you have read in the form of reflection papers, blogs, and academic essays.

Each chapter will challenge you to explore your thoughts in writing on a given thematic essay question. As you read through this chapter, keep in mind the essay question and consider how you will incorporate multiple perspectives on the issue at hand. Chapter essays will be due when your class completes the chapter.

CHAPTER PARAGRAPH QUESTION

Can human behavior be changed?

Quick Free-Write! Take out a piece of paper and write for ten minutes without stopping about what you already know about human behavior and if it can be changed.

Your Option: Once you have worked your way through the chapter readings, you are welcome to narrow down the topics covered and compose your own chapter essay question.

Previewing Psychology

Read the following questions and discuss them with your classmates. As you answer the questions, consider your personal experience and knowledge of psychology in general.

1. Geneticists hold the view that our behavior is determined to a large extent by our DNA. However, many psychologists argue that the environment determines and influences how we generally behave. Where do you stand on the nature versus nurture debate? In other words, how much of human nature do you think is genetically determined, and how much of it do you think is shaped by environmental factors such as parenting, education, and so on?

2. A famous psychologist, John Gray, wrote a book entitled *Men Are from Mars, Women Are from Venus.* His central point was that men and women think and behave as if they are from different planets. If you think this is true, first discuss in what ways men and women behave differently. Then offer some explanations to account for these differences.

3. Many studies have focused on identical twins separated at birth and raised far away from each other by different parents. Most of these studies found remarkable similarities between the twins. Do you think this is just a coincidence, or is there a reasonable explanation for these similarities?

4. Most people believe that children learn their first language mainly through the guidance of their parents, or care-givers. Children experiment with language and their parents correct their errors and teach them the correct forms. Yet, research indicates that young children all around the globe learn their first language without getting explicit instructions from their parents or teachers. How do we explain children acquiring a language so effortlessly? How do we explain the fact that adults struggle with mastering a second language while young children pick up second languages with relative ease?

5. Humans have inhabited the planet earth for thousands of years. Yet, we have not learned how to coexist in peace and harmony. Do you believe that violence is a natural part of our behavior? In other words, is conflict built into our psychological makeup?

Human beings are naturally curious about how similar or different other people's views are to theirs. As you interact with the ideas in this text, you will be asked to explore your thoughts in writing and respond to your classmates' responses to the same issues. After discussing the preview questions with your classmates, post your responses to two of them on The Wall. Then peruse The Wall and respond to at least two of your classmates' responses that pique your interest, following the guidelines below.

Etiquette for Writing on The Wall

1. **Be Civil:** It is important to be civil and courteous, even to those who may have an opposing viewpoint. You can disagree in a polite manner, choosing your words carefully. As you know, words can hurt!
2. **Be Academic:** There is a big difference between texting a friend and writing an academic response to a classmate's ideas. If your writing begins to sound like you are speaking, you are going in the wrong direction. Avoid contractions like *gonna, wanna, hafta* and slang, and follow punctuation rules. Take no shortcuts!
3. **Be Original:** Rather than using clichés and stating the obvious, repeating what you have heard somewhere else, or simply cutting and pasting text, express your independent thoughts. Find your academic voice!
4. **Be Factual:** It is one thing to base your opinion on evidence and another to base it on mere hearsay. As you respond to the preview questions and your classmates' ideas, resist the temptation to offer your opinion without sufficient support.

 OBJECTIVE
Understand and use key terms in psychology

Key Terms in Psychology

Take a moment to think about the discipline of psychology as you complete the following two exercises.

EXERCISE 2.1 **Brainstorming Vocabulary**

Directions: What associated words come to mind when you think of the world of psychology? Work with a partner and write down as many related words as you can think of in a period of five minutes, using the diagram below.

EXERCISE 2.2   **Creating Original Sentences**

EXERCISE 2.2   **Creating Original Sentences**

Directions: Choose five of the words from your brainstorming and use them to write complete and meaningful sentences.

1. _____

2. _____

3. _____

4. _____

5. _____

It has been proven that one of the most effective ways to acquire academic vocabulary is to study key terms that are thematically connected. As you launch your academic career, it will be imperative (absolutely necessary) for you to internalize vocabulary terms that are germane (relevant) to the academic disciplines that make up most 100-level credit-bearing content courses. For example, a student majoring in the discipline of psychology should be able to apply such terms as *inherited*, *assess*, and *therapy* in both spoken and written forms.

Using Synonyms and Antonyms

In every chapter of this text, you will have the opportunity not only to interact with key terms in context but also to practice finding appropriate synonyms and antonyms for those terms and others. A **synonym** is a word used to express a similar meaning to another word. For example, here are some synonyms for the word *walk*: *stroll, hike, march, pace, ramble, saunter,* and *traipse*. Although each word relates to walking, each conveys different information. An **antonym** is a word that conveys the opposite meaning of another word. For example, antonyms of *bright* could be *dark, dull,* or *dim*.

Understanding how to work with synonyms and antonyms is a critical skill, especially when you are writing a summary of a text or trying to paraphrase some of the key ideas and pieces of information contained in an original source. You cannot simply copy the same terms you see in a text, but will need to make use of synonyms and antonyms.

When you are looking for a synonym to replace a word, take into account the context in which the original word appears and its part of speech. As an example, examine the following sentence and consider replacing the word *engaged* with an appropriate synonym.

"She was fully **engaged** in her writing assignment."

From the context, you can figure out that the woman or girl mentioned in the sentence is not engaged to be married. You also can deduce that *engaged* is part of the verb phrase "was engaged." You should now be able to replace the term with a synonym that makes sense in this sentence, choosing, for example, *involved* or *focused*. If you were asked to find an antonym for *engaged*, you could now try to imagine a word that would mean the opposite of *engaged* in the context of the sentence. You might come up with such antonyms as *distracted* or *disassociated from*.

EXERCISE 2.3 **Discipline-Specific Vocabulary: Fishing for Synonyms and Antonyms**

Directions: Read the following ten (10) discipline-specific words culled from the readings in this chapter and shown in the context of the sentences in which they appeared. In the space provided after each sentence, write a synonym or antonym for the highlighted term, as directed.

Discipline-Specific Word Bank*

assess	modified	factors
nurture	lifestyle	traits
remorse	contribute	
counsel	inherited	

* The first time these discipline-specific words appear in the chapter, they are shown in bold green.

1. "Unknowingly, Bernstein and Schein had been part of a secret research project in the 1960s and '70s that separated identical twins as infants and followed their development in a one-of-a-kind experiment to **assess** the influence of nature vs. nurture in child development." (Selection 1, p. 41, para. 2)

   A synonym for *assess* is _____.

2. "Since the beginning of science, twins have offered a unique opportunity to study to what extent nature vs. **nurture** influences the way we develop, the people that we turn out to be," Wright says. (Selection 1, p. 41, para. 8)

   A synonym for *nurture* is _____.

3. "Instead, he showed no **remorse** and offered no apology." (Selection 1, p. 42, para. 11)

   An antonym for *remorse* is _____.

4. "All of these conditions can, of course, be **modified** with lifestyle changes." (Selection 2, p. 47, para. 4)

   An antonym for ***modified*** is _____.

5. "Adopting a healthier lifestyle can affect not only your **risk** for disease and the way you feel today but also your health and ability to function independently in later life." (Selection 2, p. 47, para. 2)

   An antonym for *risk* is _____.

6. "Considerable research has sought to identify factors that **contribute** to successful behavior change and to develop more effective tools for clinicians to encourage their patients to adopt healthier habits, especially in the context of a brief office visit." (Selection 2, p. 48, para. 6)

   An antonym for *contribute* is _____.

7. "Clinicians and health educators use TTM to **counsel** patients, but you don't need to be an expert." (Selection 2, p. 48, para. 9)

   A synonym for *counsel* is _____.

8. "What aspects of personality might have an **inherited** component?" (Selection 3, p. 57, para. 1)

   An antonym for *inherited* is _____.

9. "Edward L. Thorndike (1903), one of the leading psychologists of the early nineteen hundreds, staked out the nature position by claiming that 'in the actual race of life . . . the chief determining **factor** is heredity.' (Selection 3, p. 57, para. 2)

   A synonym for *factor* is _____.

10. "Researchers measure genetic contributions to personality in three ways: by studying personality **traits** in other species, by studying the temperament of human infants and children, and by doing heritability studies of twins and adopted individuals." (Selection 3, p. 58, para. 5)

    A synonym for *traits* is _____.

SUCCESS IN READING

3 OBJECTIVE

Focus your attention as you read

Getting Focused

The act of reading demands concentration. Our lives are full of distractions that range from incoming texts to loud sounds from the street to worrying thoughts. Your ability to overcome these distractions and focus as you read will determine, to a great extent, your success in college.

Complete the following reading habits questionnaire, which will give you a chance to reflect on what motivates you to read and to learn about how your peers relate to the world of reading.

EXERCISE 2.4 Reading Habits Questionnaire: What Fires Up Your Reading Neurons?

Directions: Different people read for different purposes. Ask two of your classmates the questions below to find out what inspires them to read. You may be surprised by their answers.

Reading Habits Questionnaire—Interview Two Classmates!		
Question	**Interviewee 1**	**Interviewee 2**
1. In what locations do you prefer to read? Where do you find you can best concentrate?		
2. At what time of the day do you prefer to read?		
3. What genres of reading do you most enjoy (fiction/poetry/ newspapers/magazines/online blogs/etc.)?		
4. What subject areas are you most interested in reading about?		
5. In what ways can reading make you a better person?		
6. What types of distractions make it difficult for you to sit still for an hour and focus on your reading?		

EXERCISE **2.5** **How Do You Stay Focused When You Read?**

Directions: Jot down three to four strategies you use to stay focused as you read. Discuss these strategies in a small group.

Here are some strategies you may or may not have considered that will help you focus as you read:

- **Set any distracting personal issues aside.** Whatever life dramas you are facing, try to leave them behind for a pre-determined period of time, so that you can read in peace. Think of reading as an escape, a pause from everything else going on in your life.

- **Choose a place to read that works for you.** Some people like to read in very quiet places while others enjoy reading in coffee shops. You know yourself. Experiment, and find the setting that works best for you.

- **Awaken your body.** You will be better able to focus your attention if you feel alive. If you are hungry, some protein will boost your concentration. If you did not get enough sleep, take a power nap and refresh your mind. If you feel tight, spend a few minutes stretching.

- **Practice "active reading."** Interact with the text. Jot down key points and underline key terms as you read. Annotating your textbook will help you improve your attention, concentration, and reading comprehension.

- **Take short breaks.** If you find yourself continually distracted and unable to focus on a text, give yourself a break. Getting up and walking around can make all the difference.

- **Find something interesting to focus on.** Do not convince yourself that the reading is boring before you start to read. Try to find something that interests you to focus on and hook onto it.

READING

Selection 1

Online Article from Radio Source

"Identical Strangers" Explore Nature versus Nurture

Pre-Reading Questions

Answer the following questions before exploring the text.

1. Identical twins tend to have similar personalities. How can this be explained?

2. In your encounters with identical twins, have you noticed that they have a deeper relationship than most siblings?

3. What can scientists learn from the close study of identical twins that can help us better understand the nature versus nurture debate?

Eye on Vocabulary

It may be helpful to focus on the meaning of some key words in the article before you read. Skim through the reading and look for the following key vocabulary terms in bold. Working with a partner, examine the words in context and try to guess the meaning of each. Then look up the words in a dictionary. Keep in mind that many words have multiple meanings. Write the definition that best fits the word's context in the article.

Word	Your definition	Dictionary definition
1. raised (v.)		
2. psychiatrist (n.)		
3. consensus (n.)		
4. ethical (adj.)		

"Identical Strangers" Explore Nature Vs. Nurture

by Joe Richman of Radio Diaries
October 25, 2007

Elena Seibert

Paula Bernstein (left) and Elyse Schein are identical twins who were separated at birth and were reunited in 2004, when they were 35. They are authors of a new memoir, Identical Strangers.

1　　What is it that makes us who we really are: our life experiences or our DNA? Paula Bernstein and Elyse Schein were both born in New York City. Both women were adopted as infants and **raised** by loving families. They met for the first time when they were 35 years old and found they were "identical strangers."

2　　Unknowingly, Bernstein and Schein had been part of a secret research project in the 1960s and '70s that separated identical twins as infants and followed their development in a one-of-a-kind experiment to **assess** the influence of nature vs. **nurture** in child development. Now, the twins, authors of a new memoir called *Identical Strangers*, are trying to uncover the truth about the study.

"I Have a Twin"

3　　In 2004, Paula Bernstein received a phone call from an employee of Louise Wise Services, the agency where she had been adopted. The message: She had a twin who was looking for her. The woman told Bernstein her twin's name. "And I thought, I have a twin, and her name is Elyse Schein," Bernstein says.

4　　Schein, who was living in Paris at the time, had been trying to find information about her birth mother when she learned from the adoption agency that she had a twin sister. The two women met for the first time at a cafe in New York City—and stayed through lunch and dinner, talking. "We had 35 years to catch up on. How do you start asking somebody, 'What have you been up to since we shared a womb together?' Where do you start?" Bernstein says.

Separated at Adoption

5　　Soon after the sisters were reunited, Schein told Bernstein what she had found out about why they were separated: They were part of a study on nature vs. nurture. It was the only study of its kind on twins separated from infancy. Neither parents nor children knew the real subject of the study—or that the children had been separated from their identical twin.

6　　"When the families adopted these children, they were told that their child was already part of an ongoing child study. But of course, they neglected to tell them the key element of the study, which is that it was child development among twins **raised** in different homes," Bernstein says.

A "Practically Perfect" Study

7　　Peter Neubauer, a child **psychiatrist**, and Viola Bernard, a child psychologist and consultant to the Louise Wise agency, headed up the study. Lawrence Perlman, a research assistant on the study from 1968 to 1969, says Bernard had a strong belief that twins should be raised separately. "That twins were often dressed the same and treated exactly the same, she felt, interfered with their independent psychological development," Perlman says.

8　　Lawrence Wright is the author of *Twins*, a book about twin studies. "Since the beginning of science, twins have offered a unique opportunity to study to what extent nature vs. nurture influences the way we develop, the people that we turn out to be," Wright says.

9　　Wright notes that the Neubauer study differs from all other twin studies in that it followed the twins from infancy. "From a scientific point of view, it's beautiful. It's practically the perfect study. But this study would never happen today," Wright says.

Finding the True Story

10   The study ended in 1980, and a year later, the state of New York began requiring adoption agencies to keep siblings together. At that point, Bernstein says, Neubauer realized that public opinion would be so against the study that he decided not to publish it. The results of the study have been sealed until 2066 and given to an archive at Yale University. "It's kind of disturbing to think that all this material about us is in some file cabinet somewhere. And really for ourselves, we had to figure out what the true story was," Bernstein says. The sisters attempted to reach Neubauer, a distinguished and internationally renowned psychiatrist who serves on the board of the Freud Archives. Initially, he refused to speak to them.

No **Remorse**, No Apology

11   Eventually, he granted the women an unofficial interview—no taping or videotaping allowed. Bernstein says she had hoped Neubauer would apologize for separating the twins. Instead, he showed no remorse and offered no apology.

12   Neubauer has rarely spoken about the study. But in the mid-1990s, he did talk about it with Wright, the author of *Twins*. "[Neubauer] insisted that at the time, it was a matter of scientific **consensus** that twins were better off separated at birth and raised separately," Wright says. "I never found anything in the literature to support that."

13   The author also says Neubauer was "unapologetic" about the study, even though he admits that the project raised **ethical** questions about whether one has a right to or should separate identical twins."It is very difficult to answer. It is for these reasons that these studies don't take place," Neubauer told Wright. Wright says that no such study will ever be done again—nor should it. But he acknowledges that it would be very interesting to learn what this study has to teach us.

"Different People with Different Life Histories"

14   As for Bernstein and Schein, getting to know each other has raised its own questions. "Twins really do force us to question what is it that makes each of us who we are. Since meeting Elyse, it is undeniable that genetics play a huge role—probably more than 50 percent," Bernstein says. "It's not just our taste in music or books; it goes beyond that. In her, I see the same basic personality. And yet, eventually we had to realize that we're different people with different life histories."

15   As much as she thinks the researchers did the wrong thing by separating the twins, Bernstein says she can't imagine a life growing up with her twin sister. "That life never happened. And it is sad, that as close as we are now, there is no way we can ever compensate for those 35 years," Bernstein says.

16   "With me and Paula, it is hard to see where we are going to go. It's really uncharted territory," Schein says. "But I really love her and I can't imagine my life without her." Neubauer declined to be interviewed for this story. Of the 13 children involved in his study, three sets of twins and one set of triplets have discovered one another. The other four subjects of the study still do not know they have identical twins.

Thinking about the Reading

After doing a close reading of the article, write your answers to the following questions. When you have written all of your answers, discuss them with your classmates.

1. What was the goal of the secret research project that separated the two identical twins, Paula and Elyse?

   _____

   _____

2. Do you think this type of research project is ethical? Explain your viewpoint.

   _____

   _____

3. Paula said: "We had 35 years to catch up on. How do you start asking somebody, 'What have you been up to since we shared a womb together?' Where do you start?" What is Paula's point? Paraphrase this quotation.

   _____

   _____

4. What was Viola Bernard's (a child psychologist involved in the study) opinion on how identical twins should be raised? Do you agree? Explain.

   _____

   _____

5. What does Elyse say about her relationship with her identical twin sister near the end of the article? In your opinion, is this a happy or sad story? Explain.

   _____

   _____

Reading Comprehension Check

___ 1. "It was the only study of its kind on twins separated from **infancy**." In this above context, the word *infancy* means

    a. adolescent years.   c. early childhood.

    b. babyhood.   d. birth.

___ 2. Why does Lawrence Wright, the author of a book on twins, say that a study like this "would never happen today"?

    a. It is too expensive to run.

    b. The adoption agencies wouldn't want to see the twins separated.

    c. Scientists already know enough about identical twins.

    d. This type of scientific study is considered unethical and would not be permitted.

___ **3.** After getting to know her twin sister, what is Paula Bernstein's view on the nature versus nurture question in relation to twins?

    a. Genetics determines everything.

    b. The environment you grow up in determines who you are.

    c. She believes that genetics can explain about half of the picture.

    d. She is unclear on big questions relating to the nature of identical twins.

___ **4.** Paula says: "And it is sad, that as close as we are now, there is no way we can ever **compensate** for those 35 years." The word *compensate* could be replaced by _____.

    a. make accommodations for   c. pay for

    b. make up for   d. object to

___ **5.** What is the main idea of the reading?

    a. Twins should never be separated at birth.

    b. Paula is thankful to have finally been introduced to her twin sister.

    c. Scientists do experiments to test theories related to nature versus nurture.

    d. Two identical twins who were separated at birth were reunited as adults.

___ **6.** Which of the following is not an example of how identical twins Elyse and Paula are similar?

    a. their taste in music   c. their basic personalities

    b. their taste in books   d. their life histories

___ **7.** "Twins really do force us to question what is it that makes each of us who we are. Since meeting Elyse, it is **undeniable** that genetics play a huge role—probably more than 50 percent." The word *undeniable* could be replaced by

    a. doubtful.   c. not true.

    b. without question.   d. questionable.

___ **8.** How many of the 13 original children involved in the research study know of the existence of their twin?

    a. about two-thirds   c. All of them have been informed.

    b. none   d. This information is not offered in the article.

___ **9.** What is the author's tone in this reading passage?

    a. angry   c. sad

    b. objective   d. confused

___ **10.** What can we conclude from Elyse's comment at the end of the article, "With me and Paula, it is hard to see where we are going to go. It's really uncharted territory"?

    a. She doesn't believe the twins have a future together.

    b. She is confident that they will never be separated again.

    c. She would prefer to keep the details of their reunion private.

    d. She is not sure which way this new relationship is going.

THEMATIC LINKS

If you want to learn more about the topic of identical twins, type the following words into your browser and explore the two sites that come up:

1. random noise in biology slate

2. identical twins' genes are not identical scientific american

Writing without BOUNDARIES

There Are No Checkpoints!

"Everything that irritates us about others can lead us to an understanding of ourselves."

CARL JUNG

Read the quote above and respond to Jung's idea in any way you want. Write in your notebook for ten minutes without stopping. For this activity, it is important that you focus on ideas, not words. In other words, this will be an exercise in focusing on content and not getting hung up on word choice and grammar errors. You may wish to read what you have written out loud in front of your classmates and instructor.

READING

Selection 2

Harvard Health Magazine

Why Behavior Change Is Hard—and Why You Should Keep Trying

Pre-Reading Questions

Answer the following questions before exploring the text.

1. Contrary to the popular belief that the environment mostly determines our behavior, many geneticists claim that much of human behavior is genetically determined. State your opinion on this matter using specific examples to support your position.

2. In your opinion, why are New Year's resolutions so hard to keep, especially if they are related to health behaviors such as weight loss and regular exercise?

3. If an individual is contemplating quitting smoking or consuming alcohol, what steps do you think s/he must take to change the unhealthy behavior? Be specific.

Eye on Vocabulary

It may be helpful to focus on the meaning of some key words in the article before beginning the reading. Skim through the reading and find the following key vocabulary terms in bold black. Working with a partner, examine the words in context and try to guess the meaning of these terms. Then look up the words in a dictionary. Keep in mind that many words have multiple meanings. Write the definition that fits the word's context in the article.

Word	Your definition	Dictionary definition
1. resolutions (n.)		
2. strategies (n.)		
3. regret (v.)		
4. quelling (v.)		

Why Behavior Change Is Hard—and Why You Should Keep Trying

March 2012

You will have the opportunity to read this selection in two parts. First, you will read Part I and take an inventory of what you have learned so far. Then, you will make a prediction as to what Part II of the reading will contain. Finally, you will answer some open-ended and multiple-choice questions about what you have read.

Part I

1   *Successful change comes only in stages. How long it takes is an individual matter.* You may be well on your way to making some of the changes you resolved to make back in January. If so, that's great. If not, you may understandably be feeling discouraged. New Year's **resolutions** are notoriously hard to keep, especially when they're aimed at health behaviors such as losing weight, eating better, and exercising more. In fact, no matter when we decide to make a change—or how strongly we're motivated—adopting a new, healthy habit, or breaking an old, bad one can be terribly difficult. But research suggests that any effort you make is worthwhile, even if you encounter setbacks or find yourself backsliding from time to time. Just making a New Year's resolution, for example, may boost your chances of eventual success.

2   When it comes to health recommendations, we mostly know the drill: exercise most days, eat a varied and nutritious diet, keep body mass index in the normal range (18.5 to 24.9), get enough sleep (seven to eight hours a night), don't smoke, and limit alcohol to one drink a day. What we do for ourselves in these areas is often more important than what medicine can offer us. Adopting a healthier **lifestyle** can affect not only your risk for disease and the way you feel today but also your health and ability to function independently in later life.

The Impact of lifestyle **factors** on independent living

3   In a 20-year study that followed nearly 6,500 middle-aged and elderly people, those who smoked, were obese or physically inactive, or had diabetes or uncontrolled high blood pressure when the study began were much more likely to require admission to a nursing home later on.

4   Middle-age smoking increased the chance of a nursing home admission by 56%, physical inactivity by 40%, and uncontrolled high blood pressure by 35%. Diabetes more than tripled the risk. Middle-age obesity was also associated with higher risk, but the association wasn't statistically significant—that is, the numbers could have resulted from chance. All of these conditions can, of course, be **modified** with lifestyle changes.

5   Even after a setback such as a stroke, lifestyle can make a difference. A study in the *Journal of Neurology, Neuroscience, and Psychiatry* (February 2012), which involved more than 15,000 American adults with a history of stroke, found that regular exercise and not smoking were each associated with a reduced risk of dying from any cause. Moreover, the more healthy behaviors that participants embraced (for example, eating five or more daily servings of fruits and vegetables in addition to exercising and not smoking), the lower their death rate for all causes.

ROAD STOP

Get into a small group and answer the two questions that follow.

1. What have you learned from this article so far?

2. What do you predict may be coming in the second half of the article?

Part II
What helps?

6   Considerable research has sought to identify factors that **contribute** to successful behavior change and to develop more effective tools for clinicians to encourage their patients to adopt healthier habits, especially in the context of a brief office visit. One potential roadblock: too often we're motivated by negatives such as guilt, fear, or **regret**. Experts agree that long-lasting change is most likely when it's self-motivated and rooted in positive thinking. For example, in an analysis of 129 studies of behavior change **strategies**, a British research group found that the least effective approaches were those that encouraged a sense of fear or regret. Studies have also shown that goals are easier to reach if they're specific ("I'll walk for 30 minutes every day," rather than "I'll get more exercise"). You should also limit the number of goals you're trying to reach; otherwise, you may overtax your attention and willpower. And it's not enough just to have a goal; you need to have practical ways of reaching it. For example, if you are trying to quit smoking, have a plan for **quelling** the urge to smoke (for example, keep a bottle of water nearby, chew sugarless gum, or practice deep breathing).

Change is a process, not an event

7   Research has produced several models that help account for success and failure and explain why making healthy changes can take so long. The one most widely applied and tested in health settings is the transtheoretical model (TTM). Developed in the 1980s by alcoholism researchers James O. Prochaska and Carlo C. DiClemente, TTM presupposes that at any given time, a person is in one of five stages of change: precontemplation, contemplation, preparation, action, or maintenance.

8   The idea is that each stage is a preparation for the following one, so you mustn't hurry through or skip stages. Also, different approaches and strategies (called "processes of change" in the TTM model) are needed at different stages. For example, a smoker who's at the precontemplation stage—that is, not even thinking about quitting—probably isn't ready to make a list of alternatives to smoking.

9   Most of the evidence for this model comes from studies of alcohol use, drug abuse, and smoking cessation, but it's also been applied to other health-related behaviors, including exercise and dieting. Clinicians and health educators use TTM to **counsel** patients, but you don't need to be an expert; anyone motivated to change can use this model.

It can take a few rounds

10   The path between stages is rarely straightforward. Most people relapse at some point and recycle through one or more stages. For example, if you relapse during the maintenance stage, you may find yourself back at the contemplation or preparation stage. One study found that smokers cycled through the "action" stage three or four times, on average, before they succeeded in quitting.

11   Relapse is common, perhaps even inevitable. You should regard it as an integral part of the process. Think of it this way: you learn something about yourself each time you relapse. Maybe the strategy you adopted didn't fit into your life or suit your priorities. Next time, you can use what

you learned, make adjustments, and be a little ahead of the game as you continue on the path to change.

Thinking about the Reading

After doing a close reading of the article, write the answers to the following questions. You will be asked to discuss your answers with your classmates.

1. According to many experts, what factors are most important for successfully making long-term changes in behavior?

   _____

   _____

2. The section, "The impact of lifestyle factors on independent living," refers to two research studies. Do you think the conclusions drawn are valid? Why, or why not? Explain.

   _____

   _____

3. What factors contribute to successful behavior change? Find specific examples in the reading to support your answer.

   _____

   _____

4. Why do you think the Transtheoretical Model (TTM) is most applied and tested in health settings? Explain.

   _____

   _____

5. "Relapse is common, perhaps even inevitable. You should regard it as an integral part of the process." Paraphrase this quotation.

   _____

   _____

Reading Comprehension Check

____1. "You may be well on your way to making some of the changes you **resolved** to make back in January." In the preceding sentence, the meaning of the word *resolved* is

   a. considered.   c. decided against.
   b. worked out.   d. firmly decided.

____2. "Just making a New Year's resolution, for example, may **boost** your chances of eventual success." In the preceding context, the word *boost* is opposite in meaning to

   a. improve.   c. bolster.
   b. strengthen.   d. decrease.

___ **3.** The article mentions, "if you are trying to quit smoking, have a plan for **quelling** the urge to smoke (for example, keep a bottle of water nearby, chew sugarless gum, or practice deep breathing)." The word *quelling* could be replaced by _____.

a. continuing
b. extinguishing
c. changing
d. encouraging

___ **4.** "Relapse is common, perhaps even inevitable. You should regard it as an integral part of the process." A logical conclusion to draw from this statement is that

a. we should make an effort to fail the first time we attempt behavior change.
b. we should relapse before we make a firm plan for behavior change.
c. most people will not succeed the first time they try to change behaviors.
d. relapse is an avoidable part of the process of behavior change.

___ **5.** The main idea of the article is that

a. New Year's resolutions are easy to break because they are not practical.
b. making New Year's resolutions to change behaviors such as smoking and consuming alcohol is ineffective.
c. when trying to change behavior, making an effort is important.
d. most people accept their misguided behavior and do not wish to change.

___ **6.** This article describes "action" as one of the stages of change. Which of the following is an example of an overweight person in the action stage of change?

a. a college student who keeps track of the calories she eats, strives not to go over her calorie limit, and walks daily at a brisk pace for 30 minutes or more
b. an adult woman whose body mass index is within the normal range
c. a college student who is 30 pounds overweight but hasn't thought seriously about trying to lose weight
d. a retired schoolteacher who suspects he may be overweight and has gone online a few times to read about weight loss

___ **7.** According to the information in this article, which of the following statements is *false*?

a. Each stage of change is a preparation for the one that follows it.
b. Negative motivations, such as guilt or fear, can get in the way of successful behavior change.
c. Once people truly decide to change and begin acting upon their plans, they can expect rapid progress.
d. Adopting a new habit or breaking an old one is hard to accomplish.

___ **8.** The article states that goals are easier to reach if they are specific. Which is the following is *not* a good example of a specific goal for behavior change?

   a. I will eat healthier foods in order to lessen my risk for stroke or heart disease.
   b. I will walk on the treadmill at the campus gym for forty minutes every Monday, Wednesday, Friday, and Saturday at noon.
   c. To lose weight, I will consume an average of 1150 calories or less per day for the next six weeks.
   d. I will achieve a 3.0 grade point average this semester, with no less than a C in any of my four classes.

___ **9.** According to this article, what should people expect to occur as a normal part of an effective behavior change process?

   a. to experience guilt
   b. to repeat earlier stages of the process after relapsing
   c. a fast, successful progression from stage to stage
   d. to limit alcohol to one drink per day

___ **10.** In the first paragraph, the article points out that people often fail to keep their New Year's resolutions to adopt a healthier lifestyle. This example supports the paragraph's main idea that

   a. most people are incapable of changing their behavior for longer than a few months.
   b. making a New Year's resolution is ineffective if you really want to change your lifestyle.
   c. people who set goals in January are more likely to succeed in meeting those goals.
   d. any effort to change, including making resolutions you don't end up achieving, can have a positive effect on your future accomplishments.

THEMATIC LINKS

If you want to learn more about the topic of behavior change, type the following words into your browser and explore the two sites that come up:

1. making lifestyle changes that last APA
2. qz.com/162534

READING SKILL FOCUS

OBJECTIVE
4 Determine word meanings from context

Determining Meaning from Context

Regardless of the academic career you are pursuing in college, you are likely to encounter unfamiliar words and expressions in texts and in lectures given by professors. It is, therefore, essential that you build a strong vocabulary to help you comprehend the material you read for different courses and to do well on standardized reading tests administered by most U.S. state colleges. You may not have a dictionary at your disposal all the time, so you will need to rely on **context**—the environment in which words appear—to figure out the meaning of unfamiliar words, especially when answering multiple-choice questions. Although there is no single technique that will always work, the following strategies will help you determine meaning from context without turning to a dictionary.

Denotation and Connotation

Denotation is the literal meaning of a word, which is distinct from any implied or associated ideas. For example, the word *consequence* means *a result of an action*. However, depending on the context, it can mean either a good or a bad result. When one commits a crime, one has to face the consequences, which might range from a fine to imprisonment, but in the field of chemistry, a chemical reaction could lead to the consequence of forming a gas, which might be a new and positive discovery. As a college student, you will need to determine not only the direct meaning of a word but also how a particular word is used in various contexts.

In contrast, **connotations** are the emotional and secondary meanings we associate with a word in a specific context. For example, we all know the literal meaning of *home,* but notice how the meaning of the same word changes in a different context:

> After he hit me again, I needed to get far away from *home.*

Here we can see that the connotation of *home* can vary from a place of warmth and safety to a hell inhabited by an abusive partner. As you read, you will notice that most words have either a positive or negative connotation. Even if you do not know the meaning of the new word you have just encountered, most of the time you can tell whether it has a negative or positive feel to it. Examine the following examples of words with positive and negative connotations.

Word	Denotation	Connotation
uplifting	encouraging	positive
critical	disapproving	negative
downtrend	downturn	negative
enlightening	giving knowledge	positive
optimistic	hopeful	positive

EXERCISE 2.6 **Determining Connotation**

Directions: In the table below, read the following words from Selection 1 (p. 40) in the left column and decide whether they have a positive or negative connotation. Put a check in the appropriate box.

Word	Connotation	
	Positive	**Negative**
reunited		
neglected		
distinguished		
disturbing		
interfere		

EXERCISE 2.7 **Finding Words with Positive and Negative Connotations**

Directions: Skim through Selection 2 (p. 46) and find five words that have a clear positive or negative connotation. Write them in the left column below and put a check in the appropriate box in the connotation column.

Word	Connotation	
	Positive	**Negative**

Context Clues

The context in which a word occurs also can lead you to its correct meaning. Carefully read the sentence in which an unfamiliar word appears, and look at the words that precede and follow it. If you are reading an entire passage, read the sentences that come immediately before and after the sentence that has the word in question. These adjacent sentences might also provide the context clues that will help you zero in on the correct meaning of the new word.

Let's look at an example from Selection 2 to see how this works.

> New Year's **resolutions** are notoriously hard to keep, especially when they're aimed at health behaviors such as losing weight, eating better, and exercising more.

Even if you are unfamiliar with the word *resolutions*, you can figure out its meaning from the context. In the passage above, the first clue for *resolutions* comes in its connection to "New Year's." What tradition is associated with the beginning of a New Year? If this context clue does not lead you to the word's meaning, then another hint may get you there. The verb *aimed* clearly relates to resolutions as goals or objectives. Finally, the sentence concludes with three specific examples of resolutions.

Two Strategies for Determining Meaning Using Context

1. **Identify the Word's Part of Speech.** When you come across an unfamiliar word, first identify what part of speech it is: a noun, a verb, an adjective, or an adverb. In the example above, your goal is to determine whether *resolutions* is a noun, a verb, an adjective, or an adverb. Doing so will help you understand whether the word *resolutions* has to do with the act of resolving something, an action carried out, a description of an individual, or the manner in which something is done. In this sentence, we can safely conclude that *resolutions* are acts of resolving things that are challenging. Once we understand that *resolutions* are acts, we can clearly see that the word must be a noun. Last but not least, we can confirm that *resolutions* is a noun by noticing the suffix *-tion*, which indicates action or condition, and which forms a noun when added to verbs and adjectives.

2. **Determine the Word's Connotation.** As you learned above, most words have either a positive or negative connotation. Understanding the connotation of a word will clue you in to its meaning. If you look at the context, it tells us that *resolutions* are "hard to keep" and then gives examples of health-related issues such as weight loss and healthy eating. Therefore, you can deduce that *resolutions* has a positive connotation because it relates to setting goals you wish to achieve.

Now that you have learned different strategies to determine meaning from context, let's do an exercise and apply these strategies.

EXERCISE 2.8   Using Context to Determine Meaning

Directions: Read the sentences below from Selection 3 and try to determine the meaning of the bolded words from the context in which they appear.

1. "My daughter has always been difficult, **intense**, and **testy**," she said, "but my son is the opposite, **placid** and good-natured."

Word	Part of Speech	Connotation	Your Definition
intense			
testy			
placid			

2. "When people **oversimplify**, they **mistakenly** assume that personality problems that have a genetic component are permanent—say, that someone is "born to be bad!" or to be a **miserable** grump forever."

Word	Part of Speech	Connotation	Your Definition
oversimplify			
mistakenly			
miserable			

3. "The wave of **acceptance** of genetic influence on behavior is growing into a tidal wave that **threatens** to **engulf** the second message of this research."

Word	Part of Speech	Connotation	Your Definition
acceptance			
threatens			
engulf			

EXERCISE 2.9   Vocabulary in Context

Directions: Determine the meaning of the bolded words in the following sentences without using a dictionary. Consider the part of speech and connotations of each word as you guess its meaning from context, and write down your definitions. Then, look the words up in a dictionary and write in those definitions.

1. The school psychologist realized that the failing student lacked **motivation** to do his work.
   Your definition: _____
   Dictionary definition: _____

2. At night, the woman would relive the **traumatic** episodes of her difficult childhood.
   Your definition: _____
   Dictionary definition: _____

3. The tests lacked **reliability** because the results were radically different from one to another.
   Your definition: _____
   Dictionary definition: _____

4. Recent studies have shown that **genetics** plays a much larger role in our chances of getting certain diseases than we had previously thought.
   Your definition: _____
   Dictionary definition: _____

5. Studies have shown a strong **correlation** between smoking and lung cancer.
   Your definition: _____
   Dictionary definition: _____
   _____

6. The ability to remember the past is a significant stage in a child's **development**.
   Your definition: _____
   Dictionary definition: _____

7. Some experts attribute differences between boys and girls to learned **behavior**.
   Your definition: _____
   Dictionary definition: _____

8. Through **psychoanalysis**, the patient was able to deal with his past.
   Your definition: _____
   Dictionary definition: _____

9. The war veteran found his discussions with his counselor to be very **therapeutic**.
   Your definition: _____
   Dictionary definition: _____

10. The veteran psychologist shared his years of **insight** into the workings of the human mind with his young students.
    Your definition: _____
    Dictionary definition: _____

READING

Selection 3

Textbook excerpt

Genetic Influences on Personality

Pre-Reading Questions

Answer the following questions before exploring the text.

1. Even though most siblings are raised by the same parents, grow up in the same household, and are taught more or less the same values, they are almost never alike. In your opinion, what factors cause the differences in their personalities?

2. In the past, some psychologists believed that the human mind was a blank slate and that the environment wrote on this slate, influencing human nature. Do you agree with this viewpoint? Why or why not?

3. Psychologists hope that with advancements in research on human nature, humans will someday become more accepting of who they are, their personalities. In your opinion, what specific findings will help people understand why they and their children behave a certain way?

Genetic Influences on Personality

by Carole Wade and Carol Tavris

1   A mother we know was describing her two children: "My daughter has always been difficult, intense, and testy," she said, "but my son is the opposite, placid and good-natured. They came out of the womb that way." Was this mother right? Is it possible to be born touchy or good-natured? What aspects of personality might have an **inherited** component?

2   For centuries, efforts to understand why people differ from one another have swung from biological answers ("It's in their **nature**; they are born that way") to learning and environmental ones ("It's all a matter of nurture—how they are raised and the experiences they have"). The *nature–nurture* debate has been one of the longest running either-or arguments in philosophy and psychology. Edward L. Thorndike (1903), one of the leading psychologists of the early nineteen hundreds, staked out the nature position by claiming that "in the actual race of life . . . the chief determining **factor** is heredity." But in stirring words that became famous, his contemporary, behaviorist John B. Watson (1925) insisted that experience could write virtually any message on the blank slate of human nature:

> Give me a dozen healthy infants, well-formed, and my own specified world to bring them up in and I'll guarantee to take any one at random and train him to become any type of specialist I might select—doctor, lawyer, artist, merchant—chief, and yes, even beggar man and thief, regardless of his talents, penchants, tendencies, abilities, vocations, and race of his ancestors.

3   Today, almost all psychologists would say the nature–nurture debate is over. The answer is both. Biology and experience, genes and environment, are interacting influences, each shaping the other over time (Johnson et al., 2009). In this section and the next, we will examine the interlaced influences of nature and nurture on personality.

4   How can heredity affect personality? Genes, the basic unit of heredity, are made up of elements of DNA (Deoxyribonucleic acid). These elements form chemical codes for the synthesis of proteins. Proteins, in turn affect virtually every aspect of the body, from its structure to the chemicals that keep it running. Genes can affect the behaviors we call "personality" through their effects on an infant's developing brain and nervous system. They can also affect the functioning of an adult's brain and nervous system, directly and also indirectly by switching other genes on or off. Interestingly, 98.8 percent of our total DNA, called non-coding DNA, lies outside the genes. This DNA used to be called "junk DNA" as scientists believed it was not very important, but this belief is changing fast. Non-coding DNA may also affect the expression (activity) of key genes, and mutations in it may be associated with common diseases. This existing line of research means that genes do not provide a static blueprint for development. Rather, our genetic heritage is more like a changing network of interlinked influences, including environmental ones, affecting us throughout life (Feinberg, 2008).

5   Researchers measure genetic **contributions** to personality in three ways: by studying personality **traits** in other species, by studying the temperament of human infants and children, and by doing heritability studies of twins and adopted individuals. You will be hearing lots more about genetic discoveries in the coming years, so it is important to understand what they mean and don't mean.

Evaluating Genetic Theories

6   Psychologists hope that one intelligent use of behavioral-genetic findings will be able to help people become more accepting of themselves and their children. Although we can all learn to make improvements and modifications to our personalities, most of us probably will never be able to transform our personalities completely because of our genetic disposition and temperaments.

7   Yet we should not oversimplify by assuming that "It's all in our genes!" A genetic predisposition does not necessarily imply genetic inevitability. A person might have genes that predispose him or her to depression, but without certain environmental stresses or circumstances, the person will probably never become depressed. When people oversimplify, they mistakenly assume that personality problems that have a genetic component are permanent— say, that someone is "born to be bad!" or to be a miserable grump forever. That belief can affect their behavior and actually make matters worse (Dweck, 2008). Oversimplification can also lead people to incorrectly assume that if a problem, such as depression or shyness, has a genetic contribution, it will respond only to medication, so there is no point trying other intervention.

8   It seems that nearly every year brings another report about some gene that supposedly explains a human trait. A few years back, newspapers even announced the discovery of a "worry gene." Don't worry about it! Most human traits, even such seemingly straightforward ones as height and eye color, are influenced by more than one gene. Psychological traits are especially

likely to depend on multiple genes, with each one accounting for just a small part of the variance among people. Conversely, any single gene is apt to influence many different behaviors. So at this point, all announcements of a "gene for this" or a "gene for that" should be viewed with extreme caution.

9   Robert Plomin (1989), a leading behavioral geneticist, once observed, "The wave of acceptance of genetic influence on behavior is growing into a tidal wave that threatens to engulf the second message of this research. These same data provide the best available evidence for the importance of environmental influences." Let us now see what some of those influences might be.

Thinking about the Reading

1. The article begins with a quote, "My daughter has always been difficult, intense, and testy," she said, "but my son is the opposite, placid and good-natured. They came out of the womb that way." Do you agree with the mother's view? Explain your position. When it comes to the nature–nurture debate, what do most psychologists think?

   _____

   _____

2. Feinberg states, "This existing line of research means that genes do not provide a static blueprint for development. Rather, our genetic heritage is more like a changing network of interlinked influences, including environmental ones, affecting us throughout life." What does he mean by that?

   _____

   _____

3. Why do most psychologists believe that "Although we can all learn to make improvements and modifications to our personalities, most of us probably will never be able to transform our personalities completely because of our genetic disposition and temperaments"?

   _____

   _____

4. Why do psychologists warn us that "all announcements of a 'gene for this' or a 'gene for that' should be viewed with extreme caution"?

   _____

Reading Comprehension Check

___ 1. "What aspects of personality might have an **inherited** component?" In this context, the meaning of the word *inherited* is

    a. received from one's parents' DNA.

    b. learned from one's neighbors.

    c. a behavior pattern caused by peers' influences.

    d. a characteristic learned from one's parents.

___ **2.** "In this section and the next, we will examine the **interlaced** influences of nature and nurture on personality." In this sentence, the word *interlaced* can be replaced by

    a. internal.
    b. divided.
    c. untwisted.
    d. woven together.

___ **3.** "This DNA used to be called 'junk DNA' as scientists believed it was not very important, but this belief is changing fast." We can conclude from this statement that

    a. scientists named this DNA "junk DNA" correctly.
    b. "junk DNA" is not associated with common diseases.
    c. "junk DNA" may also affect the activity of key genes.
    d. key genes are not affected by "junk DNA."

___ **4.** "A person might have genes that predispose him or her to depression, but without certain environmental stresses or circumstances, the person will probably never become depressed." We can infer from this passage that

    a. a genetic predisposition to an illness means you will always experience it.
    b. not all human behavior is genetically determined.
    c. it is reasonable to assume that it's all in the genes.
    d. depression can only be caused by environmental circumstances.

___ **5.** The main idea of the essay is that

    a. personality can be altered by changing our genetic makeup.
    b. personality develops as a result of the interaction of our genetic makeup and environment.
    c. personality is entirely influenced by environmental factors.
    d. personality usually results from behavior learned from the environment.

___ **6.** In the last paragraph of this reading, geneticist Robert Plomin is quoted as saying, "The wave of acceptance of genetic influence on behavior is growing into a tidal wave that threatens to engulf the second message of this research. These same data provide the best available evidence for the importance of environmental influences." Which of the following best restates Plomin's meaning?

    a. In addition to focusing on the idea that the genes we are born with influence our personalities, psychologists should also keep in mind that our surroundings and experiences can shape our personalities as well.
    b. The field of genetics is expanding with the same speed and destructive force as a tidal wave on the natural environment.
    c. Those who believe that our genes influence our personalities are mistaken; the environment alone is the deciding factor in explaining why we are the way we are.
    d. The primary message of the nature–nurture debate is that it is pointless to argue about what influences personality development.

___ **7.** The purpose of the anecdote about the two children in paragraph 1 is

   a. to show how intolerant parents can be of their children's personality differences.
   b. to show that the difficult daughter was naturally born that way, while the good-natured son was influenced by how he was brought up.
   c. to show that mothers prefer children who are easy going to those who are intense.
   d. to show how people often explain children's emerging personality traits as being determined by nature and present from birth.

___ **8.** In this reading, the term *nurture* most nearly means

   a. loving care provided to children.
   b. to keep a feeling alive.
   c. environmental influence.
   d. hereditary traits.

___ **9.** Which of the following is the best example of the influence of nurture?

   a. life stress that causes a person to become depressed
   b. a family history of breast cancer
   c. the belief that someone can be "born bad"
   d. the news media hyping the discovering of a "worry gene"

___ **10.** In paragraph 8, which of the following statements about the so-called worry gene is true?

   a. The worry gene is a dangerous genetic mutation that should be monitored.
   b. It is unlikely that the tendency to worry is influenced by any single gene.
   c. Every human characteristic—even the simplest traits, such as eye color—is caused by one gene only, and the worry gene is no exception to this rule.
   d. Using the phrases "a gene for this" and "a gene for that" is an informal way of expressing the valid point that the psychological trait of being anxious is caused by a specific gene.

Think to Write

Now that you have completed three readings in this chapter on psychology, think about which of the three is most interesting to you. Write a paragraph response about this reading and post it to The Wall. Here are some tips for responding to chapter readings:

A Few Tips on Responding to Chapter Readings

- You may want to discuss why you chose this particular reading as the most interesting of the chapter.
- You could zero in on a particular idea in your chosen reading and explain why this idea grabbed your attention.
- If you are feeling ambitious, you could compare the ideas in one chapter reading with those in another.

Once you have posted your response, skim your classmates' responses and write a short response to at least two of your classmates' postings.

It's SHOWTIME!

Watching a video clip related to the chapter content can be an enriching experience. Go online and find a video link with a topic that ties into one of the chapter readings (maximum length = 10 minutes). After viewing the video clip, **write** a half-page summary of the video's key points. **Post** your personal reaction to the ideas in the clip (between 150 and 400 words) on The Wall.

WRITING SKILL FOCUS

⑤ OBJECTIVE

Accurately restate the ideas of others by paraphrasing

Paraphrasing

Paraphrasing the information you hear is one way to address issues of comprehension in any language. If you are able to take a text or something that someone has said and accurately express the same ideas using different language, you have truly understood what you read. Let's take a look at what is meant by the term *paraphrasing* and how this skill might help you.

> **Definition of a paraphrase:** *An accurate restating in your own words of what someone else has written or said.*

The secret of good paraphrasing is to be flexible with *words*, not with *meaning*. Sometimes we hear someone say something, or read an article in the newspaper, and relay the information inaccurately to another person. This can get quite dangerous. Imagine you read the following excerpt in a health magazine: "If you are suffering from a severe anxiety disorder, you should immediately seek a referral to a psychiatrist." After reading this, you send the following text to a friend of yours who has been a little anxious lately about her coming exams. *"I just read that if you are feeling anxious at all, you need to see a psychiatrist."* This weak paraphrase will give your friend the wrong message.

> **Example of an Inaccurate Paraphrase**
>
> **Professor:** "If you never do your homework, you will fail my class."
>
> **Inaccurate Paraphrase:** The professor said we would fail if we missed a homework assignment.

Discuss with a classmate why this is a bad paraphrase.

> **Example of an Accurate Paraphrase from Selection 3 (para. 3, p. 57)**
>
> **Original Sentence:** "Biology and experience, genes and environment, are interacting influences, each shaping the other over time" (Johnson et al., 2009).
> **Paraphrased Sentence:** Johnson et al. (2009) contend that our genetic make-up and our acquired knowledge are bound in a reciprocal relationship.

Some Tips for Effective Paraphrasing

- **Acknowledge the source:** When you are restating someone else's ideas, it is critically important to give credit to the author of the original text. Otherwise, you will be guilty of plagiarism because you will give the reader a false impression that these are your ideas.

- **Understand what you are paraphrasing:** To be able to paraphrase a sentence, you must first fully comprehend all the information inside the sentence. Who said what to whom? What happened? Who and/or what was involved? Read the sentence or quotation you want to paraphrase a few times to gain a deeper understanding of its content.

- **Use appropriate synonyms to rephrase key words in the original sentence:** "More than half of the people who ride the subway claim …" can become "The majority of subway riders argue …"

- **Check for accuracy:** After you've paraphrased a sentence or quotation, compare your paraphrase to the original to make sure the paraphrase remains true to the ideas in the original and to check that your paraphrase does not sound just like the original.

EXERCISE 2.10   Practice with Paraphrasing

Directions: Work with a classmate. Read each of the following sentences twice, and then turn over your book and paraphrase each one orally. Take turns (and don't cheat!).

1. Parents and teachers are concerned that high school students are not able to focus their attention on their school lessons.
2. The government recently reported that alcohol and caffeine drink mixtures are very dangerous and should be taken off the market.
3. There has been an increase in crime, perhaps due to the difficult economic conditions in the country.
4. A new study indicates that more than 50 percent of NYC subway riders are connected to either an iPod or another electronic device.
5. There are now more women than men going to college in America, and the female students have higher grades.

Now write your paraphrases for items 1–5 below.

1. _____

   _____

2. _____

   _____

3. _____

   _____

4. _____

   _____

5. _____

   _____

WRITING SKILL FOCUS

6 OBJECTIVE
Write concise, accurate summaries

Summarizing

As a college student, you may be familiar with *summary writing*. Professors often ask students to summarize a specific reading, a short story, a newspaper article, or a lecture. Depending on the purpose of the writing assignment, they may ask students to write a short summary including the main idea and a few key supporting details or a long summary including the main idea, key concepts, and more details. In college, summary writing can be part of a standardized reading test, or it can be an integral part of your preparation for a final exam. It is, therefore, important that you learn how to write a concise and accurate summary of original text.

Three Important Characteristics of a Summary

If you have written a summary before, you probably know that it is difficult to restate an author's ideas in your own words. Remember that a well-written, objective summary has three important characteristics:

1. **It briefly outlines the main points of the original text without altering or modifying the meaning.**
2. **It only includes the relevant aspects of the original text.** In other words, it does not include all the supporting details in every paragraph.
3. **It is written in your own words.** The trick is to change the language significantly without changing the main idea and supporting details presented in the original text. Think of yourself as an objective information processor. Your task as a summary writer is to simply present the main ideas and supporting details of the original source in your own language. Using your own words in writing a summary is important because it demonstrates to the reader that you understood the original text correctly. If you copy sentences verbatim from the original text, you may be accused of plagiarism, an academic crime. (See the following page for more information on plagiarism.)

Writing a Summary

You have to fully understand the original text to write an accurate and objective summary. The following steps will help you to do so.

1. **Read the original text carefully, paying attention to the main idea(s) and how the reading is organized.** The reading may be divided into sections ("There are three types of volcanoes," or "The movie has four central characters"). Discussing the organization of the original text is particularly important if you are writing a summary of a long piece.

2. **Determine what type of text you are summarizing.** For example, are you writing a summary of a research paper, a short story, or a newspaper article? The purpose of identifying the genre of the original text is twofold: it helps your reader gain a better overall sense of the author's goals in the original text, and it also helps you get a better sense of the author's purpose for writing the original text (which will help guide your explanation of the author's key points).

3. **Read the text a second time, highlighting, underlining, and circling important pieces of information.**

4. **Write an introductory sentence that includes the title and author of the text you are summarizing.** Then for each section write one sentence that sums up the main point it conveys. Be careful to use your own words, retaining the original ideas.

5. **Make a list of the key major details that support each main idea.** You usually do not need to include minor details such as specific examples in your summary.

6. **Follow steps 1 through 5 a second time, revising, adding, or deleting information as you deem necessary.**

7. **Ensure that you have properly acknowledged and cited the source you are summarizing.**

Avoiding Plagiarism in Summary Writing

The term **plagiarism** is derived from the Latin word *plagiare*, which means "to kidnap." It is a writer's conscious and deliberate attempt to steal someone else's ideas and present them as her or his own. In essence, plagiarism is akin to kidnapping someone's baby and claiming that you are the baby's biological parent. Since the baby is too young to dispute the claim, most people would usually believe that you, the kidnapper, are indeed the mother or father of the baby.

Plagiarism is considered a serious academic crime in North American educational institutions. The idea is based on the assumption that an original idea is the intellectual property of its author. It is also considered disrespectful and dishonest to borrow and use the works of other authors without their consent and knowledge. A student found guilty of plagiarism can be expelled from a college or university and may find it difficult to pursue an academic career. It is, therefore, imperative that you always cite the original source in a summary.

Some novice writers forget to mention the source of an original text they are summarizing, giving their readers the impression that they are presenting their own ideas and thus unintentionally plagiarizing. To avoid this grave error, make sure that you mention the original source, as well as the main idea it contains, in the first sentence of your summary, making it explicit to the reader that you are simply restating someone else's ideas without expressing your opinion about them.

Keep in mind that at no point in a traditional, straightforward summary should you use the word *I* or express your viewpoint. For some assignments, you may be asked to write a summary blended with a personal response, but here we are focusing on strict summary writing.

Let's look at a few examples of how a summary should begin. Notice how the source is followed by the main idea:

- According to Fromkin in his article "Get it off Your Chest," men are socially conditioned to hide their feelings in public (132).
- In her article "Men Don't Cry," Smith **argues** that most men die prematurely because they keep their emotions bottled up inside (23).
- In their essay "Healthy Crying," Seliger and Sridhar **suggest** that if men can learn to express their feelings and emotions, they can live healthier lives (24–25).

Notice the use of the simple present tense (bolded) in the second and third sentences.

Note: While it is now clear that when you paraphrase or summarize, you must cite your source in the body of your essay, it is also critical that when you write an essay or research paper you cite your full source information in a separate Works Cited page (following MLA style). See "Citing Your Sources" in Chapter 9, on page 373.

Reminding the Reader

When writing a summary, your goal is to make it clear to the reader that you are not expressing your own views. You may want to remind the reader at frequent intervals that you are paraphrasing an original idea by saying one of the following:

- The author goes on to say that . . .
- The author further states that . . .
- Smalley concludes that . . .
- Johnson believes that . . .

If you are writing a long summary, it is recommended that you mention the author's name at least three times: at the beginning, in the middle, and at the end of your summary.

Inserting Transition Words

When you provide additional information to the reader, be sure to use transition words. They serve as signposts, signaling to the reader that you are about to present another idea.

Useful Transition Words		
additionally	furthermore	in fact
also	however	more important
further	in addition	moreover

EXERCISE **2.11**　　**Evaluating Summaries**

Directions: Reread "Genetic Influences on Personality" by Wade and Tavris on page 57. Then, read the four summaries below and decide which is the most accurate and objective. For each of the summaries, write at least a couple of sentences, explaining its strengths and weaknesses.

1.　　For centuries, efforts to understand why people differ from one another have swung from biological answers ("It's in their nature; they are born that way") to learning and environmental ones ("It's all a matter of nurture—how they are raised and the experiences they have"). The *nature–nurture* debate has been one of the longest running either–or arguments in philosophy and psychology. Yet we should not oversimplify by assuming that "It's all in our genes!" A genetic predisposition does not necessarily imply genetic inevitability. A person might have genes that predispose him or her to depression, but without certain environmental stresses or circumstances, the person will probably never become depressed. When people oversimplify, they mistakenly assume that personality problems that have a genetic component are permanent.

Your comments: _____

_____

_____

2.　　I really enjoyed reading the article by Wade and Tavris. In general, I agree with their assessment that the nature–nurture debate leads us clearly to the conclusion that both are major factors in determining our character. However, I disagree with their statement that people tend to simplify when they say "It's all in our genes." In my opinion, the tendency generally goes the other way. Most people forget the role of genetics and overplay environmental factors.

Your comments: _____

_____

_____

3.　　In "Genetic Influences on Personality," Wade and Tavris state that the nature–nurture debate has been going on for many, many years with scientific opinion swinging back and forth between biological and environmental interpretations of our behavior. However, the authors claim that today there is a near consensus among scientists that genetic and environmental factors both play a role in defining our personality. Wade and Tavris describe how genes influence our behavior, from their effects on a baby's brain development to their effects on how an adult's brain and nervous system functions. The authors argue that this knowledge of the influence of genetics on our behavior may lead more people to be less self-critical and less judgmental of their children. Finally, the authors warn of the dangers of oversimplifying the role of genetics, arguing that some people might then see some personality problems as impossible to change (pp. 49–50).

Your comments: _____

_____

_____

4.   The nature–nurture debate has taken a critical turn over the years in that we now have come to the understanding that both the environment and our genes play a significant role in determining our personalities. In fact, the relationship between our genetic make-up and our experiences in the world have a symbiotic relationship, demonstrating a clear influence on each other. Accepting the critical roles both nature and nurture play can lead some people to be more self-accepting, understanding that their faults, or their children's faults, are not entirely controllable. At the same time, there are those people who see everything as genetically pre-determined and thus might see personality issues as permanent defects (pp. 49–50).

Your comments: _____

_____

_____

_____

Discuss the four summaries with your classmates and find out whether they agree or disagree with your assessment.

TROUBLE SPOTS IN WRITING

Working with Reporting Verbs in a Summary

 OBJECTIVE
Use reporting verbs appropriately in summary writing

Good summary writers use a wide range of reporting verbs when referring to the original text. **Reporting verbs** are a class of verbs used to talk about or report on what other people have said (see list of "Frequently Used Reporting Verbs" on the following page). Some student writers fall into the habit of repeating "he said/she said" throughout their summaries. Others may make inappropriate use of subjective reporting verbs such as *argue* and *believe*, even when the article is factual.

You need to remind the reader frequently that you are simply paraphrasing an author's ideas without expressing your opinion about them. This is especially important if your summary is rather long. Your task is to always remain objective, leaving no confusion in the reader's mind that you are stating another writer's ideas in your summary.

Here are some of the frequently used reporting verbs.

Frequently Used Reporting Verbs			
describe	show	note	demonstrate
explain	propose	find	report
suggest	state	discuss	observe
examine	argue	contend	provide
maintain	point out	assert	develop
recommend	claim	study	emphasize

EXERCISE 2.12   Writing a Summary

Directions: Now that you have reviewed the characteristics of a winning summary, it's time to put theory into practice. Revisit Selection 1 on identical twins on page 40 and write a summary of it in your own words. Once you have finished, spend at least 20 minutes revising and editing it. Use the Summary Checklist below to guide your review work.

Summary Checklist

Topic Sentence

1. Does your topic sentence state the title of the original text, the author's name, and the main idea?

Supporting Points

2. Did you paraphrase the author's most important supporting points?
3. Did you mention the supporting points in the same order in which the author offered them?

Clarity of Thought

4. Did you convey the author's main idea and key supporting points clearly? Would someone who has never read the original understand the main idea and the supporting points?

Plagiarism

5. Did you use your own words to summarize the original? Can you find any examples of innocent plagiarism?
6. Have you correctly cited your source?

Grammar

7. Can you find any grammar mistakes? Proofread the summary and make any necessary corrections.

THEN & NOW

If you really want to understand an academic field, it is useful to gain a sense of how the academic discipline has evolved over time. This feature gives you the opportunity to do just that.

Go online and do some research to gather information about two experts in the field of psychology: one from the past and another who is contemporary. For example, learn about a prominent psychologist from the past such as Sigmund Freud or Carl Jung and a contemporary psychologist such as Steven Pinker or Elizabeth Loftus. Fill out the table provided below with pertinent information about the two psychologists.

Past Influential Psychologist	Present Influential Psychologist
Name	Name
Place of birth	Place of birth
Year of birth	Year of birth
Education	Education
What is he/she most famous for?	What is he/she most famous for?
Famous quote	Famous quote

After you fill out the table, discuss your findings with your classmates and learn from them about what they discovered on the Internet.

Working with a search engine, do the following search: "How the Mind Works, engine, Toy, W. W. Norton & Company, 1997, pp. 402–18." Peruse Steven Pinker's article to gain a deeper understanding of the complexity of the human mind. After doing a careful reading, write brief answers to the following questions about the content.

1. Pinker claims that humans are a unique species because, unlike animals, they help those who are not their relatives, including friends and strangers. In your opinion, do you believe humans help each other because they have a vested interest in doing so, or do they help others because they usually act selflessly?

   _____

   _____

2. On page 411, Pinker states that, "With threats, as with promises, communication can be a liability." Explain what he means.

   _____

   _____

   _____

   _____

3. On page 417, Pinker asks, "Why does romantic love leave us bewitched, bothered, and bewildered?" Explain.

   _____

   _____

CHAPTER PARAGRAPH ASSIGNMENT

Can human behavior be changed?

 OBJECTIVE

Read, think, plan, and write a paragraph in response to the chapter paragraph assignment

Now that you have had the opportunity to read a number of articles and a textbook excerpt, you should have a deeper understanding of the nature versus nurture debate and be prepared to compose your chapter paragraph assignment.

Scientists have believed for years that much of human behavior is genetically determined. However, many now tend to believe that the environment also plays a significant role in determining and influencing our behavior. Write a well-developed paragraph that answers the question *Can human behavior be changed?* in which you reference at least two sources, preferably from this chapter. **Remember,** you are welcome to construct your own chapter writing assignment, as long as it reflects the themes of the chapter readings.

For this early chapter, the writing assignment is limited to one paragraph. However, you have the option of writing a full essay if you feel ready for the challenge! When you are done, exchange your paragraph with that of a classmate and use the checklist below to offer constructive feedback. After you receive comments from your classmate, be sure to incorporate those suggestions you find most useful into your second draft and submit it to your instructor for further feedback on form and meaning. In future chapters, you will work with a peer review checklist, which focuses on a full essay.

Peer Review Checklist for a Paragraph

Writer: _____

Reviewer: _____

Date: _____

1. Does the paragraph begin with a clear topic sentence? If not, what suggestions do you have to improve the topic sentence?

   _____

2. Does the writer develop the topic sentence by using appropriate supporting details? If not, what types of details do you think the writer should include to develop the paragraph?

   _____

3. Is there a concluding sentence that ties everything together? If not, what would you suggest the writer do to wrap up the paragraph?

   _____

4. Are there grammar errors that impede your understanding of the writer's ideas? List a few of the errors you found:

   a. _____

   b. _____

   c. _____

5. What can be done to make this paragraph more precise and clear to the reader?

   _____

   _____

FOCUS ON FORM

Editing Reporting Verb Usage

In the Trouble Spots in Writing section on page 68, you learned how to control reporting verb usage. Now, let's put your skills into action! First, read the following paragraph on the essay topic of how the mind works. Edit the essay for errors in reporting verb usage. When you are finished, compare your edits with those of your partner.

In his critically acclaimed book entitled *How the Mind Works*, Steven Pinker confesses that much of human behavior is genetically determined and that the environment plays a minimal role in influencing how we think and behave. Pinker states the question, "Why do identical twins raised by different parents behave similarly, despite the fact that they had a different upbringing?" As you would expect, many psychologists are up in arms about his claims. In the end, Pinker talks that his critics may have a point, but that the role of environment would have to be proven based on empirical evidence.

It's Your Turn!

Now that you have had a chance to practice editing the use of reporting verbs, take a look at the paragraph you wrote for the chapter assignment and review it with new eyes. Pay close attention to the reporting verbs (if any), and be sure that you have used them correctly.

CHAPTER DEBATE

Can human behavior be changed?

You have written paragraphs and responded to your classmates' ideas on the topic of whether human behavior can be changed. Here is an opportunity for you to

participate in a debate and present, challenge and defend a position on a controversial topic. This chapter's debate topic is the same as your chapter essay assignment: *Can human behavior be changed?* Participating in this debate will provide you with a springboard for developing ideas for your essay. Refer to Appendix 8 (p. 455) for detailed guidelines on how to participate in a formal debate.

3 Criminal Justice

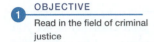
OBJECTIVE

1 Read in the field of criminal justice

Introduction to the Field of Criminal Justice

Criminal justice professionals provide vitally important services to society. From on-the-street police work to crime-scene investigations to forensic testing of criminal evidence, this is a wide-open field with an impressive variety of job descriptions.

Criminal Justice as an academic area has evolved since its beginnings in the 1920s. Scientific research has become a major element in the increasing professionalization of criminal justice, and there is a strong call for the application of evidence-based practices in the criminal justice field —that is, crime-fighting strategies that have been scientifically tested and that are based on social science research.

This chapter will primarily focus on issues related to police conduct and fair sentencing. What is the role of citizen videos in uncovering police misconduct? Should juvenile offenders be given the same sentences as adult offenders? How can corruption within the police force be checked? These provocative questions, which are explored in the readings, provide a framework for thinking critically about criminal justice.

CHAPTER 3 ESSAY QUESTION

Do you believe that the police live up to the promise of protecting and serving the community?

Quick Free-Write! Take out a piece of paper, and write for ten (10) minutes without stopping about what you already know about the theme of the chapter essay question.

As you read through the chapter, keep the essay question in focus and consider how you will integrate multiple perspectives about the issue. Chapter essays will be due when your class completes the chapter.

Your Option: Once you have worked your way through the chapter readings, you are welcome to narrow down the topics covered and compose your own chapter essay question.

Previewing Criminal Justice

Read the following questions and discuss them with your classmates. As you answer the questions, consider your personal experience and knowledge of criminal justice in general.

1. Do you generally believe in America's criminal justice system? Do you believe the system is fair? Explain. Do you have a positive view of the police force? Why or why not?

2. In your opinion, should the death penalty be legal? If yes, for what types of crimes should it be administered? Would abolishing the death penalty make America less safe? Explain.

3. Have you read or heard about a case where DNA samples provided incriminating evidence against a suspect? Describe the case.

4. Do you believe that DNA testing completely eliminates the possibility of innocent people being wrongly convicted of a crime? If yes, explain how this type of evidence reduces the margin of error.

5. In your opinion, is it a good idea for members of a community to form their own neighborhood-watch policing units? Why or why not?

After you have discussed the preview questions with your classmates, post your responses to two of them on **The Wall.** Review the postings on The Wall and respond to at least two of your classmates' postings that grab your interest. Remember the guidelines for The Wall etiquette (see p. 35)!

(see p. 35)!

OBJECTIVE

2

Understand and use key terms in criminal justice

Key Terms in Criminal Justice

Take a moment to think about the discipline of criminal justice as you complete the following two exercises.

EXERCISE 3.1   Brainstorming Vocabulary

Directions: What associated words come to mind when you think of the world of criminal justice? Work with a partner and write down as many related words as you can think of in a period of five minutes.

EXERCISE 3.2   **Creating Original Sentences**

Directions: Choose five of the words from your brainstorm list, and use them to write complete and meaningful sentences.

1. _____

2. _____

3. _____

4. _____

5. _____

Building a Strong Academic Vocabulary

An effective way to add to your academic vocabulary is to study key terms that are connected thematically. When you take your 100-level content courses, it is essential that you have a strong vocabulary base in the given academic subjects you are studying. For example, a student taking an Introduction to Criminal Justice course should be able to apply such terms as *suspect*, *parole*, and *rehabilitation* in both spoken and written forms. Sometimes, a college student will need to use other words that are similar to or are opposite in meaning to the words used in the original text when writing a brief response to a chapter or an article.

A **synonym** is a word used to express a similar meaning to another word. An **antonym** is a word that conveys the opposite meaning of another word.

In addition, understanding how to work with synonyms and antonyms is a useful skill, especially when you are writing a summary of a text and trying to paraphrase some of the key ideas and pieces of information contained in the original source. The following exercise will enable you to learn some key terms in the discipline of criminal justice and practice using synonyms and antonyms for them.

EXERCISE 3.3 **Discipline-Specific Vocabulary: Fishing for Synonyms and Antonyms**

Directions: Read the following ten (10) discipline-specific words culled from the readings in this chapter and shown in the context of the sentences in which they appeared. In the space provided after each sentence, write a synonym or antonym for each highlighted term, as directed.

Discipline-Specific Word Bank*

imposed	incarcerate	suspect	consequences
comply	corruption	parole	patrol
rehabilitation	violations		

* The first time these discipline-specific words appear in the chapter, they are shown in bold green.

1. "The city agreed to comply with a federal court order that **imposed** numerous requirements for managing the force and reviewing instances of potential abuse." (Selection 1, p. 82, para. 11)

   A synonym for *imposed* is _____.

2. "But the videos often provide an incomplete picture of events, police and law-enforcement advocates say—sometimes failing to show the actions that led to the confrontation and a **suspect**'s behavior." (Selection 1, p. 81, para. 6)

   A synonym for *suspect* is _____.

3. "The footage appears to show the deputy firing three times as the suspect begins to **comply** with orders to get up from the ground." (Selection 1, p. 82, para. 9)

   An antonym for *comply* is _____.

4. "There are more than 1,700 people in the United States serving sentences of life without **parole** for crimes committed as juveniles." (Selection 2, p. 88, para. 1)

   A synonym for *parole* is _____.

5. "Thus, at no point is there an opportunity to permit consideration of the individual circumstances of the child and the potential for **rehabilitation**." (Selection 2, p. 88, para. 6)

   An antonym for *rehabilitation* is _____.

6. "There is no question that the two juveniles, Joe Sullivan and Terrance Graham, were convicted of very serious offenses. So why is it problematic to **incarcerate** them for life?" (Selection 2, p. 88, para. 2)

   An antonym for *incarcerate* is _____.

7. "We accept the inaccuracy of using age as a measure of maturity because the **consequences** are not severe, and individual evaluations for the entire population would be impractical." (Selection 2, p. 89, para. 11)

    A synonym for *consequences* is _____.

8. "In 2006, Mayor Ron Gonzales of San Jose was indicted on public **corruption** charges, and Lynwood, California, mayor Paul Richards was found guilty of multiple counts of fraud, money laundering, extortion, making false statements to investigators, and depriving the public of honest services." (Passage Two, p. 100)

    An antonym for *corruption* is _____.

9. "Chicago, with markedly fewer people and a smaller area to **patrol**, actually has more officers than LA." (Selection 3, p. 102, para. 6)

    A synonym for *patrol* is _____.

10. "Former Illinois governor and one-time Nobel Prize nominee George Ryan was found guilty of 18 charges of racketeering, mail fraud, making false statements to FBI agents, and income tax **violations** in 2006." (Passage Two, p. 100)

    An antonym for *violations* is _____.

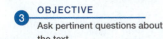

SUCCESS IN
READING

③ OBJECTIVE

Ask pertinent questions about the text

Read Actively by Asking Pertinent Questions

It is helpful to think of reading as an interactive activity. If you are sitting alone and holding a textbook or novel, you may ask, *Who exactly am I interacting with?* Good question! The answer is that if you are engaged in active reading, you are interacting with the words on the page by asking questions about the ideas and information coming at you. It is human nature to be curious, and when you start to read about a particular topic, your mind begins to formulate key questions in an effort to figure out what is going on.

So for example, you might glance at a newspaper and the headline reads:

> Three School Children Suspended for Bad Behavior in San Diego

Automatically, you begin to ask questions of the text in an effort to fill in the details of the story as shown below.

> Three Children Suspended for Bad Behavior in San Diego
> 1. What did the children do wrong?
> 2. How old were the three kids?
> 3. What caused them to act in this manner?

EXERCISE **3.4**   **Interacting with Text**

Directions: Let's read a paragraph about "Qualifications for Police Work." As you read, write down three questions about the reading that come into your head. When you are done, share your three questions with a classmate.

> One's physical and mental condition is an important factor in qualifying for police work. Generally, candidates need to have good eyesight, cannot be color blind, must have good hearing, be in average or above average physical condition, and capable of obtaining a driver's license.
>
> —From Fagin, *Criminal Justice*, p. 176.

1. _____

2. _____

3. _____

   _____

READING

Selection 1

Newspaper Article

Some Say Cop Videos Misleading

Pre-Reading Questions

Answer the following questions before exploring the text.

1. How accurate do you think videotaped recordings are when used as criminal evidence? Are there any problems you can foresee with this type of evidence?

2. Do you think the police have the right to use force under certain circumstances? Explain.

3. What other relatively recent technologies have changed the world of policing? Do you think the public any safer due to these technological innovations? Explain.

Eye on Vocabulary

Skim through the reading and find the following key vocabulary terms in bold. Working with a partner, examine the words in context and try to guess their meanings. Then look up the words in a dictionary. Keep in mind that many words have multiple meanings. Write the definition that fits the word's context in the article.

Word	Your definition	Dictionary definition
1. advent		
2. to mete out		
3. excessive		
4. at first blush		

Some Say Cop Videos Misleading

by William M. Welch

USA TODAY, November 30, 2006

1   LOS ANGELES—A series of recent videotaped arrests is providing an unfiltered look at often physical, sometimes brutal police work, due to the broadening technology of cell phone cameras and online video viewing.

2   Some law enforcement experts say the technology is shedding light on a long-standing if uncomfortable fact of life: Police frequently have to use force. And society and the law expect them to do so.

3   "The core function of police is, they're the ones who step up and use force when it is necessary," says Eugene O'Donnell, a former New York City police officer and prosecutor. "The cops are doing our dirty work. And when someone puts it on camera and shoves it out there, we say, 'Isn't this terrible.'"

4   The tape of the beating of Rodney King by police in Los Angeles in 1991 had to be handed to television stations nationwide before the public saw it. Nowadays, advances in computer technology and the **advent** of websites such as YouTube allow a person to post immediately a video online for millions of people to view. In the latest videos:

- A man is seen being pepper-sprayed by officers in Venice Beach as he is put in a squad car. The incident happened last year but was posted online in November.
- An officer is seen punching a **suspect** in the face while a fellow officer tries to handcuff him during a struggle on a Hollywood street in August.
- A UCLA student is seen being shocked with a Taser stun gun by a campus police officer during a library ID check.

Some defense lawyers say the videos are giving the American public a glimpse into brutality they never knew existed.

Incomplete Picture?

5   "I can't see how anyone would think it would be OK to **mete out** punishment to someone who has been subdued and is not any threat," says John Raphling, lawyer for the man pepper-sprayed by officers.

6   The videos have been shocking to some Americans, a more raw real-life police drama than they may have expected after countless hours of television cop shows. But the videos often provide an incomplete picture of events, police and law-enforcement advocates say—sometimes failing to show the actions that led to the confrontation and a suspect's behavior.

7   And after all, some experts say, a police officer's job is to control violent and potentially violent people. That generally requires using a level of force just above that used by the suspect. "Somewhere in America, cops are beating up on somebody right now. It's legal and justifiable, even though it may be offensive to watch," says O'Donnell, professor of law and police studies at John Jay College of Criminal Justice.

8   Los Angeles Police Chief William Bratton says his officers were using justifiable force in subduing suspects in the Hollywood and Venice Beach

incidents, even if the video strikes viewers as disturbing. In the Venice Beach pepper-spraying, Bratton said county prosecutors examined the video and cleared officers of wrongdoing because the video showed the man was clearly combative. "The officers showed remarkable restraint," Bratton said. Likewise, the officers in the Hollywood incident were cleared after a court hearing.

9.   Some experts say the number of videos is bound to increase, as will their impact on police work and the judicial system. In January, video captured a San Bernardino county sheriff's deputy shooting an unarmed Air Force airman after a chase in Chino, Calif. The footage appears to show the deputy firing three times as the suspect begins to **comply** with orders to get up from the ground. The officer was charged with attempted voluntary manslaughter.

10   A videotape of a Westminster, Colo., police takedown of a man after a seven-hour hostage drama drew attention when it was aired on TV and the Internet in 2005. The video appeared to show officers hitting the man after he was down. In Inglewood, Calif., a jury last year found in favor of two police of officers who filed suit claiming they were unfairly disciplined after a videotaped beating of a teenager in a confrontation at a gas station in 2002. "Because of the technology, everybody has a camera, and everybody's ready to use it," says Charles Whitebread, a professor of criminal procedure at the University of Southern California law school. The impact could be especially significant in Los Angeles. The city has a long and troubled history with police, use of force, and arrest videos.

11   Rodney King's arrest and beating after a traffic stop, videotaped by a bystander, made nationwide news. Four officers were charged with using **excessive** force. Their acquittal in a 1992 trial sparked riots. The Los Angeles Police Department is still feeling the effects of a 1999 scandal involving abuses by gang-control officers in the city's Rampart Division. The city agreed to comply with a federal court order that **imposed** numerous requirements for managing the force and reviewing instances of potential abuse. It is still in effect.

"Excessive force" Culture

12   Connie Rice, a civil rights lawyer who headed a review panel that investigated the scandal, credits the department with improvement in dealing with the public. "I still think LAPD has an excessive force culture," she says. "LAPD needs to tell its officers you don't get to spray people just because they mouth off." Whether the actions were justified or not, the videos have hurt the reputation of police, Whitebread says. "It may well be that there are explanations. **At first blush**, it's pretty rough to look at," he says. "It can't do LAPD any good to have these videos disseminated."

13   Police are well aware of the power of such images. One response has been a move by some police forces around the country to install video cameras in police cars—allowing law enforcement to have its own more complete visual record of confrontations. O'Donnell sees videos as possibly doing some good: They may help the public decide for itself what is reasonable force and what is not. "People become used to the idea this is the police and what they do.... That may allow people to kind of clarify misconduct from things that are not misconduct. People see the police acting in a way that may not be pretty but may be justifiable," he said.

14　　O'Donnell says the videos will also demonstrate that police are asked to bear a heavy burden in the criminal justice system, not just enforcing the law but acting as social workers with the mentally ill, the homeless and the addicted. "It's a brutal system," says O'Donnell, "and cops bear the brunt of that brutality."

Thinking about the Reading

After doing a close reading of the article, write your answers to the following questions. Then discuss your answers with your classmates.

1. Paraphrase the following quotation from Eugene O'Donnell, a former New York City police officer and prosecutor: "The core function of police is, they're the ones who step up and use force when it is necessary."

   _____

   _____

2. In what context is the Web site YouTube mentioned in the article? What role does YouTube play?

   _____

   _____

3. Paraphrase this statement by John Raphling, the lawyer for the man who was recorded on video being pepper-sprayed by police officers: "I can't see how anyone would think it would be OK to mete out punishment to someone who has been subdued and is not any threat."

   _____

   _____

   Do you agree? Explain. _____

   _____

4. What 1999 LAPD scandal is mentioned in the reading? What happened? In your opinion, how frequently do such types of police abuse occur?

   _____

   _____

5. There has been a movement across the country for some police to install video cameras inside their police cars. What would motivate a police department to install this technology?

   _____

   _____

   _____

   _____

Reading Comprehension Check

_____ **1.** "Some law enforcement experts say the technology is **shedding light on** a long-standing if uncomfortable fact of life …" (para. 2). The term *shedding light on* could be replaced with

    a. hiding information from.   c. confusing.

    b. providing information about.   d. complicating.

_____ **2.** A man being seen pepper-sprayed by the police, a suspect punched by an officer, and a student being shocked with a Taser gun are all examples of

    a. police being attacked.

    b. police responses captured on video.

    c. a crime reported but not documented.

    d. examples of political actions.

_____ **3.** What is being compared to television cop shows in paragraph 6?

    a. soap operas   c. fake video attacks

    b. violent films   d. real-life police dramas

_____ **4.** What point is offered in defense of police authorities?

    a. These videos are not official evidence.

    b. Civilians do not have the right to video private actions.

    c. Videos do not necessarily show what preceded or triggered a violent response.

    d. Substantiated claims of police abuse are rare.

_____ **5.** "Los Angeles Police Chief William Bratton says his officers were using justifiable force in **subduing** suspects in the Hollywood and Venice Beach incidents, even if the video strikes viewers as disturbing." (para. 8) In this sentence, the term *subduing* could be replaced with

    a. empowering.   c. restraining.

    b. battling.   d. injuring.

_____ **6.** According to civil rights lawyer Connie Rice, quoted in paragraph 12, what is meant by "excessive force culture"?

    a. the tendency for Los Angeles police officers to believe that the excessive use of force is justified even when a civilian's action is relatively minor

    b. the tendency for criminals to believe that violence toward police officers is justified

    c. the tendency for people to follow police officers on duty in order to catch them in acts of excessive force

    d. the tendency for our culture to condone violence in daily life

_____ **7.** The last sentence of this article quotes Eugene O'Donnell, an attorney and former officer, as saying "'It's a brutal system…and cops bear the brunt of that brutality.'" Which of the following best restates his meaning?

    a. Police officers have a responsibility to the public to be as brutal as possible.

    b. Law enforcement is an inherently difficult, sometimes violent task, and police officers experience the worst of it.

      c. Violence against police officers is far greater than violence committed by police officers.

      d. Police officers have it easy, because they are trained to be violent and thus are not affected by the psychological burdens of their work.

_____ **8.** According to paragraph 8, why were the officers cleared of wrongdoing in the case of the Venice Beach pepper-spraying?

      a. Because the officers restrained themselves from beating the man.

      b. Because no pepper spray was actually involved in the incident.

      c. Because it turned out that it was actually the suspect who pepper-sprayed the officers.

      d. Because the man was shown on video to be aggressive.

_____ **9.** According to O'Donnell in paragraph 13, why might installing video cameras in police cars be a good thing?

      a. Because video from such cameras will catch police officers who are not doing their jobs.

      b. Because viewers who are exposed to these on-the-job videos will get a better sense of the situations police face and what is excessive force versus justifiable force.

      c. Because officers can have their own records of confrontations with suspects.

      d. Because these videos can be posted online in order raise awareness of what police work is actually like.

_____ **10.** The 1991 Rodney King beating is mentioned in paragraph 4 to support the point that

      a. the Rodney King video was not spread to the general public as quickly as similar videos are today.

      b. there is no similarity between the police beating of Rodney King by police and excessive use of force by police today.

      c. the treatment of King by police was probably justified.

      d. if phones with video recorders had existed at the time, the King beating would probably not have happened in the first place.

THEMATIC LINKS

If you want to read more on the topic of police and videotaping, type the following words into your browser and explore the two sites that come up:

1. Can the cops arrest you for filming an arrest?

2. Is Filming a Police Officer a "Domestic Threat"?

Writing without BOUNDARIES

There Are No Checkpoints!

"It is better that ten guilty persons escape, than that one innocent suffer."

—Sir William Blackstone

Read the quote above and respond to the idea it expresses in any way you want. Write in your notebook for ten minutes without stopping. For this activity, it is important that you focus on ideas, not words. In other words, this will be an exercise in focusing on content and not getting hung up on word choice and grammar errors. You may wish to read what you have written out loud in front of your classmates and instructor.

READING

Selection 2

Newspaper Article

Room for Debate: Young Offenders Locked Up for Life

Pre-Reading Questions

Answer the following questions before exploring the text:

1. What are some factors that might lead minors to commit juvenile crimes?

2. How can the police work to build trust between troubled youth and neighborhood cops?

3. Should law enforcement officials treat juvenile offenders differently from adult offenders? Defend your position on this matter.

Eye on Vocabulary

Skim through the reading and find the following key vocabulary terms in bold. Working with a partner, examine the words in context and try to guess the meaning of these terms. Then look up the words in a dictionary. Keep in mind that many words have multiple meanings. Write the definition that best fits the word's context in the article.

Word	Your definition	Dictionary definition
1. banning		
2. susceptible		
3. denouncing		
4. culpability		

Room for Debate: Young Offenders Locked Up for Life

The New York Times, **November 8, 2009**

*Is life without **parole** cruel and unusual punishment for juvenile offenders convicted of non-homicide crimes?*

Marc Mauer of the Sentencing Project says Yes

Kent Scheidegger of the Criminal Justice Legal Foundation responds with a No

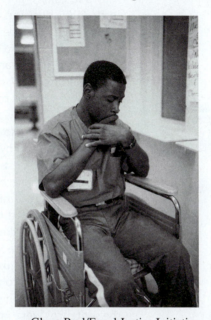

Glenn Paul/Equal Justice Initiative

Joe Sullivan, at 31 in June 2007. He was convicted at 13 for rape and sentenced in 1989 to life in prison.

Part 1

Proportionate Justice

***Marc Mauer** is the executive director of the Sentencing Project and the author of "Race to **Incarcerate**." The Sentencing Project submitted an amicus brief supporting the petitioners, Terrance Graham and Joe Sullivan.*

1   There are more than 1,700 people in the United States serving sentences of life without **parole** for crimes committed as juveniles. No other nation has even a single person serving such a sentence. Now the Supreme Court will consider an extreme outcome of this policy, two cases of juveniles serving no-parole life terms for non-homicide offenses.

2   Children do not have fully matured levels of judgment or impulse control, and they are uniquely capable of change. There is no question that the two juveniles, Joe Sullivan and Terrance Graham, were convicted of very serious offenses. So why is it problematic to **incarcerate** them for life?

3   First, children are different than adults. As the Supreme Court noted in its 2005 decision in Roper v. Simmons **banning** the death penalty for juveniles, children do not have fully matured levels of judgment or impulse control, and are more **susceptible** to peer pressure than adults. Brain imaging research documents that adolescent brains are not fully developed, particularly in areas that control reasoning and risk taking. It is for these reasons that all states already impose age restrictions on voting, driving and consuming alcohol.

4   Children are also uniquely capable of change. No matter how serious a crime committed by a 13-year-old, there is no means of predicting what type of adult he or she will become in 10 or 20 years. That's why we need professional parole boards to consider whether and at what point they are capable of returning to society.

5   The diminished capacity of young offenders renders life-without-parole sentences "cruel and unusual punishment" banned by the Eighth Amendment. As the Supreme Court noted in the Roper decision, there is a "basic precept of justice that punishment for crime should be graduated and proportioned to the offense." The two Florida cases fail on this principle because they involve non-homicide offenses and because of the way the sentences were imposed.

6   Many of the juveniles serving life without parole sentences are doing so as a result of the harsh penalties adopted by many states in the 1990s that automatically transfer certain juvenile cases to adult court. Upon conviction in adult court, they are often sentenced to mandatory life terms. Thus, at no point is there an opportunity to permit consideration of the individual circumstances of the child and the potential for **rehabilitation**.

7   The impact of these policies can be seen in the Sullivan and Graham cases, both sentenced in Florida courts. Of the 109 juveniles nationally who have been identified as serving life without parole terms for a non-homicide, 77 are in Florida alone. It is difficult to imagine that young people in Florida are so much more violent or beyond redemption than children in any other state, but it's not difficult to determine that sentencing policies in that state have produced these results.

8   Joe Sullivan was convicted of sexual battery at the age of 13. He is now 33 and confined to a wheelchair as a result of multiple sclerosis. It would seem reasonable for the court to allow for a consideration of whether he and Terrance Graham still present a threat to public safety.

Get into a small group and answer the two questions that follow.

1. What have you learned from the article so far?

2. With the understanding that Kent Scheidegger is taking an opposing position in his response to Marc Mauer's opinion, try to predict what may be coming in the second half of the reading. What might some of Mr. Scheidegger's arguments be?

Part 2

No Magic to an Age Limit

Kent Scheidegger is the legal director of the Criminal Justice Legal Foundation. He wrote an amicus brief supporting the State of Florida in the Graham and Sullivan cases. Below he responds to Marc Mauer.

9   I agree with Marc Mauer that no juvenile should be sentenced to life without parole as a result of a "mandatory minimum" sentencing statute, without an individual evaluation. But that has nothing to do with the Graham and Sullivan cases. In each of these cases, a judge evaluated the crime, the defendant's criminal record, and the failed prior efforts at rehabilitation before deciding that we could take no more chances on a young criminal who had already received two or more.

10   While **denouncing** mandatory minimum statutes that impose a sentence based on a single, rigid criterion, Mr. Mauer demands a "mandatory maximum" rule that forbids a sentence based on a single, rigid criterion. That approach is just as wrong, for the same reason. **Culpability** and potential for rehabilitation cannot be reduced to the single variable of chronological age.

11   Our society uses rigid age cutoffs for voting, driving, etc., as a matter of convenience and economy, not because we really believe there is anything magic about a particular birthday. We accept the inaccuracy of using age as a measure of maturity because the **consequences** are not severe, and individual evaluations for the entire population would be impractical.

12   For juveniles who commit major crimes of violence such as rape, armed robbery and murder, the consequences of getting it wrong are severe, and there are vastly fewer cases. We can and should evaluate each case on the merits. In a very few cases, the right answer is life in prison.

Thinking about the Reading

After doing a close reading of the articles, write your answers to the following questions. You may be asked to discuss your answers with your classmates.

1. What is Marc Mauer's most compelling argument for why juvenile offenders should get lesser sentences?

   _____

2. What statistic does Mr. Mauer offer to demonstrate how strict the state of Florida has been in sentencing juvenile offenders?

   _____

   _____

3. Do you believe that non-homicide crimes should be punished much more lightly than cases of homicide? Explain.

   _____

4. On what grounds does Kent Scheidegger disagree with Mr. Mauer's case for giving lighter sentences for juvenile offenders?

   _____

   _____

   _____

5. In your view, does Mr. Scheidegger offer a reasonable response to Mr. Mauer? Why or why not?

   _____

Reading Comprehension Check

_____ 1. According to Mr. Mauer, how is the United States unique in its sentencing of juvenile offenders?

   a. We have a tradition of lighter sentencing than most other nations.
   b. No other country gives youthful offenders life without parole.
   c. The United States and 1,700 other nations give juvenile offenders life without parole sentences.
   d. We have more people in prison than any other country.

_____ 2. What two facts were noted in the 2005 Supreme Court decision in *Roper v. Simmons*?

   a. Children resist peer pressure and mature quickly after the age of 15.
   b. Children are more susceptible to peer pressure and have excellent control of their impulses.
   c. Age restrictions are not a good idea for voting or for alcohol consumption.
   d. Children are less able to make sound judgements, and the likelihood of their being victims of peer pressure is stronger than it is for adults.

_____ 3. "Children are also **uniquely** capable of change." (para. 4) The word *uniquely* could be replaced by

a. doubtfully.　　　　　c. particularly.

b. typically.　　　　　d. unsparingly.

_____ 4. Mr. Scheidegger agrees with the judges' decisions (in the Graham and Sullivan cases) that "we could take no more chances on a young criminal" based on what factors?

a. risk of a repeat offense

b. failed past efforts at rehabilitation and mandatory sentencing

c. an evaluation of the crime, the defendant's criminal record, and failed efforts at rehabilitation

d. the defendant's criminal record only

_____ 5. Why does Scheidegger make a comparison between age rules concerning voting and driving and age rules relating to criminal sentencing?

a. His point is that the consequences of making an error with age rules is more serious in the sentencing of crimes than with voting and driving.

b. He argues that letting youth drive at a younger age is risky in the same way that letting juvenile offenders off easy can be.

c. He is strongly against bringing age cutoffs into any conversation about our laws.

d. He is trying to show that juvenile offenders should not be allowed to vote or drive.

_____ 6. According to Mauer, juveniles who commit crimes should be judged less harshly than adults who commit crimes partly because

a. juveniles typically commit less serious crimes.

b. juveniles are more easily influenced by peer pressure.

c. juveniles cannot vote, drive, or consume alcohol.

d. juveniles are less capable of change.

_____ 7. According to Mauer, which is *not* a way that a life-without-parole sentence for a juvenile offender constitutes "cruel and unusual" punishment?

a. It denies children access to age-appropriate health care while in prison.

b. The severity of the punishment is inappropriate for non-homicide offenses.

c. It fails to consider a child's potential for rehabilitation.

d. It results from automatically transferring certain juvenile cases to adult court.

_____ 8. In paragraph 7, what point does the example of the state of Florida illustrate?

a. that juveniles in Florida are more violent than in other states

b. that adults in Florida are more violent than in other states

c. that Florida has the right idea about how to sentence juvenile offenders appropriately

d. that certain states apply harsher penalties than other states when sentencing juveniles

_____ 9. According to Mauer, at the time this article was written, how many people outside the United States were serving sentences of life without parole for crimes they committed as juveniles?

a. 1,700
b. more than 1,700
c. none
d. Mauer does not say.

_____ 10. According to Mauer in paragraph 4, why is the role played by a professional parole board so important?

a. They can predict what type of adult a juvenile offender will turn out to be.
b. They can judge each child's unique capacity to return to society.
c. They can decide on a single policy that can then be applied to all juvenile offenders.
d. Volunteer parole boards tend to harbor prejudice against juvenile offenders.

THEMATIC LINKS

If you want to read more on the topic of juvenile sentencing, type the following words into your browser and explore the two sites that come up:

1. Reconsidering Life Sentences for Juveniles Who Kill Huffington Post
2. "Where Do You Think That Rage Came From?" Slate

READING SKILL FOCUS

Identifying Topics and Main Ideas (Stated and Implied)

OBJECTIVE

4 Identify the topic and main idea (stated or implied) of a reading passage

When you are asked to find the *main idea* of a reading passage or a paragraph within a reading passage, you are really being asked to identify the most important point the author wants to convey to the reader.

Movie Analogy: Understanding the Concept of *Main Idea*

Imagine a friend calls you and says she is in a hurry and would like you to recommend a film. You tell her that she should see *The Amazing Spiderman 2*, and she asks you to tell her in a sentence (there is no time to lose!) what the film is about.

You say, "Well, Spider Man has to risk the lives of the people he loves to save New York from being reduced to a pile of ashes." As you may have guessed by now, you've just offered your friend the main idea of the movie.

Main Idea versus Topic

Another way to understand the concept of *main idea* is to compare it with the idea of *topic*. A **topic** is a word, name, or phrase that tells what an author is writing about. It is more *general* than a main idea.

Examine the first three paragraphs of the opinion piece "Proportionate Justice" by Marc Mauer (p. 87).

> There are more than 1,700 people in the United States serving sentences of life without parole for crimes committed as juveniles. No other nation has even a single person serving such a sentence. Now the Supreme Court will consider an extreme outcome of this policy, two cases of juveniles serving no-parole life terms for non-homicide offenses.
>
> Children do not have fully matured levels of judgment or impulse control, and they are uniquely capable of change. There is no question that the two juveniles, Joe Sullivan and Terrance Graham, were convicted of very serious offenses. So why is it problematic to incarcerate them for life?
>
> First, children are different than adults. As the Supreme Court noted in its 2005 decision in Roper v. Simmons banning the death penalty for juveniles, children do not have fully matured levels of judgment or impulse control, and are more susceptible to peer pressure than adults. Brain imaging research documents that adolescent brains are not fully developed, particularly in areas that control reasoning and risk taking. It is for these reasons that all states already impose age restrictions on voting, driving and consuming alcohol.

The topic, or the general category, the author is writing about in the above paragraphs is *juvenile offenders*. The main idea, however, is more specific and could be stated as follows:

Juvenile offenders should not be sentenced in the same way as adult offenders.

Topic	Main Idea
Juvenile Offenders	Juvenile offenders should not be sentenced in the same way as adult offenders.

The relationship among topics, main ideas, and details is shown below as they appear on a continuum from most general to most specific. The *topic* of a reading passage is the broad subject the entire passage is about and is the most general element. The *main idea* is the writer's point about the topic, and the details and examples are the specific evidence the writer uses to explain and support his or her main point. Keeping this continuum in mind can be helpful when you are trying to locate the main idea in a reading.

Most general ⟶ **More specific** ⟶ **Most specific**

Topic (broad subject) ⟶ Main idea (point about the topic) ⟶ Details/examples (evidence that supports the main point)

Identifying the Main Idea (Stated or Implied) of a Reading

Most articles or textbook passages have a main idea. Sometimes the main idea is stated directly in a thesis statement. Other times, the author gives you the information needed to understand the main point without stating it directly in a single sentence. This is called an *implied main idea* because you the reader must use information contained in the passage to *infer* (reason out) the author's main point.

Whether the main idea is stated or implied, the key question to ask yourself in trying to distinguish the main idea is the following: What central idea do all of the paragraphs in the reading speak to and revolve around?

EXERCISE 3.5 Finding the Topic and Main Idea of Reading Passages

Directions: With a partner, review Readings 1 and 2 in this chapter, and write down the topic and main idea of each on the lines below. Keep in mind that Reading 2 contains two separate readings. Also, for each of the readings, decide whether the main idea is stated or implied and underline your choice.

1. "Some Say Cop Videos Misleading" (p. 81)

   Topic: _____

   Main idea: _____

   _____

   _____

   Stated Main Idea / Implied Main Idea

2. "Room for Debate: Young Offenders Locked Up for Life—Proportionate Justice" (p. 87)

   Topic: _____

   Main idea: _____

   Stated Main Idea / Implied Main Idea

3. "Room for Debate: Young Offenders Locked Up for Life—No Magic to an Age Limit" (p. 89)

   Topic: _____

   Main idea: _____

   _____

   Stated Main Idea / Implied Main Idea

Identifying Stated Main Ideas in Paragraphs in Readings

When we enter a reading, we first try to get a sense of the overall topic and the main idea of the entire passage. As we read further, we understand that each paragraph within a reading is organized around a central point. Writers often state their main idea—the point they are making about the topic—in a *topic sentence*. Put another way, the topic sentence includes both the topic and the controlling idea, or the main point about it, which is to be developed in the paragraph with supporting details.

Examine the following example from Selection 1 (para. 13), "Some Say Cop Videos Misleading":

> Police are well aware of the power of such images. One response has been a move by some police forces around the country to install video cameras in police cars—allowing law enforcement to have its own more complete visual record of confrontations. O'Donnell sees videos as possibly doing some good: They may help the public decide for itself what is reasonable force and what is not. "People become used to the idea this is the police and what they do. . . . That may allow people to kind of clarify misconduct from things that are not misconduct. "People see the police acting in a way that may not be pretty but may be justifiable," he said.

Topic: video cameras in police cars

Controlling Idea: Video cameras could provide a record of what actually happens during a confrontation.

Topic Sentence: One response has been a move by some police forces around the country to install video cameras in police cars—allowing law enforcement to have its own more complete visual record of confrontations.

EXERCISE 3.6 **Identifying Controlling Ideas in Topic Sentences**

Directions: Circle the topic and underline the controlling idea in the following topic sentences. The first one is done for you.

1. In each case where DNA has proven innocence beyond doubt, an overlapping array of causes has emerged—from mistakes to misconduct to factors of race and class.

2. Evidence of fraud, negligence or misconduct by prosecutors or police is disturbingly not uncommon among the DNA exoneration cases.

3. Many forensic techniques—such as hair microscopy, bite mark comparisons, firearm tool mark analysis and shoe print comparisons—have not been subjected to sufficient scientific evaluation and have resulted in error.

—The Innocence Project: www.innocenceproject.org/causes-wrongful-conviction

To help guide you toward recognition of the stated topic—or main idea—sentence in a paragraph, consider which sentence does the following:

- States the single most important point, the controlling idea, about the topic
- Is general enough to cover all the information in the paragraph
- Is explained, focused on, and supported by the other sentences

Keep in mind that the topic sentence often appears at the beginning of a paragraph, but it also can appear in the middle or at the end.

EXERCISE 3.7   Identifying Topic Sentences

Directions: In each of the following passages, try to locate the topic sentence that contains the stated main idea, using the guidelines above, and underline it.

Passage 1

As the concerns for quality policing builds, increasing emphasis is also being placed on the formal education of police officers. As early as 1931, the National Commission on Law Observance and Enforcement (the Wickerham Commission) highlighted the importance of a well-educated police force by calling for "educationally-sound" officers. In 1967, the Presidents Commission on Law Enforcement and Administration of Justice voiced the belief that "the ultimate aim of all police departments should be that all personnel with general enforcement powers should have baccalaureate degrees."

—From Schmalleger, *Criminal Justice*, p. 187

Passage 2

Often popular police shows on TV show an offender being given a rights advisement at the time of arrest. However, the Miranda decision only requires that the police advise a person of his or her rights prior to questioning. In cases where no questioning is involved, no warning is necessary. The legal system does provide law enforcement officials with some flexibility based on the circumstances of an arrest. When an officer interrupts a crime in progress, for example, it may be reasonable, based on public safety considerations, for an officer to ask a few questions before giving a rights advisement.

—From Schmalleger, *Criminal Justice*, p. 139

Passage 3

In recent years, there have been quite a number of exonerations of prisoners on death row. Whether through new testimony or DNA evidence, judges have ruled some death row inmates to be innocent of charges against them. Another controversial issue related to the death penalty has been the method of execution utilized to end the life of prisoners on death row. Flaws in the use of both the electric chair and lethal injections have resulted in disruptions to the process of execution. In sum, those against the death penalty point to a variety of flaws in America's capital punishment system.

Identifying Implied Main Ideas in Paragraphs in Readings

Most articles or textbook paragraphs have a main idea. Sometimes the main idea is stated directly in a topic sentence as noted above (for example, "Russia must do something to save its economy," or "The exact nature of the five stages of death has been disputed"). Other times, however, the author gives you the information needed to understand the main point without stating it directly in a single sentence. This is called an *implied main idea* because you the reader must use information contained in the paragraph to **infer** (reason out) the author's main point. (See Chapter 5, p. 181 for a focus on making inferences.)

Consider the following example:

> When the suspect with the dark sunglasses was brought into the police department office, Sergeant Green nodded his head twice, and said, "Let me guess, this must be a case of mistaken identity." The suspect smiled at him, and said, "Absolutely, you've got the wrong man, again. I didn't do anything."

After reading the passage above, you realize that the main idea is not directly stated. However, when you pay attention to the details that are offered, you will notice that all of the supporting sentences point you in the direction of the paragraph's main idea: *this wasn't the first time this suspect had claimed a case of mistaken identity to Sergeant Green.*

Guidelines for Finding Implied Main Ideas

- **Identify the topic.** As stated earlier, the topic is more general than the main idea, and it is critical that you first understand what the reading is about before you zero in on the implied main idea.

- **Ask yourself what larger idea the details in the text support.** Examine each detail and determine what is the most important idea the author wants you to take from the text.

- **Formulate the implied main idea in your own words.** Remember, no matter how hard you look, when the main idea is implied, you will not be able to find it written directly in the text. Make sure your expression of the main idea is neither too general nor too specific.

Let's look at another example:

> When most people picture criminal behavior, they imagine a person with a gun holding someone up or breaking into a bank. What people do not often visualize is a man in a suit committing tax fraud or large companies illegally dumping chemicals. There are many crime shows on television that dramatize violent crime and subsequent manhunts. The top-selling movies frequently focus on cops in shootouts with hard-core criminals. Our newspapers are full of horrific stories of gun-toting criminals menacing their communities.

If we first consider the general topic, the reading is about *criminal behavior*. More specifically, the paragraph focuses on the depiction of criminal behavior in the media. Now, if we examine the details, they are all examples of how the media chooses to focus on incidents involving violent crime (on TV, in the movies, and in the newspaper). Taking these combined details into account, we can infer that the implied main idea of the passage is this: *The media plays up violent crime, while playing down white-collar crime.*

EXERCISE 3.8   Identifying Implied Main Idea

Directions: Read the passages below very carefully and try to infer the main idea of each. Identify the topic, ask yourself what larger idea the details support, and then formulate and write the main idea.

Passage 1

Until the mafia boss called, the governor had a clean record of integrity and transparent leadership. He had won three regional awards for good government and was on his way to re-election. In fact, he had only recently given a speech about the sins of political **corruption**. However, that was then and this is now.

What is the topic? _____

What is the implied main idea? _____

_____

Passage 2

The state of Wyoming had to cut back on police benefits due to a tight budget that resulted from years of recession. Meanwhile, Indiana police were forced to take a 10 percent pay cut because state revenues had decreased for the fifth straight year, and even in California, where the economy hadn't taken as much of a hit, law enforcement budgets felt the crunch.

What is the topic? _____

What is the implied main idea? _____

_____

Passage 3

The officer pounded on the front door of the suspect's address. No one answered. The officer pounded again and then crouched down to the left of the house's entrance, leaning back against the brick side wall of the home. Finally, the door opened. The suspect stepped out, placing his hands up in the air. "Don't shoot, Sir . . . . I mean, Ma'am," he said.

What is the topic? _____

What is the implied main idea? _____

_____

Passage 4

Some officers go into the field for the early retirement and generous pension. Others go into policing because they are passionate about law enforcement. Some police officers get into the field because all their heroes growing up were rescuers. Finally, some people pursue a career in policing because they could not imagine working in an office from nine to five.

What is the topic? _____

What is the implied main idea? _____

_____

Passage 5

In recent years, marijuana has been legalized in several U.S. states. In the past, police officers were trained to search out and arrest marijuana dealers. The severity of the punishment for selling marijuana varied from state to state. Now in states where marijuana vending and consumption are allowed, there are still legal issues concerning permits to sell and limitations on quantities available for sale.

What is the topic? _____

What is the implied main idea? _____

_____

EXERCISE 3.9 Identifying Topics and Main Ideas

Directions: Read the following short paragraphs and identify the topic and main idea in each. If the paragraph contains a topic sentence, underline it. If it does not, formulate an implied main sentence.

Passage 1

Certain situations require immediate action by the police. If the police are chasing a person who has just committed a crime using a firearm and catch the person but fail to find the firearm on him or her, the court has ruled that the police have the right to perform a search without a warrant in places where the person may have discarded the firearm. The justification for this exception is the argument that if the search is not performed immediately, the presence of the weapon in the community may pose a serious threat to public safety.

—From Fagin, *Criminal Justice*, p. 202

Topic: _____

Main idea: _____

_____

Passage 2

Those who commit white-collar crimes include the most respected and wealthiest of persons in society, including mayors, governors, vice-presidents and presidents. In 2006, Mayor Ron Gonzales of San Jose was indicted on public corruption charges, and Lynwood, California, mayor Paul Richards was found guilty of multiple counts of fraud, money laundering, extortion, making false statements to investigators, and depriving the public of honest services. Former Illinois governor and one-time Nobel Prize nominee George Ryan was found guilty of 18 charges of racketeering, mail fraud, making false statements to FBI agents, and income tax **violations** in 2006.

—From Schmalleger, *Criminal Justice*, p. 135

Topic: _____

Main idea: _____

_____

Passage 3

New police officers learn what is considered appropriate police behavior by working with seasoned veterans. Through conversations with other officers in the locker room, in a squad car, or over a cup of coffee, a new recruit is introduced to the value-laden sub-culture of police work. This process of informal socialization plays a much bigger role than the formal police academy in determining how a rookie comes to see police work.

—From Schmalleger, *Criminal Justice*, p. 242

Topic: _____

Main idea: _____

_____

Passage 4

Corrections officers have generally been accorded low occupational status. Historically, the role of prison guard required minimal formal education and held few opportunities for professional growth and career advancement. Such jobs were typically low-paying, frustrating and often boring. Growing problems in our nation's prisons, including emerging issues of legal liability, however, increasingly require a well-trained and adequately equipped force of professionals.

—From Schmalleger, *Criminal Justice*, p. 470

Topic: _____

Main idea: _____

_____

EXERCISE **3.10** Recognizing Topic Sentences

Directions: Reread the first article in this chapter, "Some Say Cop Videos Misleading," on page 81, and go through each paragraph, underlining the topic sentences. Keep in mind that not every paragraph includes a topic sentence. For those that do not, see if you can identify the topic and main idea and write an implied main idea sentence for each. When you are done, compare your work with that of a classmate.

READING

Selection 3

Textbook Reading

LAPD Adds Officers and Crime Falls—But Is There a Connection?

Pre-Reading Questions

Answer the following questions before exploring the text:

1. Considering your understanding of the crime rate in your community, do you think the number of police officers on the street should be increased, decreased, or kept at about the same level? Explain.

2. In your view, is increasing the police presence the best method to reduce crime? If yes, explain why. If no, what methods might prove more effective?

3. If you chose a career in law enforcement, would you be willing to police the streets of a high-crime city? Explain your answer in detail.

LAPD Adds Officers and Crime Falls—But Is There a Connection?

1   Ever since he successfully ran for office in 2005, Los Angeles Mayor Antonio Villaraigosa has been intent on adding more sworn officers to the Los Angeles Police Department and reaching a record level of 10,000.

2   Battling huge budget shortfalls, he succeeded in adding a few hundred new officers through 2012, putting the LAPD just shy of the 10,000 mark. Facing the end of his tenure due to term limits, the mayor finally reached his goal on Jan. 1, 2013, through a maneuver that didn't put any new officers on the streets. The LAPD simply annexed the city's General Services Department, which oversees parks, libraries, and other municipal buildings, and its 60 officers were sworn into the LAPD.

3   "I know some people think that 10,000 cops is a magical illusion, a meaningless number, that more officers don't necessarily lead to a reduction in crime," the mayor said. "Those critics talk a lot, but they're just plain wrong."

4   City officials noted that from 2011–2012, gang crime, one of the city's greatest scourges, fell by 10.5%. By 2012, Los Angeles had the lowest overall crime rate of any major city. Using extra officers early in Villaraigosa's tenure, the LAPD could put more of them on the streets and open new stations, and response times fell from 8–9 minutes to 6–7 minutes for calls for assistance.

5   But were extra officers the key factor in reducing crime? Skeptics point to other factors, such as a nationwide decline in crime rates and reshuffling existing officers into a new LAPD office targeting gang violence. Also, the city's budget shortages led to cutbacks in overtime, reducing the possible positive impact of having more officers on the payroll.

6   And if more officers reduce crime, then why do Chicago and New York, which have much higher ratios of officers to residents, have higher crime rates than LA? In 2005, the LAPD's ratio of officers to residents was about half the rate of the NYPD, even though Los Angeles has a much larger geographic area that should make it harder to **patrol**. Chicago, with markedly fewer people and a smaller area to patrol, actually has more officers than LA.

7   The varying circumstances among big-city police departments show there is no single ratio of officers to population that can be applied to all cities. The optimal ratio depends on local conditions, according to the International Association of Chiefs of Police (IACP). "Defining patrol staffing allocation and deployment requirements is a complex endeavor which requires consideration of an extensive series of factors and a sizable body of reliable, current data," the group says.

8   Therefore, a low crime rate might allow a city to have fewer officers. But without a universal standard for officer-to-population ratios, there will always be debate on what the right level for a city should be. For example, Charlie Beck, the current LAPD chief, insisted in a 2010 interview that LA should have 12,000 officers. With a lower number, "You're not able to spend any time working on solutions," he said. "You're just constantly chasing the symptoms."

9   But by January 2013, Beck was concerned about just maintaining the 10,000-officer level. If voters do not approve a sales tax increase in an upcoming ballot initiative, Beck warned that the number of officers might have to be cut.

—From Schmalleger, *Criminal Justice*, p. 148

Thinking about the Reading

After doing a close reading of the article, write your answers to the following questions. You may be asked to discuss your answers with your classmates.

1. What obstacle stood between Los Angeles mayor, Antonio Villaraigosa, and his goal of bringing the police force up to 10,000?

2. Paraphrase former Mayor Villaraigosa's quote in paragraph three. Do you agree with his point? Why or why not?

3. What statistics are offered by the city of LA to demonstrate the positive effect of a larger police force?

4. What evidence did skeptics point to as the real reason crime declined in LA?

_____

_____

5. Paraphrase the current LAPD chief, Charlie Beck's quote defending the idea of building the LA police force to 12,000 officers. "With a lower number, 'You're not able to spend any time working on solutions. You're just constantly chasing the symptoms.'"

_____

_____

Reading Comprehension Check

_____ **1.** According to the reading, how did Mayor Villaraigosa figure out a way to bring the LA police force up to 10,000 by the beginning of 2013?

    a. He found some loopholes in the city budget.

    b. He made sure all new officers were placed into high-crime neighborhoods.

    c. He was able to annex the city's General Services Department.

    d. He made a deal with his opponents.

_____ **2.** What is the topic of the reading?

    a. community policing issues

    b. the history of large city policing

    c. heroes of the police force

    d. the correct size of an urban police force

_____ **3.** According to the International Association of Chiefs of Police (IACP), the optimal ratio of officers to population

    a. depends on local conditions and a variety of factors.

    b. should be the same in all big cities.

    c. depends on factors related to the presence of drugs and gang-related violence on the street.

    d. is higher than the ratio most politicians suggest.

_____ **4.** What is the main idea of the reading passage?

    a. The situation in LA clearly points to the fact that an increase in the police force lowers crime.

    b. Crime in Chicago remained high despite the fact that the city has a large police presence.

    c. While increasing the size of a city's police force may play a role in reducing crime, a host of other factors may also contribute.

    d. The former mayor of Los Angeles realized his dream of building the city's police force to 10,000.

_____ 5. What warning does LAPD chief, Charles Beck, offer in the last paragraph of the reading?

    a. The police force would have to be reduced based on insufficient evidence that a higher police presence was reducing the crime rate.

    b. He would step down as chief if the police force was reduced to 9,000.

    c. If sales tax were not raised, the city could not increase the police force to 12,000.

    d. The LA police force would have to be reduced if the city could not make budget.

_____ 6. Paragraph 6 compares Los Angeles to Chicago and New York to explore the idea that

    a. big cities typically have high crime rates.

    b. maintaining a high ratio of police officers to residents might not cause crime rates to fall.

    c. mild winters are a good indicator of lower crime rates.

    d. east-coast police officers are less honest and less motivated than officers on the west coast.

_____ 7. According to this reading, what is a major factor that effects whether a city can add more officers to its police force?

    a. budget shortfalls   c. officers to population ratios

    b. crime rates   d. gang violence

_____ 8. In paragraph 2, the word _annexed_ most nearly means

    a. stole.   c. took over.

    b. detached.   d. divided.

_____ 9. According to this reading, which of the following sentences about Los Angeles is _false_?

    a. In 2012, Los Angeles had the lowest overall crime rate of the nation's major cities.

    b. Then-mayor Antonio Villaraigosa objected to adding more officers to the Los Angeles Police Department.

    c. Los Angeles has a larger geographic area for officers to patrol than either Chicago or New York.

    d. At the time this article was written, Chicago had more police officers than Los Angeles.

_____ 10. According to the reading, Mayor Villaraigosa believes that

    a. the more people complain about gang violence, the more likely it is to continue.

    b. it is more desirable to fund parks and libraries than it is to increase the number of police officers in Los Angeles.

    c. criminals are more violent in Chicago and New York than they are in Los Angeles.

    d. the more police officers a city has, the less crime that city will have.

THEMATIC LINKS

If you want to read more on the topic of increasing the police force, type the following words into your browser and explore the two sites that come up:

1. LAPD force exceeds 10,000 LA Times
2. LAPD chief: The thin blue line CNN

Think to Write

Now that you have completed three readings in this chapter on Criminal Justice, think about which of the three is most interesting to you. Write a paragraph response about this reading and post it to The Wall.

It's SHOWTIME!

Watching a video clip related to the chapter content can be an enriching experience. Go online and find a video link whose topic ties into one of the chapter readings (maximum length = 10 minutes). After viewing the video clip, write a half-page summary of the video's key points. Post your personal reaction to the ideas in the clip (between 150 and 400 words) on The Wall.

WRITING SKILL FOCUS

 OBJECTIVE

5 Write an introductory paragraph with a thesis statement

Writing an Introduction with a Thesis Statement

The introductory paragraph is one of the most important parts of an essay. It should draw the reader in and lead him or her smoothly into the body of the essay. It should convince the reader that you offer an original approach to an interesting topic. An introduction should be a sneak preview to the entirety of your essay. When it is not, it is disappointing for the reader to discover that the focus of the composition is something other than what was promised. In fact, this is a good way of thinking about the introduction: as a promise to the reader.

The chief goals of an introduction are to grab your attention and to introduce the main topic and the writer's central idea about it—the thesis statement. The first sentence may include a hook, or attention grabber, to catch the reader's attention. After writing this opening sentence, you may want to include a few sentences that provide background information about the topic. Finally, most introductory paragraphs conclude with a circumscribed (narrow) thesis statement, which is the main statement of the entire essay. Although there is no law that requires the writer to include the thesis statement in the first paragraph, it is usually found in the introduction. After all, it is the thesis statement that is explored and supported in the body paragraphs.

EXERCISE 3.11   Evaluating the Effectiveness of Two Introductory Paragraphs

Directions: Examine the following two examples of introductory paragraphs with a partner. Discuss which introduction is more effective and why.

Introductory Paragraph A

Imagine spending twenty years of your life behind bars before being declared innocent by the government. Well, this has been the reality for over three hundred prisoners who have been exonerated based on DNA evidence. This essay will focus on the noble mission of an organization called The Innocence Project, which works to illuminate cases in which innocent people have been locked away. The Innocence Project plays an important role in the criminal justice system in exposing suspicious guilty verdicts, playing on the media to write about these unjust cases, and educating Americans about the unequal treatment of poorer criminal suspects.

Introductory Paragraph B

What happened in Minnesota should not be hidden from the public by America's biased media. This police officer's heroic actions saved a family with three young children from a violent attack on their home. Everyone who happened to learn of this incredible story is in shock that the rest of the nation has been kept in the dark. We, as a united people, must bring to light such incidents so that everyone understands the dangers our police force come into contact with daily and the bravery they must display in the face of these tremendous challenges.

Composing Introductory Paragraphs: Problems to Avoid

To write an effective introduction, you should try to avoid the following:

- **The one-sentence introduction.** Your introduction needs to flow smoothly from your opening sentence through your thesis statement. You cannot do the job in one sentence.

- **The "spill-all-your-beans" introduction.** Keep in mind as you introduce the topic of your essay that this is not the place to share many specific details. If you share all the key points and examples in your introductory paragraph, you will have little to say in the remaining sections of your essay. Try to be general, and only make mention of what you will cover later on.

- **The "assumption-of context" introduction.** Introductory Paragraph B above is a classic example of what happens when a writer does not provide context or necessary background information about the topic being covered. In this paragraph, the writer assumes the reader knows something about media bias and the heroic police action in Minnesota, but because the writer provides no specifics about either, the reader doesn't know enough about the situation being referred to or why the author chose to focus on this particular case. As a writer, you cannot assume that your reader has background knowledge of the topic you are writing about; it is your job to clearly lay it out.

- **The "where the heck is the thesis" introduction.** A writer may do an excellent job of generating interest and introducing the topic of an essay, but the reader surely wants to know the writer's central point about the topic. Be sure to include a clear thesis statement.

Writing a Thesis Statement

The **thesis statement**, usually a one-sentence assertion of your main idea, is the bedrock upon which you build your essay. It signals to your audience the approach you are going to take to the topic of your essay.

Earlier in the chapter, you learned the critical reading skill of identifying the main idea of a given reading. As a writer, your job is to orient your reader in the direction of the main point you are trying to make in your essay. A solid thesis statement sharpens the focus of a writer's ideas by committing the writer to a certain essay structure, and it limits the scope of arguments employed to keep the essay on topic. So, for example, if your thesis statement is *There are three principal issues in community policing: safety, trust, and commitment*, you as a writer are delivering a promise to your reader that your essay will be centered around these three issues. If suddenly, the reader finds a fourth issue discussed, such as budgeting concerns, he or she will be baffled, and wonder why this fourth idea has been introduced.

A good thesis statement narrows the focus of your essay, so that you are setting yourself up for a task you can accomplish. If a thesis statement is too vague or general, you are going to get stuck trying to corral a five hundred-pound gorilla! Imagine a thesis statement like the following: *There are many, many causes of violence in the world, and hundreds of ways of making the world safer.* Do you really have enough time to write a seventy-five-page essay? Well, if you promise your reader that you are going to discuss all the causes of violence that exist around the globe, in addition to the infinite number of ways to reduce violence, you may have just set yourself up for an impossible task.

EXERCISE 3.12   **Evaluating the Effectiveness of Thesis Statements**

Directions: Examine the four pairs of example thesis statements below. In each set, one of the thesis statements is effective and the other is not. In the space provided, write down which of the thesis statements is effective and why.

1. a. The rising crime rate in the city scares me and my neighbors.
   b. Three solutions to curbing crime in urban areas have been proposed by the mayor, but only two of them can be effective.

_____

_____

2. a. While some people in my neighborhood see police officers as a threat, the
        police can sometimes be helpful in protecting and serving local residents.
    b. There is a police officer on my street named Robert who once bought my
        sister a chocolate-chip cookie on her birthday.

        _____

        _____

        _____

3. a. Structured criminal sentencing offers a number of advantages and disad-
        vantages to the criminal justice system.
    b. Two bank robbers in different parts of the country got different sentences
        for the same crime.

        _____

        _____

        _____

4. a. Violence in prisons makes for trouble.

    b. Violence in women's prisons is less frequent than it is in institutions
        for men.

        _____

        _____

        _____

        _____

EXERCISE 3.13   Writing Narrow Thesis Statements

Directions: Review the Previewing Criminal Justice questions at the beginning
of the chapter (p. 76). Choose three of them and try to write narrow thesis statements in reaction to each one. Remember, the goal here is to set up an essay
response to each question by providing a clear viewpoint, which will serve to
guide your essay forward.

1. In reaction to Preview Question # _____.

    Thesis statement_____

    _____

2. In reaction to Preview Question # _____.

    Thesis statement_____

    _____

3. In reaction to Preview Question # _____.

    Thesis statement_____

    _____

EXERCISE 3.14 **Putting It All Together: Writing an Introductory Paragraph for Your Chapter Essay**

Directions: There is no better way to wrap up a lesson on writing an introductory paragraph with a clear thesis statement than to practice putting one together! You have the task of composing a chapter essay, so why not work on developing your introductory paragraph here.

If you remember, your essay question for this chapter is: *Do you believe that the police live up to the promise of protecting and serving the community?* Using what you have learned and the following tips, write an introduction for your essay. When you are done, turn in your work to your instructor for review.

As you draft your introduction, consider that it should do the following:

1. Provide an interesting opening sentence that grabs the reader's attention

2. Introduce the topic and provide any necessary background information or context

3. Indicate to the reader how the topic is going to be developed

4. Contain the thesis statement, which should make a clear point about the topic

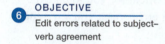
TROUBLE SPOTS IN WRITING

6 **OBJECTIVE**
Edit errors related to subject-verb agreement

Editing for Subject–Verb Agreement

Many developmental writers often leave the letter *s* off third-person present verbs that demand its presence. A student might follow colloquial speech and write, "He don't know what he is doing," but this does not work on paper. *He* is a third-person singular subject and demands a third-person singular verb, like *doesn't* or *wants* or *likes*.

Errors in subject–verb agreement frequently result from a writer mistaking a plural noun for a singular one. Mixing singular nouns with plural verb forms distracts the reader, so you will need to pay close attention to this distinction between singular and plural noun forms if you want your sentences to flow smoothly. Once again, if a noun is singular, do not forget to put an *s* on the end of your base verb (e.g., he *claims*). Pay attention to subjects such as *no one*, *everyone, nobody*, and *everybody*, which "feel plural" but are considered singular and thus need an *s* added to the base verb (e.g., everybody *knows*). In most cases, students make these subject–verb agreement errors because they are rushing and do not take the time to check their work. So, remember to edit your sentences each and every time you write!

EXERCISE 3.15 Subject–Verb Agreement

Directions: Work with a classmate to fill out the following chart with nouns and verbs that agree with their counterpart noun or verb. The first three are done for you.

Subject (noun)	Present tense verb
Maria	likes
all of them	smell
one of my friends	works
somebody	
	are
no one	
every student	
	don't
	needs
dancing	
	make
both Jim and his cousin	
last-minute assignments	

EXERCISE 3.16 Editing for Subject–Verb Agreement

Directions: Most subject–verb agreement mishaps are the result of careless oversight on the part of the writer who is more likely focusing most of his or her attention on content, not form. This is why it is critical for you to take the time to edit your writing for subject–verb agreement errors once you have completed your writing assignments.

Edit the following paragraphs about identity theft for errors in subject–verb agreement. See if you can locate and edit the ten errors in the paragraphs. Once you have identified each error and edited the verb form, circle the noun that now agrees with this verb.

Identity theft, which involve obtaining credit, merchandise, or services by fraudulent personal representation is a special kind of larceny. Information from the Bureau of Justice Statistics (BJS) show that 7.0% of all households in the United States had at least one member who had been a victim of one or more types of identity theft in 2010. The BJS also say that identity theft is the fastest-growing type of crime in America.

Identity theft became a federal crime in 1998 with the passage of the Identity Theft and Assumption Deterrence Act. The law make it a crime whenever anyone "knowingly transfer or uses, without lawful authority, a means of identification of another person with the intent to commit, or aid or abet, any unlawful activity which constitute a violation of federal law, or that constitutes a felony under any applicable state or local law."

According to the National White Collar Crime Center, identity thieves uses several common techniques. Some engages in "dumpster diving," going through trash bags, cans or dumpsters to get copies of checks, credit cards and bank statements, credit card applications, or other records that typically bears identifying information. Others use a technique called "shoulder surfing," which involves looking over the victim's shoulder as he or she enter personal information into a computer or on a written form.

— From *Criminal Justice*, Schmalleger, p. 51

THEN & NOW

Go online and do some research to gather information about two experts in the field of Criminal Justice: one from the past such as Allan Pinkerton or Clarence Darrow and another contemporary expert such as Christopher Stone or David Onek. Fill out the table provided below with pertinent information about the two experts.

Past Influential Expert	Present Influential Expert
Name	Name
Place of birth	Place of birth
Year of birth	Year of birth
Education	Education
What is s/he most famous for?	What is s/he most famous for?
Famous quote	Famous quote

After you fill out the table, discuss your findings with your classmates and learn from them about what they discovered on the Internet.

Bryan Stevenson is the founder and executive director of the Equal Justice Initiative, which fights poverty and challenges racial discrimination in the criminal justice system. Working with a search engine, type in the following search query: *"Bryan Stevenson we need to talk about an injustice transcript."* This is the transcript of a TED Talk Stevenson gave. After doing a careful reading, write brief answers to the following questions about the content. You may also choose to listen to his video presentation as well.

1. How does Stevenson describe the home he grew up in?

_____

_____

2. When Stevenson was a young child, his grandmother took him aside and asked him to promise to do three things. What were these three promises?

_____

_____

3. What does Stevenson mean when he says, "Wealth, not culpability, shapes outcomes"? How does he back up his claim?

_____

_____

_____

_____

CHAPTER ESSAY ASSIGNMENT

Do you believe that the police live up to the promise of protecting and serving the community?

OBJECTIVE

Think, plan, and write an essay in response to the chapter essay assignment

Now that you have had the opportunity to read a number of articles and a textbook excerpt, you should have a deeper understanding of the topic area and be prepared to compose your Chapter Essay Assignment.

Write a one- to two-page essay on the above question, or compose your own essay question that reflects the themes in this chapter. You have already written your introductory paragraph, so you are well on your way! When you are done, hand in your essay to your instructor. After you have received constructive feedback from your instructor, be sure to incorporate some of his or her suggestions into your second draft and submit the revised second draft to your instructor for further feedback on form and meaning.

FOCUS ON FORM

Editing Subject–Verb Agreement Usage

In the Troublespots on Writing section on page 109, you learned how to make sure that your subjects and verbs agree with each other. Now let's put your skills into action. First, read the following paragraph on the essay question "Why do people commit violent crime?" Edit the paragraph for errors in subject–verb agreement, by crossing out errors and writing in the correct forms. When you are finished, compare your edits with those of your partner.

There is many factors which may lead someone toward committing a violent crime. Poverty often play a significant role in determining the choices people has. If someone is in need of resources and don't have the means to obtain them, crime may seem like a final option. Mental instability is another factor that can influence someone to commit rash acts of violence. Finally, if a person have suffered violent abuse in the past, he or she may carries turns toward a life of violence.

It's Your Turn!

Now that you have had a chance to practice editing the use of subject–verb agreement, take a look at the introductory paragraph you wrote for the chapter essay assignment and review it with new eyes. Pay close attention to how your subjects match up with their corresponding verb forms.

CHAPTER DEBATE

Do you believe that the police live up to the promise of protecting and serving the community?

This chapter's debate topic is the same as your chapter essay assignment. Refer to Appendix 8, page 455, for detailed guidelines on how to set up and participate in a formal debate.

4 Environmental Science

Learning Objectives

IN THIS CHAPTER, YOU WILL LEARN TO . . .

1 Read in the field of environmental science

2 Understand and use key terms in environmental science

3 Interpret graphics

4 Write effective topic sentences

5 Identify and develop supporting details

6 Write well-developed body paragraphs

7 Revise and edit your essay

8 Read, think, plan, and write an essay in response to the chapter essay assignment

Introduction to the Field of Environmental Science

OBJECTIVE

1

Read in the field of Environmental Science

Environmental Science is the study of interactions among physical, chemical, and biological components of the environment. Environmental scientists use their knowledge of the physical makeup and history of the earth to protect the environment. Major focuses in the field are on developing clean, renewable energy resources; conducting environmental site assessments; and providing advice in such areas as how to improve indoor air quality and clean up hazardous waste in rivers, industrial sites, and abandoned waste-disposal sites.

The great scale and complexity of environmental problems is creating a growing need for scientists with rigorous, interdisciplinary training in environmental science. Many environmental scientists work at consulting firms, helping businesses and government agencies comply with environmental policy. They are usually hired to solve problems. Environment-related jobs are found in industry, environmental protection agencies, local and central government, media, international organizations, and environmental consultancy. The opportunities are endless. Environmental science graduates could be managing tropical rain forests, monitoring coral reef biodiversity, or practicing environmental law.

This chapter focuses primarily on one of the greatest challenges facing not only environmental scientists but all of us who inhabit the earth: global warming. You will read about some of the devastating effects global warming has already caused and will cause to our ecosystem. This chapter also will explore some ways in which we can all play a role in conserving energy, making sure that most, if not all, forms of life are preserved. The role of the government in placing stricter controls on preserving various forms of life on earth is a critical question, and one that serves as this chapter's subject for debate.

CHAPTER ESSAY QUESTION

What role should the US government and the American people play in preserving various forms of life on earth?

Quick Free-Write! Take out a piece of paper, and write for ten minutes without stopping about what you already know about the theme of the chapter essay question.

Your Option: Once you have worked your way through the chapter readings, you are welcome to narrow down the topics covered and compose your own chapter essay question.

Previewing Environmental Science

Read the following questions and discuss them with your classmates. As you answer the questions, consider your personal experience and knowledge of environmental science in general.

1. Do you feel that summers and winters are often warmer than they used to be during your childhood? If so, then what do you think is causing the climate to change?

2. Most scientists studying climate change believe that human activity is causing global temperatures to rise. Do you agree with their view that global warming is caused by humans, or do you believe that human activities have no impact on global warming? If you agree with the scientists, describe specific human activities that might contribute to warming the earth. If you do not agree, explain why.

3. Climate scientists have found evidence that increases in greenhouse gases, including carbon dioxide, methane, and nitrous oxide, are caused by human activities, mainly the burning of fossil fuels. Discuss effective ways of reducing the greenhouse gas emissions that have driven climate change recently.

4. A report of the Intergovernmental Panel on Climate Change (IPCC) concludes that further climate change is inevitable and that the earth's future depends on how humans act now. Is it the government's responsibility to make people aware of how their activities are harming the earth? If so, how can the government best educate citizens to become more environmentally friendly?

5. Most environmental scientists are concerned that the continued depletion of earth's natural resources and the destruction of biodiversity, its flora and fauna, are caused by human activities. In your opinion, what can people do to ensure that most forms of life, including plants and animals, are respected and preserved?

After you have discussed the preview questions with your classmates, post your responses to two of them on **The Wall.** Peruse The Wall and respond to at least two of your classmates' responses that pique your interest. Remember to make The Wall your romping ground!

OBJECTIVE

2   Understand and use key terms in environmental science

Key Terms in Environmental Science

Take a moment to think about the discipline of environmental science as you complete the following two exercises.

EXERCISE 4.1   Brainstorming Vocabulary

What associated words come to mind when you think of the world of environmental science? Work with a partner and write down as many related words as you can think of in a period of five minutes.

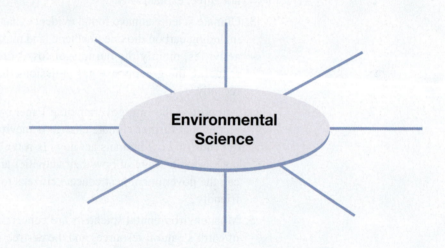

Environmental Science

EXERCISE 4.2   Creating Original Sentences

Directions: Choose five of the words from your brainstorm list and use them to write complete and meaningful sentences.

1. _____

2. _____

3. _____

4. _____

5. _____

A **synonym** is a word used to express a similar meaning to another word. An **antonym** is a word that conveys the opposite meaning of another word.

As a discipline, environmental science has its own jargon and technical terms. A student majoring in this discipline will need to acquire and use terms such as *ecosystems, species, extinct,* and *sustaining* in both spoken and written forms. The following exercise will help you learn some key terms in the discipline of environmental science and practice using synonyms and antonyms for them. Understanding how to work with synonyms and antonyms is a useful skill, especially when you are writing a summary of a text and trying to paraphrase some of the key ideas and pieces of information contained in the original source.

EXERCISE 4.3 Discipline-Specific Vocabulary: Fishing for Synonyms and Antonyms

Directions: Read the following ten (10) discipline-specific words culled from the readings in this chapter and shown in the context of the sentences in which they appeared. In the space provided after each sentence, write a synonym or antonym for the highlighted term, as directed.

Discipline-Specific Word Bank*

precipice	extinct	sustaining	toxic
species	adverse	afflict	reforms
ecosystems	invasive		

* The first time these discipline-specific words appear in the chapter, they are shown in bold green.

1. "'We may be sitting on a **precipice** of a major extinction event,' said Douglas J. McCauley, an ecologist at the University of California, Santa Barbara, and an author of the new research, which was published on Thursday in the journal Science." (Selection 1, p. 123, para. 1)

   A synonym for *precipice* is _____.

2. "It's much harder for researchers to judge the well-being of a **species** living under water." (Selection 1, p. 123, para. 3)

   A synonym for *species* is _____.

3. "Fragile **ecosystems** like mangroves are being replaced by fish farms, which are projected to provide most of the fish we consume within 20 years." (Selection 1, p. 124, para. 7)

   A synonym for *ecosystems* is _____.

4. "The fossil record indicates that a number of large animal species became **extinct** as humans arrived on continents and islands. For example, the moa, a giant bird that once lived on New Zealand, was wiped out by arriving Polynesians in the 1300s …" (Selection 1, p. 124, para. 10)

   An antonym for *extinct* is _____.

5. "No level of diversity loss can occur without **adverse** effects on ecosystem functioning." (Selection 2, p. 129, para. 2)

   A synonym for *adverse* is _____

   _____.

6. "The primary drivers of biodiversity loss are, in rough order of impact to date: habitat loss, overharvesting, **invasive** species, pollution and climate change." (Selection 2, p. 130, para. 3)

   A synonym for *invasive* is _____.

7. "Ghosts of species past haunt ecosystems worldwide, which have already lost not just one or another type of grass or roundworm but also some of their strength at **sustaining** life as a whole." (Selection 2, p. 130, para. 7)

   A synonym for *sustaining* is _____.

8. "After painting this idyllic picture, the chapter goes on to describe 'a strange blight' that began to **afflict** the town and its surrounding area." (Selection 3, p. 134, para. 2)

   An antonym for *afflict* is _____.

9. "Many thousands of songbirds were recovered dead and analyzed in laboratories for DDT content; all had **toxic** levels in their tissues." (Selection 3, p. 135, para. 3)

   A synonym for *toxic* is _____.

10. "She is credited not only with major **reforms** in pesticide policy, but with initiating an environmental awareness that eventually led to the modern environmental movement and the creation of the EPA." (Selection 3, p. 135, para. 6)

    A synonym for *reforms* is _____.

SUCCESS IN READING

OBJECTIVE

3 Interpret graphics

Interpreting Graphics

Whether you are studying environmental science, nursing, computer science, business, education, biology, or another subject, most content-area textbooks contain graphic aids. Information can be presented in a variety of formats, including bar graphs, line graphs, pie charts, maps, tables, diagrams, or photos; all visual representations of how different sets of data are interrelated. The ability to interpret graphic material is an essential college reading skill your instructors will expect you to perform, and it is only through practice that you will begin to interpret graphic information smoothly and accurately.

Interpreting a Bar Graph

While there are many types of graphics, one of the most frequently used in academic texts is the bar graph. Remember that learning to read a graph is a matter of interpreting different pieces of information that go together. The following guidelines will help you interpret a bar graph accurately:

1. **Read the title of the graph, the legend, and the caption (if there is one) carefully.** The title should tell you the subject of the graph; the legend will explain what different colors, symbols, or patterns refer to; and the caption can provide additional information and/or explanations of what is being shown.

2. **Check the scale for each graph element.** Units of time such as days, weeks, months, or years are usually listed on the *x*-axis (horizontal), and quantity measurements such as numbers, percentages, feet, or meters are usually listed on the *y*-axis (vertical). For example, the *x*-axis may represent the months in a calendar year, and the *y*-axis might represent the number of babies born in a state, country, or the world.

3. **Read the graph to find the information you require.** For example, you may need to know how many babies were born in the month of July in the United States. To do this, you would find "July" on the *x*-axis, go to the top of the vertical bar and read directly across to the left until you hit the *y*-axis (vertical). The number that intersects with the straight line is the number of babies born in July.

4. **Interpret the information.** Study the entire graph carefully to identify trends or patterns. Look for correlations between the information on the *x*- and *y*-axes. For example, does the graph show that more babies were born in one month than another? If so, think about why this might be.

The following bar graph shows the benefits and costs of environmental regulations. Keeping the above guidelines in mind, examine the graph with a partner and answer the questions that follow.

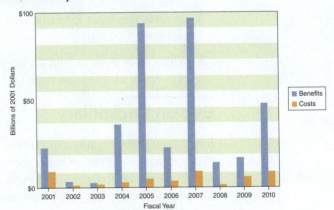

Benefits and costs of major regulations, 2000-2010. Clearly, the benefits of regulations far outweigh the costs of implementing the rules.

(Source: Office of management and budget, 2011 Report to Congress on the Benefits and Costs of Federal Regulations and Unfunded Mandates on State, Local and Tribal Entities, June 2011.)

—From Cummings, *Environmental Science: Toward a Sustainable Future*, 12e, p. 43

1. What were the cost savings of environmental regulations in the 2000–2010 decade?

    _____

2. What were the costs of environmental regulations in the same period?

    _____

3. Which years saw the maximum benefits as compared to the costs?

    _____

4. Which years saw the minimum increase in benefits as compared to the costs?

    _____

READING

Selection 1

Newspaper Article

Ocean Life Faces Mass Extinction, Broad Study Says

Pre-Reading Questions

Before reading the following article, answer these questions in pairs or small groups. Discussing the questions will help prepare you to analyze the text with relative ease.

1. How will the potential extinction of all ocean species affect our lives? In other words, how will our lives change if there is nothing left living in our seas?

2. In what ways are humans harming the world's oceans? Give specific examples.

3. What can be done to limit the human-caused damage to ocean life?

Eye on Vocabulary

Skim through the reading and find the following key vocabulary terms in bold. Working with a partner, examine the words in the context in which they appear, and try to guess the meaning of each. Then look up the words in a dictionary. Keep in mind that many words have multiple meanings. Write the definition that best fits the word's context in the article.

Word	Your definition	Dictionary definition
1. intact (adj.)		
2. prognosis (n.)		
3. habitat (n.)		
4. terrestrial (adj.)		

Ocean Life Faces Mass Extinction, Broad Study Says

by Carl Zimmer

Jan. 15, 2015, New York Times

A dead whale in Rotterdam, the Netherlands, in 2011. As container ships multiply, more whales are being harmed, a study said.

1   A team of scientists, in a groundbreaking analysis of data from hundreds of sources, has concluded that humans are on the verge of causing unprecedented damage to the oceans and the animals living in them. "We may be sitting on a **precipice** of a major extinction event," said Douglas J. McCauley, an ecologist at the University of California, Santa Barbara, and an author of the new research, which was published on Thursday in the journal *Science*.

2   But there is still time to avert catastrophe, Dr. McCauley and his colleagues also found. Compared with the continents, the oceans are mostly **intact**, still wild enough to bounce back to ecological health. "We're lucky in many ways," said Malin L. Pinsky, a marine biologist at Rutgers University and another author of the new report. "The impacts are accelerating, but they're not so bad that we can't reverse them."

3   Scientific assessments of the oceans' health are dogged by uncertainty: It's much harder for researchers to judge the well-being of a **species** living underwater, over thousands of miles, than to track the health of a species on land. And changes that scientists observe in particular ocean **ecosystems** may not reflect trends across the planet. Dr. Pinsky, Dr. McCauley and their colleagues sought a clearer picture of the oceans' health by pulling together data from an enormous range of sources, from discoveries in the fossil record to statistics on modern container shipping, fish catches and seabed mining. While many of the findings already existed, they had never been juxtaposed in such a way.

4   A number of experts said the result was a remarkable synthesis, along with a nuanced and encouraging **prognosis**. "I see this as a call for action to close the gap between conservation on land and in the sea," said Loren McClenachan of Colby College, who was not involved in the study.

5   There are clear signs already that humans are harming the oceans to a remarkable degree, the scientists found. Some ocean species are certainly overharvested, but even greater damage results from large-scale **habitat** loss, which is likely to accelerate as technology advances the human foot-print, the scientists reported. Coral reefs, for example, have declined by 40 percent worldwide, partly as a result of climate-change-driven warming.

6   Some fish are migrating to cooler waters already. Black sea bass, once most common off the coast of Virginia, have moved up to New Jersey. Less fortunate species may not be able to find new ranges. At the same time, carbon emissions are altering the chemistry of seawater, making it more acidic. "If you cranked up the aquarium heater and dumped some acid in the water, your fish would not be very happy," Dr. Pinsky said. "In effect, that's what we're doing to the oceans."

7   Fragile **ecosystems** like mangroves are being replaced by fish farms, which are projected to provide most of the fish we consume within 20 years. Bottom trawlers scraping large nets across the sea floor have already affected 20 million square miles of ocean, turning parts of the continental shelf to rubble. Whales may no longer be widely hunted, the analysis noted, but they are now colliding more often as the number of container ships rises.

8   Mining operations, too, are poised to transform the ocean. Con-tracts for seabed mining now cover 460,000 square miles underwater, the researchers found, up from zero in 2000. Seabed mining has the potential to tear up unique ecosystems and introduce pollution into the deep sea.

9   The oceans are so vast that their ecosystems may seem impervious to change. But Dr. McClenachan warned that the fossil record shows that global disasters have wrecked the seas before. "Marine species are not immune to extinction on a large scale," she said. Until now, the seas largely have been spared the carnage visited on **terrestrial** species, the new analysis also found.

10   The fossil record indicates that a number of large animal species became **extinct** as humans arrived on continents and islands. For example, the moa, a giant bird that once lived on New Zealand, was wiped out by arriving Polynesians in the 1300s, probably within a century. But it was only after 1800, with the Industrial Revolution, that extinctions on land really accelerated. Humans began to alter the habitat that wildlife depended on, wiping out forests for timber, plowing under prairie for farmland, and laying down roads and railroads across continents. Species began going extinct at a much faster pace. Over the past five centuries, researchers have recorded 514 animal extinctions on land. But the authors of the new study found that documented extinctions are far rarer in the ocean.

11   Before 1500, a few species of seabirds are known to have vanished. Since then, scientists have documented only 15 ocean extinctions, includ-ing animals such as the Caribbean monk seal and the Steller's sea cow.

While these figures are likely underestimates, Dr. McCauley said that the difference was nonetheless revealing. "Fundamentally, we're a terrestrial predator," he said. "It's hard for an ape to drive something in the ocean extinct." Many marine species that have become extinct or are endangered depend on land—seabirds that nest on cliffs, for example, or sea turtles that lay eggs on beaches.

12   Still, there is time for humans to halt the damage, Dr. McCauley said, with effective programs limiting the exploitation of the oceans. The tiger may not be salvageable in the wild—but the tiger shark may well be, he said. "There are a lot of tools we can use," he said. "We better pick them up and use them seriously."

13   Dr. McCauley and his colleagues argue that limiting the industrialization of the oceans to some regions could allow threatened species to recover in other ones. "I fervently believe that our best partner in saving the ocean is the ocean itself," said Stephen R. Palumbi of Stanford University, an author of the new study. The scientists also argued that these reserves had to be designed with climate change in mind, so that species escaping high temperatures or low pH would be able to find refuge. "It's creating a hopscotch pattern up and down the coasts to help these species adapt," Dr. Pinsky said.

14   Ultimately, Dr. Palumbi warned, slowing extinctions in the oceans will mean cutting back on carbon emissions, not just adapting to them. "If by the end of the century we're not off the business-as-usual curve we are now, I honestly feel there's not much hope for normal ecosystems in the ocean," he said. "But in the meantime, we do have a chance to do what we can. We have a couple decades more than we thought we had, so let's please not waste it."

Thinking about the Reading

After doing a close reading of the article, write your answers to the following questions. You may be asked to discuss your answers with your classmates.

1. In paragraph 1, Douglas J. McCauley, an ecologist, says, "We may be sitting on a precipice of a major extinction event." What message is McCauley trying to get across? What evidence backs up his claim?

   _____

   _____

2. What methods did Dr. Pinsky and Dr. McCauley's team employ in getting a clearer picture of the oceans' health?

   _____

   _____

3. In paragraph 8, we learn that mining operations are causing great damage to the deep seas. What benefits do we derive from deep-sea mining? In your opinion, are these benefits worth the costs? Explain.

   _____

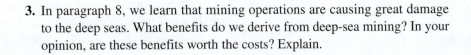

4. Explain the last quote of the article (para. 14). "We have a couple decades more than we thought we had, so let's please not waste it."

_____

Reading Comprehension Check

_____ **1.** The main idea of the article is that

a. human activity only affects terrestrial animals.

b. ocean damage caused by human activities is threatening many ocean species.

c. polar bears and penguins have been the most threatened.

d. damage to the ocean is ignored by mining interests.

_____ **2.** According to Loren McClenachan (para. 4), it is time to close the gap

a. between the conservation of land and sea.

b. between extinct and living creatures.

c. between global efforts and local efforts to save the oceans.

d. between temperatures on land and in the sea.

_____ **3.** "At the same time, carbon emissions are **altering** the chemistry of seawater, making it more acidic" (para. 6). The word _altering_ could be replaced by which of the following?

a. destroying   c. changing

b. preserving   d. maintaining

_____ **4.** "The scientists also argued that these reserves had to be designed with climate change in mind, so that species escaping high temperatures or low pH would be able to find **refuge**." A synonym for the word _refuge_ is

a. cooler water.   c. safe haven.

b. food.   d. other animals of the same species.

_____ **5.** In what context are the Caribbean monk seal and the Steller's sea cow mentioned?

a. as ocean animals that have been saved from extinction

b. as examples of sea creatures that are now extinct

c. as sea creatures that are thriving

d. as animal species that have done damage to the ocean floor

_____ **6.** "If you cranked up the aquarium heater and dumped some acid in the water, your fish would not be very happy," Dr. Pinsky said. "In effect, that's what we're doing to the oceans" (para. 6). What is Dr. Pinsky's main point in the above statement?

a. Recent human activity is threatening ocean sea life.

b. Fish have adapted to acid dumped in their habitat.

c. Fish are generally not a contented species.

d. If we do not stop dumping acid in our seas, climate change will be pronounced.

_____ **7.** "The tiger may not be **salvageable** in the wild—but the tiger shark may well be" (para. 12). The word *salvageable* could be replaced by which of the following?

a. savage   c. able to be rescued

b. dangerous   d. extinct

_____ **8.** "I **fervently** believe that our best partner in saving the ocean is the ocean itself" (para. 13). What does the word *fervently* mean as it is used here?

a. hotly   c. passionately

b. grudgingly   d. barely

_____ **9.** "Marine species are not **immune** to extinction on a large scale" (para 9). A synonym for the word *immune* in the above sentence is

a. susceptible.   c. vulnerable.

b. exempt.   d. inoculated.

_____ **10.** The author of this article would most likely agree that

a. there is still plenty of time to find solutions to the long-term effects of human activity on the oceans.

b. only professionals working in the field of conservation biology should be concerned about the devastation of ocean species.

c. it is far too costly to invest in ocean conservation.

d. a large-scale effort of ocean conservation is absolutely necessary.

THEMATIC LINKS

If you want to learn more about the topic of the growing threat to ocean life, type the following words into your browser: Threats to Oceans and Coasts WWF.

Writing without BOUNDARIES

There Are No Checkpoints!

"Destroying rainforest for economic gain is like burning a Renaissance painting to cook a meal."

—EDWARD O. WILSON

Read the quote above and respond to E. O. Wilson's idea in any way you want. Write for ten minutes without stopping. It is important that you focus on ideas, not words; this will be an exercise in focusing on content and not getting hung up on word choice and grammar errors. You may wish to read what you have written out loud in front of your classmates and instructor.

READING

How Biodiversity Keeps Earth Alive

Pre-Reading Questions

Answer the following questions before exploring the text:

1. How do you think the degree of biodiversity—variety of plants and animals— affects how much life the planet can support? Be specific.

2. Biologists believe that human activity has caused the elimination of many plants, animals, and other forms of life. In your opinion, what types of human activity have caused the extinction of some plants and animals? Give specific examples to support your answer.

3. What can be done to mitigate the severity of biodiversity loss? In other words, what can humans do to ensure that most forms of life on earth thrive?

Eye on Vocabulary

Skim through the reading and find the following key vocabulary terms in bold. Working with a partner, examine the words in context and try to guess the meaning of each. Then look them up in a dictionary. Keep in mind that many words have multiple meanings. Write the definition that best fits the word's context in the article.

Word	Your definition	Dictionary definition
1. biomass (n.)		
2. abundance (n.)		
3. traits (n.)		
4. drought (n.)		

How Biodiversity Keeps Earth Alive

by David Biello
May 3, 2012

*Species loss lessens the total amount of **biomass** on a given parcel, suggesting that the degree of diversity directly impacts the amount of life the planet can support.*

Part 1

1   In 1994 biologists seeded patches of grassland in Cedar Creek, Minn. Some plots got as many as 16 species of grasses and other plants—and some as

few as one. In the first few years, plots with eight or more species fared about as well as those with fewer species, suggesting that a complex mix of species—what is known as biodiversity—didn't affect the amount of a plot's leaf, blade, stem and root (or biomass, as scientists call it). But when measured over a longer span—more than a decade—those plots with the most species produced the greatest **abundance** of plant life.

2   "Different species differ in how, when, and where they acquire water, nutrients and carbon, and maintain them in the **ecosystem**. Thus, when many species grow together, they have a wider set of **traits** that allow them to gain the resources needed," explains ecologist Peter Reich of the University of Minnesota, who led this research to be published in *Science* on May 4. This result suggests, "no level of diversity loss can occur without **adverse** effects on ecosystem functioning." That is the reverse of what numerous studies had previously found, largely because those studies only looked at short-term outcomes.

3   The planet as a whole is on the cusp of what some researchers have termed the sixth mass extinction event in the planet's history: the wiping out of plants, animals and all other forms of life due to human activity. The global impact of such biodiversity loss is detailed in a meta-analysis led by biologist David Hooper of Western Washington University. His team examined 192 studies that looked at species richness and its effect on eco-systems. "The primary drivers of biodiversity loss are, in rough order of impact to date: habitat loss, overharvesting, **invasive** species, pollution and climate change," Hooper explains. Perhaps unsurprisingly, "biodiver-sity loss in the 21st century could rank among the major drivers of ecosys-tem change," Hooper and his colleagues wrote in *Nature* on May 3.

Get into a small group and answer the two questions that follow.

1. What have you learned from the article so far?

2. Try to predict what may be coming in the second half of the article.

Part 2

4   Losing just 21 percent of the species in a given ecosystem can reduce the total amount of biomass in that ecosystem by as much as 10 percent—and that's likely to be a conservative estimate. And when more than 40 percent of an ecosystem's species disappear—whether plant, animal, insect, fungi or microbe—the effects can be as significant as those caused by a major **drought**. Nor does this analysis take into account how species extinction can both be driven by and act in concert with other changes—whether warmer average temperatures or nitrogen pollution. In the real world environmental and biological changes "are likely to be happening at the same time," Hooper admits. "This is a critical need for future research."

5   The major driver of human impacts on the rest of life on this planet—whether through clearing forests or dumping excess fertilizer on fields—is our need for food. Maintaining high biomass from farming ecosystems, which often emphasize monocultures (single species) while also preserving biodiversity—some species now appear only on farmland—has become a "key issue for sustainability," Hooper notes, "if we're going to grow food for nine billion people on the planet in the next 40 to 50 years."

6   Over the long term, maintaining soil fertility may require nurturing, creating and sparing plant and microbial diversity. After all, biodiversity itself appears to control the elemental cycles—carbon, nitrogen, water— that allow the planet to support life. Only by acting in conjunction with one another, for example, can a set of grassland plant species maintain healthy levels of nitrogen in both soil and leaf. "As soil fertility increases, this directly boosts biomass production," just as in agriculture, Reich notes. "When we reduce diversity in the landscape—think of a cornfield or a pine plantation or a suburban lawn—we are failing to capitalize on the valuable natural services that biodiversity provides."

7   At least one of those services is largely unaffected, however, according to Hooper's study—decomposition. Which means the bacteria and fungi will still happily break down whatever plants are left after this sixth extinction. But thousands of unique species have already been lost, most unknown even to science—a rate that could halve the total number of species on the planet by 2100, according to entomologist E. O. Wilson of Harvard University. Ghosts of species past haunt ecosystems worldwide, which have already lost not just one or another type of grass or round-worm but also some of their strength at **sustaining** life as a whole.

Mt. Rainier, Washington State

Thinking about the Reading

After doing a close reading of the article, write your answers to the following questions. You may be asked to discuss your answers with your classmates.

1. What did the biologists discover after seeding patches of grassland in Cedar Creek, Minnesota?

2. Based on his research, what did ecologist Peter Reich of the University of Minnesota conclude about biodiversity loss?

_____

3. Why do Hooper and his colleague believe that "biodiversity loss in the 21st century could rank among the major drivers of ecosystem change"?

_____

_____

_____

4. According to the article, what will happen when more than 40 percent of an ecosystem's species disappear?

_____

5. What is the primary reason for human activity that has an adverse affect biodiversity? In your opinion, what needs to be done to reverse or at least lessen the adverse effects on the rest of life on the planet?

_____

_____

Reading Comprehension Check

_____ 1. "Species loss lessens the total amount of biomass on a given parcel, suggesting that the degree of diversity directly **impacts** the amount of life the planet can support." In this context, the word _impacts_ means

a. hits on.   c. has no influence on.

b. has an effect on.   d. has no effect on.

_____ 2. The main idea of the reading is that

a. humans will continue to hurt or destroy other forms of life for their own benefit.

b. biodiversity loss is good for the planet because it allows new species to evolve.

c. human activity has little or no impact on the amount of life the planet can support.

d. there is a correlation between biodiversity and the amount of life the planet can support.

_____ 3. Which of the following examples supports the researchers' definition of the term _mass extinction_?

a. the wiping out of plants

b. the killing of animals

c. the destruction of all forms of life

d. the destruction of many forms of plant and animal life

_____ **4.** In paragraph 3, which of the following is not a primary driver of biodiversity loss?

a. overharvesting

c. ecosystems

b. invasive species

d. climate change

_____ **5.** In paragraph 4, the reading states "And when more than 40 percent of an ecosystem's species disappear—whether plant, animal, insect, fungi or microbe—the effects can be as significant as those caused by a major drought." Which of the following best restates this quotation's meaning?

a. Loss of biodiversity is a major crisis comparable to the damage caused by extended periods without rainfall.

b. Overall, a major drought is a more severe problem than the disappearance of an ecosystem's species.

c. The disappearance of plant and animal species from an ecosystem has more of an impact than the disappearance of insect, fungi, or microbes.

d. Loss of species in an ecosystem affects rainfall.

_____ **6.** What is the main idea of paragraph 6?

a. Maintaining soil fertility does not help the planet as a whole support life.

b. Encouraging a variety of plants and microbes is necessary to maintain soil fertility.

c. Increasing soil fertility depletes biomass production.

d. Biodiversity is unrelated to elemental cycles.

_____ **7.** Biodiversity among species, as described in this reading, can best be compared to

a. warring armies battling for resources.

b. a group of individuals working together for the common good.

c. a small town where everyone is related and everyone looks alike.

d. a kingdom dominated by a selfish ruler who takes all the resources away from everyone else.

_____ **8.** According to paragraph 6, which statement about biodiversity is true?

a. It is a characteristic of cornfields, pine plantations, and suburban lawns.

b. It decreases soil fertility.

c. It helps grassland plant species maintain healthy soil and leaves.

d. Elemental cycles, such as the nitrogen cycle, control biodiversity.

_____ **9.** According to paragraph 7, which of the following is *not* affected by the presence of biodiversity?

a. plant decomposition by bacteria and fungi

b. the spread of disease by bacteria

    c. a suburban lawn

    d. sustaining life as a whole

_____**10.** What does the author mean when he writes "Ghosts of species past haunt ecosystems worldwide, which have already lost not just one or another type of grass or roundworm but also some of their strength at sustaining life as a whole"?

    a. Past extinctions of plants and animals around the world had little effect on the ecosystems of today.

    b. Losing types of grass and roundworms can cause some negative effects but not enough to cause concern.

    c. Around the world, ecosystems are so impacted by the loss of plant and animal diversity that it is no longer possible for them to sustain life.

    d. Past extinctions of species have already negatively affected the ability of ecosystems around the world to sustain life.

THEMATIC LINKS

If you want to learn more about the topic of biodiversity, type the following words into your browser and explore the two sites that come up:

1. Science Daily and Biodiversity News

2. Postcard from Norway's magical Lofoten Islands Discover

READING

Selection 3

Textbook Excerpt

Science and the Environment

Pre-Reading Questions

Answer the following questions before exploring the text:

1. Do you live in a town or city where all forms of life live in harmony, or do you think there is a conflict between humans and other forms of life such as plants and animals? Be specific.

2. Humans spray pesticides and herbicides on the landscape to control pests in agricultural crops, towns, and cities. The spraying kills many pests and weeds, but the crops, towns, and cities are protected. Do you think there is a way humans and other species can coexist in harmony and share the earth's natural resources?

3. Do you believe that humans, plants, and animals have equal rights to exist on the planet, or do you hold the view that humans are superior to other creatures and have the right to hurt and kill other species for food? Explain your position with solid reasoning.

Science and the Environment

by Richard T. Wright and Dorothy F. Boorse

1   "There was once a town in the heart of America where all life seemed to live in harmony with its surrounding. The town lay in the midst of a checkerboard of prosperous farms, with fields of grain and hillsides of orchards where, in spring, white clouds of blossom drifted above the green fields… The countryside was, in fact, famous for the abundance and variety of its bird life, and when the flood of migrants was pouring through in spring and fall people traveled from great distances to observe them… . So it had been from the days many years ago when the first settlers raised their houses, sank their wells, and built their barns."[1]

2   These are words from the classic book *Silent Spring*, written by biologist Rachel Carson to open her first chapter, titled "A Fable for Tomorrow." After painting this idyllic picture, the chapter goes on to describe "a strange blight" that began to **afflict** the town and its surrounding area. Fish died in streams, farm animals sickened and died, families were plagued with illnesses and occasional deaths. The birds had disappeared, their songs no longer heard—it was a "silent spring." And on the roofs and lawns and fields remnants of a white powder could still be seen having fallen from the skies a few weeks before.

---

1   Rachel Carson, *Silent Spring*. Boston: Houghton Mufflin Company, pp. 1, 2.

3   Rachel Carson explained that no such town existed, but that all of the problems she described had already happened somewhere, and that there was the very real danger that "... this imagined tragedy may easily become a stark reality we all shall know."[2] She published her book in 1962, during an era when pesticides and herbicides were sprayed widely on the landscape to control pests in agricultural crops, forests, and towns and cities. In *Silent Spring*, Carson was particularly critical of the widespread spraying of DDT. This pesticide was used to control Dutch elm disease, a fungus that invades trees and eventually kills them. The fungus is spread by elm bark beetles, and DDT was used to kill the beetles. In towns that employed DDT spraying, birds began dying off, until in some areas people reported their yards were empty of birds. Many thousands of songbirds were recovered dead and analyzed in laboratories for DDT content; all had **toxic** levels in their tissues. DDT was also employed in spraying salt marshes for mosquito control, and the result was a drastic reduction in the fish-eating bald eagle and osprey.

4   FALLOUT. Rachel Carson brought two important qualities to her work: she was very careful to document every finding reported in the book, and she had a high degree of personal courage. She was sure of her scientific claims, and she was willing to take on the establishment and defend her work. In spite of the fact that her work was thoroughly documented, the book ignited a firestorm of criticism from the chemical and agricultural establishment. Even respected institutions such as the American Medical Association joined in the attack against her.

5   Despite the criticism, Carson's book caught the public's eye, and it quickly made its way to the President's Science Advisory Committee when John F. Kennedy read a serialized version of it in the *New Yorker*. Kennedy charged the committee with studying the pesticide problem and recommending changes in public policy.

6   In what must be seen as a triumph of Rachel Carson's work, DDT was banned in the United States, and most other industrialized countries, in the early 1970s. Unfortunately, Rachel Carson did not live long after her world-shaking book was published; she died of breast cancer in 1964. Her legacy, however, is a lasting one: she is credited not only with major **reforms** in pesticide policy, but with initiating an environmental awareness that eventually led to the modern environmental movement and the creation of the EPA.

Thinking about the Reading

After doing a close reading of the article, write your answers to the following questions. You may be asked to discuss your answers with your classmates.

1. Why did Rachel Carson name her book *Silent Spring*?

_____

_____

_____

2   Ibid., p. 3.

2. What inspired Rachel Carson to conceive the imaginary town?

_____

_____

_____

3. Why was Rachel Carson so critical of the widespread spraying of DDT?

_____

_____

4. What two important qualities did Rachel Carson bring to her work?

_____

_____

5. Why did President Kennedy recommend changes in public policy regarding DDT spraying?

_____

_____

Reading Comprehension Check

_____ **1.** "There was once a town in the heart of America where all life seemed to live in **harmony** with its surrounding." In this sentence, the word *harmony* means

    a. disagreement.   c. peace.

    b. discord.   d. accord.

_____ **2.** The main idea of the essay is that

    a. one person does not have much impact on public policy.

    b. Rachel Carson's book significantly impacted public policy.

    c. although the book was popular, the events in it were not supported by facts.

    d. DDT is a dangerous chemical that needed to be banned.

_____ **3.** Which of the following statements is not true?

    a. DDT was employed to kill bald eagles.

    b. DDT was sprayed to control mosquitoes.

    c. DDT was used to control Dutch elm disease.

    d. DDT was used to kill elm bark beetles.

_____ **4.** Which of the following is not one of the problems discussed in paragraph 2?

    a. Fish died in streams.   c. Farm animals died.

    b. Crops died in the fields.   d. Some humans died.

_____ **5.** According to paragraph 6, which of the following statements is not true about Carson's legacy?

  a. DDT was banned in the United States in the early 1970s.
  b. Her work caused reforms in pesticide policy.
  c. Her work led to the creation of the EPA.
  d. She received the Biologist of the Year award in 1970.

_____ **6.** According to the reading, Rachel Carson's work not only brought about the banning of the pesticide DDT but also

  a. brought about the environmental movement of today.
  b. prompted then President Kennedy to criticize her outspokenness.
  c. caused the chemical industry to applaud her efforts on their behalf.
  d. brought about a major crop failure when insects overran an apple orchard.

_____ **7.** In her famous book chapter "A Fable for Tomorrow," described in this reading, Rachel Carson most likely used the hypothetical example of an imaginary town because

  a. she had to keep the name of the real town a secret so that the chemical company that had harmed its inhabitants would not sue her.
  b. she did not believe in using emotion to sway her readers and wanted to keep her narrative strictly factual.
  c. she wanted to show the damaging effects of pesticides on the environment in a way people could relate to personally.
  d. she was interested in writing a science fiction story about the imaginary town and wanted to see how readers reacted to the made-up scenario.

_____ **8.** Shortly after the publication of her classic book _Silent Spring_, the author

  a. was arrested for libel.
  b. started an environmentally friendly company.
  c. reversed her position on the dangers of pesticides.
  d. died of cancer.

_____ **9.** In the subheading at the beginning of paragraph 4, the word _fallout_ most nearly means

  a. consequences.   c. volcanic ash.
  b. radioactive particles. d. misunderstanding.

_____ **10.** According to paragraph 3, it is ironic that DDT, a pesticide used to protect _____, ended up harming so many living things.

  a. elm trees   c. bald eagles and osprey
  b. crops, trees, and people d. songbirds and elm trees

THEMATIC LINKS

If you want to learn more about Rachel Carson's life and work type the following words into your browser and explore the two sites that come up:

  1. US Fish and Wildlife Service and Rachel Carson
  2. Silent Spring Ignites the Environmental Movement New York Times

Think to Write

Now that you have completed three readings in this chapter on Environmental Science, think about which of the three is most interesting to you. Write a paragraph response about this reading and post it to The Wall.

It's SHOWTIME!

Watching a video clip related to the chapter content can be an enriching experience. Go online and find a video link whose topic ties into one of the chapter readings (maximum length = 10 minutes). After viewing the video clip, write a half-page summary of the video's key points. Post your personal reaction to the ideas in the clip (between 150 and 400 words) on The Wall.

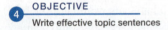

WRITING SKILLS FOCUS

OBJECTIVE
④ Write effective topic sentences

Writing Topic Sentences

In the previous chapter, you practiced identifying the topic and the controlling idea in topic sentences. Now, let's focus on developing topic sentences with controlling ideas. Before you begin, let's examine an example thesis statement and how a writer generates supporting ideas to elaborate on the central idea of an essay.

> **Thesis Statement:** There are effective measures the government can take to reduce the problem of air pollution.

See below how the writer brainstormed ideas to support his thesis statement.

> 1. Require people to wear face masks outdoors.
> 2. Encourage people to use public transportation more often.
> 3. Initiate a car-sharing program.
> 4. Offer subsidies to electric-car manufacturers.
> 5. Invest more in alternative energy sources.
> 6. Spend more on solar energy.
> 7. Put a higher tax on gasoline.
> 8. Revoke driver licenses for speeding.
> 9. Ask residents to help clean the air.
> 10. Offer free bikes to all workers.

Having brainstormed, the writer then had to choose which supporting ideas would work best as the bases for topic sentences for well-developed body paragraphs. Upon review, he realized that #1 and #9 did not support the thesis statement. He also concluded that the idea in #6 was already covered in #5. In the end, he chose to work with the three most relevant ideas to elaborate on the thesis statement: #2, #4, and #5. Notice how he then revised his thesis statement based on these three supporting ideas and developed a topic sentence for each.

Revised Thesis Statement: Some measures the government can take to reduce the problem of air pollution are encouraging people to use public transportation, offering subsidies to electric-car manufacturers, and investing more in alternative-energy sources.

Body Paragraph 1 Topic Sentence: One way the government can reduce air pollution is to promote the use of public transportation.

Body Paragraph 2 Topic Sentence: Another effective way to address the issue of air pollution is to offer subsidies to electric-car manufacturers.

Body Paragraph 3 Topic Sentence: Finally, investing more in alternative energy could be a successful method of reducing air pollution.

EXERCISE 4.4   Developing Supporting Ideas for a Thesis Statement

Directions: For the following thesis statements, first brainstorm as many supporting ideas as you can. Make your lists on a separate sheet of paper. Then, carefully choose the three best ideas that would serve as topic sentences for your body paragraphs, and write them below.

1. Environmental scientists claim that global warming is caused by human activity.
   a. _____
   b. _____
   c. _____
      _____

2. There are many benefits of recycling.
   a. _____
   b. _____
   c. _____

Writing Manageable Topic Sentences: Neither Too General, Nor Too Specific

When writing a topic sentence, you must envision how it will lead to a well-balanced paragraph of a manageable length. On the one hand, if your topic sentence is too general, you will have a difficult time covering all aspects of it in one paragraph. On the other hand, if your topic sentence is too narrow, you will be challenged to find supporting details to add to it. Consider the following two example topic sentences:

Water issues will be the defining environmental problem for the twenty-first century.

One resident, Michael Powers, is concerned about the decreasing level of potable water in his house.

If you have not guessed already, it would be difficult to develop either of the above topic sentences into an effective paragraph. In the case of the first topic sentence, one could write a 15-page essay on such a broad topic, covering many kinds of water issues across the globe, and still only scratch the surface. In contrast, a writer would get stuck with the second topic sentence because it is basically a fact, and there is little else to be said about it. Writing is a process, so you need to be aware of this general versus specific concern and revise accordingly when a topic sentence is not well balanced. Examine the revisions below:

Too General: Water issues will be the defining environmental problem for the twenty-first century.

Revised: One environmental concern in the twenty-first century is the lack of potable water in poorer regions of the world.

Too Specific: One resident, Michael Powers, is concerned about the decreasing level of potable water in his house.

Revised: The residents of Alameda County have complained to the mayor about declining amounts of potable water in the area.

Lake Oroville, CA, 2015

Helpful Hints: The following hints will help you determine whether a topic sentence is manageable or not.

1. If you look at a draft of your topic sentence and you notice that you can go in a hundred different directions with it, it is time for you to narrow your topic down!

2. If you are staring at your topic sentence draft and you cannot come up with anything to add, your best bet is to start moving toward a more general focus.

EXERCISE 4.5   **Assessing the Scope of a Topic Sentence**

Task 1: Examine the following topic sentences and label them based on whether they are too general (G), too specific (S), or effective (E).

_____ **1.** The number of polar bears in Alaska continues to decrease.

_____ **2.** Many animals are threatened by a host of environmental issues.

_____ **3.** Human activity is causing global warming.

_____ **4.** Carbon emissions went up 12 percent last year in California.

_____ **5.** Poachers have become the target of many environmentalists.

Task 2: After reviewing the effectiveness of the above topic sentences with your instructor, revise the examples that were "too general" and "too specific" to make them effective.

    1. _____

    2. _____

    3. _____

READING SKILL FOCUS

OBJECTIVE

Identify and develop supporting details

Supporting Details

Supporting details are a key element in a reading passage because they provide additional information to explain, illustrate, or prove the main idea of a particular paragraph. Supporting details answer the questions readers naturally formulate as they interact with a given text. For example, the first sentence of paragraph 10 (p. 124) of "Ocean Life Faces Mass Extinction, Broad Study Says" is "The fossil record indicates that a number of large animal species became extinct as humans arrived on continents and islands." Clearly, this is the topic sentence, or main point, of the paragraph. The reader can then predict how the paragraph will continue—in other words, what supporting details the paragraph will consist of—by formulating questions.

> **Main idea:** The fossil record indicates that a number of large animal species became extinct as humans arrived on continents and islands.
>
> **Questions:** Which large animal species became extinct? Why did the arrival of humans precipitate extinctions?

Reading through the full paragraph, the reader's questions are answered, as shown here:

The fossil record indicates that a number of large animal species became extinct as humans arrived on continents and islands. For example, the moa, a giant bird that once lived on New Zealand, was wiped out by arriving Polynesians in the 1300s, probably within a century. But it was only after 1800, with the Industrial Revolution, that extinctions on land really accelerated. Humans began to alter the habitat that wildlife depended on, wiping out forests for timber, plowing under prairie for farmland, and laying down roads and railroads across continents. Species began going extinct at a much faster pace. Over the past five centuries, researchers have recorded 514 animal extinctions on land. But the authors of the new study found that documented extinctions are far rarer in the ocean.

Types of Supporting Details

Supporting details most often come in the form of the following:

- **Characteristics** (Three characteristics of gene mutation are …)
- **Steps** (First, the kangaroo emerges from its hiding place. Then, it …)
- **Examples** (Another example of dyslexic behavior is …)
- **Reasons** (These religions are often in conflict because …)
- **Results** (A consequence of this action is that the night owl …)
- **Descriptions** (Sharp, rocky coasts contrast with the smooth blue Aegean Sea.)
- **Dates** (The battles that occurred in the winter of 1943 and summer of 1944 were critical.)
- **Places** (Some cities with high rates of violence include Washington, Miami, and Detroit.)
- **Names** (Such leaders as Franklin, Washington, and Hamilton are most remembered from this period.)
- **Statistics** (Americans consume nearly a quarter of the world's energy supply.)

Let's practice predicting supporting details by trying to formulate questions from main idea sentences related to our chapter theme.

EXERCISE 4.6   Predicting Supporting Details

Directions: Work with a partner to formulate *Who? What? Why? Where?* and *How?* questions about the main ideas offered below. The first one has been done for you.

1. **Main Idea:** The president's proposal to drill for oil in Alaska has been defeated by Congress.

   Questions: a. Why did Congress reject the president's proposal?

   b. What prompted the president to offer this proposal?

   c. What were the exact details of the drill-for-oil project?

2. **Main Idea:** A basic law of thermodynamics is that energy is never completely efficient.

   Questions: a. _____

   b. _____

3. **Main Idea:** In the 1940s, the properties of the new insecticide DDT seemed close to miraculous.

   Questions: a. _____

   b. _____

   c. _____

4. **Main Idea:** Chains of carbon atoms form the framework of all organic molecules, the building blocks of life.

   Questions: a. _____

   b. _____

5. **Main Idea:** Many of the environmental problems that plague modern society have resulted from human interference in ecosystem function.

   Questions: a. _____

   b. _____

   c. _____

   d. _____

6. **Main Idea:** Many scientists believe that global warming is already affecting our ecosystem.

   Questions: a. _____

   b. _____

   c. _____

Major and Minor Details

Read the following paragraph (para. 5) from the reading "Ocean Life Faces Mass Extinction, Broad Study Says" (p. 124), and underline the main idea.

There are clear signs already that humans are harming the oceans to a remarkable degree, the scientists found. Some ocean species are certainly overharvested, but even greater damage results from large-scale habitat loss, which is likely to accelerate as technology advances the human footprint, the scientists reported. Coral reefs, for example, have declined by 40 percent worldwide, partly as a result of climate-change-driven warming.

The main focus of this paragraph is spelled out in the first sentence ("There are clear signs already that humans are harming the oceans to a remarkable degree, the scientists found."), so you should look for a *supporting detail* that could explain *what* signs researchers found that indicate humans are damaging the oceans. Here it is:

Supporting Detail (major): Some ocean species are certainly overharvested, but even greater damage results from large-scale habitat loss, which is likely to accelerate as technology advances the human footprint, the scientists reported.

This kind of detail is known as a **major detail** because it directly supports the main idea. The paragraph continues by explaining more about the *major detail* (answering the question, What kinds of damage results from habitat loss?).

Supporting Detail (minor): Coral reefs, for example, have declined by 40 percent worldwide, partly as a result of climate-change-driven warming.

The above sentence represents a minor detail because it provides additional information that supports and illustrates the major detail.

This relationship between main point and major and minor details is diagrammed below.

Main Point = The main idea or central focus
There are clear signs already that humans are harming the oceans to a remarkable degree, the scientists found.

$\downarrow$

Major Detail = Supports the main idea
Some ocean species are certainly overharvested, but even greater damage results from large-scale habitat loss, which is likely to accelerate as technology advances the human footprint, the scientists reported.

$\downarrow$

Minor Detail = Supports and explains the major detail
Coral reefs, for example, have declined by 40 percent world-wide, partly as a result of climate-change-driven warming.

EXERCISE 4.7 Predicting Supporting Details

Directions: With a partner, imagine some logical minor details that follow from the main point and the major detail offered below. Turn the questions you might have into statements, providing the minor details in the table below.

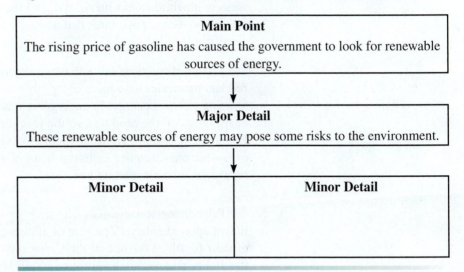

Main Point
The rising price of gasoline has caused the government to look for renewable sources of energy.

Major Detail
These renewable sources of energy may pose some risks to the environment.

Minor Detail	Minor Detail

EXERCISE 4.8 Practice Identifying Major and Minor Details

Directions: In the following short paragraphs, work with a partner to identify both the major and minor details. First, identify and highlight the main idea (called a topic sentence when you are writing). Then, underline the major details and double-underline the minor ones. The first one has been done for you.

1. During aggressive displays, animals may exhibit weapons such as claws and fangs and they often do things to make them appear larger. Competitors often stand upright and erect their fur, feathers, ears, or fins. The displays are typically accompanied by intimidating sounds (growls, croaks, roars, chirps) whose loudness can help decide the winner. Fighting tends to be a last resort when displays fail to resolve a dispute.

—From Audesirk, Audesirk, and Byers, *Biology*, p. 577

2.   In addition to observing natural selection in the wild, scientists have also devised numerous experiments that confirm the action of natural selection. For example, one group of evolutionary biologists released small groups of Anolis sagrei lizards onto fourteen small Bahamian islands that were previously uninhabited by lizards. The original lizards came from a population on Staniel Cay, an island with tall vegetation, including plenty of trees. In contrast, the islands to which the small colonial groups were introduced had few or no trees and were covered mainly with small shrubs and other low-growing plants.

—From Audesirk, Audesirk, and Byers, *Biology*, p. 291

3.   The scientific name of an organism is formed from the two smallest categories, the genus and the species. Each genus includes a group of closely related species, and each species within a genus includes populations of organisms that can potentially interbreed under natural conditions. Thus, the genus Sialia (bluebirds) includes the eastern bluebird (Sialia sialis), the western bluebird (Sialia mexicana), and the mountain bluebird (Sialia currucoides)—very similar birds that normally do not interbreed.

—From Audesirk, Audesirk, and Byers, *Biology*, p. 358

4.   Chemical reactions fall into two categories. In exergonic reactions, the reactant molecules have more energy than do the product molecules, so the reaction releases energy. In endergonic reactions, the reactants have less energy than do the products, so the reaction requires an input of energy. Exergonic reactions can occur spontaneously; but all reactions, including exergonic ones, require an initial input of energy to overcome electrical repulsions between reactant molecules.

—From Audesirk, Audesirk, and Byers, *Biology* p. 114

5.   Paleontologists (scientists who study fossils) have cataloged the extinction of approximately 70 percent of all living species by the disappearance of their fossils at the end of the Cretaceous Period. In sites from around the globe, researchers have found a thin layer of clay deposited around 65 million years ago; the clay has about 30 times the typical levels of a rare element called iridium, which is found in high concentrations in some meteorites.

—From Audesirk, Audesirk, and Byers, *Biology*, p. 130

EXERCISE 4.9   More Practice with Supporting Details

Directions: The following excerpts are taken from an introductory biology text. Read the paragraphs carefully, and answer the multiple-choice questions that follow. Remember to apply the skills you learned earlier to identify the major and minor details supporting the main idea.

Passage 1

Biodiversity refers to the total number of species within an ecosystem and the resulting complexity of interactions among them; in short, it defines the biological "richness" of an ecosystem. Rain forests have the highest biodiversity of any ecosystem on Earth. Although rain forests cover only 6% of Earth's total land area, ecologists estimate that they are home to between 5 million and 8 million species, representing half to two-thirds of the world's total. For example, a recent survey of a 2.5 acre site in the upper Amazon basin revealed 283 different species of trees, most of which were represented by a single individual. In a 3-square-mile (about 5-square-kilometer) tract of rain forest in Peru, scientists counted more than 1300 butterfly species and 600 bird species. For comparison, the entire U.S. is home to only 400 butterfly and 700 bird species.

—From Audesirk, Audesirk, and Byers, *Biology*, p. 588

_____ **1.** The main idea of the passage is that

    a. there are 400 butterfly and 700 bird species in the United States.

    b. the Amazon basin has 283 tree species.

    c. the rich flora and fauna of an ecosystem and their complex interactions are called biodiversity.

    d. rain forests contain approximately 8 million species of trees, birds, and butterflies.

_____ **2.** The first major detail presented in the passage is which of the following?

    a. A survey of a large area in the Amazon basin was recently conducted.

    b. The highest biodiversity is found in rain forests.

    c. Scientists found 1,300 butterfly and 600 bird species in Peru.

    d. Rain forests cover 6 percent of earth's land area.

_____ **3.** Which of the following is a minor detail?

    a. The Amazon basin has 283 different species of trees.

    b. _Biodiversity_ is a term used to define the richness of an ecosystem.

    c. Biodiversity refers to the complex interactions between plants and animals in an ecosystem.

    d. Rain forests have the highest biodiversity of an ecosystem.

Passage 2

Because of infertile soil and heavy rains, agriculture is risky and destructive in rain forests. If the trees are carried away for lumber, few nutrients remain to support crops. If the nutrients are released to the soil by burning the natural vegetation, the heavy year-round rainfall quickly dissolves and erodes them away, leaving the soil depleted after only a few seasons of cultivation. The exposed soil, which is rich in iron and aluminum, then takes on an impenetrable, brick-like quality as it bakes in the tropical sun. As a result, secondary succession on cleared rain-forest land is slow; even small forest cuttings take about 70 years to regenerate. Despite their unsuitability for agriculture, rain forests are being felled for lumber or burned down for ranching or farming at an alarming rate. The demand for biofuels (fuels produced from biomass, including palm and soybean oil) is driving rapid destruction of rain forests to grow these crops. Estimates of rain-forest destruction range up to 65,000 square miles (42 million acres, or about 170,000 square kilometers) per year, or about 1.3 acres each second. In recent years Brazil alone has lost about 10,000 square miles (6000 square kilometers) annually. For comparison, the state of Connecticut occupies about 5000 square miles.

—From Audesirk, Audesirk, and Byers, _Biology_, pp. 589–590

_____ **1.** Which of the following is the main idea of the passage?

    a. Agriculture can thrive in rain forests.

    b. Heavy rains have caused a boom in Brazil's agricultural growth.

    c. Rain forests are unsuitable for agriculture.

    d. Infertile soil helps the natural vegetation to grow rapidly.

_____ **2.** According to the passage, which of the following statements is not true?

a. Deforestation deprives the soil of its rich nutrients.

b. Brazil has lost approximately 10,000 square miles of rain forests annually.

c. Humans cutting down rain forests for lumber and farming is not a cause for concern.

d. Heavy rains deplete the soil.

_____ **3.** According to the passage, biofuels

a. have sparked an interest in protecting rain forests.

b. are helping decrease global warming.

c. have saved 42 million acres of rain forests.

d. have accelerated deforestation.

Passage 3

Although they are as diverse as terrestrial ecosystems, aquatic ecosystems share three general features. First, because water is slower to heat and cool than air, temperatures in aquatic ecosystems are more moderate than those in terrestrial ecosystems. Second, water absorbs light; even in very clear water, below 650 feet (200 meters) little light is left to power photosynthesis. Suspended sediment (nonliving particles carried by moving water) or microorganisms greatly reduce light penetration. Finally, nutrients in aquatic ecosystems tend to be concentrated near the bottom sediments, so where nutrients are highest, the light levels are lowest. Of the four requirements for life, aquatic ecosystems provide abundant water and appropriate temperatures. Thus, the availability of energy and nutrients largely determines the quantity of life and the distribution of life in aquatic ecosystems.

—From Audesirk, Audesirk, and Byers, *Biology*, p. 598

_____ **1.** Which of the following sentences best states the main idea of the passage?

a. Aquatic ecosystems share three general characteristics.

b. Energy and nutrients influence the quantity of life in aquatic ecosystems.

c. Aquatic ecosystems are incredibly diverse.

d. Water absorbs light in clear water.

_____ **2.** The first major detail that supports the topic sentence is which of the following?

a. Terrestrial ecosystems are diverse.

b. There are three general features of aquatic ecosystems.

c. Aquatic temperatures are moderate because water heats and cools slowly.

d. Aquatic ecosystems have lower temperatures than terrestrial ecosystems

_____ **3.** The second major detail discussed by the author is which of the following?

    a. Aquatic ecosystems have insufficient light for photosynthesis.

    b. Aquatic ecosystems have moderate temperatures.

    c. There are four requirements for life in aquatic ecosystems.

    d. Water absorbs light, so there is little photosynthesis below 650 feet.

_____ **4.** The third major detail that the author discusses is that

    a. microorganisms greatly reduce light penetration.

    b. the greatest concentration of nutrients occurs where there is the least light.

    c. photosynthesis does not occur in aquatic ecosystems.

    d. aquatic ecosystems provide water and appropriate temperatures.

_____ **5.** Which of the following is not a major detail?

    a. Because most nutrients are in sediments, they appear where there is the least light.

    b. Water cools and heats slowly, so temperatures remain moderate.

    c. Suspended sediment or microorganisms greatly reduce light penetration.

    d. Water absorbs light, which affects where photosynthesis can occur.

EXERCISE 4.10 Identifying Main Ideas and Major and Minor Details in Readings

Directions: Identify the main idea and major and minor supporting details in each of the three major chapter readings, using what you have learned in this and preceding chapters, and create an outline for each. Start by writing the title and the main idea (thesis) of the entire reading. Then list the major details, each followed by their minor supporting details, in the order they appear.

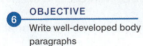

**WRITING
SKILL FOCUS**

OBJECTIVE

6

Write well-developed body paragraphs

Developing Body Paragraphs

Let's summarize what you have learned so far. A body paragraph usually begins with a topic sentence that introduces the topic and controlling idea of the paragraph. The controlling idea is further developed in the paragraph through supporting details: both major and minor. In Chapter 1, you learned that a body paragraph should be unified and coherent—that is, all of the sentences in the paragraph should be related to each other and relevant to the topic, and the information should be presented in a logical order, and connected by transitions to ensure a smooth flow of ideas (see p. 23 for more on unity and coherence). Notice how the following paragraph is developed following these principles.

> It is important to understand that science and its outcomes take place in the context of a scientific community and a larger society. There is no single authoritative source that makes judgments on the validity of scientific explanations. Instead, it is the collective body of scientists working in a given field who, because of their competence and experience, establish what is sound science and what is not. They do so by communicating their findings to each other and to the public, so they publish their work in peer reviewed journals. The process of peer review is crucial; it requires experts in a given field to analyze the results of their colleagues' work. Careful scrutiny is given to research publications, with the objective of rooting out poor or sloppy science and affirming work that is clearly meritorious.
>
> —From Wright and Boorse, *Environmental Science: Toward A Sustainable Future*. p 16

Notice that the topic of the paragraph you just read is *science and its outcomes*, and the controlling idea is that scientific results *take place in the context of a scientific community and a larger society*. The rest of the paragraph contains supporting details as the authors explain that scientists circulate their work by publishing it and by communicating the results to other scientists. We can say that this paragraph follows the principles of paragraph development listed below.

Principles of Paragraph Development

1. A body paragraph should have only one topic sentence.
2. A body paragraph should be unified.
3. A body paragraph should be coherent.
4. A body paragraph should have clear supporting details.

EXERCISE **4.11**   Revising a Paragraph

Directions: The following paragraph is poorly developed. Some sentences do not belong in the paragraph and make it incoherent. Your first task is to identify the irrelevant sentences and cross them out. Then, brainstorm a list of appropriate supporting details to elaborate on the controlling idea.

People in all walks of life—scientists, sociologists, workers, and executives, economists, government leaders and clergy, as well as traditional environmentalists—are recognizing that "business as usual" is not sustainable. Although business is important and provides many career opportunities. A finite planet cannot continue to grow by 80 million persons annually without significant detrimental effects.

—From Wright and Dorothy, *Environmental Science*, p. 20

EXERCISE 4.12   **Challenge on The Wall**

Directions: Post your rewrite of the paragraph in Exercise 4.11 to The Wall. Keep the topic sentence intact, but delete the irrelevant sentences and provide appropriate supporting details to develop the controlling idea. You may have to do some online research to find relevant supporting information.

EXERCISE 4.13   **Writing Well-Developed Paragraphs**

Directions: Refer to the free-writing you created at the beginning of the chapter, and write the introduction to this chapter's essay. (See Chapter 3, p. 105 for more on introductory paragraphs.) You may or may not wish to include all of the ideas you brainstormed during the free-writing exercise. Remember to include a clear thesis statement that indicates to the reader the main focus of your essay. Then, make an outline of your essay by writing three to five topic sentences that support your thesis statement and list supporting details that elaborate on each. Keep in mind that you need to use specific examples as supporting details.

Chapter Essay Question from Environmental Science: How can we best preserve all forms of life on earth?

Thesis statement: _____

_____

Topic sentence: _____

_____

Topic sentence: _____

_____

Topic sentence: _____

_____

Topic sentence: _____

_____

Topic sentence: _____

_____

Once you have created an outline of your essay, draft the body paragraphs. Remember that after you write the body paragraphs, you will need to write the concluding paragraph and create a title. (See Chapter 5, p. 199, for instructions on how to write the conclusion.)

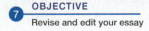

OBJECTIVE

7 Revise and edit your essay

Revising and Proofreading

After you write the first draft of an essay, you need to go through the introductory, body, and concluding paragraphs reading like a reviewer and thinking how best to revise and edit your writing.

Revising Your Essay

It helps to wait a little before revising, so you have some distance from your work and can look at it more objectively. Reread carefully, keeping in mind your assignment. Revision, in this sense, is rethinking your essay, taking time to assess the thesis statement, the supporting topic sentences with controlling ideas, the supporting details in each body paragraph, the overall organization and structure, flow of thoughts, and unity and coherence. It can often involve reorganizing content, refining the thesis statement and topic sentences, adding transitions, and adding or cutting details.

Use the following checklist to guide your revision process.

Revision Checklist

Introductory Paragraph

1. Does my introduction grab the reader's attention? Does it begin with an effective hook?

2. Does my introduction offer background information?

3. Does my introduction have a circumscribed thesis statement?
   Write the thesis statement here and revise it so that it is sufficiently narrowed down.

   _____

   _____

   _____

   _____

4. Write below how you will improve the introduction.

   _____

   _____

Body Paragraphs

For each body paragraph, ask and answer the following questions:

5. Does the paragraph begin with a topic sentence?

6. Does the topic sentence have a clear controlling idea?

7. Does the topic sentence support the thesis statement?

8. Do the details support the topic sentence?

9. Does the paragraph have unity and coherence? In other words, are all of the sentences in the paragraph relevant to the topic sentence, logically organized, and smoothly connected?

10. Write below what you need to do to improve your body paragraphs.

_____

_____

_____

Conclusion Paragraph

11. Have I summarized the main points of the essay?

12. Have I restated the thesis statement?

13. Does the conclusion leave a lasting impression on the reader? Explain how.

14. Write below how you will improve the conclusion.

_____

_____

Overall Evaluation

15. What is the best part of the essay?

16. What parts need to be improved or revised?

Proofreading Your Essay

Now that you have done the revisions, you should focus on the mechanical aspects of writing such as grammar and spelling errors. When you submit an essay that is not proofread properly, your instructor may find it difficult to follow your thoughts. For this reason, it is imperative that you go through your essay very carefully, find grammar and spelling errors, and correct them appropriately. Refer to the following questions as you proofread your essay. You also may wish to refer to the editing questions in Chapter 1 (p. 27).

Editing Checklist
1. Are there incomplete thoughts in my essay, such as run-ons, comma splices, and fragments? (See p. 244)
2. Are there subject–verb agreement errors? (See p. 109.)
3. Are all of the words spelled correctly?
4. Have I used the correct verb tense? (See p. 201.)
5. Have I eliminated all instances of contractions such as "won't" and "don't"? (See p. 28.)

EXERCISE 4.14   Revising and Proofreading Your Chapter Essay

Directions: Once you have completed the first draft of your chapter essay, put it aside for a short while, and then carefully reread and revise it. Using the Revision (p. 152) and Editing (p. 153) Checklists, move, add, and delete content to produce a well-organized, well-developed, and unified and coherent essay. Once you are satisfied with your revisions, be sure to go over your writing sentence by sentence as you proofread.

THEN & NOW

Go online and do some research to gather information about two experts in the field of environmental science: one from the past such as Barry Commoner or Chico Mendes and another contemporary environmentalist such as Adam Werbach or Edward Osborne Wilson. Fill out the table provided below with pertinent information about the two experts.

Past Influential Environmentalist	Present Influential Environmentalist
Name	Name
Place of birth	Place of birth
Year of birth	Year of birth
Education	Education
What is s/he most famous for?	What is s/he most famous for?
Famous quote	Famous quote

After you fill out the table, discuss your findings with your classmates and learn from them about what they discovered on the Internet.

Working with a search engine, do the following search, "TED Talks Edward O. Wilson My Wish" and click on "View Interactive Transcript." Peruse the talk to gain a deeper understanding of biodiversity. After doing a careful reading, write brief answers to the following questions about the content.

1. At the beginning of the talk, why does Wilson tell his audience members that they are the great hopes for the whole world?

   _____

   _____

2. In the second paragraph, what discovery did Wilson make during his college years?

   _____

   _____

3. In the conclusion, what does Wilson hope the "Encyclopedia of Life" will accomplish?

   _____

   _____

   _____

CHAPTER ESSAY ASSIGNMENT

What role should the US government and the American people play in preserving various forms of life on earth?

OBJECTIVE

8 Read, think, plan, and write an essay in response to the chapter essay assignment

Now that you have had the opportunity to read a number of articles and a textbook excerpt, you should have a deeper understanding of *biodiversity* and be prepared to compose your chapter essay assignment.

Write a one- to two-page essay on the chapter essay assignment, or compose your own essay question that reflects the themes in this chapter. When you are done, hand in your essay to your instructor. Be sure to incorporate some of his or her suggestions into your second draft and submit the revised draft to your instructor for further feedback on form and meaning.

FOCUS ON FORM	# Revising and Proofreading

In the Trouble Spots in Writing section on page 152, you learned how to revise and proofread the preliminary draft of your essay. Now practice what you have learned about revising and proofreading a rough draft. First, read the following introductory paragraph written by a student on the topic of air pollution in Beijing, China, and make corrections to it. Consider the hook and thesis statement and see if you can revise the introduction to make it more appealing to the reader. Also, look for grammar errors and make the necessary corrections. When you are done, write out the revised paragraph, and compare your edits with those of a classmate.

People are wearing face masks in Beijing. Heavy air pollution in China's biggest commercial city has made it increasingly difficult for the people to breathe easily. Critics say that Chinese government is not done enough to reduce air pollution in Beijing and other cities throughout the country. The air is severely polluted, according to Beijing's environmental center, which issued a warning for children, the elderly, and the sick asking them to stay indoors. It also urge people to refrain from do outdoor activities. However, asking people to remain indoors were not a practical solution to air pollution. I believe that Chinese government should done something about it.

_____

_____

_____

_____

_____

_____

_____

_____

_____

It's Your Turn!

You have practiced revising and proofreading a student's introductory paragraph. Now read the essay you wrote for the chapter essay assignment and revise and proofread it. Consider if you need to rewrite or slightly revise your hook, thesis statement, and topic sentences. Pay attention to the details you have offered to support the topic sentences.

END OF CHAPTER DEBATE OPTION

What role should the US government and the American people play in preserving various forms of life on earth.

This chapter's debate topic is the same as your chapter essay assignment. Refer to Appendix 8, page 455, for detailed guidelines on how to set up and participate in a formal debate.

5 Literature

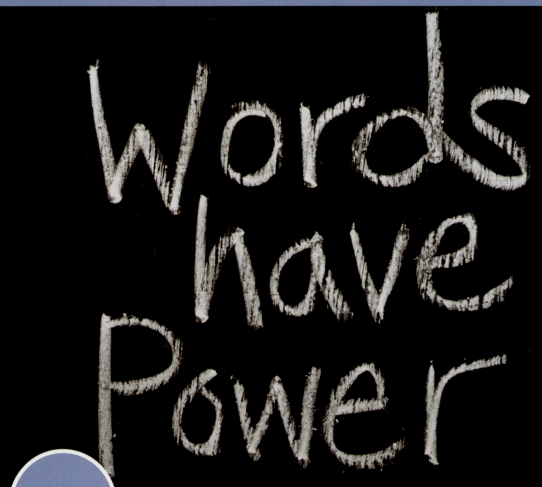

Learning Objectives

IN THIS CHAPTER, YOU WILL LEARN TO . . .

1 Read in the field of literature

2 Understand and use key literary terms

3 Reread to deepen understanding

4 Make inferences and draw logical conclusions

5 Write a concluding paragraph

6 Control verb tense through careful editing

7 Draft a piece of creative writing

8 Write about literature

9 Read, think, plan, and write an essay in response to the chapter essay assignment

OBJECTIVE
1
Read in the field of literature

Introduction to the Field of Literature

Literature depicts life in all its shining colors. Whether we are reading a poem or a play, a story or a novel, love and hate, romance and tragedy, jealousy and compassion take center stage and challenge the way we see the world around us. In this chapter, you will have the opportunity to explore some poems and a suspenseful short story about a boy who gets into trouble while playing on a subway train. You will also read a scene from a play filled with family intrigue, the first pages of a popular novel set in Afghanistan, and an essay about the importance of literature in our lives. Finally, you will be given the chance to create your own original work of fiction.

CHAPTER ESSAY QUESTION

Taking into consideration all of the chapter readings, which character, setting, or plot movement is most significant to you?

Quick Free-Write! Chapter essays will be due when your class completes this chapter. As you have not read the readings yet, take out a piece of paper and write for ten minutes without stopping about a book you have read or a movie or play you have watched recently that you found especially interesting. Think about the characters, the plot, and the places the story was set in.

Your Option: Once you have worked your way through the chapter readings, you are welcome to narrow down the topics covered and compose your own chapter essay question.

Previewing Literature

Read the following questions and discuss them with your classmates. As you answer the questions, consider your personal experience and knowledge of literature in general.

1. Do you have a favorite novel, a favorite poem, or a favorite author? What book or author would you recommend to a friend, and why?

2. What are the purposes of reading, beyond having to do so for a class assignment or in preparation for an exam?

3. Many teachers and parents are concerned that America is becoming a nation of nonreaders. Why do you think this is the case? What can be done to inspire more people to read for pleasure?

4. Bookstores across America are worried that traditional printed books are going to disappear because of the increasing popularity of audiobooks and e-books. Do you think paper-based text will become extinct? Given the choice, would you prefer reading a printed book or a technology-based text, such as an audiobook, an e-book, or an online article? Explain your preference.

5. If you were asked to write a creative piece for a literature class, what topics do you think you would write about? Explain your choices.

After discussing the preview questions with your classmates, post your responses to two of them on The Wall. Review the postings on The Wall and respond to at least two of your classmates' responses that grab your interest. Remember the guidelines for The Wall etiquette!

OBJECTIVE

Understand and use key literary terms

Key Terms in Literature

Take a moment to think about the field of literature as you complete the following two exercises.

EXERCISE 5.1 **Brainstorming Vocabulary**

Directions: What associated words come to mind when you think of the world of literature? Work with a partner and write down as many related words as you can think of in a period of five minutes.

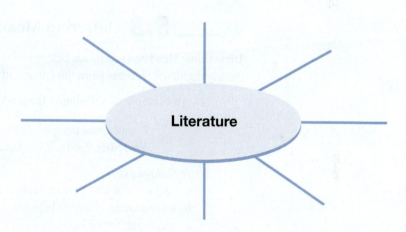

Literature

EXERCISE 5.2 **Creating Original Sentences**

Directions: Choose five of the words from your brainstorm list, and use them to write complete and meaningful sentences.

1. _____

2. _____

3. _____

4. _____

5. _____

A **synonym** is a word used to express a similar meaning to another word. An **antonym** is a word that conveys the opposite meaning of another word.

The following terms are frequently used in literary analysis. If you take a college-level literature course, it will be important for you to fully understand them and to be able to use them in your writing. Unlike in other chapters of this text, these words do not appear directly in the context of readings. However, you will be expected to make use of these literary terms in your discussions of the chapter readings. Review the words below and answer the multiple-choice questions that follow.

Discipline-specific Word Bank

alliteration	irony	scene
character	metaphor	setting
conflict	personification	stanza
dialogue	plot	symbolism
foreshadowing	point of view	tone

EXERCISE 5.3   Inferring Meaning from Context

Directions: Read each sentence below and try to derive the correct meaning of the highlighted key terms from the context in which they appear.

_____ 1. An example of a **dialogue** from a William Faulkner story follows:

> "I want some poison," she said to the druggist.
> "Yes, Miss Emily. What kind? For rats and such?"

A *dialogue* is
a. two lines of text that are related to each other.
b. an exchange of words between characters.
c. a comparison of ideas.
d. a term used only in poetry.

_____ 2. An example of **symbolism** follows: "After my girlfriend left, the sky grew dark and cold." *Symbolism* is when

a. a writer uses objects or situations to suggest emotions or states of mind.
b. the meaning of one's life is lost because of a broken heart.
c. a scene is both tragic and comic.
d. the world becomes unreal and unpleasant.

_____ 3. The new play has three principle **characters**. A *character* is

a. always evil.
b. an object of affection.
c. played by an actor.
d. a part or a role in a literary work.

_____ 4. The **plot** of a romantic novel often involves four stages: finding love, enjoying love, losing love, and regaining love. A *plot* is

a. a secret plan to do something.
b. a particular scene in a story.

c. the main story of a novel, play, or short story.

d. the story of how an innocent person learns something.

_____ **5.** The novel I am reading is told from the **point of view** of a single mother in New Orleans around the time of Hurricane Katrina. *Point of view* means

a. the opinion of the main character.

b. the perspective from which a story is told.

c. what can be seen within a certain distance.

d. the way a single mother sees the world.

_____ **6.** The **setting** of his new play is Paris, France, on a rainy winter afternoon. The *setting* is

a. what happens in a story.

b. why a character acts the way he or she does.

c. the time and place in which a play occurs.

d. related to the weather.

_____ **7.** The central **conflict** of the play is that the husband is jealous of his new tenant's sex appeal because he thinks his wife is attracted to him. The term *conflict* means

a. a struggle between a character and some obstacle.

b. a difficult solution to a problem.

c. a physical fight between characters.

d. a prolonged struggle.

_____ **8.** Here is an example of **alliteration**: The fruit-loving forager followed my footsteps. Which of the following is the correct definition of *alliteration*?

a. personifying an object

b. repetition of consonant sounds

c. repeated rhyming words

d. use of figurative language

_____ **9.** This is an example of **irony**: Bob is tired of all of his neighbors and wants to be left alone. The door rings, he answers it and says to his neighbor Joe, "It is so great to see you!" Irony means

a. an example of humorous dialogue.

b. predictable behavior by a particular person in a specific situation.

c. having difficulty telling the truth.

d. the contrast between what is said and what is meant.

_____ **10.** My favorite **scene** in the novel is when Santiago meets the alchemist. What does the term *scene* mean?

a. the part of a chapter where the most action happens

b. a unit of a play or story

c. a pause from any action or dialogue in a dramatic work of fiction

d. a display of emotion, which takes place early in a work of fiction and steers the story in one direction or another

_____11. Here are two examples of **metaphor**:
- That book is garbage.
- Her smile lights up the sky.

A *metaphor* can be described as

a. a type of literary writing.
b. an unusual use of language.
c. describing something by comparing it to something else.
d. an inaccurate description.

_____12. An example of **foreshadowing** in the play is when Julius Caesar receives the kiss of death in an early scene. *Foreshadowing* means

a. a suggestion of what is to come.
b. making something darker or less pleasant.
c. an act of kindness followed by an act of ill will.
d. making an event more important than it really is.

_____13. I love the third **stanza** of the poem when he writes, "life is the death of life." What is a *stanza*?

a. a chapter
b. the rhyming scheme of a poem
c. an instance of plot in poetry
d. a group of lines forming a unit in a poem

_____14. The following is an example of **personification**: The trees ached and cried out for love. The term *personification* refers to

a. when a writer gives a person characteristics of nonliving objects.
b. when a writer gives an inanimate object, animal, or other nonhuman, human traits.
c. an ongoing dialogue between nature and humans.
d. dialogue between two unrelated characters in a play or other dramatic work.

_____15. In the Langston Hughes poem we read in class, the author's **tone** was lighthearted and comical. What does *tone* refer to?

a. attitude or mood
b. purpose
c. dialogue and setting
d. writing that has a musical quality

SUCCESS IN READING

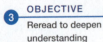

OBJECTIVE

Reread to deepen understanding

Rereading

It is one thing to say that you have completed a reading and another thing to say that you understood what you have read. Just because your eyes have passed over a text does not mean that you have comprehended all, or even most, of the ideas contained within it. How you interpret the ideas in a given reading depends on many factors: your mood during the particular reading session; your level of focus and interest in the topic; your personal bias on the subject matter; the particular sections of the text you happen to pay more attention to during a given reading, and so on. For this reason, rereading a section of a textbook, a story, or an article can prove very helpful. You may find that you see things during a second read that you didn't pick up on the first time around.

Try to set up different goals for the first and second reading of a text. For example, you can first read straight through without stopping to get an overall sense of what the author is saying and then go back and reread, but this time to highlight key terms and concepts and maybe work on sections you did not fully understand.

EXERCISE 5.4 Rereading Fiction: Comparing Interpretations of First and Second Readings

Directions: Read the first two pages of Khaled Hosseini's recent novel *And the Mountains Echoed*, share your interpretation of the ideas in the text with a classmate (see questions and directions that follow), and then reread the same pages to see if and/or how your second read has broadened your perspective.

One

FALL 1952

1   So, then. You want a story and I will tell you one. But just the one. Don't either of you ask me for more. It's late, and we have a long day of travel ahead of us, Pari, you and I. You will need your sleep tonight. And you too, Abdullah. I am counting on you, boy, while your sister and I are away. So is your mother. Now. One story, then. Listen, both of you, listen well. And don't interrupt.

2   Once upon a time, in the days when *div*s and *jinn*s and giants roamed the land, there lived a farmer named Baba Ayub. He lived with his family in a little village by the name of Maidan Sabz. Because he had a large family to feed, Baba Ayub saw his days consumed by hard work. Every day, he labored from dawn to sundown, plowing his field and turning the soil and tending to his meager pistachio trees. At any given moment you could spot him in his field, bent at the waist, back as curved as the scythe he swung all day. His hands were always callused, and they often bled, and every night sleep stole him away no sooner than his cheek met the pillow.

3   I will say that, in this regard, he was hardly alone. Life in Maidan Sabz was hard for all its inhabitants. There were other, more fortunate villages to the north, in the valleys, with fruit trees and flowers and pleasant air, and streams that ran with cold, clear water. But Maidan Sabz was a desolate place, and it didn't resemble in the slightest the image that its name, Field of Green, would have you picture. It sat in a flat, dusty plain ringed by a chain of craggy mountains. The wind was hot, and blew dust in the eyes. Finding water was a daily struggle because the village wells, even the deep ones, often ran low. Yes, there was a river, but the villagers had to endure a half-day walk to reach it, and even then its waters flowed muddy all year round. Now, after ten years of drought, the river too ran shallow. Let's just say that people in Maidan Sabz worked twice as hard to eke out half the living.

4   Still, Baba Ayub counted himself among the fortunate because he had a family that he cherished above all things. He loved his wife and never raised his voice to her, much less his hand. He valued her counsel and found genuine pleasure in her companionship. As for children, he was blessed with as many as a hand has fingers, three sons and two daughters, each of whom he loved dearly. His daughters were dutiful and kind and of good character and repute. To his sons he had taught already the value of honesty, courage, friendship, and hard work without complaint. They obeyed him, as good sons must, and helped their father with his crops.

5   Though he loved all of his children, Baba Ayub privately had a unique fondness for one among them, his youngest, Qais, who was three years old. Qais was a little boy with dark blue eyes. He charmed anyone who met him with his devilish laughter. He was also one of those boys so bursting with energy that he drained others of theirs. When he learned to walk, he took such delight in it that he did it all day while he was awake, and then, troublingly, even at night in his sleep. He would sleepwalk out of the family's mud house and wander off into the moonlit darkness. Naturally, his parents worried. What if he fell into a well, or got lost, or, worst of all, was attacked by one of the creatures lurking the plains at night? They took stabs at many remedies, none of which worked. In the end, the solution Baba Ayub found was a simple one, as the best solutions often are: He removed a tiny bell from around the neck of one of his goats and hung it instead around Qais's neck. This way, the bell would wake someone if Qais were to rise in the middle of the night. The sleepwalking stopped after a time, but Qais grew attached to the bell and refused to part with it. And so, even though it didn't serve its original use, the bell remained fastened to the string around the boy's neck. When Baba Ayub came home after a long day's work, Qais would run from the house face first into his father's belly, the bell jingling with each of his tiny steps. Baba Ayub would lift him up and take him into the house, and Qais would watch with great attention as his father washed up, and then he would sit beside Baba Ayub at suppertime. After they had eaten, Baba Ayub would sip his tea, watching his family, picturing a day when all of his children married and gave him children of their own, when he would be proud patriarch to an even greater brood.

6   Alas, Abdullah and Pari, Baba Ayub's days of happiness came to an end.

—*And the Mountains Echoed*, by Khalled Hosseini, 2013

Discuss the following two questions with a classmate:

1. What is this story about? What is happening in these first few pages of the novel?

2. What images and or ideas in these pages grab your attention?
   Now, go back and reread the first pages of this novel with fresh eyes. Try not to rush through the reading. When you are done, discuss the same questions you focused on after your first reading, as well as question 3 below.

3. Describe how your second reading of these pages differed from your first. What images, ideas, and/or interpretations came into your mind during the second reading that didn't come as much into focus during the first?

READING

Selection 1

Poetry

Two Poems

Pre-Reading Questions

1. The first poem you are going to read offers a welcoming message for new immigrants coming to America. In your opinion, does America welcome its new immigrants with open arms? Explain.

2. The second poem concerns the topic of death. Why do you think so many poems deal with this theme? What can a poet gain from sharing his or her feelings about death?

3. Although you have not read the two poems yet, how is the process of reading a poem different from reading a short story?

Eye on Vocabulary

It may be helpful to focus on the meaning of some key words in the poems before you read them. Skim through both and look for the following key vocabulary terms in bold. Working with a partner, examine the words in context and try to guess the meaning of each. Then look up the words in a dictionary. Keep in mind that many words have multiple meanings. Write the definition that best fits the word's context in the article.

Word	Your definition	Dictionary definition
1. huddled		
2. wretched		
3. ceased		
4. rendered		

Poem 1: "The New Colossus"

Emma Lazarus (1849–1877) was an American poet from New York City best known for her sonnet, "The New Colossus," which she wrote for an auction held to raise money to build a pedestal for the Statue of Liberty. The poem appears on a plaque inside the pedestal.

The New Colossus

by Emma Lazarus

1 Not like the brazen giant of Greek fame,
    With conquering limbs astride from land to land;
    Here at our sea-washed, sunset gates shall stand
    A mighty woman with a torch, whose flame

5 Is the imprisoned lightning, and her name
    Mother of Exiles. From her beacon-hand
    Glows world-wide welcome; her mild eyes command
    The air-bridged harbor that twin cities frame.
    "Keep, ancient lands, your storied pomp!" cries she

10 With silent lips. "Give me your tired, your poor,
    Your **huddled** masses yearning to breathe free,
    The **wretched** refuse of your teeming shore.
    Send these, the homeless, tempest-tossed to me,
    I lift my lamp beside the golden door!"

Poem 2: "Failures of Alchemy"

Carol Edelstein of Northampton, Massachusetts, is a poet (The World Is Round, *1994, Amherst Writers and Artists Press,* The Disappearing Letters, *2005, Perugia Press, Florence, MA), fiction writer, and essayist whose work has appeared in numerous literary magazines and anthologies, including* The Massachusetts Review, The Georgia Review, Denver Quarterly, *and* Flash Fiction *(W.W. Norton, Inc).*

Ms. Edelstein lives within a mile of where she was born. With her husband, Robin Barber, she leads writing workshops and organizes a reading series that features local writers. She has led a weekly Thursday writing group in Northampton, Massachusetts since September, 1988, and she is a founding member of Gallery of Readers.

Failures of Alchemy

by Carol Edelstein

[2005]

1 In the pearl of this April morning
    I have just learned of your death.
    You are freshly dead, hours gone,
    without yet the shelter of wood, earth,
5 or cleansing, consumptive fire.

    How could you have hanged yourself
    from a wooden beam
    when the lilac bush in your own yard
    was just getting dressed,
10 and your youngest daughter's flock
    of memories will have to land
    during each migration, exactly here?

I must mix Animal Stone with Vegetable Liquor.
I must send the soul of Saturn whirling

15 into an Oily Clot. None of us will say
we knew you well — not now.
Did you think we'd know you better
If you put a stop to conversation,
or if, at the pond's putrefying edges,

20 you ceased finding beauty?
I know you once found it there,
for you rendered wings and filaments,
fronds and pods, cilia so delicate
they required you to load your color

25 onto a brush made of only three hairs.

When I was twenty and not so sure
it was good to live, you were the man
who stood by the completed painting,
placed a magnifying glass in my hand,

30 and said, "Look what I made."

Where were you last night?
Your answer better be good.
I mean I want to hear
you mixed Leafy Water with Leathery Water

35 and drank it down under the fattest moon,
thinking it was the sturdy donkey
who would carry you
like a load of salt to the sea.
Perhaps I am casting nonsense spells

40 to prove nothing can bring you back.
I'm afraid I will always fault you
for not trying hard enough.

Why didn't you try Burnt Copper
with Blackened Copper?

45 A thick slash of blue in the upper left?
Something hammered in, or stuck on with glue —
shards of glass, old cutlery, anything at all —
you of all people knew how full this world is

Of matter to break and fix, melt down, build up.

50 It didn't have to be new — couldn't you,

have set out to duplicate any one

of the old recipes, or simply rested

into this milky light that comes

even when nobody calls.

Post-Reading Activity: Discussing poetry demands a close reading and rereading of a poem, line by line. Working with the "Responding to Poems" checklist will guide you toward a better understanding of the two poems you have just read.

Work with a partner and try to answer the checklist questions about each of the poems.

Responding to Poems	
First response	☐ What was your response to the poem on first reading?
Speaker and tone	☐ Who is the speaker? ☐ Do you think the speaker is fully aware of what he or she is saying, or does the speaker unconsciously reveal his or her personality and values? ☐ Is the speaker narrating on an earlier experience or attitude?
Audience	☐ To whom is the speaker speaking?
Structure and form	☐ Does the poem proceed in a straightforward way, or at some point or points does the speaker reverse course, altering his or her tone or perception? ☐ Is the poem organized into sections? ☐ What is the effect on you of the form—say quatrains (stanzas of four lines) or blank verse (unrhymed lines of ten syllables of iambic pentameter)?
Center of interest and theme	☐ What is the poem about? ☐ Is the theme stated explicitly (directly) or implicitly?
Diction	☐ How would you characterize the language? ☐ Do certain words have rich and relevant associations that relate to other words and help to define the speaker or the theme or both? ☐ What is role of figurative language, if any? ☐ What do you think is to be taken figuratively or symbolically and what literally?

—From Barnet, Burto, and Cain, *An Introduction to Literature*, 16th edition, p. 12

Thinking about the Reading

Now that you have completed a close reading of the two poems, write your answers to the following questions. You may be asked to discuss your answers with your classmates.

1. After reading "The New Colossus," what kind of ideas do you think the poet, Emma Lazarus, had about new immigrants and American culture? Do you agree with her? Explain.

   _____

   _____

2. The famous lines, "Give me your tired, your poor, / Your huddled masses yearning to breathe free," are some of the most celebrated in American culture. In your view, why do these words get so much attention? What ideals are expressed in these lines?

   _____

   _____

3. What is the relationship between the narrator of the poem and the deceased? What clues inform you to the nature of this relationship.

   _____

   _____

   _____

4. Why do you think the narrator inquires, "Where were you last night? It better be good."

   _____

   _____

5. Which poem did you enjoy more? What was it that you liked better about this poem?

   _____

   _____

Reading Comprehension Check

____ 1. In the poem "The New Colossus," what is the purpose of the reference to the "huddled masses yearning to be free"?

   a. to express how some immigrants take advantage of the American system
   b. to express why many immigrants choose to come to America
   c. to show how many people want to come to America
   d. to make the point that some immigrants have in sufficient resources

_____ **2.** Who is the "mighty woman with a torch" referenced in the second stanza of first poem?

    a. the Statue of Liberty

    b. an immigrant mother

    c. a symbol of people from all over the world

    d. a sculpture of a large woman

_____ **3.** What is one of the main messages of "The New Colossus"?

    a. Immigrants should think twice before coming to America.

    b. Immigrant children want to learn English.

    c. America is refuge for immigrants in search of freedom.

    d. America is already overcrowded.

_____ **4.** The reference to "wood, earth / or cleansing, consumptive fire" in the first stanza is a reference to

    a. methods of suicide.

    b. lack of shelter.

    c. the hunger for life.

    d. after-death rituals.

_____ **5.** The narrator mentions "the pond" as representing a place of _____ to the deceased artist?

    a. creativity   c. conflict

    b. hate   d. edges

_____ **6.** What does the narrator of "Failures of Alchemy" imply at the beginning of the fourth stanza?

    a. that she was once in love with this artist

    b. that she too once contemplated suicide

    c. that she is now twenty years-old

    d. that this was the narrator's first painting

_____ **7.** The tone of the narrator in "Failures of Alchemy" can best be described as

    a. proud and apologetic.

    b. nostalgic and gentle.

    c. humorous and joyous.

    d. shocked and angry.

_____ **8.** In the final line of "The New Colossus," *I lift my lamp beside the golden door!* the phrase *golden door* most likely symbolizes

    a. an investment opportunity.

    b. memories of a shining past.

    c. a bright future in the United States.

    d. exile.

_____ **9.** In the second-to-last line of "The New Colossus," the phrase *tempest-tossed* most likely means

    a. having experienced suffering and turmoil.

    b. suffering from seasickness.

    c. angry and defensive.

    d. having become disoriented.

_____**10.** The speaker's tone in "The New Colossus" can best be described as

    a. scolding and threatening.

    b. unsure and tentative.

    c. lighthearted and teasing.

    d. sincere and earnest.

THEMATIC LINKS

If you want to learn more about the works of Emma Lazarus and Maya Angelou, type the following words into your browser and explore the two sites that come up:

1. Emma Lazarus Miriam's Cup

2. Poems inspired by paintings

Writing Without BOUNDARIES

There Are No Checkpoints!

"Love all, trust a few, do wrong to none."

WILLIAM SHAKESPEARE
All's Well That Ends Well,"
Act 1 Scene 1

Read the quote above and respond to the idea in any way you want. Write in your notebook for ten minutes without stopping. For this activity, it is important that you focus on ideas, not words; this will be an exercise in focusing on content and not getting hung up on word choice and grammar errors. You may wish to read what you have written out loud in front of your classmates and instructor.

READING

Selection 2

Short Story

"Samuel"

Pre-Reading Questions

Answer the following questions before reading the story:

1. What are the greatest potential dangers to young children growing up in big cities?

2. What do you think is an appropriate age for parents to permit their children to travel around on mass transit without an adult chaperone? Explain your opinion.

3. The story you are about to read is suspenseful. Do you enjoy suspenseful movies, stories, or TV programs? If yes, share a few examples.

Eye on Vocabulary

Skim through the reading and find the following key vocabulary terms in bold. Working with a partner, examine the words in context and try to guess their meanings. Then look up the words in a dictionary. Keep in mind that many words have multiple meanings. Write the definition that fits the word's context in the article.

Word	Your definition	Dictionary definition
1. accelerated		
2. blushed		
3. hiss		
4. abandoned		

Grace Paley (1922–2007) was born in New York City. While raising two children, she first focused on writing poetry and later began to write fiction. The main subject of Paley's writing is the life of little people struggling in the big city.

Pre- and Post-Reading Checklist

Before jumping into the story, it might be helpful to consider the many different ways to interpret a short story. Read through the checklist questions below with a partner. Some of the literary terms mentioned in the checklist are included in this chapter's discipline-specific word bank on page 162.

To make sure you fully understand each item, try to rephrase each question in your own words. After reading the story, you will be asked to go back to the checklist and answer each of the questions.

	Responding to Stories
Plot	☐ Does the plot grow out of the characters, or does it depend on chance or coincidence? ☐ Does surprise play an important role, or does fore-shadowing? ☐ What conflicts does the story include? ☐ Are certain episodes narrated out of chronological order?
Character	☐ Which character chiefly engages your interest? ☐ What purposes do minor characters serve? ☐ How does the author reveal character? ☐ Is the behavior plausible—that is, are the characters well motivated? ☐ If a character changes, why and how does he or she change? ☐ Are the characters round or flat? ☐ How has the author caused you to sympathize with certain characters?
Point of view	☐ Who tells the story? ☐ How does the point of view help shape the theme? ☐ Does the narrator's language help you to construct a picture of the narrator's character, class, attitude, strengths, and limitations?
Setting	☐ Do you have a strong sense of time and place? ☐ What is the relation of the setting to the plot and characters?
Theme	☐ Is the title informative? ☐ Do certain passages—dialogue or description—seem to you to point especially toward the theme? ☐ Is the meaning of the story embodied in the whole story, or does it seem conveyed chiefly by certain passages of editorializing? ☐ Suppose someone asked you to state the point—the theme—of the story. Could you?

—From Barnet, Burto, and Cain, *An Introduction to Literature*,
16th edition, pp. 10–11

Samuel (1974)

By Grace Paley

Part One

1   Some boys are very tough. They're afraid of nothing. They are the ones who climb a wall and take a bow at the top. Not only are they brave on the roof, but they make a lot of noise in the darkest part of the cellar where even the super hates to go. They also jiggle and hop on the platform between the locked doors of the subway cars.

2   Four boys are jiggling on the swaying platform. Their names are Alfred, Calvin, Samuel, and Tom. The men and the women in the cars on either side watch them. They don't like them to jiggle or jump but don't want to interfere. Of course some of the men in the cars were once brave boys like these. One of them had ridden the tail of a speeding truck from New York to Rockaway Beach without getting off, without his sore fingers losing hold. Nothing happened to him then or later. He had made a compact with other boys who preferred to watch: Starting at Eighth Avenue and Fifteenth Street, he would get to some specified place, maybe Twenty-third and the river, by hopping the tops of the moving trucks. This was hard to do when one truck turned a corner in the wrong direction and the nearest truck was a couple of feet too high. He made three or four starts before succeeding. He had gotten his idea from a film at school called *The Romance of Logging*. He had finished high school, married a good friend, was in a responsible job and going to night school.

3   These two men and others looked at the four boys jumping and jiggling on the platform and thought, It must be fun to ride that way, especially now the weather is nice and we're out of the tunnel and way high over the Bronx. Then they thought, These kids do seem to be acting sort of stupid. They *are* little. Then they thought of some of the brave things they had done when they were boys and jiggling didn't seem so risky.

4   The ladies in the car became very angry when they looked at the four boys. Most of them brought their brows together and hoped the boys could see their extreme disapproval. One of the ladies wanted to get up and say, Be careful you dumb kids, get off that platform or I'll call a cop. But three of the boys were Negroes and the fourth was something else she couldn't tell for sure. She was afraid they'd be fresh and laugh at her and embarrass her. She wasn't afraid they'd hit her, but she was afraid of embarrassment. Another lady thought, Their mothers never know where they are. It wasn't true in this particular case. Their mothers all knew that they had gone to see the missile exhibit on Fourteenth Street.

5   Out on the platform, whenever the train **accelerated**, the boys would raise their hands and point them up to the sky to act like rockets going off, then they rat-tat-tatted the shatterproof glass pane like machine guns, although no machine guns had been exhibited.

6   For some reason known only to the motorman, the train began a sudden slowdown. The lady who was afraid of embarrassment saw the boys jerk forward and backward and grab the swinging guard chains. She had her own boy at home. She stood up with determination and went to the door. She slid it open and said, "You boys will be hurt. You'll be killed. I'm going to call the conductor if you don't just go into the next car and sit down and be quiet."

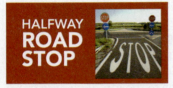

Get into a small group and answer the two questions that follow.

1. What do you understand about this story so far?

2. Try to predict what may be coming in the second half of the story. What will happen with this group of boys?

Part 2

7   Two of the boys said, "Yes'm," and acted as though they were about to go. Two of them blinked their eyes a couple of times and pressed their lips together. The train resumed its speed. The door slid shut, parting the lady and the boys. She leaned against the side door because she had to get off at the next stop.

8   The boys opened their eyes wide at each other and laughed. The lady **blushed**. The boys looked at her and laughed harder. They began to pound each other's back. Samuel laughed the hardest and pounded Alfred's back until Alfred coughed and the tears came. Alfred held tight to the chain hook. Samuel pounded him even harder when he saw the tears. He said, "Why you bawling? You a baby, huh?" and laughed. One of the men whose boyhood had been more watchful than brave became angry. He stood up straight and looked at the boys for a couple of seconds. Then he walked in a citizenly way to the end of the car, where he pulled the emergency cord. Almost at once, with a terrible **hiss**, the pressure of air **abandoned** the brakes and the wheels were caught and held.

9   People standing in the most secure places fell forward, then backward. Samuel had let go of his hold on the chain so he could pound Tom as well as Alfred. All the passengers in the cars whipped back and forth, but he pitched only forward and fell head first to be crushed and killed between the cars.

10   The train had stopped hard, halfway into the station, and the conductor called at once for the trainmen who knew about this kind of death and how to take the body from the wheels and brakes. There was silence except for passengers from other cars who asked, What happened! What happened! The ladies waited around wondering if he might be an only child. The men recalled other afternoons with very bad endings. The little boys stayed close to each other, leaning and touching shoulders and arms and legs.

11   When the policeman knocked at the door and told her about it, Samuel's mother began to scream. She screamed all day and moaned all night, though the doctors tried to quiet her with pills. Oh, oh, she hopelessly

cried. She did not know how she could ever find another boy like that one. However, she was a young woman and she became pregnant. Then for a few months she was hopeful. The child born to her was a boy. They brought him to be seen and nursed. She smiled. But immediately she saw that this baby wasn't Samuel. She and her husband together have had other children, but never again will a boy exactly like Samuel be known.

—Excerpted from The Collected Stories, *by Grace Paley*

Thinking about the Reading

1. After doing a close reading of this short story, return to the checklist on page 176 and see how many questions about this story you are able to answer. Then, discuss the following questions to review the content of the story you have just read.

2. How does race play a role in this story?

_____

_____

_____

3. The author keeps shifting the point of view of who is watching the boys from the older men to the angry women and finally to the embarrassed woman. Why do you think the author tells the story in this way?

_____

_____

_____

_____

4. How do you feel about the way the writer ended the story? Could you think of a more interesting ending?

_____

_____

5. This story was written about fifty years ago. What evidence in the story points to the fact that this narrative is not taking place in our time?

_____

_____

6. Considering race relations in our present time, do you think this scene would play out any differently today? Explain.

_____

_____

Reading Comprehension Check

_____ 1. What is the setting of this story?

   a. the countryside
   b. someone's home
   c. a city subway train
   d. on a street

_____ 2. Who is the narrator of the story?

   a. one of the boys
   b. The narrator is not a physical character in the story.
   c. one of the older men watching
   d. a woman who felt bad for the victim

_____ 3. What do we learn in the second paragraph about some of the older men watching?

   a. They are angry at the boys.
   b. They are jiggling, too.
   c. They are listening to music on their headphones.
   d. They used to do similarly dangerous things.

_____ 4. What caused the accident to happen?

   a. The boys were jiggling too much.
   b. The embarrassed woman called the conductor.
   c. One of the men watching pulled the emergency cord.
   d. The boys got stuck between the train cars.

_____ 5. What is the meaning of the last line of the story, "She and her husband together have had other children, but never again will a boy exactly like Samuel be known"?

   a. The mother was able to continue her life by having other children.
   b. A lost child can never be replaced.
   c. The mother was unable to conceive again.
   d. Samuel would one day be forgotten.

_____ 6. When Samuel says, " Why you bawling? You a baby, huh?," the word "bawling" could be replaced with

   a. angry.   c. crying.
   b. pounding.   d. laughing.

THEMATIC LINKS

If you want to learn more about the works of Grace Paley, type the following words into your browser and explore the two sites that come up:

1. An Interview With Poet and Fiction Writer Grace Paley Poets&Writers
2. Grace Paley, Writer and Activist, Dies NYT

READING SKILL FOCUS

Making Inferences

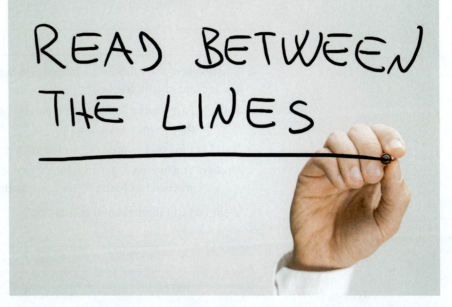

Reading does not just involve understanding the literal meaning of the words on a page or screen. Good readers are able to comprehend what an author is implying or suggesting. An *inference* is an educated guess based on information provided, or omitted, from a text. Just as in face-to-face interactions, telephone conversations, or text communications, we are always trying to go beyond what people say (or write) and figure out what they actually mean.

EXERCISE 5.5 Making Inferences in Everyday Situations

Directions: Work with a partner to make inferences based on the everyday situations below.

1. You see a professionally dressed woman running full-speed up the stairs of a business office, her résumé in hand. What can you infer?

   _____

   _____

2. You overhear a man and a woman speaking:

   Woman: "You can have her on weekends only. Do you hear me?"

   Man: "Okay, but I want the right to take her for some holidays as well."

   What can you infer about the topic of this conversation?

   _____

   _____

3. You are in a department store in line at the customer service counter. A man with a very frustrated expression on his face is walking away from the counter holding a broken lamp. What can you infer about his situation?

_____

_____

4. You overhear the following conversation between a mother and her teenage son in front of a high school.

Mother: How could you have gotten 100 percent on your math test if you didn't study even five minutes for the exam?

Son: I got lucky. I figured out all the answers. That's all.

Mother: You weren't getting lucky two days ago when you failed the practice test based on the same material."

What you can infer about this situation?

_____

_____

Making Inferences from Written Text

Making inferences as a reader can be more challenging than inferring meaning in oral communication, as one cannot depend on facial expression and/or tone of voice to get a sense of what is going on. However, readers have the advantage of being able to slow things down and closely examine the written text in order to make accurate inferences. Words on a page, unlike spoken words, do not disappear into the air the moment they are expressed.

Examine the example below of implied meaning taken from Carol Edelstein's poem "Failure of Alchemy" (p. 169). Try to determine which of the four choices is the logical inference you can make based on her words and a rereading of the poem.

Example

When the narrator looks back and says, "When I was twenty and not so sure / it was good to live, you were the man / who stood by the completed painting, / and placed the magnifying glass in my hand, / and said, 'Look what I made,'" it can be inferred from the narrator's statement that

   a. the young narrator was confident about life.

   b. the narrator was appreciating a new work by the great artist.

   c. the older artist was showing the narrator the potentially life-saving power of creative vision.

   d. the older artist was pompous and distant.

1. Choice (a) is not true, since in the fourth stanza of the poem, the narrator states that he/she was "not so sure it was good to live." This is not the voice of a confident person.

2. Choice (b) looks correct on first glance. After all, we know the deceased person painted, so why wouldn't it be his painting here? However, if you re-read the stanza, you will realize that something else is being implied.

3. We already know that the young narrator is feeling insecure and is in need of a vote of confidence. The respected artist hands the narrator a magnifying glass and says," Look what I made" to show the narrator that she could gain confidence and pride in herself through creating works of art. This was the narrator's painting! Choice C is correct.

4. The older artist is anything but pompous and distant in this scene. He is showing respect and support to the young artist. Choice D is incorrect.

When making inferences, think like a detective, read the main idea, and look at the details closely. It is important that you abstain from bringing your own opinion of the topic into consideration and that you focus on what is stated. By relying on the facts, details, and clues in the passage, you will arrive at a logical conclusion.

Strategies for Making Inferences

Your success in making accurate inferences has much to do with your ability to follow the author's thought process as you read. You need to pay attention to ideas that are suggested, but not directly stated. When good readers make an inference, they draw logical conclusions based on implied information. One needs to ask oneself, what exactly is going on in this moment in the text? If you do a close reading and follow the logical flow presented in the text, you will be able to "read between the lines" and make correct inferences.

Here are a few key strategies to bear in mind as you try to go beyond the surface level of a text and understand what is being implied.

Key Strategies for Making Inferences

- **First, understand the general flow of the reading:** You need to have a grasp of the writer's main idea and point of view before you can make correct inferences.

- **Pay attention to details:** Some details will clue you into the author's intended meaning. When you notice a surprising detail, ask yourself, why did the author include this particular piece of information here?

- **Examine the writer's choice of words:** The author may be implying something by his or her choice of descriptive words. Some words hold emotional weight. You can often gain insight into the author's attitude toward the subject through evaluating his or her choice of words.

- **Consider the author's purpose (see Chapter 6):** Is the author trying to support an argument? Is the author sympathetic to a particular character? The author may not state so directly, but may lead you to this conclusion through certain details.

- **Confirm that the inference you make is evidence-based:** Double-check that there is sufficient evidence to back up whatever conclusions you draw.

EXERCISE 5.6   Working with Fiction: Drawing Logical Conclusions

Directions: Let's revisit the short story "Samuel" on page 177. This is a wonderful work of fiction to practice making inferences from, as the author often does not directly state what is going on, and leaves it to the reader to figure things out.

Practice making inferences by reading the following passages with a classmate and trying to arrive at a logical conclusion based on the clues offered within them. Underline the key words or sentences that clue you in to the intended meaning. It may be useful to first reread the whole story to refresh your memory about the characters and their motivations.

1.   "These two men and others looked at the four boys jumping and jiggling on the platform and thought, It must be fun to ride that way, especially now the weather is nice and we're out of the tunnel and way high over the Bronx. Then they thought, These kids do seem to be acting sort of stupid. They *are* little. Then they thought of some of the brave things they had done when they were boys and jiggling didn't seem so risky" (para. 3).

What can we infer about how the men view the boys, actions?

_____

_____

2.   "The ladies in the car became very angry when they looked at the four boys. Most of them brought their brows together and hoped the boys could see their extreme disapproval. One of the ladies wanted to get up and say, Be careful you dumb kids, get off that platform or I'll call a cop. But three of the boys were Negroes and the fourth was something else she couldn't tell for sure. She was afraid they'd be fresh and laugh at her and embarrass her. She wasn't afraid they'd hit her, but she was afraid of embarrassment. Another lady thought, Their mothers never know where they are" (para 4).

What can we infer about the lady who wanted to tell the boys to stop and from the last sentence of this paragraph?

_____

_____

3. "For some reason known only to the motorman, the train began a sudden slowdown. The lady who was afraid of embarrassment saw the boys jerk forward and backward and grab the swinging guard chains. She had her own boy at home" (para. 6).

What can we infer about what this lady is thinking now?

_____

_____

4. "The door slid shut, parting the lady and the boys. She leaned against the side door because she had to get off at the next stop. The boys opened their eyes wide at each other and laughed. The lady blushed. The boys looked at her and laughed harder."

What can we infer from the lady's blushing (para. 7 and para. 8)?

_____

_____

5. "She did not know how she could ever find another boy like that one. However, she was a young woman and she became pregnant. Then for a few months she was hopeful. The child born to her was a boy. They brought him to be seen and nursed. She smiled. But immediately she saw that this baby wasn't Samuel. She and her husband together have had other children, but never again will a boy exactly like Samuel be known" (para. 11).

What can we infer about Samuel's mother's feelings?

_____

_____

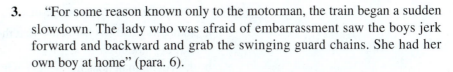

EXERCISE 5.7 Working with Fiction: Determining the Most Accurate Inference

Directions: Read the following excerpts from a variety of poems and stories, and try to infer their meaning from the given context. Keep in mind the strategies for making inferences as you work to choose the correct answer.

A. Excerpt from *Kill the Witch* by Judith Cook

The young couple stood together, looking out over the gently rolling parkland. The sun had not yet burned away the mist, and it still lay in pools in the hollows. Under the tree, red deer were grazing: a tranquil scene.

"You're quite certain?" he asked her.

She nodded. "Last month I was unsure, but now … oh!"

Her eyes filled, and she began to cry.

Her lover put his arm around her and hugged her to him. "Come now, dry your eyes—there's no need for tears. It's not as if we're not already promised to each other. At worst there will be a little talk heareabouts, but it will soon pass."

_____ **1.** We can infer from the passage that

    a. something bad has happened that the young woman is afraid people will talk about.

    b. the young man does not believe what the young woman is saying.

    c. the young woman has realized she does not really love the young man.

    d. the young couple are not married and she is pregnant.

B. Excerpt from "Schoolsville" by Billy Collins (1985)

1 Glancing over my shoulder at the past,

    I realize the number of students I have taught

    is enough to populate a small town.

    I can see it nestled in a paper landscape,

5 chalk dust flurrying down in winter,

    nights dark as a blackboard.

    The population ages but never graduates.

    On hot afternoons they sweat the final in the park

    and when it's cold they shiver around the stoves

10 reading disorganized essays out loud.

    A bell rings on the hour and everybody zigzags

    in the streets with their books.

—From *The Apple That Astonished Paris*, Billy Collins, 1999

_____ **2.** It can be inferred that in this poem

    a. a teacher is on a quest to find all of his former students.

    b. most of the students this teacher taught never graduated.

    c. a teacher is feeling nostalgic about his many former students.

    d. all of his students had the habit of writing organized essays.

C. "wahbegan" by Jim Northrup (1993)

1 Didja ever hear a sound,

    smell something,

    taste something,

    that brought you back

5 to Vietnam, instantly?

    Didja ever wonder

    when it would end?

    It ended for my brother

    he died in the war

10 but didn't fall

    down for fifteen tortured years

His flashbacks are over,

another casualty whose name

will never be on the Wall

15 some can only find peace

in death

The sound of his family

crying hurt

The smell of the flowers

20 didn't comfort us

The taste in my mouth

still sours me

How about a memorial

for those who made it

through the war

but still died

before their time?

—From Walking the Rez Road, by Jim Northrup, 1993

_____ **3.** It can be inferred from the poem that

    a. the narrator believes that veterans whose lives were destroyed by Vietnam but did not die there should also be memorialized.

    b. the narrator's brother died in Vietnam.

    c. the narrator's brother is still alive but is suffering from his memories of war.

    d. the narrator was never really very close with his brother.

D. From "The Raven" by Edgar Allen Poe (1845)

1 Once upon a midnight dreary, while I pondered, weak and weary,

Over many a quaint and curious volume of forgotten lore—

    While I nodded, nearly napping, suddenly there came a tapping,

As of some one gently rapping, rapping at my chamber door.

5 "'Tis some visitor," I muttered, "tapping at my chamber door—

    Only this and nothing more."

_____ **4.** We can infer that beneath the narrator's outer sense of calm, there is a feeling of

    a. tranquility.

    b. doubt and fear.

    c. anger.

    d. contentment.

Selection 3

A Scene from a Play

A scene from The Piano Lesson by August Wilson

August Wilson is one of America's most celebrated playwrights. He was born in 1945 and grew up in the Hill District of Pittsburgh, Pennsylvania. His childhood experiences in this poor black community would later influence his dramatic writings. Wilson set the goal of writing a ten-play cycle that captured each decade of the black experience in the twentieth century. The Piano Lesson *takes place in the 1930s. Wilson completed his goal with the opening of his final theater work,* Radio Golf, *in April of 2005. Two months later, he was diagnosed with liver cancer, and on October 2, 2005, August Wilson passed away at the age of 60.*

Pre-Reading Questions

1. Consider how "reading" a play might differ from "seeing" a play. How would the experience be different?

2. The play begins with some guests showing up at a home without notice. What kinds of tensions might "unexpected guests" present to a host?

3. One of the themes of *The Piano Lesson* deals with the responsibility siblings hold for each other. Does a brother or sister have to stand by their sibling, even if their sibling means trouble? Share your view.

Eye on Vocabulary

Before beginning the reading, skim through the reading and find the following key vocabulary terms in bold. Working with a partner, examine the words in context and try to guess the meaning of each. Then look up the words in a dictionary. Keep in mind that many words have multiple meanings. Write the definition that fits the word's context in the play.

Word	Your Definition	Dictionary Definition
1. sparsely		
2. portent		
3. apt		
4. brash		
5. haul		

A Scene from *The Piano Lesson*

by August Wilson

Note to Students: Choose a role to play and play-act this classic theater scene out loud in groups of five. If you are bold enough, present your theater scene in front of the entire class.

Doaker Charles: Main character, an older man
Berniece: Doaker's niece, and mother of Maretha
Maretha: Berniece's eleven-year-old daughter
Boy Willie: Bernice's brother, Doaker's nephew, who shows up unexpected from the South
Lymon: Boy Willie's "business partner"

The Setting: The action of the play takes place in the kitchen and parlor of the house where DOAKER CHARLES lives with his niece, BERNIECE, and her eleven-year-old daughter, MARETHA in Pittsburgh. The house is **sparsely** furnished, and although there is evidence of a woman's touch, there is a lack of warmth and vigor. BERNIECE AND MARETHA, occupy the upstairs rooms. DOAKER'S room is prominent and opens onto the kitchen. Dominating the parlor is an old upright piano. On the legs of the piano, carved in the manner of African sculpture, are mask-like figures resembling totems. The carvings are rendered with a grace and power of invention that lifts them out of the realm of craftsmanship and into the realm of art. At left is a staircase leading to the upstairs.

Act One

(The lights come up on the Charles household. It is five o'clock in the morning. The dawn is beginning to announce itself, but there is something in the air that belongs to the night. A stillness that is a **portent**, a gathering, a coming together of something akin to a storm. There is a loud knock at the door.)

BOY WILLIE: (Off stage, calling.) Hey, Doaker ... Doaker! (He knocks again and calls.)

Hey, Doaker! Hey, Berniece! Berniece!

(DOAKER enters from his room. He is a tall, thin man of forty-seven, with severe features, who has for all intents and purposes retired from the world though he works full-time as a railroad cook.)

DOAKER: Who is it?

BOY WILLIE: Open the door, nigger! It's me … Boy Willie!

DOAKER: Who?

BOY WILLIE: Boy Willie! Open the door!

(DOAKER opens the door and BOY WILLIE and LYMON enter. BOY WILLIE is thirty years old. He has an infectious grin and a boyishness that is **apt** for his name. He is **brash** and impulsive, talkative and somewhat crude in speech and manner. LYMON is twenty-nine. BOY WILLIE's partner, he talks little, and then with a straightforwardness that is often disarming.)

DOAKER: What you doing up here?

BOY WILLIE: I told you, Lymon. Lymon talking about you might be sleep. This is Lymon. You remember Lymon Jackson from down home? This my Uncle Doaker.

DOAKER: What you doing up here? I couldn't figure out who that was. I thought you was still down in Mississippi.

BOY WILLIE: Me and Lymon selling watermelons. We got a truck out there. Got a whole truckload of watermelons. We brought them up here to sell. Where's Berniece? (Calls.)

Hey, Berniece!

DOAKER: Berniece up there sleep.

BOY WILLIE: Well, let her get up. (Calls.)

Hey, Berniece!

DOAKER: She got to go to work in the morning.

BOY WILLIE: Well she can get up and say hi. It's been three years since I seen her.

(Calls.)

Hey, Berniece! It's me … Boy Willie.

DOAKER: Berniece don't like all that hollering now. She got to work in the morning.

BOY WILLIE: She can go on back to bed. Me and Lymon been riding two days in that truck … the least she can do is get up and say hi.

DOAKER: (Looking out the window.) Where you all get that truck from?

BOY WILLIE: It's Lymon's. I told him let's get a load of watermelons and bring them up here.

LYMON: Boy Willie say he going back, but I'm gonna stay. See what it's like up here.

BOY WILLIE: You gonna carry me down there first.

LYMON: I told you I ain't going back down there and take a chance on that truck breaking down again. You can take the train. Hey, tell him Doaker, he can take the train back. After we sell them watermelons he have enough money he can buy him a whole railroad car.

DOAKER: You got all them watermelons stacked up there no wonder the truck broke down. I'm surprised you made it this far with a load like that. Where you break down at?

BOY WILLIE: We broke down three times! It took us two and a half days to get here. It's a good thing we picked them watermelons fresh.

LYMON: We broke down twice in West Virginia. The first time was just as soon as we got out of Sunflower. About forty miles out she broke down. We got it going and got all the way to West Virginia before she broke down again.

BOY WILLIE: We had to walk about five miles for some water.

LYMON: It got a hole in the radiator but it runs pretty good. You have to pump the brakes sometime before they catch. Boy Willie have his door open and be ready to jump when that happens.

BOY WILLIE: Lymon think that's funny. I told the nigger I give him ten dollars to get the brakes fixed. But he thinks that funny.

LYMON: They don't need fixing. All you got to do is pump them till they catch.

(BERNIECE enters on the stairs. Thirty-five years old, with an eleven-year-old daughter, she is still in mourning for her husband after three years.)

BERNIECE: What you doing all that hollering for?

BOY WILLIE: Hey, Berniece. Doaker said you was sleep. I said at least you could get up and say hi.

BERNIECE: It's five o'clock in the morning and you come in here with all this noise. You can't come like normal folks. You got to bring all that noise with you.

BOY WILLIE: Hell, I ain't done nothing but come in and say hi. I ain't got in the house good.

BERNIECE: That's what I'm talking about. You start all that hollering and carry on as soon as you hit the door.

BOY WILLIE: Aw hell, woman, I was glad to see Doaker. You ain't had to come down if you didn't want to. I come eighteen hundred miles to see my sister I figure she might want to get up and say hi. Other than that you can go back upstairs. What you got, Doaker? Where your bottle? Me and Lymon want a drink.

(To BERNIECE.)

This is Lymon. You remember Lymon Jackson from down home.

LYMON: How you doing, Berniece. You look just like I thought you looked.

BERNIECE: Why you all got to come in hollering and carrying on? Waking the neighbors with all that noise.

BOY WILLIE: They can come over and join the party. We fixing to have a party. Doaker, where your bottle? Me and Lymon celebrating. The Ghosts of the Yellow Dog got Sutter.

BERNIECE: Say what?

BOY WILLIE: Ask Lymon, they found him the next morning. Say he drowned in his well.

DOAKER: When this happen, Boy Willie?

BOY WILLIE: About three weeks ago. Me and Lymon was over in Stoner County when we heard about it. We laughed. We thought it was funny. A great big old three hundred-and-forty-pound man gonna fall down his well.

LYMON: It remind me of Humpty Dumpty.

BOY WILLIE: Everybody say the Ghosts of the Yellow Dog pushed him.

BERNIECE: I don't want to hear that nonsense. Somebody down there pushing them people in their wells.

DOAKER: What was you and Lymon doing over in Stoner County?

BOY WILLIE: We was down there working. Lymon got some people down there.

LYMON: My cousin got some land down there. We was helping him.

BOY WILLIE: Got near about a hundred acres. He got it set up real nice. Me and Lymon was down there chopping down trees. We was using Lymon's truck to **haul** the wood. Me and Lymon used to haul wood all around them parts.

(To BERNIECE.)
Me and Lymon got a truckload of watermelons out there.

(BERNIECE crosses to the window to the parlor.)

Doaker, where your bottle? I know you got a bottle stuck up in your room. Come on, me and Lymon want a drink.

(DOAKER exits into his room.)

BERNIECE: Where you all get that truck from?

BOY WILLIE: I told you it's Lymon's.

BERNIECE: Where you get the truck from, Lymon?

LYMON: I bought it.

BERNIECE: Where he get that truck from, Boy Willie?

BOY WILLIE: He told you he bought it. Bought it for a hundred and twenty dollars. I can't say where he got that hundred and twenty dollars from

… but he bought that old piece of truck from Henry Porter. (To LYMON.) Where you get that hundred and twenty dollars from, nigger?

LYMON: I got it like you get yours. I know how to take care of money.

(DOAKER brings a bottle and sets it on the table.)

BOY WILLIE: Aw hell, Doaker got some of that good whiskey. Don't give Lymon none of that. He ain't used to good whiskey. He liable to get sick.

LYMON: I done had good whiskey before.

BOY WILLIE: Lymon bought that truck so he have him a place to sleep. He down there wasn't doing no work or nothing. Sheriff looking for him. He bought that truck to keep away from the sheriff. Got Stovall looking for him too. He down there sleeping in that truck ducking and dodging both of them. I told him come on let's go up and see my sister.

BERNIECE: What the sheriff looking for you for, Lymon?

BOY WILLIE: The man don't want you to know all his business. He's my company. He ain't asking you no questions.

LYMON: It wasn't nothing. It was just a misunderstanding.

BERNIECE: He in my house. You say the sheriff looking for him, I wanna know what he looking for him for. Otherwise you all can go back out there and be where nobody don't have to ask you nothing.

LYMON: It was just a misunderstanding. Sometimes me and the sheriff we don't think alike. So we just got crossed on each other.

BERNIECE: Might be looking for him about that truck. He might have stole that truck.

BOY WILLIE: We ain't stole no truck, woman. I told you Lymon bought it.

DOAKER: Boy Willie and Lymon got more sense than to ride all the way up here in a stolen truck with a load of watermelons. Now they might have stole them watermelons but I don't believe they stole that truck.

BOY WILLIE: You don't even know the man good and you calling him a thief. And we ain't stole them watermelons either. Them old man Pitterford's watermelons. He give me and Lymon all we could load for ten dollars.

DOAKER: No wonder you got them stacked up out there. You must have five hundred watermelons stacked up out there.

BERNIECE: Boy Willie, when you and Lymon planning on going back?

BOY WILLIE: Lymon say he staying. As soon as we sell them watermelons I'm going on back.

BERNIECE: (Starts to exit up the stairs.) That's what you need to do. And you need to do it quick. Come in here disrupting the house. I don't want all that loud carrying on around here. I'm surprised you ain't woke Maretha up.

BOY WILLIE: I was fixing to get her now. (Calls.)

Hey, Maretha!

DOAKER: Berniece don't like all that hollering now.

BERNIECE: Don't you wake that child up!

BOY WILLIE: You going up there … wake her up and tell her her uncle's here. I ain't seen her in three years. Wake her up and send her down here. She can go back to bed.

BERNICE: I ain't waking that child up … and don't you be making all of that noise. You and Lymon need to sell those watermelons and go on back.

(BERNIECE exits up the stairs.)

Excerpted from *The Piano Lesson*, by August Wilson, 1990

Thinking about the Reading

Discuss the following questions with a classmate to review the content of the play excerpt you have just read:

1. How would you describe Doaker's relationship with his niece, Berniece?

   _____

2. From what you know about Boy Willie and Lymon from this scene, do you trust these guys? Why or why not?

   _____

   _____

3. Why did the two men come north from Mississippi? What can you infer about Boy Willie and Lymon's economic situation?

   _____

   _____

4. What can be inferred about Berniece's relationship with her brother, Boy Willie?

   _____

   _____

5. What predictions can you make about what will happen in later acts of this play?

   _____

   _____

Reading Comprehension Check

_____ **1.** What is Doaker's first feeling when Boy Willie comes knocking on his door?

a. happiness   c. sadness

b. surprise   d. disgust

_____ **2.** Where did the two guests, Boy Willie and Lymon, begin their journey?

a. West Virginia   c. Mississippi

b. Pittsburgh   d. New York City

_____ **3.** Why is Berniece upset with her brother?

a. He came unexpectedly.

b. It's 5 AM, and he is making a lot of noise.

c. Because he bought the watermelons.

d. She doesn't get along with him.

_____ **4.** We can infer that Berniece asks twice about where they got the truck because

a. she is hard of hearing.

b. the boys are making too much noise.

c. she wants to buy it from them.

d. she fears that they stole it.

_____ **5.** It can be inferred from the way Berniece speaks with Boy Willie that she

a. doesn't trust his intentions.

b. misses her cousin.

c. is nostalgic for her past life.

d. wishes he would stay and move in with the family.

READING

Selection 4

Textbook Reading

What Is Literature, and Why Do We Study It?

Pre-Reading Questions

Answer the following questions before exploring the text:

1. Try to answer the two questions in the title of this reading.

2. Do you prefer hearing or reading a good story? Explain.

3. How hard would it be for you to go one year without reading any literature (poems, stories, novels)? Explain.

What Is Literature, and Why Do We Study It?

by Edgar V. Roberts

1   We use the word literature, in a broad sense, to mean compositions that tell stories, dramatize situations, express emotions and analyze and advocate ideas. Before the invention of writing five thousand years ago, literary works were necessarily spoken or sung, and they were retained only as long as living people continued to repeat them. In some societies, the oral tradition of literature still exists, with many poems and stories designed exclusively for spoken delivery. Even in our modern age of writing, printing, and electronic communication, much literature is still heard as told by living speakers. Parents delight their children with stories and poems and storywriters read their works directly before live audiences; plays and scripts are interpreted on stages and before movie and television cameras for the benefit of a vast public.

2   No matter how we assimilate literature, we gain much from it. In truth, readers can often not explain why they enjoy reading, for goals and ideals are not always easily articulated. There are, however, areas of general agreement about the value of systematic and extensive reading.

3   Literature helps us to grow, both personally and intellectually. It opens doors for us. It stretches our minds. It develops our imagination, increases our understanding and enlarges our power of sympathy. It helps us to see beauty in the world around us. It links us with the cultural, philosophical and religious world of which we are a part. It enables us to recognize human dreams and struggles in different places and times. It helps us to develop mature sensibility and compassion for all living beings. It nurtures our ability to appreciate the beauty of order and arrangement—gifts that are also bestowed by a well-structured song, a beautifully painted canvas, or a skillfully chiseled statue.

4   Literature enables us to see worthiness in the aims of all people. It exercises our emotions through interest, concern, sympathy, tension, excitement, regret, fear, laughter, and hope. It encourages us to assist creative and talented people who need recognition and support. Through our cumulative experiences in reading, literature shapes our goals and values by clarifying our own identities—both positively, through acceptance of the admirable in human beings, and negatively, through rejection of the sinister. It enables us to develop perspectives on events that are occurring locally and globally, and thereby it gives us understanding and control. It is one of the shaping influences of our lives. It makes us human.

—From Edgar V. Roberts, *Writing About Literature*,
13th edition, pp. 1–2

Thinking about the Reading

After doing a close reading of the text, write your answers to the following questions. You may be asked to discuss your answers with your classmates.

1. What argument does the author make about the value of oral storytelling in today's modern world? Do you agree?

   _____

   _____

2. The author believes that reading literature "enlarges our power of sympathy." What do you think he means by this?

   _____

   _____

3. Clearly, the author takes the position that literature plays a huge role in our lives. Yet, there are many perfectly happy people for whom literature means very little. What do you think the author would say to those who choose to live without literature?

   _____

   _____

4. Paraphrase this line from the reading (para. 3): "It enables us to recognize human dreams and struggles in different places and times."

   _____

   _____

5. When the author writes, "There are, however, areas of general agreement about the value of systematic and extensive reading," what can be inferred about the author's position on children spending a lot of time with books?

   _____

   _____

Reading Comprehension Check

_____ 1. The author refers to a time five thousand years ago when
   a. not many people were literate, and only a few could read texts.
   b. poetry did not exist.
   c. literature could only be preserved by repeated storytelling.
   d. movies did not feature stories.

_____ **2.** The author writes that literature "nurtures our ability to appreciate the beauty of order and arrangement—gifts that are also bestowed by a well-structured song, a beautifully painted canvas, or a skillfully chiseled statue." What can you infer from this statement?

    a. He believes that reading and painting are very similar activities.

    b. He values law and order.

    c. He believes songs, paintings, and statues are more beautiful than written texts.

    d. He believes that works of art encourage us to enjoy the beauty of order and arrangement.

_____ **3.** You can infer from the author's tone that

    a. he places literature among the highest ranks of human achievement.

    b. he has written many novels and poems.

    c. he sees both the dark side and light side of reading literature.

    d. he is disappointed that many young people today choose not to read.

_____ **4.** What is the main idea of the reading passage?

    a. TV and movies allow us to listen to stories.

    b. Parents enjoy reading their children stories and poems.

    c. Oral storytelling goes back over five thousand years.

    d. Reading, or hearing, literature helps us grow as human beings.

_____ **5.** Which of the following does the author *not* mention as one of the benefits of reading literature?

    a. It encourages us to see the worthiness in others.

    b. It prepares us for our careers.

    c. It links us with a larger world.

    d. It stretches our minds.

Think to Write

Now that you have completed four literary readings and an excerpt from the textbook, *Writing About Literature*, in this chapter, think about which of the five readings was most interesting to you. Write a paragraph response about this reading and post it to The Wall.

It's SHOWTIME!

Watching a video clip related to the chapter content can be an enriching experience. Go online and find a video link whose topic ties into one of the chapter readings (maximum length = ten minutes). After viewing the video clip, write a half-page summary of the video's key points. Post your personal reaction to the ideas in the clip (between 150 and 400 words) on The Wall.

WRITING SKILL FOCUS

Writing a Concluding Paragraph

You are writing an essay. You have already written an introductory paragraph with a circumscribed thesis statement and a number of well-detailed body paragraphs, each focused around a clear topic sentence. Now, you need to bring your essay to a satisfactory close.

Your concluding paragraph serves to remind the reader of the ideas you have discussed in your essay. You want to make the reading of your essay a user-friendly experience; to wrap things up in a smooth fashion. To do this, you should *summarize the key points* of your essay and then *rephrase the thesis statement*. To spice up your conclusion and leave a lasting impression on your reader, you may want to finish with a *final thought* about the topic at hand, which could come in the form of a suggestion or a prediction.

Compare the following two examples of effective conclusions. After you have read them both, answer the questions that follow.

Example One

In conclusion, suspense novels are perfect for high school students. They are page-turners that motivate otherwise distracted readers, and they are often written as part of a series, so that students are directed toward their next reading choice even before they have put the first one down. High school English teachers should take note of the benefits of suspense novels when choosing the reading material for their next class

Example Two

Suspense novels work very well with high school readers. As we have discussed, students are motivated to keep reading because they want to know what will happen to the characters in the story. Secondly, many suspense novels are written in a series of three to eight books, the advantage being that if a student enjoyed the novel he or she has just finished, there are others in the series to continue with. Clearly, if more high school students are directed toward reading suspense novels, we will see many more teenagers with their heads in a book.

1. First, circle the rephrasing of the thesis statement in each example, and underline the essay's key points. Then, put brackets around the suggestion or prediction.

2. Which concluding paragraph example do you like better? Explain your choice.

It may be wise to delay writing your conclusion until you have had a chance to carefully read over and revise your essay. Firstly, upon review you may make significant changes in both content and organization, which may very well affect your conclusion. Secondly, you need to have a clear understanding of the ideas you expressed in your essay, so as not to contradict your main point or to introduce irrelevant information in your conclusion.

EXERCISE 5.8   Evaluating Three Concluding Paragraphs

Directions: In reviewing the following three concluding paragraphs, work with the "Guidelines for a Clear Conclusion" taken from the "Essay Checklist" you have worked with in previous chapters. Give each conclusion a rating from 1–5, with 5 being the best.

Guidelines for a Clear Conclusion

1. Does the writer summarize the main points of the essay?

2. Does the writer restate the thesis statement?

3. Does the conclusion leave a lasting impression on the reader? Explain why or why not.

Concluding Paragraph 1

Thesis Statement: While good-natured characters can be interesting, readers are more captivated by evil ones.

Evil characters portrayed in novels grab our attention more than kind and caring ones. This has been seen on television programs and movies we love to watch. For example, Magneto or Doctor Doom are memorable villains and keep us going to the cinema to find out if they can be defeated. There is no doubt, books with nasty villains are always going to be popular.

Rating (from 1–5): _____

Explain your rating (offer at least two points about strengths or weaknesses):

_____

_____

_____

Concluding Paragraph 2

Thesis Statement: Reading fiction on an electronic device, such as a Kindle, can be beneficial in many ways.

Reading novels on an e-reader offers a number of advantages. Firstly, think of all the trees you are saving by making this choice. Secondly, there is an economic plus as you can store thousands of books and documents on one e-reader. Finally, it is a whole lot easier to carry a backpack with one e-reader inside as compared with half a dozen paper books. For all of these reasons, I think it is safe to say that paper books will soon only be seen in museum exhibits.

Rating (from 1–5): _____

Explain your rating (offer at least two points about strengths or weaknesses):

_____

_____

Concluding Paragraph 3

Thesis Statement: Research indicates that reading extensively to young kids encourages them to read for pleasure as they get older.

A study conducted in Canada showed that middle-school children whose parents read to them extensively when they were very young are much more likely to read for pleasure. These students not only read much more than their counterparts, but fare better on standardized reading exams. Clearly, government agencies and pediatric offices should make the effort to advise new parents to invest more time in reading to their young kids. The only bad side to this is that some studies have shown that early exposure to music before bed also has positive effects. So, which should parents choose, the story or the CD?

Rating (from 1–5): _____

Explain your rating (offer at least two points about strengths or weaknesses):

_____

_____

TROUBLE SPOTS IN WRITING

OBJECTIVE

6 Control verb tense through careful editing

Controlling Verb Tense

When you are writing, it is important to be aware of the verb choices you are making in terms of whether you are referring to the past or the present. You should be careful not to randomly switch verb tenses, as this can confuse the reader and make it difficult for him or her to follow your writing. Examine the paragraph below, and underline the location in the paragraph where the writer loses control of verb tense. Discuss your choice with a classmate.

> The main character in the story brings home the point that parents should never spank their children. Children were our gifts, and had to be treated with more respect. While in the old days, hitting children was common, things have changed and corporal punishment is now frowned upon.

In this paragraph, the writer starts in the present tense but then switches to the past tense, which is jarring and confusing. A general rule to consider is to set the present tense as your default, and only switch into the past tense when you are giving an example that takes place in the past. Examine how this works in the paragraph below. The verb forms are bolded to make this tense switch more evident.

> The message of this short story **is** that it **is** better to communicate disapproval to a child than to physically punish him or her. Nowadays, many parents **are making** more of an effort to understand their children's motivations. When I **was** a child, things **were** different. If I **spoke** back to my father, I **could expect** a hard slap on the cheek.

In the paragraph above, the writer begins in the present tense and appropriately shifts into the past tense when giving an example from his childhood.

As it is quite common for writers to make a few verb tense errors as they compose a piece of writing, it is critical that you spend some time editing for verb control issues once you have completed a draft of your work.

EXERCISE 5.9   Editing for Verb Tense Control

Directions: Edit the following paragraph with a classmate for errors in verb tense. See if you can find and correct all **five** of the errors in the paragraph.

In the play *The Piano Lesson*, unexpected guests from the South turn a relatively stable household in Pittsburgh upside down. Boy Willie and his partner, Lyman are escaping the ghosts, which haunt their past, but were bringing these troubles into Doaker's home. The partners make the claim that they were simply businessmen trying to sell some watermelon, but their hosts understood that there were crimes looming behind their guest's pretense that this is a simple visit.

Doaker and his niece Bernice have migrated north and made lives for themselves, and would do everything in their power to maintain their newfound status.

THEN & NOW

Go online and do some research to gather information about two great writers or poets: one from the past and another contemporary. Fill out the table provided below with pertinent information about the two writers.

Past Influential Writer	Present Influential Writer
Name	Name
Place of birth	Place of birth
Year of birth	Year of birth
Education	Education
What is s/he most famous for?	What is s/he most famous for?
Famous quote	Famous quote

After you fill out the table, discuss your findings with your classmates and learn from them about what they discovered on the Internet.

Lisa Bu has built a career helping people find great stories to listen to. Born and raised in Hunan, China, she spent seven years as a talk show producer and a digital media content director at Wisconsin Public Radio. She's also a computer programmer, with a PhD in Journalism and an MBA in Information Systems from the University of Wisconsin.

Working with a search engine, type in the following search query: "**Lisa Bu How Books Can Open Your Mind transcript**." This is the transcript of a talk she gave on TED Talks. After doing a careful reading, write brief answers to the following questions about the content. You may also choose to listen to this video presentation as well.

1. Lisa Bu writes, "I was afraid that for the rest of my life some second-class happiness would be the best I could hope for." What did she mean by this?

   _____

   _____

2. Why did Lisa start to read books in pairs? What are some examples of these paired books?

   _____

   _____

3. Paraphrase the following lines from Lisa Bu's speech: "I have come to believe that coming true is not the only purpose of a dream. Its most important purpose is to get us in touch with where dreams come from, where passion comes from, where happiness comes from. Even a shattered dream can do that for you."

   _____

   _____

   _____

   _____

SPECIAL WRITING FEATURE 1

Writing a Short Creative Work of Fiction

7 OBJECTIVE
Draft a piece of creative writing

In this chapter, you have sampled some great works of fiction, from novels to poetry to a play. Now it is your chance to share your creative imagination through the composition of a poem or a one- to three-page short story.

Brainstorming Ideas for Your Creative Work

Jot down quick answers to the following questions before beginning to write:

1. Would you rather try to compose a poem or a short story?

   _____

   _____

2. What themes/types of characters might you be interested in including in your piece?

   _____

   _____

3. What tone do you want your creative work to take (humorous/dramatic/scary/ romantic/other)?

   _____

   _____

4. If you have chosen to write a story, what will be the setting (time and place) of your work?

   _____

   _____

5. What narrative voice would you like to write your story or poem in (first person = I, second person = you, and third person = he/she/it)?

   _____

   _____

EXERCISE 5.10   Creative Writing

Directions: Write a one- to three-page story, or a poem, edit your work, and post it to The Wall. When you have completed this task, respond to two of your classmates' creative postings.

SPECIAL WRITING FEATURE 2

OBJECTIVE

Write about literature

Writing About Literature

Writing about literature is unique in the sense that more attention must be paid to symbolic meaning and an author's use of literary devices such as character, setting, and plot. As your chapter essay assignment involves literary analysis, this special section should help prepare you for this task. Your analysis of literature will rely on your ability to make inferences and your close attention to an author's choice of words.

Writing an analysis of a piece of fiction can be a confusing process. First, literary analyses rely on the assumption that stories have meaning. How does a story mean something? Isn't a story just an arrangement of characters and events? And if the author wanted to convey a meaning, wouldn't he or she be much better off writing an essay just telling us what he or she meant?

Clearly, works of fiction would not be as interesting if the meanings of the stories were obvious to everyone who read them. Part of the beauty of literature is that the ideas presented are open to different interpretations. Meaningful literature uses characters, settings, and actions to illustrate issues that have no easy resolution. They show different sides of a problem, and they can raise new questions. In short, the stories we read in class have meanings that are arguable and complicated, and it is our job to sort them out.

Here are some guidelines to keep in mind as you write about literature:

Guidelines for Writing About Literature

To write a good interpretation of a piece of literature or fiction, do the following:

1. Avoid the obvious (in other words, try not to say what you imagine everyone else will say).

2. Support your main points with strong evidence from the story, play, poem, or novel.

3. Use careful reasoning to explain how that evidence relates to the main points of your interpretation.

EXERCISE 5.11   Guiding Questions for Character, Setting, and Plot

Directions: The chapter essay question asks you to choose a literary selection from this chapter and to focus your writing on the use of character, setting, or plot in the work of literature.

1. Choose the literary selection you would like to focus on. Write the name of the literary work and the page number it appears on here: _____

   _____

2. Choose the literary device you would like to explore in your essay: character, setting, or plot. If you choose a character, write the name of the character you will focus on.

   Literary Device / character: _____

3. Answer the Guiding Questions that follow for the literary device you have chosen to focus on in your essay. Your response notes will serve as material for your essay.

Guiding Questions for Character	Response Notes
Which character (include the name of the piece of literature) have you chosen to focus on? Why does this particular character interest you?	
How does the author reveal the character, or personality, of the person you are writing about?	
Is your chosen character a plausible figure; that is, does the author make this character believable?	

Guiding Questions for Setting	Response Notes
Which setting (include the name of the piece of literature) have you chosen to focus on? Why does this particular setting grab your interest?	
Do you feel a strong sense of place and time in this piece of writing? How does the author convey this sense to the reader?	
What is the relation of the setting to the plot and characters?	

Guiding Questions for Plot	Response Notes
Which plot movement (include the name of the piece of literature) has drawn your attention? Why?	
What conflict does the plot movement build or shed light on?	
Does this plot movement grow out of the characters, or does it depend on chance or coincidence?	

CHAPTER ESSAY ASSIGNMENT

Taking into consideration all of the chapter readings, which character, setting, or plot movement is most significant to you?

OBJECTIVE

9 Read, think, plan, and write an essay in response to the chapter essay assignment

Now that you have had the opportunity to read a number of works of fiction, you should have a deeper understanding of the topic area and be more prepared to compose your chapter essay. (You are also welcome to compose your own chapter essay question.)

Write a one- to two-page essay. Be sure to include a clear thesis statement in your opening paragraph, which focuses your essay around a central idea. When you are done, hand in your essay to your instructor. After you have received constructive feedback from your instructor, be sure to incorporate some of the suggestions into your second draft and submit the revised second draft to your instructor for further feedback on form and meaning.

As writing about literature can be a challenging task, before rushing into the composition of your chapter essay, carefully review the "Writing about Literature" section on page 205. You will have a chance to jump-start the writing assignment by taking some critical notes, which will guide your way forward.

FOCUS ON FORM

Editing for Verb-Tense Control

In the Trouble Spots in Writing section on page 201, you learned how to check for verb-tense control in your writing. Now it's time to put your skills into action! First, read the following paragraph on the essay topic of "How can a poem connect to our life realities?" Edit the essay for errors in verb-tense control, by crossing out errors and writing in the correct forms. When you are finished, compare your edits with a partner.

In the opening scene of William Shakespeare's play *All's Well That Ends Well*, a mother gives the following advice to her son. "Love all, trust a few, do wrong to none." I find these to be words of true wisdom. When I was a child, I trust everyone. No matter what people say to me, regardless of who said it, I will believe everything they say. Now that I am older, I understood that trust had to be earned. As for love, who can argue with the idea of sharing it with everyone? You can show love to others, while not completely trusting them. I remember some years back, there were some bully kids in my Math class. Even though they are not kind to me, I did my best to find some positive qualities in both of them. This connects with the last idea in the quote, "do wrong to none." It took a lot of patience to control bad feelings you might have towards others, and we must always keep in mind that two wrongs do not make a right.

It's Your Turn!

Now that you have had a chance to practice editing for verb-tense control, take a look at chapter essay and review it with new eyes. Pay close attention to your verb forms and make sure they are written in the correct tense.

CHAPTER DEBATE

What is the future of lending libraries?

Refer to Appendix 8, page 455, for detailed guidelines on how to set up and participate in a formal debate.

6 Education

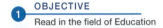

OBJECTIVE

1 Read in the field of Education

Introduction to the Field of Education

Teaching is one of the most challenging, demanding, and rewarding of professions. Teachers are not only expected to educate our children and provide them with an academically enriching environment but they also play a role in students' social development. Teachers have the huge task of preparing young minds for the world ahead of them. They model collaborative learning and critical thinking, and they introduce students to the technological tools that they will need to navigate the twenty-first-century classroom and beyond.

The system of American education faces many challenges in the twenty-first century. In this chapter, you will read about some of the issues that educators today must consider. Should new immigrant students be offered a bilingual curriculum? Is our education system failing underprivileged students? What kinds of innovative teaching methods can help improve American students' low performance in the sciences and inspire more interest in scientific inquiry? Finally, what factors are influencing teachers to change the way they deliver instruction?

CHAPTER ESSAY QUESTION

Is a college education worth it?

Quick Free-Write! Take out a piece of paper, and write for ten minutes without stopping about what you already know about the theme of the chapter essay question.

As you read through the chapter, keep in mind this essay question and consider how you will incorporate multiple perspectives on the issue into your writing. Chapter essays will be due when your class completes the chapter.

Your Option: Once you have worked your way through the chapter readings, you are welcome to narrow down the topics covered and compose your own chapter essay question.

Previewing Education

Read the following questions and discuss them with your classmates. As you answer the questions, consider your personal experience and knowledge of education in general.

1. Do you believe that you received a quality education at your high school? Describe some of the positive aspects and some of the shortcomings of your high school experience.

2. Many people argue that American public education is in crisis. If you agree, then who is to blame? In other words, who is most responsible for students' academic progress—students, teachers, parents, or the state educational system? Please give specific reasons for your answer.

3. When you hear that someone is "educated," what image comes to your mind about this person? In your opinion, what are some of the characteristics of an "educated" person?

4. In your many years of schooling, which of your teachers left the most lasting impression on you? What made this teacher so special?

5. Do you feel that you learn more when the teacher is lecturing to the class or when the teacher assigns small-group problem-solving tasks?

After discussing the preview questions with your classmates, post your responses to two of them on The Wall. Peruse The Wall and respond to at least two of your classmates' responses that pique your interest. Remember to make The Wall your romping ground!

Key Terms in Education

OBJECTIVE

Understand and use key terms in education

Take a moment to think about the discipline of education as you complete the following two exercises.

EXERCISE 6.1   Brainstorming Vocabulary

Directions: What associated words come to mind when you think of the world of *education*? Work with a partner and write down as many related words as you can think of in a period of five minutes. Add more lines to the cluster diagram if you need them.

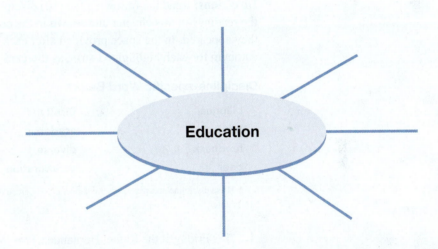

EXERCISE 6.2   Creating Original Sentences

Directions: Choose five of the words from your cluster list, and use them to write complete and meaningful sentences.

1. _____

2. _____

3. _____

4. _____

5. _____

As with any area of specialization, there are specific terms that are germane to the discipline of education. As you read the selections in this chapter, learn these terms and incorporate them into your academic work when appropriate. For example, a student taking an introduction to education course should be able to apply such terms as *individualistic, curricula,* and *acculturation* in both spoken and written forms.

As in previous chapters, you will also practice finding appropriate synonyms and antonyms for these terms and others. Understanding how to work with synonyms and antonyms is a useful skill, especially when you are writing a summary of a text and trying to paraphrase some of the key ideas and pieces of information contained in the original source.

> A **synonym** is a word used to express a similar meaning to another word. An **antonym** is a word that conveys the opposite meaning of another word.

EXERCISE 6.3   Discipline-specific Vocabulary: Fishing for Synonyms and Antonyms

Directions: Read the following ten (10) discipline-specific words culled from the readings in this chapter and shown in the context of the sentences in which they appeared. In the space provided after each sentence, write a synonym or antonym for each highlighted term, as directed.

Discipline-specific Word Bank*

bilingual	faculty	accountable
curricula	academic	reform
feedback	diverse	
peer	acculturation	

* These discipline-specific words are shown in bold green the first time they appear in the chapter readings.

1. "It's Friday at the Rafael Hernandez Two-Way **Bilingual** School in Roxbury and a sign on the door of the four kindergarten and first-grade classrooms tells students they will speak English today." (Selection 1, p. 222, para. 1)

   An antonym for *bilingual* is _____.

2. "Within each grade, the teachers design parallel **curricula** in each language."(Selection 1, p. 222, para. 6)

   A synonym for *curricula* is _____.

3. "'We sneak into each other's classrooms as often as we can' to watch each other teach to learn from each other and give honest **feedback**, Mulvihill says." (Selection 1, p. 222, para. 7)

   A synonym for *feedback* is _____.

4. "**Peer** critiquing can be intimidating, but the confidence they have in each other and their drive to improve helps them use criticism constructively." (Selection 1, p. 222, para. 8)

   An antonym for *peer* is _____.

5. "Gates, the Microsoft founder whose Bill & Melinda Gates Foundation has spent roughly a half billion dollars on higher education, made his case to college business officers Monday that colleges must hold themselves more **accountable**—or someone else will bring them to account." (Selection 2, p. 227, para. 2)

    A synonym for *accountable* is _____.

6. "He painted a future in which a small number of top-quality online courses in key disciplines replace home-grown lectures on many campuses (as leading textbooks have historically done), fretted about what **faculty** unions could do to interfere with changes in higher education, and said nonprofit colleges could learn something from for-profit colleges about providing support to students." (Selection 2, p. 227, para. 4)

    A synonym for *faculty* is _____.

7. "By contrast, Gates said, when public institutions lose state funding, they do whatever they can to protect the 'academic core' but often don't count services that support students outside the classroom in that core, so those services end up being cut." (Selection 2, p. 228, para. 12)

    An antonym for *academic* is _____.

8. "As students face the obstacles associated with acculturation into U.S. society, teachers are facing the challenge of meeting the needs of their increasingly **diverse** classrooms." (Selection 3, p. 239, para. 3)

    An antonym for diverse is _____.

9. "As students face the obstacles associated with **acculturation** into U.S. society, teachers are facing the challenge of meeting the needs of their increasingly diverse classrooms." (Selection 3, p. 239, para. 3)

    A synonym for *acculturation* is _____.

10. "Changes in society spur new efforts in educational research, which in turn propel **reform** movements, new legislation driven by increased youth obesity drives 'junk food' out of schools; new technology leads to new educational research and development, which in turn fuels new legislation." (Selection 3, p. 239, para. 5)

    A synonym for *reform* is _____.

SUCCESS IN READING

OBJECTIVE

Read actively through highlighting and annotating

Read Actively Through Highlighting and Annotating Relevant Text

There are a number of productive ways of interacting with text. We have already discussed the role of outlining. Active readers can also incorporate the critical skills of highlighting and annotation to improve their ability to comprehend reading material.

Highlighting

Highlighting key terms and concepts in a reading passage with brightly colored highlighters (red, green, and blue) serves a number of purposes. First, it motivates you to seek out the most relevant points in a given section of a text upon first read (a very similar skill to note taking when listening to a lecture!) Second, when exam time approaches, highlighted text will guide you toward the key terms and concepts that you need to review.

Here are some hints about highlighting:

- Highlight main ideas, not minor points.
- Highlight key terms that connect to important concepts.
- Highlight points that you feel would be helpful to remember upon review.

As you highlight the different parts of a text, avoid over-highlighting, as it will make it difficult for you to locate the most relevant points for further reflection. Remember to highlight only the main ideas, not minor details or examples.

Challenge Activity: Highlighting

Directions: Now read and highlight the following biographical profile of Dr. Ruth Simmons, the first African American and female president of Brown University, keeping the hints listed above in mind.

Biographical Profile: Dr. Ruth Simmons

Dr. Ruth J. Simmons is the first African American educator ever to be president of an Ivy League institution and the first female president of Brown University. Ruth J. Simmons was born in 1945 in Grapeland, Texas. She grew up on a farm in East Texas and had a life of deprivation and hardship. Yet she recounts her life in Texas fondly: "My journey has not been all that arduous, contrary to the way that my life is often presented. I had this wonderful grounding by my parents, and then an extraordinary streak of luck."

Despite her meteoric rise to prominence in the field of education, she remains humble and grateful to her mentors who challenged, supported, and encouraged her to pursue her dreams. One of the most influential mentors was her mother, whom Ruth Simmons watched as a child pressing fabric for hours. She recalls, "I remember thinking what a horrible, horrible thing to have to do. And yet she would see a crease invisible to everyone else, and she would work on it until it disappeared." Her mother passed away when Simmons was 15 but not before teaching her the value of perseverance, a precious lesson that has stayed with her since then. Simmons studied at Dillard University and later at Wellesley College where she was inspired by President Margaret Clapp to view traditional gender roles in a different perspective. "That was defining for me, the notion that women didn't have to play restricted roles, that you didn't have to hold back at all," recounts Simmons. "The **faculty** demanded that you work up to your potential." She went on to earn a PhD at Harvard University in Romance Languages.

Simmons admits that shaking the traditional notion of gender was not easy for her. She recalled that her mother "believed herself to be subservient to the interests of men. I expected that in my relationship with men. I should pretend not to be smart. I never wanted to be valedictorian because I thought it was very important for a boy to be valedictorian." She got married at the age of 22, had two children, and is now divorced. She was the director of studies at Princeton University and rejuvenated black culture on campus by hiring prominent black scholars such as Cornel West, Henry Louis Gates, and Toni Morrison to teach in the Department of African American Studies.

Simmons became president of Brown University in 2001. She is known to be a pioneer. As president of Brown University, she has taken on an ambitious $1.4 billion initiative known as the Campaign for **Academic** Enrichment to boost Brown University's academic programs. She remains dedicated to the cause of education and encourages students to succeed in their academic endeavors: "The best thing any parent can do for a child is to give your child a sense of love and support to be open to the idea that they need to learn."

Compare what you highlighted with a colleague, and discuss your choices.

Learning Implications

The more you interact with a text, the more connected you will feel to the ideas and information contained within it. Highlighting is a way of breaking a text down into comprehensible points.

Highlighting also provides a visual aid for a later review of a text and gives you the opportunity to distinguish between major and minor points offered in a reading. This is especially helpful with a high-level reading that is hard to comprehend.

Annotating

Reading is often thought of as a passive activity whereby the reader simply reads sentences in silence. Contrary to popular belief, reading is actually a complex process, and active readers are fully aware of the fact that they must use their writing skills while reading. Annotating your textbook is an effective way to respond to what you are reading. **Annotating** involves adding notes to the text, explaining difficult concepts, and commenting on controversial issues for future reference.

As you read your textbook, write notes in the margins of the pages, underline main ideas and supporting details, circle unfamiliar vocabulary items, and put question marks next to statements you find confusing. As you get used to making annotations, you will notice that your attention, concentration, and reading comprehension improve significantly. Annotating a text also enables you to revisit a reading, understand the main idea and key concepts, and review the material with relative ease.

Techniques for Annotating Textbooks

There are various ways to annotate a text. Here are a few techniques, but you can create your own methods for marking your textbook for clarification and further reflection.

- Use markers to highlight the main ideas, key concepts, numbered items, definitions, and examples. You may use different colors for different purposes. For example, you might use a blue marker for the main idea, or thesis, yellow for topic sentences and/or important points, and green for vocabulary.

- Circle or underline terms and their definitions.

- Put a question mark next to a difficult sentence, an unfamiliar word, or a confusing passage. You can always go back to the passage later. The question mark will remind you that you had difficulty understanding something.

- Mark key concepts with an asterisk or a checkmark or underline them.

- If the author has used the process analysis pattern of organization or is listing important points, use numbers to denote the steps in a process or the items in a series.

- As you read the text, write questions in the margin for further analysis. These recall questions will help you comprehend the material.

- As mentioned previously, reading is an active process. Unlike watching TV, active reading requires your involvement. Feel free to disagree with the author and write your thoughts in the margin.

- Finally, if you are reading a long selection, write a summary including the main idea and a few major details at the end of each main section and a summary of the entire reading at the end.

Example of an Annotated Text

What follows is a passage from an education textbook for college students. Notice how the text has been annotated. Keep in mind that there is no single way of annotating a text. Depending on what works best for you, you may develop your own technique of annotating a text.

Teaching in a Changing World

What are these perspectives?   As you read this book you will find <u>many different perspectives</u> on education as well as much information about our changing world, especially those aspects that affect the lives of educators and their schools. As an aspiring teacher, you are now hopefully in the process of develop-

Unsure/uncertain   ing your own tentative perspectives on what the job of teaching entails and what you need to know and be able to do to become an excellent and successful teacher. This chapter also will help you learn more about successfully completing your teacher education program and eventu-

What are the related important questions?   ally finding a position as an educator and about the salary and benefits that you may receive. Answering these and related important questions about the profession of teaching are the topics of Chapter 1.

Although people hold many different perspectives on education, most agree that teaching is a profession that is critical to the well-being

A good point to refer to in the chapter essay! Interesting point!

of youth and of society. Many students indicate that they have chosen teaching as a career because they care about children and youth. Teaching requires caring, but it also requires competence in the subject being taught and in the teaching of that subject. *Teachers' knowledge and skills should lead to the ultimate goal of successful student learning.

Important point to remember

Educators must undergo stringent assessments and meet high standards to ensure high quality in the teaching profession. The teaching profession includes at least three stages of quality assurance, beginning, most commonly, with college-level teacher preparation programs, such as the one in which you are likely now enrolled. Next, state teacher licensing systems give the public assurance that teachers are qualified and competent to do their work as educators. The third stage of continuing professional development is tied to retaining the

How is performance assessed?

state license and seeking national certification. Each of these stages is accompanied by performance assessments to determine whether individuals are qualified for the important job of teaching.

Another good point

Reflection is one of the important characteristics of successful teachers. Professionals who reflect on and analyze their own teaching are involved in a process that is critical to improving as an educator. Individuals who are making a commitment to teaching, whether lifelong or short-term, should consider the responsibilities and expectations of a teaching career. In this chapter, you will begin exploring the realities of what it means to be a teacher.

Why do I want to be a teacher?

In addition to these concepts, Chapter 1 presents a number of big ideas about teaching. These include the facts that education is extremely important in our society, that educators are members of an established profession, that educators are generally well respected and valued by the public, and that the future job market for educators is complex but promising.

How is it that the job market is both complex and promising?

Today's Teachers

Thought the number would be larger.

Strict? Tough?

More than three million teachers provide the instructional leadership for public and private schools in the United States. Today's new teachers must meet rigorous national and state standards for entering the profession that did not exist a decade ago. Requirements for entering teacher education programs in colleges and universities are now more

Strict/severe

stringent than admission requirements for most other professions. Grade point averages of 3.0 and higher are becoming more common requirements for admission; tests and other assessments must be passed before admission, at the completion of a program, and for state licensure. Clearly, not everyone can teach. Teaching is becoming a profession that attracts the best and brightest college students into its ranks.

And I thought teaching was easy!

Teacher candidates today are diverse in age and work experience. Some of you are eighteen to twenty-two years old, the traditional age of college students, but still more of you are nontraditional students who are older and have worked for a number of years in other jobs or professions. Some of your classmates may have worked as teachers' aides in classrooms for years. Others may be switching careers from the armed forces, engineering, retail management, or public relations.

Welcome to a profession in which new teachers represent such wonderfully diverse work experiences, as well as varying educational, cultural and economic backgrounds.

The Importance of Teachers to Society

Society has great expectations for its teachers. "Nine out of ten Americans believe the best way to lift student achievement is to ensure a qualified teacher in every classroom," according to a national survey. In addition to guiding students' academic achievement, teachers have some responsibility for students' social and physical development. They are expected to prepare an educated citizenry that is informed about the many **issues** critical to maintaining a democracy. They help students learn to work together and try to instill the values that are critical to a just and caring society. Teachers are also asked to prepare children and youth with the knowledge and skills necessary to work in an information age.?

Given these challenging responsibilities, teaching is one of the most important careers in a democratic society. Although critics of our education system sometimes give the impression that there is a lack of public support for schools and teachers, the public now ranks teaching as the profession that provides the most important benefit to society. Public perceptions of the importance of teaching have improved over the past years. In fact, respondents to a survey ranked teachers first by more than a three-to-one margin over physicians, nurses, businesspeople, lawyers, journalists, politicians, and accountants.

Teachers were also given a vote of confidence in a July 2002 Gallup Poll that asked people to indicate if most of the people in certain groups could be trusted or if you can't be too careful in dealing with them. This public trust should be both encouraging and perhaps a bit frightening to you as a future educator—encouraging because you will be entering a highly regarded and trusted professional group and frightening because you will be responsible for helping to uphold this public trust.

From Johnson et al., *Foundations of American Education*, pp. 4–8

Teaching is a demanding and socially responsible profession! Are teacher compensated well for their services?

Surprising that teachers rank higher than lawyers.

I'm glad I'm pursuing teaching as a career!

EXERCISE 6.4 ## Highlighting and Annotating "Learning and Teaching a Two-Way Calle in Boston"

Directions: As you read Selection 1, "Learning and Teaching a Two-Way Calle in Boston" (p. 222), highlight and annotate the text. Use the techniques mentioned above, refer to the annotated text above, or create your own techniques to mark the text. Highlight main ideas and underline or circle unfamiliar words, write in the margin, place question marks next to things you do not understand,

and write open-ended questions about the content. You can discuss these questions with your peers and instructor to understand the reading more clearly.

Learning Implications

As you annotate a text, you interact with the material. Furthermore, you take a multisensory approach to reading—you use kinesthetic and visual learning styles. Annotating your textbook will help you improve your attention, concentration, and reading comprehension. Keep annotating text, and you will gradually develop a consistent marking system, which will become an effective study aid for you.

READING

Selection 1

Newspaper Article

Learning and Teaching a Two-Way Calle in Boston*

Pre-Reading Questions

Before reading the following article, answer these questions in pairs or small groups. Discussing the questions will help prepare you to analyze the text with relative ease.

1. What kinds of challenges do recently arrived immigrant children face in American public schools?

2. How do you think the school system can help these students to overcome the challenges that they experience?

3. Do you think children whose first language is not English benefit more from bilingual instruction than they do from English-only instruction? Explain.

Eye on Vocabulary

Working with a partner, skim through the reading and find the following key vocabulary terms in bold. Examine the words in context and try to guess the meaning of each. Then look up the words in a dictionary. Keep in mind that many words have multiple meanings. Write the definition that best fits the word's context in the article.

Word	Your definition	Dictionary definition
1. environment (n.)		
2. dominant (adj.)		
3. literacy (n.)		
4. accolades (n.)		

---

* *Calle* is Spanish for *street*.

Learning and Teaching a Two-Way Calle in Boston

by Michelle Lefort, Special for *USA TODAY*

December 20, 2005

1   BOSTON—It's Friday at the Rafael Hernandez Two-Way **Bilingual** School in Roxbury and a sign on the door of the four kindergarten and first-grade classrooms tells students they will speak English today.

2   When they return their homework Monday, everyone will learn songs, math and science in Spanish.

3   In one of Boston's poorest neighborhoods, and named for a Puerto Rican poet who addressed the isolation of migration, Rafael Hernandez School was founded in the early 1970s to serve the children of Boston's growing Puerto Rican immigrant community. After Boston's 1974 desegregation order, Hernandez became a two-way language school.

4   Today, the school is highly sought after, with 250 applicants for 50 kindergarten slots. Although three-quarters of the students get free or reduced-priced lunches and many start school with little language in either English or Spanish, the kindergarten/first-grade team of Martine Lebret, Naomi Mulvihill, Brenda Rosario and Jessie Auger gets them off to a successful start.

5   Of last year's 50 first-graders, 45 were reading at or above grade level; 88% were meeting or exceeding math standards. But state standards are only one measure of success for the teachers, who work long hours to build an **environment** of respect, pride, community and continual learning.

6   Lebret and Mulvihill teach kindergarten, and Rosario and Auger teach first grade. In each classroom, about half of the students are **dominant** in English and half dominant in Spanish. During the 90-minute morning **literacy** blocks, students change classrooms to work in their dominant language. Within each grade, the teachers design parallel **curricula** in each language.

7   The teachers, who average $13\frac{1}{2}$ years teaching experience and have numerous individual **accolades**, each have distinct styles that are both loving and demanding. But it's their teamwork that makes them click. They write almost all of their materials, coordinate plans and help one another improve. "We sneak into each other's classrooms as often as we can" to watch each other teach to learn from each other and give honest **feedback**, Mulvihill says.

8   **Peer** critiquing can be intimidating, but the confidence they have in each other and their drive to improve helps them use criticism constructively. Their ability to learn from each other is the key, says principal Margarita Muniz. "They can listen to each other, critique each other without hard feelings." "We are all different people, but we all have a desire to learn, a desire to share," Auger explains. "We're very proud of each other."

9   They also work together to help each child meet his or her own goals.

10   Carlos Piedad, now 8, wanted to move from the English-dominant group to the Spanish-dominant group. Over his two years with the team, the teachers developed individual assignments, gave ideas to his parents to work with him at home and nurtured his writing skills. He made the move midway through last year, ending the year fluent in both languages.

11   Parents Javier Piedad and Patti Lautner say Carlos wasn't particularly driven. "They motivated him," Lautner says. The team didn't spend any more time working with Carlos than they did with the other students, Lautner adds. It's not unusual for any of the teachers to work 12-hour days. Even though they each teach classes of 24 or 25 students, each teacher sends regular progress reports home or makes daily calls home if the parent requests. They also host small dinner parties for families where students write and illustrate their own books.

12   In keeping with the school's "expeditionary learning" approach, the team uses class projects to teach responsibility while meeting academic standards. Former eighth-grade classes transformed an abandoned lot into a community garden. Now, kindergarteners plant the garden each spring. The following September, both the first-graders and the new kindergarteners harvest plants for use in crafts such as swan gourd maracas or in making vegetable soup.

13   Learning and teaching in two languages may be doubly difficult, but also doubly rewarding. Says Auger: "Learning two languages is incredibly intellectually stimulating."

Michelle Lefort, "Learning and Teaching
a Two-Way Calle in Boston," *USA Today*, December 20, 2005

Thinking about the Reading

After doing a close reading of the article, write your answers to the following questions. You may be asked to discuss your answers with your classmates.

1. In paragraph 4 of the article, the author writes, "Today, the school is highly sought after, with 250 applicants for 50 kindergarten slots." Based on the information in the reading, why is the Rafael Hernandez School so popular?

_____

_____

2. In paragraph 5, the author writes, "But state standards are only one measure of success for the teachers." In your opinion, how much do these state exams tell us about an elementary school student's progress in reading and math?

_____

_____

3. The school principal, Margarita Muniz, says (para. 8), "They can listen to each other, critique each other without hard feelings." In this quotation, what is the principal trying to say?

_____

_____

4. Who is Carlos Piedad? What can we learn about the school from his example?

_____

_____

_____

_____

5. In the last line of the article, a first-grade teacher in the school, Jessie Auger, says, "Learning two languages is incredibly intellectually stimulating." What are the benefits of being bilingual in twenty-first-century America?

_____

_____

_____

Reading Comprehension Check

Write the letter of the best answer for each question on the lines provided.

_____ **1.** The term *two-way* in paragraph 3 could be replaced with _____.

    a. alternative   c. English-only

    b. Hispanic-only   d. bilingual

_____ **2.** What becomes clear about the school profile from the information in paragraphs 3 and 4?

    a. Many of the students speak English only.

    b. Most of the students do not live in Boston.

    c. The vast majority of the students are poor.

    d. All of the students share the same first language.

_____ **3.** It can be inferred from paragraph 6 that

    a. students learn completely different material in each language.

    b. students cover the same material regardless of the language used.

    c. students do not learn much when they study content in two languages.

    d. bilingual students are slower to learn.

_____ **4.** The term *peer critiquing*, as used in paragraph 8, refers to a collaboration between _____.

    a. students and teachers

    b. a group of students

    c. two teachers

    d. both teachers and their bilingual students

_____ **5.** What is Carlos's mother's main point about his teachers?

    a. They can teach in both English and Spanish.

    b. They work hard for the students.

    c. The teachers are not strict enough in America.

    d. Carlos is progressing.

_____ **6.** What was the result of Carlos working for two years with the team of teachers?

    a. His English improved while his Spanish got weaker.

    b. He ended the school year fluent in both English and Spanish.

    c. He was able to skip a whole grade.

    d. He improved all of his academic skills.

_____ **7.** In paragraph 7, we read, "They write almost all of their materials, **coordinate** plans and help one another improve." A synonym for the word _coordinate_ is

    a. vary.   c. outline.

    b. discuss.   d. harmonize.

_____ **8.** As used in the sentence, "Parents Javier Piedad and Patti Lautner say Carlos wasn't particularly **driven,**" the term, _driven_ means

    a. lackadaisical.   c. motivated.

    b. stubborn.   d. uninterested.

_____ **9.** What is one example of how the school implemented an "expeditionary learning" approach?

    a. Former students transformed an abandoned lot into a community garden.

    b. Former eight-graders produced seeds for the community garden.

    c. The students played an instrumental role in training new teachers.

    d. Teachers host small parties for students and parents.

_____ **10.** In the final sentence of the article, one of the bilingual teachers says, "Learning two languages is incredibly intellectually **stimulating**." The word _stimulating_ could be replaced with the word _____.

    a. boring   c. challenging

    b. interesting   d. enabling

THEMATIC LINKS

If you want to learn more about the topic of bilingual education, type the following words into your browser and explore the two sites that come up:

1. NABE - Bilingual Education

2. Unknown Struggles of a Bilingual Student Huffington Post

Writing Without BOUNDARIES

There Are No Checkpoints!

"He who knows not and knows not that he knows not is a fool; avoid him.

He who knows not and knows that he knows not is a student; teach him.

He who knows and knows not that he knows is asleep; wake him.

He who knows and knows that he knows is a wise man; follow him."

— PERSIAN SAYING

Read the quote above and respond to it in any way you want. Write in your notebook for ten minutes without stopping. For this activity, it is important that you focus on ideas, not words. In other words, this will be an exercise in focusing on content and not getting hung up on word choice and grammar errors. You may wish to read what you have written out loud in front of your classmates and instructor.

READING

Selection 2

Magazine Article

A More Nuanced Bill Gates

Pre-Reading Questions

Answer the following questions before exploring the text:

1. Do you believe that colleges and universities in the United States are doing a good job providing a quality education to students? Explain.

2. In your opinion, does everyone have equal access to higher education, or do you think higher education is only for students from affluent backgrounds?

3. Who is more likely to earn a higher salary—a high school graduate or a college graduate? Give specific reasons for your answer.

Eye on Vocabulary

Working with a partner, skim through the reading and find the following key vocabulary terms in bold. Examine the words in context and try to guess the meaning of each. Then look up the words in a dictionary. Keep in mind that many words have multiple meanings. Write the definition that best fits the word's context in the article.

Word	Your definition	Dictionary definition
1. ironic (adj.)		
2. institutions (n.)		
3. disciplines (n.)		
4. voracious (n.)		

A More Nuanced Bill Gates

by Doug Lederman and Ry Rivard

July 22, 2014

Part 1

1   SEATTLE—It is **ironic**, says Bill Gates, that academic **institutions** are so good at studying the world around them but not themselves.

2   Gates, the Microsoft founder whose Bill & Melinda Gates Foundation has spent roughly a half billion dollars on higher education, made his case to college business officers Monday that colleges must hold themselves more **accountable**—or someone else will bring them to account.

3   "The sooner you drive this the better it is than having it brought down from on high in a way that is not appropriate," Gates told members of the National Association of College and University Business Officers during the group's annual conference here, which is also home to "the foundation," as those here call it.

4   It will surprise few that Gates said more than a few things that would rile many a faculty member. He painted a future in which a small number of top-quality online courses in key **disciplines** replace home-grown lectures on many campuses (as leading textbooks have historically done), fretted about what faculty unions could do to interfere with changes in higher education, and said nonprofit colleges could learn something from for-profit colleges about providing support to students.

5   But his remarks, and his answers to a set of questions posed by Miami Dade College's Rolando Montoya, displayed a level of nuance and sophistication about higher education that would probably surprise those who have read his well-publicized comments urging state governors to emphasize disciplines that create jobs and envisioning a wholesale embrace of massive open online courses by community colleges.

6   In a clear critique of the Obama administration's proposed college rating system, he warned against simplistic efforts to judge colleges' quality: he discouraged a single-minded focus on college "completion." He described as "over-simplistic" the view that higher education is "just about getting a job with a certain salary"—"Citizenship, developing deeper understanding, other things, are all important," he said.

7   He also emphasized the impact that state budget cuts were having on public higher education, and particularly on institutions' ability to provide support services to students. And he acknowledged that most MOOCs are "mediocre."

The Gates Agenda

8   Gates, whose multibillion-dollar foundation funds global health and education projects, is known as a **voracious** reader who reads both grand treatises and bone-dry technical reports. He said he was willing to read any college's report, however complicated, that explains how much it spends to subsidize unprofitable sports programs, on luxurious dorms, or why it is employing increasing numbers of administrators who play no role in directly helping students.

9   But colleges are not good at giving such explanations, Gates said, urging campus business officers to better-explain what happens inside the "black box" of higher ed. "Being able to pull the numbers out and contrast yourself with other institutions, in for-profit companies is done all the time," Gates said. But most colleges are opaque—except, he said, for for-profits.

10   Because for-profits take some of the toughest students to educate and pay a steep price from a regulatory standpoint if too many of them drop out, the institutions have built up student support systems that are top-notch, he said, citing Kaplan chairman Andy Rosen's book *Change.edu*.

11   "For-profits know within 10 minutes when a student hasn't gone to class so they can figure out why," Gates said. Nonprofit institutions, by contrast, tend to have a sophisticated understanding of "how much their alumni give and whether they went to a basketball game."

12   By contrast, Gates said, when public institutions lose state funding, they do whatever they can to protect the "academic core" but often don't count services that support students outside the classroom in that core, so those services end up being cut. Can they explain why? He singled out a few nonprofit institutions for praise, including Arizona State University.

13   Gates laid out a difficult scenario ahead for the vast majority of colleges that are not Harvard and Stanford or closely linked with local employers, like some community colleges. Their revenue sources will be challenged and they will find strings attached to taxpayer dollars.

14   But he warned against too-simple efforts to hold colleges accountable. As lawmakers fund public colleges based on how many students

they graduate—an emphasis that many critics would lay at least partially at the feet of Gates' own foundation and the organizations it supports—colleges may shun the hardest-to-educate students or start making it too easy to skate through.

15   "Amazingly," Gates said, "someone will have a 100 percent graduation rate, and it won't be too hard."

16   Too much emphasis on graduates' salary data will also create "huge problems," Gates warned, because it could create unfair comparisons between salaries in New York and Utah. "All these really simple measures are really difficult," Gates said.

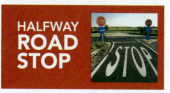

HALFWAY ROAD STOP

Get into a small group and answer the two questions that follow.

1. What have you learned from the article so far?

2. Try to predict what may be coming in the second half of the article.

Part 2

The Role of Technology

17   Some of Gates's critics have accused him of glorifying technology's role as "the" answer if higher education is to fulfill its role as an engine of equal opportunity for all Americans. Some have gone so far as to suggest that he does so to help the technology company that provided his riches.

18   His comments on Monday were relatively moderate on that score. Massive open online courses will not, in and of themselves, change much, he said. He said some were good but most were "mediocre" and MOOCs in general are useful only "for the most motivated students."

19   This will change, though, Gates predicted, because competition is "heating up dramatically." MOOCs will become like a textbook rather than a replacement for college: a tool for the motivated student to learn from on their own, or as a supplement for professors.

20   In "five or six years," he said, digital offerings that are now "pretty crummy" will greatly improve, with online forums, links to tutors or peers, and other tools that can help underprepared students in remedial courses at scale.

21   A few such courses in each field will emerge and "will be as clearly excellent as the standard textbook in those fields," and at that point it will be very difficult for the average professor at a typical campus to make the case that he or she can teach that course as well as that cream-of-the-crop digital course.

22   It's going to be, he said, "like one of us standing up and singing compared to Madonna giving one of her tour-type performances."

23   That language—and the fact that Gates did not really address what would happen to those average instructors who now give those lectures on the many typical campuses—sounded like the vintage Bill Gates that has driven some faculty advocates to the edges of their sanity.

24   But then he said this: "But you still have to connect [that content], particularly to kids whose parents didn't go to college, who are having a tough time with the [traditional college] schedule, who lack the whole motivational piece. You could lose some of that as you transition to online.

25   "If you tell a low-income student, you don't get to sit with anybody like you, you just get to sit in front of a computer terminal, they will drop out. How you create those face-to-face opportunities is an unsolved piece that is absolutely critical.

26   "I still believe in physical places of learning for a fairly significant part of what goes on."

Thinking about the Reading

After doing a close reading of the article, write your answers to the following questions. You may be asked to discuss your answers with your classmates.

1. Why does Gates state "that academic institutions are so good at studying the world around them but not themselves"?

_____

_____

2. Discuss why Gates is so critical of the Obama administration's proposed college rating system.

_____

_____

_____

3. Why does Gates say that "nonprofit colleges could learn something from for-profit colleges about providing support to students"?

_____

_____

_____

4. Why does Gates warn "against too-simple efforts to hold colleges accountable"?

_____

_____

5. According to Gates, how will technology help students in remedial courses in five or six years?

_____

_____

Reading Comprehension Check

_____ **1.** "It will surprise few that Gates said more than a few things that would **rile** many a faculty member." In the context above, the word *rile* means

a. delight.

c. calm.

b. appease.

d. exasperate.

_____ **2.** Mr. Gates's main idea is that

a. only a special group of students can pursue a higher education and succeed.

b. colleges must hold themselves more accountable for student success.

c. higher education should only be for students who come from an affluent background.

d. our education system should focus those students with the most needs.

_____ **3.** Why does Bill Gates says that nonprofit colleges should learn from for-profit colleges?

a. because for-profit colleges provide better teacher benefits

b. because for-profit colleges screen potential students more effectively

c. because for-profit colleges do not admit some of the toughest students

d. because for-profit colleges provide top-notch student support systems

_____ **4.** "By contrast, Gates said, when public institutions lose state funding, they do whatever they can to protect the 'academic core' but often don't count services that support students outside the classroom in that core, so those services end up being cut. Can they explain why? He singled out a few nonprofit institutions for praise, including Arizona State University." It can be inferred from the above passage that

a. Arizona State University recently phased out their student support services because of limited funding.

b. unlike other nonprofit institutions, Arizona State University provides good student support services.

c. nonprofit institutions are doing their best to support at-risk students by offering them extra tutoring.

d. despite losing state funding, most nonprofit institutions provide excellent student support services.

_____ **5.** The author's purpose is

a. to inform.

c. to entertain.

b. to persuade.

d. to amuse.

_____ **6.** According to the reading, what is one of the practical reasons that for-profit institutions tend to provide students with excellent academic support?

    a. Students at for-profit institutions tend to come from wealthy families who are willing to pay extra for academic support.

    b. For-profit institutions have a stake in student success because they receive a bonus from the Bill & Melinda Gates Foundation for each student who graduates.

    c. For-profit institutions find it too expensive to focus on constructing luxury dorms or costly sports programs, so they focus on academic support for students instead.

    d. Regulators penalize for-profit institutions if too many of their students drop out, so it pays to help students succeed.

_____ **7.** In paragraph 9, when the author says that "most colleges are opaque," he most nearly means

    a. most colleges are a dark and depressing environment for students

    b. most colleges refuse to offer remedial courses to help under-prepared students, leaving them in the dark academically.

    c. most colleges are reluctant to reveal how much they spend and on what.

    d. most colleges make it too easy for their students to graduate.

_____ **8.** According to the article, in what way does Bill Gates say that a MOOC (massive open online course) is like a textbook?

    a. Students can learn from MOOCs on their own, or professors can use them as supplements.

    b. Current digital offerings are "pretty crummy," like substandard textbooks.

    c. Top-quality online courses will replace casual lectures, just as leading textbooks have done in the past.

    d. Just like a textbook, a MOOC that is well designed and authoritative can take the place of a professor and the college campus itself.

_____ **9.** The reading suggests that the overly simplistic view of judging the quality of a college by its completion rate is held by

    a. Bill Gates.   c. Kaplan's Any Rosen.

    b. parents of at-risk students.   d. President Obama.

_____ **10.** According to the reading, why may public colleges avoid accepting students who are the hardest to educate?

    a. because they believe such students cannot succeed

    b. because they receive funding based on how many of their students graduate

    c. Bill Gates is a major financial backer of higher education, and he would prefer that public colleges enroll only those students with a proven track record for high achievement.

    d. Students who end up dropping out might damage the reputations of public colleges who took a chance on admitting them by critiquing them harshly on social media.

THEMATIC LINKS

If you want to learn more about the topic of higher education, explore the homepage of the Chronicle of Higher Education, browse through the articles, and choose one or two that interest you or visit the Stanford News site by typing the words into your browser:

1. Chronicle of Higher Education homepage
2. Stanford explores the future of higher education Stanford News

READING SKILL FOCUS

Recognizing Author's Purpose and Tone

4 OBJECTIVE

Identify an author's purpose and tone

Fluent readers can determine an author's purpose and tone by carefully reading a text, and, as a college student, you will need to develop the same skill. Complete the following exercise before reading more about how to recognize an author's purpose (reason for writing) and tone (expression of feeling and/or emotion).

EXERCISE 6.5 Understanding Purpose and Tone

Directions: Working in a small group, examine the following four short paragraphs, all focusing on the same topic—the future of cell phones—and consider what makes each paragraph different from the others.

Passage 1

Most teachers teach their content areas without any orientation in education. For example, a college professor teaches history because s/he has a PhD in history. However, most content teachers have never taken courses in classroom management, issues in reading and writing, supervision, assessment, and test preparation. The same goes for foreign language teachers. They teach a foreign language simply because it happens to be their native language. They have little or no background in second language acquisition, educational research, and applied linguistics. The government ought to mandate that all teachers take some foundational courses in education before they teach their subject matter.

Passage 2

In the twenty-first century, American teachers have to change their lesson plans to address the diverse social, cultural, and linguistic needs of their students. As change happens in the country, it is also reflected in the teaching profession. Changes in teaching are influenced by many factors such as immigrant students' learning backgrounds, changes in society, groundbreaking educational research findings, and children's health issues such as obesity and malnutrition.

Passage 3

Teaching English as a Second Language (ESL) has its moments of humor. ESL students get their ideas about American culture mostly from Hollywood movies and learn expressions such as "What's up," "Howdy," "Hey baby," and "Man." These students often misuse these expressions while addressing their teachers, thinking it is normal to call a female instructor "Hey baby." Although this misunderstanding can sometimes cause confusion, most ESL teachers understand their students' innocent mistakes.

Passage 4

Here is a lesson plan to teach academic reading to college students. First, choose a short story that you think most students will be interested in reading. Make a list of key vocabulary items and go over them in class before you ask students to read the short story. As students take turns reading parts of the story, ask both comprehension and open-ended questions about the story. After they read the story, ask students to answer multiple-choice questions. Finally, tell them that their homework assignment is to write a short response paper regarding the story.

Recognizing an Author's Purpose

An **author's purpose** is simply his or her reason for writing a text. When we are reading, it is easy to forget that a real person, with a specific purpose in mind, at some point sat down and wrote what is now in front of us. When the author wrote the text, he or she had an **intended audience** in mind—a specific group of people the author was writing for. For instance, an economist writing a first-year macro-economics textbook may assume that his or her audience will be students taking an introductory course in this discipline. A journalist for *Vogue* magazine knows his or her intended audience consists of people interested in the latest fashion.

Let's reread paragraph 3 from "Learning and Teaching a Two-Way Calle in Boston" (p. 222) by Michelle Lefort to better understand how to determine purpose.

> In one of Boston's poorest neighborhoods, and named for a Puerto Rican poet who addressed the isolation of migration, Rafael Hernandez School was founded in the early 1970s to serve the children of Boston's growing Puerto Rican immigrant community. After Boston's 1974 deseg-regation order, Hernandez became a two-way language school.

Notice that the author has refrained from expressing her personal view in the passage. She simply provides information about a bilingual school in Boston. If the author's purpose were to convince or persuade the reader that this was a particularly good school, the passage would contain sentences such as "I think Rafael Hernandez School is the best in the country" or "I believe that immigrant parents should send their children to Rafael Hernandez School." Based on the content, it is safe to conclude that the author's purpose in the above paragraph is to inform the reader, not to convince, or entertain, or instruct him or her.

Now reread paragraph 4 from "Teaching in a Changing World," which is taken from an education textbook (see p. 218).

> Reflection is one of the important characteristics of successful teachers. Professionals who reflect on and analyze their own teaching are involved in a process that is critical to improving as an educator. Individu-als who are making a commitment to teaching, whether lifelong or short-term, should consider the responsibilities and expectations of a teaching career. In this chapter, you will begin exploring the realities of what it means to be a teacher.

The purpose of this passage is clearly not to just to inform the reader. Notice the use of phrases such as "important characteristics of successful teachers," "a process that is critical to improving as an educator," and "In this chapter," which indicate information is being taught. The purpose of this passage is to instruct students in how to become successful teachers.

So, an author's purpose is very much related to his or her intended audience and the genre, or type of writing, he or she is doing. Common purposes for writing are to inform, to entertain, to instruct, or to persuade the reader, which lend themselves to different genres, as shown in the following chart.

Purpose	Genre
■ To inform	newspaper articles, textbooks, legal documents, reference materials
■ To persuade or convince	advertising, editorials, music/art criticism, political speeches
■ To instruct	how-to manuals, technical guides, math- and lab-related textbooks
■ To entertain	novels, poems, jokes, gossip columns

When trying to determine an author's purpose, read the text carefully and ask yourself, "Why did the author write this? What was he or she trying to accomplish?"

EXERCISE 6.6   Identifying an Author's Purpose

Directions: In the same groups as before, re-examine passages 1 to 4 and try to determine the author's purpose in each. In your earlier discussion, you may have touched upon the different purposes of each passage.

Passage 1 _____

Passage 2 _____

Passage 3 _____

Passage 4 _____

Understanding Tone

Authors carefully choose words to convey a *tone* or feeling. An author's tone reflects his or her *attitude* toward a topic. In a conversation, you can tell if the person you are speaking with is angry, serious, sympathetic, or just kidding around by the intonation, volume, and pitch of that person's voice and his or her facial expression (if you can actually see him or her). In writing, however, one has to rely on the author's choice of words and style of writing to determine the tone. For example, read the following introductory paragraph from the biographical profile of Ruth Simmons on page 216:

Dr. Ruth J. Simmons is the first African American educator ever to be president of an Ivy League institution and the first female president of Brown University. Ruth J. Simmons was born in 1945 in Grapeland, Texas. She grew up on a farm in East Texas and had a life of deprivation and hardship. Yet she recounts her life in Texas fondly: "My journey has not been all that arduous, contrary to the way that my life is often presented. I had this wonderful grounding by my parents, and then an extraordinary streak of luck."

If you just read the highlighted words, you get the impression that the writer is both impressed and enthusiastic about Ruth Simmons, who has excelled despite "a life of deprivation and hardship," speaks "fondly" of her upbringing in Texas, credits her parents with giving her a "wonderful grounding," and refers to her later success as an "extraordinary streak of luck."

If you understand an author's purpose, you are halfway to identifying the author's tone. If the author's purpose is simply to inform, then perhaps the tone is somewhat unemotional, perhaps neutral or objective. If the author is trying to persuade the reader of something, then perhaps the tone will be critical or disapproving, or supportive and encouraging, or enthusiastic and upbeat, as in the example above. If the writer is trying to entertain, the tone might be lighthearted, comic, or sarcastic.

In mastering the reading skill of identifying author's tone, it is important that you build up a rich vocabulary of adjectives that describe tone.

Recognizing Tone Through Adjectives

Below is a list of useful words that describe tone. They are a small sampling of the adjectives that convey tone and are valuable vocabulary to have in your inventory. Many of them you may already know. They are grouped into general categories to make it easier for you to become familiar with them.

Objective Tones These are often used in textbooks, newspaper and magazine articles, and reference materials.	
neutral	not taking a particular side
straightforward	simple and easy to understand
indifferent	not having any feelings or opinions about something
serious	earnestly stated, with a sense that what is being said is important
instructional	providing information about a particular concept

Emotional Tones These are found in persuasive writings, such as editorials and political writing.	
angry	outraged or upset about something
concerned	worried about something
sentimental	expressing emotions such as love, pity, or sadness too strongly
nostalgic	longing for things or situations in the past
remorseful	feeling sorry for something one has done
inspirational	motivating the reader to act

Disapproving Tones These may be found in movie and art reviews, editorials, political speeches, and blogs.

critical	severely judging people or things
pessimistic	having a negative outlook
intolerant	not being willing to accept ways of thinking that are different from one's own
gloomy	a dark, hopeless feeling
bitter	a sour reaction

Supportive Tones These may be found in reviews and editorials, self-help books and articles, as well as in inspirational writing.

encouraging	showing support
optimistic	having a bright view of the future
sympathetic	showing understanding of how someone feels and being supportive of his or her actions
enthusiastic	exhibiting a lot of interest and excitement about something
convincing	trying to persuade the reader

Humorous and Sarcastic Tones These may appear in many kinds of writing, including cartoons, literature and criticism, poetry, and newspaper columns.

ironic	using words that are the opposite of what is really meant in order to be amusing or show annoyance
skeptical	doubting or not believing something
cynical	unwilling to believe that someone has good or honest intentions for doing something
mocking	laughing at something to make it seem silly
lighthearted	cheerful, not intended to be serious
comic	funny, especially in a strange and unexpected way
tongue-in-cheek	said or done seriously, but meant as a joke

EXERCISE 6.7 Identifying Tone

Directions: Let's return one last time to the beginning of this section and Passages 1 to 4 (p. 233). From what we have just reviewed, try to determine what the author's tone is for each of the paragraphs. Pay close attention to the use of language, and highlight the key words that clue you in to the author's tone.

	Author's Tone	**Key Clue Words**
Passage 1		
Passage 2		
Passage 3		
Passage 4		

EXERCISE 6.8   Identifying Authors' Purpose and Tone

Directions: Now practice identifying an author's purpose and tone at the same time. In the table below, fill in the appropriate box for purpose and tone for each of the three chapter selections. You may need to review Selections 1 and 2 again and preview Selection 3 to answer the questions correctly.

Readings	Author's Purpose	Author's Tone
Selection 1: "Learning and Teaching a Two-Way Calle in Boston," page 222		
Selection 2: "A More Nuanced Bill Gates," page 227		
Selection 3: "How Is Teaching Changing?," page 239		

READING

Selection 3

Textbook

How Is Teaching Changing?

Pre-Reading Questions

Answer the following questions before exploring the text:

1. With the advancements in science and technology in the twenty-first century, what changes do you think teachers need to make to teach their students more efficiently?

2. More and more people continue to immigrate to the United States every year. Discuss how teachers can meet the social, cultural, and linguistic needs of their diverse classrooms.

3. Technology is shaping our lives in many ways. How do you think the Internet and cell phones are influencing how students think and learn?

How Is Teaching Changing?

George S. Morrison

1 Rapid change, a characteristic of American society in general, also is reflected in the teaching profession. The changing nature of teaching results from a variety of factors: new knowledge derived from educational research; changes in society; state and national school **reform** efforts (including legislation); children's health issues, such as obesity and nutrition; immigration; rapidly changing technology; and safety concerns.

2 Obesity and nutrition are influencing lesson plans, school lunch programs, and school funding as childhood obesity levels continue to rise. As a result, school food programs are on a diet! As schools scramble to comply with federal requirements that every school district develop a wellness plan to provide students with healthier foods, many are banning a wide array of unhealthy food options. California is a case in point; it has banned deep fryers and now serves baked fries and chicken nuggets.

3 Immigration and the changing composition of American society also is affecting teaching and learning. As students face the obstacles associated with **acculturation** into U.S. society, teachers are facing the challenge of meeting the needs of their increasingly **diverse** classrooms.

4 New technologies are changing the way we think and live. The Internet, cell phones, and social networking are all influencing how students think, learn, and socialize, both inside and outside of the classroom. Cell-phone-accessorized teens may think that is just "GR8," but as the lexicon spawned by a 160-character message limit starts to spill off the cell phone screen into written work, some of their English teachers are not exactly "ROFL." Nor does seeing text-message abbreviations in essays bring a smiley face to college admission officers. Veteran high school English teacher Ruth Maenpaa started noticing how much text messaging was affecting her students, in both subtle and not-subtle ways. The first time Maenpaa flagged the use of "4" for "for" in an essay, the student said she was so used to text messaging that she did not even think about it. "As I watch students texting, I see them routinely using abbreviations to the point that they do not know how to spell the word correctly."

5 You need to prepare for how such changes, as well as new ones, will affect the teaching profession. Changes in society spur new efforts in educational research, which in turn propel reform movements; new legislation driven by increased youth obesity drives "junk food" out of schools; new technology leads to new educational research and development, which in turn fuels new legislation. All of these factors impact the day-to-day lives of teachers and the way public schools function in the United States. Being a teacher means living with and adapting to change.

—Morrison, *Teaching in America*, p. 27

Thinking about the Reading

After doing a close reading of the article, write your answers to the following questions. You may be asked to discuss your answers with your classmates.

1. Why does the author think that rapid change is a characteristic of American society?

_____

_____

_____

2. According to the author, what factors affect and change the nature of teaching?

_____

_____

_____

3. Why is every school district trying to provide students with healthier foods?

_____

_____

4. How is immigration changing teaching and learning?

_____

_____

_____

5. According to Ruth Maenpaa, how is text messaging affecting her students?

_____

Reading Comprehension Check

_____ **1.** "**Rapid** change, a characteristic of American society in general, also is reflected in the teaching profession." In the above sentence, the word *rapid* is opposite in meaning to _____.

    a. brisk   c. dizzy

    b. slow   d. quick

_____ **2.** What is the main idea of the essay?

    a. The government has started a special training program for novice teachers in America.

    b. Most teachers know how to deal with the increasingly diverse classrooms in America.

    c. Teaching is changing as classrooms are becoming increasingly diverse in America.

    d. Students in American schools come from diverse social and linguistic backgrounds.

_____ **3.** According to the passage, which of the following does *not* cause teaching to change?

    a. children's health issues
    b. changing technology
    c. the rate of inflation
    d. new educational research

_____ **4.** The author's purpose is

    a. to convince.   c. to persuade.
    b. to amuse.   d. to inform.

_____ **5.** The overall tone of the passage is

    a. sarcastic.   c. sardonic.
    b. humorous.   d. neutral.

_____ **6.** Which of the following statements about this reading selection is *false*?

    a. California schools refuse to change school lunch programs despite rising childhood obesity levels.
    b. Teachers these days must be flexible and able to respond to changing times.
    c. English teacher Ruth Maenpaa noticed that her students' poor spelling was related to frequent texting.
    d. Immigrant students face challenges at school as they attempt to become acculturated into U.S. society.

_____ **7.** According to the reading, new technology influences how students

    a. text, email, and tweet.
    b. think, learn, and socialize.
    c. feel about educational reform.
    d. combat childhood obesity.

_____ **8.** The audience for this reading selection is most likely which of the following?

    a. students who text frequently
    b. advocates of combating childhood obesity
    c. education reformers
    d. people interested in entering the teaching profession

_____ **9.** What characteristic of U.S. society does Morrison say is reflected in the teaching profession?

    a. acculturation   c. change
    b. wellness   d. dieting

_____ **10.** According to the reading, which of the following is *not* a cause of "the changing nature of teaching"?

    a. parental involvement
    b. new knowledge gained from research
    c. immigration
    d. new technology

Think to Write

Now that you have completed three readings in this chapter on education, think about which of the three is most interesting to you. Write a paragraph response about this reading and post it to The Wall.

It's SHOWTIME!

Watching a video clip related to the chapter content can be an enriching experience. Go online and find a video link whose topic ties into one of the chapter readings (maximum length = ten minutes). After viewing the video clip, write a half-page summary of the video's key points. Post your personal reaction to the ideas in the clip (between 150 and 400 words) on The Wall.

WRITING SKILL FOCUS

 OBJECTIVE

Develop your purpose and tone based on your audience

Awareness of Audience: Purpose and Tone

When authors write, they usually have a specific audience in mind. Writing that does not address a specific audience can be confusing or hard to follow. For example, a computer professional writing an article for other computer professionals can use technical language and reference theories without defining every term or explaining every concept, as she can safely assume they are familiar with the discipline. However, the same computer professional writing a textbook for entry-level computer science students will need to define terms and give ample examples to illustrate them in order to ensure her audience understands the vocabulary and concepts pivotal to learning the subject. Clearly, writers' awareness of their audience helps them refine their purpose and influences how they write.

As you write, it is important for you to be aware of your audience: Who you write for will determine your purpose, and it will certainly influence what and how you write. Before you begin to write your preliminary draft, use the following questions to help you determine what information your audience needs to know and how you should present that information:

Considering Audience Before You Write

1. **Who is your audience?** Your audience is the people who will read your written work. They may be a narrow audience such as your instructor and classmates, or they may be part of a wider audience such as your neighbors, workmates, or fellow citizens. It is important to be mindful of your audience so that you can determine what format to use (paragraph, essay, letter, memo, letter of complaint, etc.), whether to use formal or informal language, what kinds of details to include, and the overall tone to employ (informative, friendly, angry, etc.).

2. **What does your audience expect from you?** If your audience is your instructor, find out what his or her expectations are before you write your essay. (How long should it be? What is the topic and format? Should it be documented, and if so, using what style? When is it due?) However, if you are posting a response to a classmate's academic work, writing a letter to the editor of your local paper, or disputing your electric bill, you need to find out the guidelines for these projects before you start writing.

3. **What does your audience already know about the topic of your essay? What do they need to know?** If your audience is familiar with your topic, you can safely assume they have the information they need to follow your thinking. However, if your audience is unfamiliar with your topic, you will need to provide the necessary background information, define key terms, and use examples and analogies that are familiar to your readers so that they can connect their prior knowledge to the new information you are providing.

4. **How does the audience feel about your topic?** Some readers in your audience may have strong feelings for or against a controversial topic such as gun control or euthanasia—assisted suicide—and others may have a neutral position on the topic. Knowing how your audience feels about your topic beforehand will help you write a well-reasoned essay. For instance, if your audience is not in agreement with your stance, you have to take this into account and not only present your argument and support for it but also acknowledge their perspective and arguments against it.

5. **If you are writing an argument paper, do you think you will be able to convince your audience? Will you use only opinions, or will you use facts to sway your audience?** If you use opinions unsubstantiated with hard evidence, your audience will not respect your points of view. However, if you use verifiable facts to support your position, your audience is more likely to be swayed by your argumentation.

Addressing these questions will give you a sense of your audience and prepare you to better write your essay. As you participate in class discussions frequently and respond to each other's posts on The Wall, you will become familiar with opposing points of view and with your classmates' feelings toward sensitive and controversial topics.

Suppose, for example, that you are prochoice and support abortion, but you also know that some of your classmates are prolife and oppose abortion. Being cognizant of their position on this topic, you will have to choose your words carefully and write a well-reasoned essay supporting a woman's right to an abortion. In your essay, you will avoid using inflammatory and offensive language and defend your position in a respectful way. If you are unsure about how your instructor and classmates will respond to your opinion, you can easily ask them.

EXERCISE 6.9   Writing for an Intended Audience

Directions: Based on your reading of the three readings in this chapter, write the intended audience for each of them in the chart below.

Readings	Intended Audience
Selection 1: "Learning and Teaching a Two-Way Calle in Boston," page 222	
Selection 2: "A More Nuanced Bill Gates," page 277	
Selection 3: "How Is Teaching Changing?," page 239	

WRITING SKILL FOCUS

Correcting Fragments and Run-On Sentences

If a sentence you write does not contain both a subject and a verb, it is not a complete sentence, it is a fragment. Run-on sentences are two independent (main) clauses joined without using a comma and a coordinating conjunction (*for, and, nor, but, or, yet,* and *so*).

OBJECTIVE

6   Correct fragments and run-on sentences

As a college student, you should avoid these errors as you write your academic essays. One strategy that can help is to carefully read what you have written out loud, and to consider where the natural pauses are in your narrative. Where there are pauses in speech, there should be punctuation.

Fragments

As mentioned above, a fragment is an incomplete idea presented as a complete sentence, for example,

> * And taught at the University of Massachusetts for thirty years.
>
> (The asterisk before the sentence is a linguistic convention to denote that it is ungrammatical.)

Do you know why it is ungrammatical? Remember that a sentence must consist of a subject and a verb. The problem with the example is that even though it has a verb (taught), it does not have a subject. Most readers will find the sentence confusing, because it does not clearly state *who* taught at the University of Massachusetts. You can repair the fragment easily by including a subject at the beginning of the sentence:

> *Professor Kay Harker* taught at the University of Massachusetts for thirty years.

Run-On Sentences

Unlike sentence fragments, run-on sentences are two independent clauses joined without appropriate punctuation. Consider the following example:

> * According to some projections, by 2020 the US will have three million fewer college graduates than the economy will need making college attendance increasingly expensive now will further increase this trend in the future.

This is a run-on sentence, because two complete sentences are presented as one without correct punctuation. Can you tell where one sentence ends and the other begins?

You can revise a run-on sentence by separating the two independent sentences with a period, semicolon, or a comma and a coordinating conjunction (use the mnemonic FANBOYS—*for, and, nor, but, or, yet,* and *so*—to remember the coordinating conjunctions).

With a period

According to some projections, by 2020 the US will have three million fewer college graduates than the economy will need. Making college attendance increasingly expensive now will further increase this trend in the future.

With a semicolon

According to some projections, by 2020 the US will have three million fewer college graduates than the economy will need; making college attendance increasingly expensive now will further increase this trend in the future.

With a comma and a coordinating conjunction

According to some projections, by 2020 the US will have three million fewer college graduates than the economy will need, and making college attendance increasingly expensive now will further increase this trend in the future.

EXERCISE 6.10   Recognizing Fragments and Run-On Sentences

Directions: Read the following examples carefully and determine whether they are fragments or run-on sentences. Write F for a fragment and R for a run-on.

_____ 1. There are pros and cons to educational testing people tend to feel strongly about the issue.

_____ 2. May lead you to the wrong academic decision.

_____ 3. That you can pursue that will bring you success in both your career and your personal life.

_____ 4. MOOCs (massive open online courses) are growing in popularity and offer a range of benefits there appear to be two distinct categories: those based on the connectivist approach and those based on more traditional courses.

_____ 5. Although a degree is a prerequisite for many careers, it is important to position yourself well in the job market use the following six tips for success.

EXERCISE 6.11   Writing Complete Thoughts

Directions: The paragraph below contains both sentence fragments and run-ons. Revise it by making the sentence fragments complete thoughts and, in the cases of run-ons, by dividing the sentences up. You will have to add words in, capitalize words, and add punctuation.

Many students begin their college studies without. Because they are not sure of which career path they would like to follow, students will often take general required courses this is a practical plan, which will save students from wasting time. a wise idea. Although a student with an undeclared major might feel a certain amount of pressure to quickly figure out what they want to study. What often ends up happening is a student takes an introductory course they really like and then decide to major in that academic area and later on, they take the upper level courses in that respective field and continue onward toward a career in that discipline.

Learning Implications

It is important to know how basic sentences work in order to address common errors that may occur when you are constructing your own sentences. As you write essays, avoiding sentence fragments and run-ons and writing complete thoughts will help you communicate clearly with your readers. For a more in-depth focus on punctuating your sentences, turn to page 378, in Chapter 9, and review the Trouble-Spots in Writing feature.

TROUBLE SPOTS IN WRITING

OBJECTIVE

7

Use transitions to connect ideas and indicate purpose

A Bumpy Road Without Transition Words

If a road is full of speed bumps, the ride is very uncomfortable, tiring, and sometimes painful. However, if they are removed, the ride becomes smooth, pleasant, and enjoyable. Similarly, if you write without transition words, the reader will not enjoy the reading ride because your sentences will be choppy. As a result, he or she will not have a sense of how your ideas connect.

An effective way to help a reader follow your movement of thoughts with ease is to use transition words within and between sentences. Transition words can be a single word, phrase, or even an entire sentence. It is important to remember that transitional words and phrases can appear at the beginning, in the middle, and at the end of a sentence.

The primary purpose of using transition words is twofold:

1. They signal the writer's movement from one thought to another, improving coherence.
2. They also indicate the pattern of organization the writer is using, which provides clues as to what to look for as you read.

Using transition words in a paragraph helps a writer achieve coherence and tells the reader how the sentences in the paragraph are related to each other. It should be noted that writers use transitional words, phrases, and sentences not only to connect ideas within paragraphs but also to connect paragraphs to each other and to the thesis statement. What follows is a list of transition words for your reference. Notice how they are used for different purposes.

Purpose	Transitions
Comparison	also, by the same token, in comparison, similarly, likewise
Contrast	in contrast, on the contrary, on the other hand, by contrast, however, nevertheless, otherwise, whereas, although, even though, and yet, instead, rather
Addition	in addition, also, furthermore, moreover, also, finally, first, next
Concession	although it is true, at the same time, granted, I admit, of course, while it is true, I concede

(Continued)

Purpose	Transitions
Example/illustration	for instance, for example, in fact, in other words, by way of illustration, in particular, specifically
Results	consequently, as a result, accordingly, hence, therefore, thus, in short,
Summary	to conclude, in conclusion, as I have said, to sum up, to summarize, on the whole, in brief, in other words, in short
Show time	since, shortly, afterward, in the meantime, lately, meanwhile, of late, thereafter, thereupon, soon, since

It is important to remember that you should not use transition words excessively. However, when you think you need to indicate to the reader how one sentence is related to another, use transition words.

EXERCISE 6.12   Using Transition Words

Directions: Read the following passages and underline the transition words in each. After each passage, write the transition words and the purpose for which they are used. The first transition in Example 1 is done for you.

Passage 1

To keep up with the media and technology environment today's students inhabit outside school, teachers must integrate technology into their teaching. For example, students of Neelam Mishra, who teaches Hindi at Edison High School in New Jersey, uses Skype to interact with Hindi-speaking students at St. Gregorios High School in Mumbai, India. Her students ask their peers about Hindi words, after-school activities, and Indian history. According to Mishra, "My students enjoy my class, but when they talk to their peers, they feel more comfortable sharing." In addition to online collaboration with native Hindi speakers, Mishra's students use technology to develop projects on topics such as Gandhi's life, school days in India, or Indian tourism. Her students share many of these projects with the Mumbai students, for example, performing a skit during a Skype videoconference (George Lucas Educational Foundation, April 2010).

— Parkay, *Becoming a Teacher*, p. 19

Transition Words	Purpose
For example	example and illustration

Passage 2

When you think ahead to a career in teaching, a question you are likely to ask yourself is, "What is the job outlook for teachers? From time to time, teacher supply and demand figures have painted a rather bleak picture for those entering the teaching profession. At other times, finding a position has not been difficult. Even during times of teacher surplus, talented, qualified teachers are able to find jobs. Teaching is one of the largest professions in the United States; out of a national population of about 310 million, about 49.3 million attended public elementary and secondary schools during 2008—2009, where they were taught by about 3.2 million teachers (National Center for Education Statistics, August 2010). Public elementary and secondary enrollment is projected to increase to 52 million students by 2019–2020 (U.S. Department of Labor, 2010). The job outlook is brightest for teachers in high-demand fields such as science, mathematics, and bilingual and special education, and in less desirable urban or rural school districts. In addition, the number of teachers retiring is expected to reach an all-time high in 2011–2012, and this will create many job openings (Ingersoll & Merrill, 2010).

—Parkay, *Becoming a Teacher*, pp. 21–23

Transition Words	Purpose

Passage 3

When teachers are preparing to teach or reflecting on previous teaching, they can afford to be consistently deliberate and rational. Planning for lessons, grading papers, reflecting on the misbehavior of a student—such activities are usually done alone and lack the immediacy and sense of urgency that characterize interactive teaching. While working face-to-face with students, however, you must be able to think on your feet and respond appropriately to complex, ever-changing situations. You must be flexible and ready to deal with the unexpected. During a discussion, for example, you must operate on at least two levels. On one level, you respond appropriately to students' comments, monitor other students for signs of confusion or comprehension, formulate the next comment or question, and remain alert for signs of misbehavior. On another level, you ensure that participation is evenly distributed among students, evaluate the content and quality of students' contributions, keep the discussion focused and moving ahead, and emphasize major content areas.

—Parkay, *Becoming a Teacher*, p. 46

Transition Words	Purpose

EXERCISE 6.13   Using Transition Words for Purpose

Directions: Now that you have identified the transition words in the three passages above, practice writing appropriate transition words based on the writer's purpose in the following passages. Read the passages carefully and insert transition words wherever you feel the writer needs to indicate to the reader how one sentence is related to another. Use the chart on page 247 to guide you.

Passage 1

In most professions, new members must undergo a prescribed induction period. Physicians must serve an internship or a residency before beginning practice, and most lawyers begin as clerks in law firms. Teachers usually do not go through a formal induction period before assuming full responsibility for their work. Practice teaching courses comes closest to serving as an induction period, but it is often relatively short, informal, and lacking in uniformity.

—Parkay, *Becoming a Teacher*, p. 55

Passage 2

In team-teaching arrangements, teachers share the responsibility for two or more classes, dividing the subject areas between them, with one preparing lessons in mathematics, science, and health while the other plans instruction in reading and language arts. The division of responsibility may also be made in terms of the performance levels of the children, so one teacher may teach the lowest—and highest—ability reading groups and the middle math group, while the other teaches the middle-ability reading groups and the lowest and highest mathematics group.

—Parkay, *Becoming a Teacher*, p. 67

Passage 3

In *The Life of Reason*, George Santayana said, "Those who cannot remember the past are condemned to repeat it." Adlai Stevenson, presidential candidate in 1952 and 1956, said, "We can chart our future clearly and wisely only when we know the path which has led us to the present."

For teachers, the implication of these statements is clear—the past has an impact on teaching and schools today. Accomplished teachers learn from our nation's educational past. They know that educational practices from the past have not disappeared—they continue to evolve, and they shape the present, as well as the future. We cannot understand schools today without a look at what they were yesterday. Today's teachers must be students of our educational future. The history of education in the United States reveals countless examples of how political forces and special interest groups have influenced schools, and professional teachers understand these influences.

—Parkay, *Becoming a Teacher*, p. 146

THEN & NOW

If you really want to understand an academic field, it is useful to get a sense of how the discipline has evolved over time. This feature gives you the opportunity to do just that. Go online and do some research to gather information about two experts in the field of education: one educator from the past such as Paulo Freire or John Locke and another contemporary educator such as Noam Chomsky or Henry Louis Gates, Jr. Fill out the table provided below with pertinent information about the two experts.

Past Influential Expert	Present Influential Expert
Name	Name
Place of birth	Place of birth
Year of birth	Year of birth
Education	Education
What is s/he most famous for?	What is s/he most famous for?
Famous quote	Famous quote

After you fill out the table, discuss your findings with your classmates and learn from them about what they discovered on the Internet.

Working with a search engine, do the following search, "TED Talks Geoffrey Canada Our failing schools. Enough is enough!" and click on "View Interactive Transcript." Peruse the transcript to gain a deeper understanding of the education system. After doing a careful reading, write brief answers to the following questions about the content.

1. Why is Geoffrey Canada so angry? As a student, do you feel the same way?

   _____

   _____

2. According to Geoffrey Canada, why hasn't the education system embraced technology wholeheartedly?

   _____

   _____

   _____

   _____

3. What does Canada think educators need to do to help the young students?

   _____

   _____

   _____

   _____

Is a college education worth it?

OBJECTIVE

Read, think, plan, and write an essay in response to the chapter essay assignment

Now that you have had the opportunity to read a number of articles and a textbook excerpt, you should have a deeper understanding of the discipline of education and be prepared to compose your chapter essay assignment.

Write a two-page essay in response to the above question. Remember that your first paragraph should have a clear thesis statement that tells the reader what you will focus on in the rest of the essay. Develop your thesis statement in the body paragraphs. Finally, summarize the main points of your essay in the concluding paragraph, restate the thesis statement, and leave a lasting impression on the reader by writing a concluding sentence.

When you are done, hand in your essay to your instructor. After you have received constructive feedback from your instructor, be sure to incorporate some of his or her suggestions into your second draft and submit the revised second draft to your instructor for further feedback on form and meaning.

FOCUS ON FORM

Using Transition Words

In the Trouble Spots in Writing section in this chapter, you learned that reading an essay that does not use transition words appropriately can be a bumpy road for the reader. In this section, your task is to read the following paragraph, find places where transition words are needed, and provide them to make the sentences run more smoothly. When you are finished, compare your revised paragraph with that of a partner.

> Bilingual education has been a highly controversial and political issue. Opinion is sharply divided between those who believe it is beneficial for students and those who argue that it is not useful. Many states have passed English-only initiatives and have abandoned bilingual programs. California, Arizona, and Massachusetts provide instruction in English only and no longer offer bilingual programs. They require that non-native English speaking children learn core content areas in English rather than in

their native language. This practice is contradictory to research findings.
Stephen Krashen, professor at the University of Southern California, and
an expert in theories of language acquisition and development, argues
that children learn better in their first language. He presents strong evidence that children must be literate in their native language before they
embark on learning a second language.

It's Your Turn!

You have practiced using transition words appropriately. It is time for you to
review the written work you did for the chapter essay assignment. Read your
essay carefully, and see if you need transition words in some places. While the
purpose of this exercise is to focus on transition words, you may find other
errors such as run-on sentences and fragments. Pay a close attention to grammar
errors, and make sure that your essay is error free.

CHAPTER DEBATE OPTION

Is a college education worth it?

This chapter's debate topic is the same as your chapter essay assignment. Refer
to Appendix 8, page 455, for detailed guidelines on how to set up and participate
in a formal debate.

7 Health and Nutrition

Learning Objectives

IN THIS CHAPTER, YOU WILL LEARN TO . . .

1 Read in the field of health and nutrition

2 Understand and use key terms in health and nutrition

3 Skim and scan a reading to find specific information

4 Conduct Internet searches and evaluate online sources

5 Understand and apply the art of argumentation

6 Avoid faulty argumentation

7 Read, think, plan, and write an essay in response to the chapter essay assignment

Introduction to the Field of Health and Nutrition

When we think of health as a discipline, many subtopics come to mind: nutrition, exercise, weight loss, living a long life, and so on. Eating a healthy diet, exercising regularly, working in a stress-free environment, and keeping a positive outlook on life all contribute to our health. This chapter, however, focuses on the topic of nutrition, showing how food has a definitive effect on our health.

The readings included in this chapter cover a wide range of health- and nutrition-related issues such as banning fast-food ads on television in an attempt to curb America's obesity crisis; investigating the secrets of why Japanese women have the highest life expectancy on earth; and understanding the complexities involved in the debate on the benefits of genetically modified organisms (GMOs).

A careful examination of the articles in this chapter will enable you to understand how you can make smart nutrition choices to attain health and longevity.

CHAPTER ESSAY QUESTION

What are the secrets to living a long and healthy life?

Quick Free-Write! Take out a piece of paper, and write for ten minutes without stopping about what you already know about the theme of the chapter essay question.

As you read through this chapter, keep in mind this essay question and consider how you might incorporate multiple perspectives on the issue into your writing. Chapter essays will be due when your class completes the chapter.

Your Option: Once you have worked your way through the chapter readings, you are welcome to narrow down the topics covered and compose your own chapter essay question.

Previewing Health and Nutrition

Read the following questions and discuss them with your classmates. As you answer the questions, consider your personal experience and knowledge of nutrition in general.

1. How would you describe someone who maintains an *unhealthy lifestyle*? What are some of the characteristics of *healthy* people?

2. Do you know of someone who maintains an absolutely healthy lifestyle? Describe this person's health and nutrition habits. Do you consider yourself a health nut? Explain.

3. Do you have a positive or negative view of fast-food restaurants? Explain. What adjectives come to mind when you hear the term *fast food*?

4. Some health advocates believe that unhealthy foods should not be available in certain places. Do you think that our eating habits should be regulated by the government? For example, should vending machines containing soda and candy be banned from public schools?

5. Beyond maintaining a healthy diet, what can individuals do to live a long and fruitful life?

After discussing the preview questions with your classmates, post your responses to two of them on The Wall. Peruse The Wall and respond to at least two of your classmates' responses that grab your interest.

Key Terms in Health and Nutrition

Take a moment to think about the discipline of health and nutrition as you complete the following two exercises.

EXERCISE **7.1**   Brainstorming Vocabulary

Directions: What associated words come to mind when you think of the world of *nutrition*? Work with a partner and write down as many related words as you can think of in a period of five minutes. Add more lines to the cluster diagram if you need them.

EXERCISE **7.2**   Creating Original Sentences

Directions: Choose five of the words from your cluster list, and use them to write complete and meaningful sentences.

1. _____
2. _____
3. _____
4. _____
5. _____

A **synonym** is a word
used to express a similar meaning to another
word. An **antonym** is a
word that conveys the
opposite meaning of
another word.

One of the most effective ways to build your academic vocabulary is to study key terms that are connected thematically. When you take your 100-level credit-bearing content courses, it will be critical that you have a strong vocabulary base in the given academic subjects you are studying. For example, a student taking an introduction to health course should be able to apply such terms as *mortality*, *lifestyle*, and *genetic* in both spoken and written forms. As in previous chapters, you will also practice finding appropriate synonyms and antonyms for these terms and others.

EXERCISE 7.3   Discipline-specific Vocabulary: Fishing for Synonyms and Antonyms

Directions: Read the following ten (10) discipline-specific words in context culled from the readings in this chapter and shown in the context of the sentences in which they appeared. In the space provided after each sentence, write a synonym or antonym for the highlighted term, as directed.

Discipline-Specific Word Bank*

obesity	lifestyle	organisms
inactive	trend	starvation
moderate	risks	
mortality	genetic	

*The first time these discipline-specific words appear in the chapter, they are shown in bold green.

1. "A little less 'I'm Lovin' It' could put a significant dent in the problem of childhood **obesity**, suggests a new study in the U.S. that attempts to measure the effect of TV fast-food ads." (Selection 1, p. 264, para. 1)

   An antonym for *obesity* is _____.

2. "They also took steps to account for the possibility that some children may already have been overweight and **inactive** regardless of their TV-watching habits." (Selection 1, p. 265, para. 5)

   A synonym for *inactive* is _____.

3. "A lot of people consume fast food in **moderate** amounts and it doesn't harm their health." (Selection 1, p. 265, para. 7)

   An antonym for *moderate* is _____.

4. "Eriko Maeda could be forgiven for succumbing to occasional thoughts about her own **mortality**." (Selection 2, p. 269, para. 1)

   A synonym for *mortality* is _____.

5. "Maeda . . . attributes her impeccable health, and the prospect of easily outliving her male peers, to a **lifestyle** that would shame people at least 30 years her junior." (Selection 2, p. 270, para. 5)

   A synonym for *lifestyle* is _____.

6. "According to the health ministry, the upward **trend** in life expectancy is largely down to improvements in the diagnosis and treatment of cancer, cardiac disorders and strokes, Japan's three biggest killers." (Selection 2, p. 270, para. 7)

   A synonym for *trend* is _____.

7. "The health of Japan's seniors is not without **risks**." (Selection 2, p. 270, para. 9)

An antonym for *risks* is _____.

8. "Supporters envision an ever-expanding role for **genetic** engineering in food production." (Selection 3, p. 280, para. 2)

An antonym for *genetic* is _____.

9. "Genetically modified **organisms** (GMOs) represent arguably one of the most controversial topics in food science." (Selection 3, p. 280, para. 1)

A synonym for *organisms* is _____.

10. "[These benefits include] increased food security for countries struggling with food insecurity and **starvation** by increasing the income of small farmers, improving crop yields, and producing food crops with greater resistance to drought." (Selection 3, p. 281, para. 2)

An antonym for *starvation* is _____.

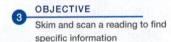

SUCCESS IN READING

OBJECTIVE
3 Skim and scan a reading to find specific information

Skimming and Scanning

Skimming and *scanning* are two reading techniques that enable you to read a passage quickly to determine the main idea and to locate specific bits and pieces of information without having to read the function words.

Skimming

When you **skim** a passage, your goal is to find and understand the main idea without reading every single word. As you skim, skip the function words such as prepositions (*to, into, on, at*), articles (*a, an, the*), and conjunctions (*so, but, yet, and*), and pay attention to the content words such as nouns (*government, policy, citizens, law*), verbs (*approve, penalize, allow*), adjectives (*mandatory, strict,* *legitimate*), and adverbs (*temporarily, permanently, momentarily*). You will notice that function words are not that important and that content words carry the meaning. When you skim, follow these steps to determine the main idea:

Steps for Skimming

1. *Skim the introductory paragraph quickly without reading every single word.* Usually, the main idea is found in the first paragraph. Sometimes, the main idea may not be in the first paragraph, in which case you will need to skim down a few more paragraphs. Keep in mind, also, that in some cases the main idea is offered in the final paragraph of a text.

2. *While skimming, pay attention to the content words such as nouns and verbs.* These will give you a clue as to the main idea of the entire passage.

3. *Go all the way to the last paragraph and read it quickly.* Most authors usually summarize the main ideas in the last paragraph.

4. *Keep in mind that skimming will help you get a general sense of what the reading is about.* It will not help you find specific details. For that purpose, you will need to use another reading technique called *scanning*.

Challenge Activity: Skimming

Use skimming as a reading technique to locate the key points and to get the gist of the following passage. Read it carefully, pay attention to content words, and underline the key points.

> You probably know the symptoms well. Your nose runs like a leaky faucet and turns beet red from constant wiping. Your head seems stuffed with cotton, and it feels like someone is playing bongo drums under your scalp. Between coughing and sneezing, you can't get the rest you need to relieve what feels like constant fatigue. The diagnosis? At least one of the more than 200 varieties of cold virus has invaded your body, and you have a cold that can last as long as two weeks.
>
> You're never alone if you have a case of the common cold—Americans will suffer a billion of them this year alone. Students miss more than 22 million school days every year battling the common cold.
>
> Contrary to popular belief, you can't catch a cold from being outside on a cold day without a coat or hat. Rather, the only way to catch a cold is to come into contact with a cold virus. Contact can be direct, such as when you hug or shake hands with someone who is carrying the virus; or indirect, such as when you touch an object like a keyboard or telephone contaminated with a cold virus. The next time you touch your nose or rub your eyes, you transfer these germs from your hands into your body. You can also catch a cold virus by inhaling virus-carrying droplets from a cough or sneeze of someone with a cold.

—From *Nutrition and You*, by Joan Salge Blake, 3rd edition, p. 262

Scanning

Unlike skimming, which is used to find the main idea, **scanning** is used to find specific details. Try to focus on the content words such as nouns, verbs, and adjectives to find the specific bits and pieces of information you need to answer a question about the passage. Take the following steps to scan a passage.

Steps for Scanning

1. *First, read the title and subtitle of the passage.* Then read the sections and subheadings, if any, to focus your search for specific details.
2. *As you scan the passage, constantly ask yourself questions you need to answer.* For example, ask *who* if you are looking for names, *where* if you need to know the place where something happened such as a meeting or an accident, *what* if you want to know what actually happened, *when* if your focus is the time of an event or an incident, and *why* if you are looking for reasons.
3. *Keep scanning and look for specific words that answer your questions.*
4. *When you find the information you are looking for, stop scanning and read the surrounding text carefully to understand the context better and ensure you have identified the correct data.*

The following questions will help you scan a passage to find specific information with relative ease and success. Keep in mind that you can create your own questions and that the type of questions you create will depend on the material and information you are looking for, so some of the questions below may not be relevant to all the readings in this chapter.

Questions to Ask When Scanning

1. *Why* did something (an event, incident, accident, natural calamity) happen?
2. *How* does something (passing an exam, writing a good essay) happen?
3. *How* much time or money is involved in this process?
4. *Which* of the two options/topics/decisions is more appropriate?
5. *When* does something (a semester, a restaurant opening, a political event) happen?
6. *How* often does something (an event, a publication, a grant or scholarship, an award) happen?
7. *Where* did/does this (an important political meeting, an international event, a violent crime) happen?
8. *Who* did/does this (a cook, a teaching assistant, director of a foundation, an author, a university professor)?

Challenge Activity: Scanning

Now use scanning as a reading technique to look for supporting details. Scan the following passage for the answers to the questions listed below. Once again, skip the function words such as the articles, prepositions, and conjunctions, and focus on the content words such as nouns, verbs, adjectives, and adverbs.

1. What percentage of your daily calorie intake should come from added sugar, according to the DRI?

2. Which groups of people would particularly benefit from reducing the amount of added sugars in their diet?

_____

3. Why is eating large amounts of food with added sugars, such as soda, a bad choice?

_____

_____

The DRI recommends that added sugars make up no more than 25 percent of your daily calories, but the Dietary Guidelines for Americans, 2010 suggest that no more than 5 to 15 percent of your daily calories come from a combination of added sugars and solid fats. Americans, on average, consume 16 percent of their daily calories from added sugars alone! Many Americans, especially women, sedentary individuals, and older adults who have lower daily calorie needs, would benefit from reducing the amount of added sugars in their diet. These individuals need to make sure that they are getting a substantial amount of nutrition from each bite of food. Eating excess amounts of food with added sugars, such as soda, can displace more nutritious food choices, such as skim milk, in the diet.

—From *Nutrition and You*, by Joan Salge Blake, 3rd edition, p. 126

READING

Selection 1

Newspaper Article

Study: Ban on Fast-Food TV Ads May Cut Obesity

Pre-Reading Questions

Before reading the article, discuss the following questions in small groups and share your answers with your classmates.

1. In your opinion, do you think your eating habits are influenced by TV ads for fast food? If yes, can you think of a TV ad that prompted you to buy the food product?

2. Do you think young children below the age of ten beg their parents to purchase food items that they see on TV commercials? Discuss how parents can educate their young children about the consequences of unhealthy eating.

3. Some people argue that the government is being irresponsible by allowing fast-food companies to advertise their unhealthy products on TV. In your opinion, should the government ban fast-food TV ads?

Eye on Vocabulary

Skim through the reading and look for the following key vocabulary terms in bold. Working with a partner, examine the words in context and try to guess the meaning of each. Then look up the words in a dictionary. Keep in mind that many words have multiple meanings. Write the definition that best fits the word's context in the article.

Word	Your definition	Dictionary definition
1. deduction (n.)		
2. link (n.)		
3. implications (n.)		
4. pondering (v.)		

Study: Ban on Fast-Food TV Ads May Cut Obesity

USA Today, **November 20, 2008**

1   ATLANTA (AP)—A little less "I'm Lovin' It" could put a significant dent in the problem of childhood obesity, suggests a new study in the U.S. that attempts to measure the effect of TV fast-food ads. A ban on such commercials would reduce the number of obese young children by 18%, and the number of obese older kids by 14%, researchers found. They also suggested that ending an advertising expense tax **deduction** for fast-food restaurants could mean a slight reduction in childhood obesity.

2   Some experts say it's the first national study to show fast-food TV commercials have such a large effect on childhood obesity. A 2006 Institute of Medicine report suggested a **link**, but concluded proof was lacking. "Our study provides evidence of that link," said study co-author Michael Grossman, an economics professor at City University of New York.

3   The study has important **implications** for the effectiveness of regulating TV advertising, said Lisa Powell, a researcher at the University of Illinois at Chicago's Institute for Health Research and Policy. She was not involved in the research but was familiar with it. The percentage of US children who are overweight or obese rose steadily from the 1980s until recently, when it leveled off. About a third of American kids are overweight or obese, according to US Centers for Disease Control and Prevention estimates.

4   The causes of childhood obesity are complicated, but for years researchers have been **pondering** the effects of TV advertising. Powell, for example, found fast-food commercials account for as much as 23% of the food-related ads kids see on TV. Others have estimated children see fast-food commercials tens of thousands of times a year. The new study is based in part on several years of government survey data from the late 1990s that involved in-person interviews with thousands of US families.

5   The researchers also looked at information about local stations in the 75 largest TV markets, including locally seen fast-food commercials and the size of viewing audiences. The researchers used a statistical test that presumes TV ads lead to obesity but made calculations to address other influences such as income and the number of nearby fast-food restaurants. They also took steps to account for the possibility that some children may already have been overweight and **inactive** regardless of their TV-watching habits.

6   The study is being published this month in the *Journal of Law & Economics*. The authors, funded by a federal grant, included Grossman and researchers from Lehigh University and Georgia State University. The authors stopped short of advocating an advertising ban or eliminating the advertising tax deduction.

7   Grossman said it is possible that some families benefit from advertising by finding out what restaurants are nearby and what they're serving. "A lot of people consume fast food in **moderate** amounts and it doesn't harm their health," he said.

8   McDonald's Corp., the giant fast-food chain responsible for the widely seen "I'm Lovin' It" ad campaign, referred questions about the study to the National Council of Chain Restaurants. Officials with that organization could not be reached Wednesday evening.

Thinking about the Reading

After doing a close reading of the article, write your answers to the following questions. You may be asked to discuss your answers with your classmates.

1. The article begins with the claim that a ban on fast-food TV ads could reduce the rate of obesity among young children by 18 percent. Do you believe that fast-food TV commercials actually cause young children to consume more unhealthy food? Why, or why not?

   _____

   _____

2. In paragraph 5, Michael Grossman claims that his study provides evidence of a link between fast-food TV commercials and childhood obesity. In your opinion, what kind of evidence linking fast-food commercials and childhood obesity would be credible? Be specific.

   _____

   _____

3. Other than the fast-food commercials, what else could account for childhood obesity? Give specific reasons to support your answer.

   _____

   _____

Reading Comprehension Check

_____ 1. What is the topic of the article?

    a. advertising targeted at children

    b. fast-food and TV advertising

    c. TV advertising

    d. McDonald's TV ads

_____ 2. What do some experts suggest about childhood obesity in the second paragraph?

    a. Banning fast-food TV ads would dramatically reduce the obesity rate among older and younger children.

    b. A ban on fast-food TV ads would result in lower obesity rates for older children, but not for younger ones.

    c. There is no relationship between fast-food TV ads and childhood obesity.

    d. Research has indicated there is a link between fast food TV ads and obesity but no conclusive proof.

_____ 3. In the sentence beginning "The study has important **implications** for the effectiveness of regulating TV advertising said Lisa Powell, a researcher at the University of Illinois at Chicago's Institute for Health Research and Policy" (paragraph 3), the word _implications_ could be replaced by

    a. possible truths.   c. suggested possibilities.

    b. presumptions.   d. proofs.

_____ 4. According to the article, what percentage of American kids are overweight or obese?

    a. 14 percent   c. 50 percent

    b. 33 percent   d. 75 percent

_____ 5. The main idea of the article is that

    a. fast-food TV advertising is the sole cause of childhood obesity.

    b. the majority of American children eat unhealthy food.

    c. a study suggests that fast-food TV advertising has a significant effect on childhood obesity rates.

    d. causes of childhood obesity are complicated.

_____ 6. Besides fast-food TV advertising, the study researchers also looked at other possible factors related to childhood obesity such as _____.

    a. family income and the proximity of fast-food restaurants

    b. the location of fast-food restaurants and parental eating habits

    c. peer pressure and family income

    d. cigarette smoking and sugar consumption

_____ 7. Michael Grossman, one of the study's coauthors, believes which of the following statements?

    a. There should be an absolute ban on fast-food TV advertising.

    b. Many families consume fast food in moderate amounts.

c. Most families benefit from fast-food ads.

d. There is still no absolute proof of a link between fast-food commercials and childhood obesity.

_____ **8.** In the sentence, "They also took steps **to account for** the possibility that some children may already have been overweight and inactive regardless of their TV-watching habits," the expression *to account for* could be replaced by

a. take responsibility for.

b. do the math.

c. find an explanation for.

d. justify.

_____ **9.** In the sentence, "The authors **stopped short** of advocating an advertising ban or eliminating the advertising tax deduction," the expression *stopped short* means

a. did not complete their argument.

b. did not go so far as to say.

c. provided limited information about.

d. gave limited support to.

_____ **10.** What is the main point of the last paragraph?

a. McDonald's Corp. is pleased by the findings of the study.

b. McDonald's Corp. is protesting the results of the study.

c. Neither McDonald's Corp. nor the National Council of Chain Restaurants commented on the study.

d. Only the National Council of Chain Restaurants refused to comment.

THEMATIC LINKS

If you want to learn more about the topic of fast food and obesity, type the following words into your browser and explore the two sites that come up:

1. Cheap Food Blamed for America's Obesity Crisis NBC News

2. See More, Eat More: The Geography Of Fast Food

Writing Without BOUNDARIES

There Are No Checkpoints!

"The food you eat can be either the safest and most powerful form of medicine or the slowest form of poison."

—Ann Wigmore

Read the quote above and respond. Write in your notebook for ten minutes without stopping. For this activity, it is important that you focus on ideas, not words. In other words, this will be an exercise in focusing on content and not getting hung up on word choice and grammar errors. You may wish to read what you have written out loud in front of your classmates and instructor.

READING

Selection 2

Newspaper Article

Japan's Women Toast Their Own Health as Life Expectancy Rises Again

Pre-Reading Questions

Answer the following questions before exploring the text:

1. How can we explain the fact that women live longer than men in every country of the world? What contributes to women's longevity?

   _____

   _____

2. What factors may explain why Japanese women have the highest life expectancy on earth?

   _____

   _____

3. In which part of the world do you think people have the lowest life expectancies? What factors might contribute to their shorter life spans?

   _____

   _____

Eye on Vocabulary

Working with a partner, scan the reading and find the following key vocabulary terms in bold. Examine the words in context and try to guess the meaning of each. Keep in mind that many words have multiple meanings. Write the definition that best fits the word's context in the article.

Word	Your definition	Dictionary definition
1. factor (n.)		
2. attribute (v.)		
3. impeccable (adj.)		
4. shrugs off (v.)		

Japan's Women Toast Their Own Health as Life Expectancy Rises Again

by Justin McCurry

www.theguardian.com, Sunday 1 August 2010 10.09 EDT

Part 1

Tokyo: Now living to an average of 86.4, Japanese women say longevity down to a fishy diet, exercise and sleep. And sake.

Japanese women have enjoyed the longest life expectancy in the world for more than two decades.

1   Eriko Maeda could be forgiven for succumbing to occasional thoughts about her own **mortality**. But even as she prepares to turn 70, she has every reason to expect she'll be around for at least another two decades. Aside from an exemplary low-fat diet and regular exercise, she has one other important **factor** on her side in the longevity stakes: her nationality.

2   Japanese women have enjoyed the longest life expectancy in the world for a quarter of a century, according to government figures. In 2009,

they could expect to live, on average, a record 86.4 years—up almost five months from the previous year—followed by women in Hong Kong and France. Japanese men, meanwhile, added almost four months to their life expectancy to 79.5 years, although they fell from fourth to fifth place in the global rankings behind Qatar, Hong Kong, Iceland and Switzerland.

3   Experts **attribute** Japan's extraordinary longevity statistics to a traditional diet of fish, rice and simmered vegetables, easy access to health care and a comparatively high standard of living in old age.

4   If Maeda is typical, then Japanese women will continue to outlive the rest of us. "I never eat meat and avoid fried food . . . with the occasional exception," she says as she nods, a little guiltily, at her lunch of rice and a pair of tempura prawns. "I eat lots of oily fish, like mackerel and sardines, I've never smoked and I hardly ever drink," she adds between mouthfuls at a restaurant in the elderly shopping and entertainment neighbourhood of Sugamo, in Tokyo.

5   Diet aside, Maeda, who lives with her son and his family, attributes her **impeccable** health, and the prospect of easily outliving her male peers, to a **lifestyle** that would shame people at least 30 years her junior. "I get up at 4:30, do the washing and the rest of the housework," she says. "I make a Japanese-style dinner for me and usually something western for my son's family, and I'm in bed well before 9 pm."

HALFWAY ROAD STOP

Get into a small group and answer the two questions that follow.

1. What have you learned from the article so far?

2. Try to predict what may be coming in the second half of the article.

Part 2

6   In contrast, Sachiko Yasuhara is almost blasé about her diet and confesses to being a regular sake drinker. Yet at 81, she is the picture of health as she **shrugs off** Tokyo's stifling humidity and sips—of all things— a Coke outside McDonald's. "I eat just about anything, but I draw the line at western food," she says, adding that regular exercise comes in the form of outings with friends in Sugamo.

7   According to the health ministry, the upward **trend** in life expectancy is largely down to improvements in the diagnosis and treatment of cancer, cardiac disorders and strokes, Japan's three biggest killers.

8   Takao Suzuki, general director of the National Institute of Geriatrics and Gerontology in Nagoya, believes that Japan's almost perfect literacy rate is also a factor. "Older people are able to consume a huge amount of health and lifestyle advice in the media," he says. "Although women live longer, they experience longer periods of ill-health than men before they die because they lose bone and muscle strength more easily than men. If the government addresses that problem, Japanese women will live even longer."

9   The health of Japan's seniors is not without **risks**. If left unaddressed, the greying of the population combined with the low birth rate will lead to a pension crisis, ballooning healthcare costs and a labour shortage that could endanger Japan's economic status.

10   "I can see why people like me might be a problem in the future," Yasuhara says. "Look around you; there are too many old people in Japan. We need more children."

Thinking about the Reading

After doing a close reading of the article, write your answers to the following questions. You may be asked to discuss your answers with your classmates.

1. How does Eriko Maeda describe her diet? How similar are her daily eating habits to yours?

   _____

   _____

2. How do Sachiko Yasuhara's daily habits contrast with Ms. Maeda's? Given Ms. Yasuhara's lifestyle, does it surprise you that she has lived so long? Explain.

   _____

   _____

3. What potential negative effects of Japan's high life expectancy are mentioned in the article?

   _____

   _____

   _____

Reading Comprehension Check

_____ 1. Experts attribute Japan's high life expectancy to all of the following factors except

    a. access to good health care.
    b. a tradition of heavy exercise.
    c. a diet rich in fish and simmered vegetables.
    d. a high standard of living.

_____ 2. For how long have Japanese women had the highest life expectancy in the world?

    a. since 2009
    b. forever
    c. only in the last few years
    d. about twenty-five years

_____ 3. What point does Takao Suzuki, general director of the National Institute of Geriatrics and Gerontology in Nagoya, make about Japan's high life expectancy?

    a. Diet is the key factor.
    b. Due to an almost perfect literacy rate, Japanese people are well-informed about new health and lifestyle information.

c. Not all Japanese people maintain a healthy diet.

d. You cannot always trust information coming from the media.

_____ 4. The main idea of the reading is that

a. a healthy lifestyle and other key factors result in Japanese women having the world's highest life expectancy.

b. Japanese women live longer than Japanese men even though they experience more end of life illness.

c. Ms. Maeda eats very healthy food and keeps fit.

d. the health of Japan's seniors is not without risks.

_____ 5. We can infer from the reading that

a. the author of the article is Japanese.

b. the author appreciates Japan's healthy diet.

c. some Japanese are worried about their aging population.

d. all Japanese women maintain a healthy lifestyle.

_____ 6. Which of the following statements about the content of this reading selection is *true*?

a. If older people in Japan continue to live longer, a pension crisis or a labor shortage might result.

b. Elderly Japanese people are not influenced by the latest trends in health and well being.

c. Older Japanese women rarely exercise, living an essentially sedentary lifestyle.

d. Sachiko Yasuhara is healthy and fit at 81 years old, yet she eats McDonald's hamburgers regularly.

_____ 7. In paragraph 5, what does McCurry mean when he says that Maeda's lifestyle "would shame people at least 30 years her junior"?

a. People younger than Maeda would be embarrassed to get up early, work hard, and go to bed early.

b. People younger than Maeda work a lot harder and stay up a lot later than she does, and they would think that her minimal effort and going to bed early is shameful.

c. People younger than Maeda would be embarrassed to get up early, work hard, and go to bed early.

d. People younger than Maeda probably believe that they work hard, but the amount of work she does each day thoroughly surpasses them.

_____ 8. According to the reading, how does Japan's high literacy rate contribute to long life expectancy?

a. Literacy contributes to higher wages, which means that the Japanese can spend more on health care and medications.

b. The relaxation and enjoyment that the Japanese gain from reading for pleasure relieves harmful stress before it can impact their health and longevity.

c. A high literacy rate means that Japanese people are able to read health and lifestyle advice in the media, thus keeping up with trends and new information that can help them live healthier lives.

d. A high literacy rate means that the Japanese population can avoid accidental injury and exposure to dangerous chemicals by being able to read warning signs and safety precautions.

_____ 9. Which of the following is *not* one of Japan's three most fatal diseases?

    a. epilepsy   c. stroke

    b. cancer   d. cardiac disorders

_____ 10. Although McCurry does not define the word *sake*, we can infer that it means

    a. a caffeinated soft drink.

    b. an alcoholic drink.

    c. green tea.

    d. a brand of bottled water.

THEMATIC LINKS

Directions: If you want to learn more about the topic of longevity and global life expectancy, type the following words into your browser and explore the two sites that come up:

1. Mediterranean Diet Boosts Lifespan, Cuts Chronic Disease: Harvard

2. Longevity on Beyond 100 National Geographic

READING SKILL FOCUS

Researching and Evaluating Internet Sources

OBJECTIVE

4

Conduct Internet searches and evaluate online sources

While you might have a lot of experience working with various Internet search engines and navigating the Web, you may not have as much experience in doing academic research online and distinguishing between credible and less credible sources. The ability to evaluate Web sources is a critical skill as anyone can publish on the Internet, and you want to ensure that the source information you are working with is accurate and reliable. Unlike most print sources such as books and journals where a lot of filtering takes place—peer review or editing, for example—the information you get from many Internet resources is unfiltered.

The guidelines that follow provide a starting point for doing Internet research and evaluating Web sites.

Guidelines for Internet Research

Before you start an Internet search, consider the following:

1. **What type of site would be most likely to provide the information you are looking for?** In most cases, you can categorize Web site types by examining the last three letters in the URL. Sites ending in *.edu* or *.gov* are probably quite reliable and can provide authoritative information on the topic you are researching. Sites ending in *.biz* or *.com* are designed to sell products and may provide a one-sided perspective on a topic.

URL Abbreviation	Website Category
.biz	business organizations
.com	commercial products or commercially sponsored sites
.edu	educational or research material
.gov	government resources
.int	international organizations
.mil	U.S. Department of Defense
.name	personal use
.net	networks
.org	nonprofit organizations

2. **What type of information are you looking for?** If you are writing an essay focusing on the relationship between obesity and diabetes in children, make sure your search terms are specific to this narrow topic. If you simply do a search on "obesity" or "diabetes," you will receive thousands of Web results that have nothing to do with your essay topic. Don't waste your time! Search efficiently.

3. **Do not simply click on the first set of results that appear on your screen.** Accepting whatever sources come your way is lazy research. Take the time to carefully read the title and description of your Web results. Scroll down and go to the next page of results until you find Web sites that seem relevant to your particular research needs.

Evaluating Web Sources

Use the following guidelines to aid you in assessing the authority, accuracy, currency, purpose, audience for, and coverage provided by the sites you review as possible sources. We will investigate source quality by applying these guidelines to the second reading of this chapter, "Japan's Women Toast Themselves as Life Expectancy Rises Again," on page 269.

Guidelines for Evaluating Web Sites

1. **Authority:** Before investing your time and conducting research on a given Web site, you should first get a clear sense of who is the author, or sponsor, of the Web site. Here are some useful questions to ask:
   - Who is the author or producer of the document?
   - Is the author or producer an expert on the subject?
   - Is there a link to information about the author or the sponsor?
   - If the page includes neither a signature nor indicates a sponsor, is there any other way to determine its origin?

   The author of "Japan's Women Toast Themselves as Life Expectancy Rises Again," on page 269 is Justin McCurry, and the article was published on the Web site of *The Guardian*, a British newspaper that won a Pulitzer Prize for public service stories in 2014 for reporting on Edward Snowden's leaks of national security surveillance activities. There are links to both the author (*The Guardian*'s Tokyo correspondent, who has a master's in Japanese studies and reports for many well-known publications) and the publisher, so it is safe to say that this is an authoritative source.

2. **Accuracy:** When you are doing online research, you want to read carefully and think critically about the information on your screen. Remember: Just because it's there doesn't mean it's true! Ask the following questions to help you assess the accuracy of a site:
   - Does the information seem reliable or is it full of obvious errors?
   - Is there a way to verify the information?
   - Can you detect political, ideological, or religious bias?
   - How does the source of the information bear on the accuracy of the material presented (e.g., a cigarette company lobbying group would most likely play down the negative effects of secondhand smoke)?

   Consider the above set of questions as you reread the first three paragraphs of "Japan's Women Toast Themselves as Life Expectancy Rises Again,". Note that the article is professionally written with no errors, and the author lays out a set of logically ordered facts and statistics that can be researched and confirmed. There is no hint of bias, and the author is an expert in Japanese affairs, so it is fair to assume that the information is accurate.

3. **Currency:** Much of what you read online is not up-to-date information. It is important to verify that the source of the information you are using as supporting details is not outdated. Some useful questions to ask are the following:
   - Is there a date for when the information was first published and/or written?
   - Is there a date for when the information was placed on the Web?
   - Is there a date for when the information was last revised?
   - How current are the links? Have some expired or moved?

   The article was published August 1, 2010, which is relatively recent, and the links are relevant, current, and functional. You might ask yourself, if this reporting was done seven or eight years ago, is it still relevant today? In the case of the topic in focus here—Japanese women living longer—it most likely still is. However, if the topic were about the U.S. government's goal of building a new space station within two years, you might want to search for more up-to-date information.

4. **Purpose:** Try to get a sense of the author's purpose for writing the article or creating the Web page. Is it the author's purpose to do one of the following:

- Inform others of new research
- Summarize the current status of a research interest
- Advocate a particular position on the subject
- Stimulate further discussion on the topic
- Publicize a product
- Other

   Let's consider the purpose of the article on Japanese women. Clearly, the author is informing readers of a recent phenomenon and offering information to help explain the possible reasons Japanese women are living longer lives. As the author is mostly stating facts on the topic, we cannot deduce that he is advocating a particular position on the subject.

5. **Audience:** As you review a Web site, pay attention to who the intended audience is for the information being offered. Knowing who the intended audience is will give you a better sense of whether the Web site suits your research needs. Is the intended audience one of the following:

- Beginners
- Consumers
- Other
- Experts
- Professionals

   In trying to understand the intended audience of a reading, consider the market for the source. *The Guardian* is a high-level British newspaper, written for a general audience of educated readers. Unlike a trade publication or academic source, it is not intended for a narrow audience of experts or professionals in a specific area.

6. **Coverage:** Very often you will find information on a Web site that is either too basic for your research needs or too technical for you to understand. If the coverage of your research topic does not work for you, choose another site. Here are some questions to investigate:

- Does the information provided fully cover what you need to know?
- Is the information too simple?
- Is the information too technical or complicated?
- Are there links to similar pages that will provide more information?

   Clearly, if you were writing an essay on the secrets of longevity, or more specifically on the health status of Japanese women, this article could prove to be a useful source. Would the information in this article fully cover your research needs? Well, of course not! You would need to work with multiple sources to get a wider range of information on your research subject.

EXERCISE **7.4** Evaluating Web Site Information

Directions: Imagine you are doing online research for an essay on *the benefits of vegetarianism*. With a partner, evaluate the credibility and usefulness of the information excerpted from the following three Web sites by visiting each site and asking and answering the questions listed in the Guidelines for Evaluating Web Sites.

A. URL: http://www.brown.edu/Student_Services/Health_Services/Health_Education/nutrition_&_eating_concerns/being_a_vegetarian.php

> Broadly defined, a vegetarian is a person who does not eat meat, poultry, and fish. Vegetarians eat mainly fruit, vegetables, legumes, grains, seeds, and nuts. Many vegetarians eat eggs and/or dairy products but avoid hidden animal products such as beef and chicken stocks, lard, and gelatin.
>
> The American Dietetic Association (ADA) classifies vegetarians more specifically in the following ways:
>
> - *Vegans or total vegetarians* exclude all animal products (e.g. meat, poultry, fish, eggs, milk, cheese, and other dairy products). Many vegans also do not eat honey.
> - *Lacto vegetarians* exclude meat, poultry, fish, and eggs but include dairy products.
> - *Lacto-ovo vegetarians* exclude meat, poultry, and fish but include dairy products and eggs. Most vegetarians in the United States are lacto-ovo vegetarians.

1. Comment on the credibility and reliability of the information given:

_____

_____

2. How could you make use of this source information in your essay?

_____

_____

B. URL: www.herheartlandsoul.com/why-im-no-longer-a-vegetarian/

Why I'm No Longer a Vegetarian

> I don't think I've ever been so nervous to write a post before. After two years of being a vegetarian (and loving it!), I recently introduced chicken and turkey back into my life. It was something I never thought I would do but something I feel absolutely certain I needed to do.
>
> The reason I'm sharing this with you guys is because I always want to be 100% honest on here. I want you to know whether I'm writing about my life or reviewing a product I am always going to be real with you guys. This blog is about my journey through life, so it only feels right I document a major roadblock along the way.

3. Comment on the credibility and reliability of the information given:

    _____

    _____

    _____

4. How could you make use of this source information in your essay?

    _____

    _____

C. **URL:** www.wholefoodsmarket.com/healthy-eating/special-diets/vegetarian

    Vegetarian Shopping at Whole Foods Market

    The produce aisle and bulk bins are a wonderland for vegetarian shoppers. In fact, in just those two sections of the store, you can find almost everything you need to follow the Four Pillars of Healthy Eating. From leafy greens, bright peppers and colorful root vegetables to whole grains, nuts and dried beans, we have almost all you need to put together a phytonutrient-rich, plant-strong diet.

    Have questions about how to put together the healthiest vegetarian diet? Many of our stores have Healthy Eating Specialists, who can suggest healthy recipes, help with good-for-you meal plans, and more. And you can always find products marked with our Health Starts Here® logo in any store. That's our guide to—and your guarantee of—the healthiest food choices.

5. Comment on the credibility and reliability of the information given:

    _____

    _____

6. How could you make use of this source information in your essay?

    _____

    _____

    _____

Practicing the Skill

Imagine you are writing an essay on the topic "The Secret to Living to 100" and you would like to include some relevant source information from the Internet. Working with a search engine, do a search and evaluate three Web site sources using a Website Evaluation Chart like the one shown on the next page.

> **Web site Evaluation Chart (Check box for "Yes" responses)**
>
> ☐ 1. **Authority:** Is the author or sponsor a reliable source?
>   Explain: _____
>
> ☐ 2. **Accuracy:** Does the information seem reliable/credible?
>   Explain: _____
>
> ☐ 3. **Currency:** Is the information up to date?
>   Explain: _____
>
> ☐ 4. **Purpose/Audience:** Is the author's purpose and intended audience
>   clear to you?
>   Explain: _____
>
> ☐ 5. **Coverage:** Is the information suited to your research needs (not too
>   simple/too complicated)?
>   Explain: _____

READING

Selection 3

Textbook Excerpt

Genetically Modified **Organisms:** *A Blessing or a Curse?*

Pre-Reading Questions

Answer the following questions before exploring the text:

1. How has technology changed the way we eat? How does our daily eating routine differ from that of Americans who lived a hundred years ago?

_____

_____

2. Some vegetarians argue that the habit of eating meat is both a health risk and an environmental disaster. What is your position on the potential consequences of meat production and the consumption of meat?

_____

_____

3. The genetic production of food holds the promise of increasing the food supply and feeding the world's hungry. What might be some of the risks of genetically modified organisms (GMOs)?

_____

_____

4. The way we eat has changed dramatically in the last one hundred years. Refrigerated foods, microwave ovens, and genetically modified foods are just a few examples. Can you make a few predictions about how the way we eat will be different a hundred years from now?

_____

_____

Genetically Modified Organisms: A Blessing or a Curse?

Janice Thompson and Melinda Manore

1   Genetically modified organisms (GMOs) represent arguably one of the most controversial topics in food science. GMOs are created through **genetic** engineering, a process in which foreign genes are spliced into a non-related species, creating an entirely new (transgenic) organism. Many GMOs are, of course, animal and plant foods. The terms for those foods—biotech foods, gene foods, and frankenfoods—suggest divergent views of their potential benefits and **risks** to the environment and to human health.

2   Supporters envision an ever-expanding role for genetic engineering in food production. They identify numerous potential benefits resulting from the application of this technology. These benefits include:

- Enhanced taste and nutritional quality of food.
- Crops that grow faster, have higher yields, can be grown in inhospitable soils, and have increased resistance to pests, diseases, herbicides and spoilage.
- Increased production of high-quality meat, eggs, and milk.
- Improved animal health due to increased disease resistance and overall hardiness.
- Environmentally responsible outcomes such as a reduction in use of an insecticide called Bt; use of less harmful pesticides; conservation of water due largely to the development of drought-tolerant species of corn; reduced use of energy and emission of greenhouse gases

because of reduced need for ploughing and pesticide spraying; and conservation of soil due to higher productivity.

- Increased food security for countries struggling with food insecurity and **starvation** by increasing the income of small farmers, improving crop yields, and producing food crops with greater resistance to drought.

3   Despite these claims, there is significant opposition to genetic engineering. Detractors cite a wide range of concerns related to environmental hazards, human health risks, and economic instability. These include the following:

- Genes have been transferred to non-target species through cross-pollination, resulting in the spread of undesirable plants, including super-weeds that tolerate conventional herbicides. Indeed, from 1996 to 2011, despite the decline in the use of the insecticide Bt, the rapid spread of herbicide-resistant super-weeds in the United States led to an overall 7% increase in pesticide use. In short, the magnitude of the increase in the use of herbicides on these superweeds has dwarfed the more modest reductions in insecticide use, and the problem is estimated to increase dramatically in the future.
- Genes have been transferred from non-crop foods to crops intended for food, tainting them with non-food-grade ingredients. This was demonstrated when traces of a type of maize that was approved for use only in animal feed appeared in food products in the United States.
- Undesirable genes could be transferred from genetically modified foods to cells of the body or to the gastrointestinal flora, adversely affecting human health. For example, if antibiotic-resistant genes were transferred, susceptibility to infectious disease could increase.
- There is a potential for significant loss of biodiversity. Not only could GMOs, superweeds and increased use of herbicides decimate populations of beneficial insects, microorganisms, and native plants and animals, but also the diversity of food crops in cultivation could be reduced.
- Monopolization and privatization of farming has reduced economic opportunity. For example, the seed industry has become increasingly controlled by just three bioengineering firms that have bought up small, local seed companies, then increased prices to farmers for their genetically engineered seed. At the same time, the firms require farmers to sign contracts promising that they will not save the seeds from their future crops. Critics say that monopoly control of genetically modified, non-renewable seed has had tragic consequences. By one estimate, a quarter million farmers have taken their lives because of debt induced by the high cost of non-renewable genetically engineered seed.

4   Other concerns commonly cited include the potential for the creation of new biological weapons, and an increased risk for bioterrorism as well as the development of new diseases that can attack plants, animals and humans. Many argue that, at the very least, all genetically modified foods should be labeled so that consumers know what they are purchasing. As of 2012, the US Food and Drug Administration did not require that all genetically engineered foods be identified as such; however, nationwide polls over the past several years have continually shown that more than 90% of Americans support labeling of GMO foods.

5   Because GMOs and genetically modified foods have been available only since 1996, we do not as yet have any long-term human health or environmental impact studies of genetically engineered foods or crops. It may thus be many years before we begin to understand their impact in the world.

—From Thompson and Manore, *Nutrition: An Applied Approach*, 4e

Thinking about the Reading

After doing a close reading of the article, write your answers to the following questions. You may be asked to discuss your answers with your classmates.

1. After reading this article, and based on your prior knowledge of GMOs, do you support their production inside the United States and around the world? Explain.

   _____

   _____

2. Should genetically modified foods be clearly labeled for consumers? What are some pro and con arguments for identifying them?

   _____

   _____

   _____

3. According to the article, how has the monopolization and privatization of farming reduced economic opportunity?

   _____

   _____

   _____

   _____

Reading Comprehension Check

_____ 1. What is the author's purpose for writing this article?

   a. to convince readers not to consume genetically modified foods
   b. to show both sides of a controversial issue
   c. to demonstrate the benefits of producing a larger food supply through genetic engineering
   d. to entertain

_____ 2. What is the author's tone?

   a. optimistic and thoughtful
   b. comical and pessimistic

c. factual and informative

d. excited and enthusiastic

_____ **3.** What is the main idea of the reading?

    a. Monopolization and privatization of farming have reduced economic opportunity.

    b. Changing technology affects our lives in both positive and negative ways.

    c. Inflation has caused a surplus of farm produce.

    d. While GMOs enhance food production, many fear they pose a host of serious risks.

_____ **4.** Which of the following was not mentioned as a potential negative consequence of GMOs?

    a. increased prices for food

    b. reduced economic opportunity

    c. the tainting of food crops with genes from nonfood crops

    d. a loss of biodiversity

_____ **5.** It can be inferred from the passage that most small-time farmers would

    a. have a favorable view of GMOs.

    b. simply choose not to get involved with GMOs.

    c. take a balanced view of the benefits and shortcomings of GMOs.

    d. feel threatened by GMOs.

_____ **6.** Which of the following statements about the content of this reading selection is _true_?

    a. Genetically modified foods have been available since the 1950s.

    b. Opponents of genetically modified foods fear that they present the possibility for the creation of new biological weapons.

    c. Fewer than 10% of Americans support the labeling of genetically modified foods.

    d. GMOs are sometimes referred to as _vampire foods_ because they suck the life out of a food's flavor.

_____ **7.** Which of the following is _not_ a potential benefit of genetic engineering in food technology, according to supporters?

    a. monopolization of farming

    b. increased disease resistance in animals

    c. food of better nutritional quality

    d. crops that can resist pests

_____ **8.** According to opponents of genetically engineered foods, which of the following is one of its disadvantages?

    a. Farmers might begin growing genetically modified marijuana and opium to sell on the black market, increasing drug-related crime.

    b. The popularity of genetically modified foods could cause supermarkets to run out of stock on certain items, driving up prices and causing food shortages.

    c. The transference of undesirable genes from genetically modified foods to human cells could endanger human health.

    d. World hunger will increase because only wealthy nations will be able to afford to import genetically modified foods.

9. According to the reading, what is the reason for the argument that all genetically modified foods should be labeled?

    a. Sellers will know how much to charge for a given food item.

    b. Consumers will know what kind of food they are buying.

    c. Retailers can choose to opt out of selling genetically modified foods.

    d. The Food and Drug Administration can use bar codes to track a food's progress through the marketplace.

10. In paragraph 3, we can infer that the term *superweed* means

    a. a weed that is hard to kill with chemical herbicides.

    b. a weed that is much larger than most weeds.

    c. a weed that is edible.

    d. a weed that attracts insects.

THEMATIC LINKS

Directions: If you want to learn more about the topic of GMOs, type the following words into your browser and explore the two sites that come up:

1. GMOs of the Future Discover

2. GMO Labeling Battle Is Heating Up National Geographic

Think to Write: Summary/Response

Now that you have read the three readings on health and nutrition in this chapter, think about which of the three is most interesting to you. Write a one-paragraph summary and one-paragraph response of this reading and post it to The Wall. Try to include at least three discipline-specific words in your writing. Once you have posted, respond to at least two of your classmates' postings.

It's SHOWTIME!

Watching a video clip related to the chapter content can be an enriching experience. Go online and find a video link with a topic that ties into one of the chapter readings (maximum length = ten minutes). After viewing the video clip, write a half-page summary of the video's key points. Post your personal reaction to the ideas in the clip (between 150 and 400 words) on The Wall.

WRITING SKILL FOCUS

OBJECTIVE
Understand and apply the art of argumentation

The Art of Argumentation

The goal of argumentation in a formal essay is to take a position on an issue and to defend your position with convincing supporting ideas. If you imagine that your audience may perhaps disagree with your position, you will have to work hard to persuade your reader to accept your point of view.

Example Debatable Topic: Is giving up meat a wise dietary choice?

You may have a strong opinion on this controversial topic and have many arguments in your head that you would like to use to prove that your position is the wisest one. However, while you may be able to talk the talk, the question is, can you walk the walk in terms of expressing these ideas clearly in writing?

Before you begin an argumentative essay, it would first make sense to brainstorm the pros and cons of your debatable topic.

EXERCISE **7.5** Brainstorming Pros and Cons

Directions: With a partner, fill in the columns with pro and con arguments on the subject of, "Is giving up meat a wise dietary choice?"

Pros of Giving Up Meat	Cons of Giving Up Meat

Thesis Statement

In Chapter 4, you had a lesson on building a circumscribed thesis statement into your essay introduction. When offering your position on a debatable topic, an effective thesis has a clear controlling idea and may include a list of specific arguments you will make in your essay to support it.

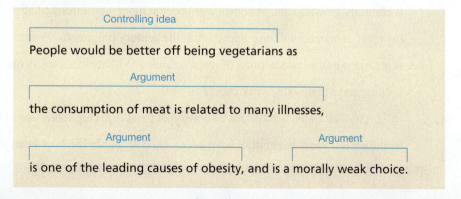

Controlling idea

People would be better off being vegetarians as

Argument

the consumption of meat is related to many illnesses,

Argument   Argument

is one of the leading causes of obesity, and is a morally weak choice.

Build in Supporting Evidence to Strengthen Your Arguments

It is not enough to simply take a position and come up with a list of arguments to support it. You need to provide several types of supporting evidence, like the following, to win over your reader.

- **Include hard facts:** Facts, unlike opinions, can be verified. Double-check your sources to make sure you've got your facts straight, and work only with reliable sources in obtaining facts. Statistics are one type of fact often used to back up an argument. Keep in mind that statistics can be manipulated to support different points of view, so assess them carefully for accuracy.

- **Use informed opinions:** Integrating opinions from experts in a given field can reinforce your argument.

- **Quote a respectable source in the field:** To persuade your reader, make use of a relevant quote(s) from an expert(s) in the field. When you include a quote as supporting evidence, do not forget to mention your source.

- **Knock down the opposition's argument with facts:** Find research-based facts that contradict the opposing side's position.

- **Add anecdotes and/or real life examples:** It is valid to include specific personal experiences to support your point of view.

Read the following essay on the debatable topic we have been focusing on.

Note to students: This essay is being shown without citations and a Works Cited list as the authors would like to put the onus on you to locate the supporting evidence without any citation clues.

Rupert Walker   Walker 1

Professor Rothman

English 090

4 March 2015

Is Giving Up Meat a Wise Dietary Choice?

1   In this day and age, many young people are concerned about their health and are beginning to question the traditional meat and potato diets they have been brought up on. The vegetarian movement is certainly growing, and as consumers become more well-informed about the shortcomings of eating meat, this trend will only speed up as the century progresses. People would be better off being vegetarians as the consumption of meat is related to many illnesses, is one of the leading causes of obesity, and is a morally weak choice as well.

2   First of all, many studies have shown that meat consumption is one of the leading causes of certain illnesses. Meat-based diets have been linked to higher levels of heart disease and a number of

Walker 2

different forms of cancer. A 2009 report from the National Cancer Institute found that people who consumed heavy amounts of red meat—which can have high levels of cholesterol-rising saturated fat—were 27 percent more likely to die of heart disease. The same report also found that heavy meat eaters were 20 percent more likely to die of cancer—pancreatic, liver, and colon cancer—than those who consumed the least amount of meat. Marjorie McCullough, ScD, strategic director of nutritional epidemiology with the American Cancer Institute, recently pointed to a consistent association between red and processed meats and a risk of colon cancer. While meat lovers will argue that meat adds to our health and provides us with essential forms of protein, the facts speak otherwise, as the risk of getting potentially fatal illnesses is not worth the gain in protein, a source that easily be replaced through milk and bean consumption.

3   America's obesity crisis is clearly being helped along by our carnivorous habits. Many studies have pointed to the correlation between heavy meat consumption and weight gain. In fact, a 2011 study by the New Hampshire Department of Health found that those who stated that they consume more than ten portions of meat a week in a 2010 state survey were three times more likely to be obese. The facts are clear. Red meat is heavy in saturated fat. While chicken is generally less fattening, most Americans choose to eat chicken fried up in fattening batter. If you visit a large vegetarian meeting, as I did in the summer of 2011, you will notice that the great majority of those in attendance are slim. Fruits and vegetables, unlike meat, are low in calories and are mostly fat free. According to Dr. Michael Fisher, a leading expert on healthy diets, "America's obesity crisis could be solved if we just learned to focus on eating plants and not animals."

4   Finally, there are moral reasons for giving up meat as part of your diet. Vegetarians are not only healthier, they also can feel good about not contributing to the ugly, industrial factory industry of animal slaughtering. The film *Fast Food Nation* provides graphic details into the barbaric procedure of meat production. Cows are treated horribly before their heads are chopped off on their path to becoming your next hamburger or steak. To enjoy a healthy salad or a hearty bowl of lentil soup, no blood must be spilt.

5   In conclusion, we as Americans have the freedom to eat as we please. However, a close attention to facts has led many people toward a vegetarian lifestyle. Meat consumption is detrimental to our health in that it has been clearly correlated with potentially fatal diseases as well as serving as a key link to obesity. It is also a morally vacuous choice. Why not live better as humans while allowing our fellow animals to live without the fear of human slaughter?

EXERCISE 7.6   Locating Types of Supporting Evidence

Directions: Find examples in the above essay of each of the following types of support. Write the number of the paragraph and write out the example you have identified. The first example is done for you.

Hard fact: Paragraph #: __3__

A 2011 study by the New Hampshire Department of Health found that those who stated

that they consume more than ten portions of meat a week in a 2010 state survey were

three times more likely to be obese.

1. **Hard fact:** Paragraph #: ___

   _____

   _____

2. **Informed opinion:** Paragraph #: ___

   _____

   _____

   _____

3. **Quote from a respected source:** Paragraph #: ___

   _____

   _____

4. **Facts knocking down opponents' arguments:** Paragraph #: ___

   _____

   _____

   _____

   _____

5. **Anecdote/real-life example:** Paragraph #: ___

   _____

   _____

THEN & NOW

If you really want to understand an academic field, it is useful to get a sense of how the academic discipline has evolved over time. This feature gives you the opportunity to do just that.

Go online and do some research to gather information about two experts in the field of nutrition: one from the past such as Robert Atkins or Paul Bragg and another contemporary such as Jenny Craig or Joel Fuhrman. Fill out the table provided with pertinent information about the two experts.

Past Influential Expert	Present Influential Expert
Name	Name
Place of birth	Place of birth
Year of birth	Year of birth
Education	Education
What is s/he most famous for?	What is s/he most famous for?
Famous quote	Famous quote

After you fill out the table, discuss your findings with your classmates and learn from them about what they discovered on the Internet.

TROUBLE SPOTS IN WRITING

OBJECTIVE
6
Avoid faulty argumentation

Faulty Argumentation

When you are writing, as in the real world when you are interacting with others, the arguments you put forth have to stand up logically; that is, your arguments have to make sense. If you asked a friend why he or she arrived an hour late for a planned meeting you had set up, and your friend responded, " Sorry, I woke up ten minutes late, so I was running a few minutes behind," you would most likely offer your friend a puzzled look. They haven't clearly explained why they were late by an hour.

The importance of offering logical argumentation in writing is that much more critical because you do not have the luxury of clarifying your point later on (as your friend probably would have in conversation when you offered that puzzled stare). What you write in the paper is all your audience has to go by, so you need to make sure your arguments are not faulty.

Paths to Faulty Argumentation: A Top Five List

Here are five common errors in reasoning (also known as logical fallacies) that you should avoid in order to provide a strong, logical argument.

1. **Appeal to popular opinion** This is when someone claims that an idea or belief is true simply because it is what most people believe.

   Example: "Lots of people like that movie, so it must be good."

2. **False analogies** Just because two items, ideas, things, places, and so on share one or more points of similarity, you cannot assume they are similar in other ways.

> **Example:** "Rice and couscous have a similar taste, so they must come from the same plant."

3. **Illogical correlation** Just because X + Y has a positive result, you cannot assume that adding Z will have the same result. Put in more concrete terms, if peanut butter and jelly taste good together, and mayonnaise tastes good, it is not necessarily true that adding mayo to your peanut butter and jelly mix will also taste good.

> **Example:** It has been shown that lifting weights and then doing a short run afterward is a good exercise combination. Biking is a healthy activity, so it can definitely fit in between the other two exercises in your routine.

4. **Absolute statements** Beware of statements written in absolute form. These are oversimplifications, and as we all know, life is nuanced and usually more complicated.

> **Example:** All dogs are evil. Teachers always give too much homework. Cell phones never let you down.

5. **Circular argumentation** This fallacy is when an argument takes its proof from a factor within the argument itself, rather than from an external one.

> **Example:** I know that this soup is great because it is a quality soup.

EXERCISE 7.7 **Recognizing Faulty Reasoning**

Directions: Read the following ten examples with a classmate and discuss which claims hold up logically. If you decide that an example is based on faulty logic, offer a short explanation of why on the line below it.

1. Fruit and vegetables are healthy because they are good for you.

_____

_____

2. Adding more fish to your diet may be a good choice as many types of fish contain essential vitamins and are a good source of low-fat proteins.

_____

_____

3. Eating rice together with beans is a good combo as it forms a high-fiber vegetarian protein. So, if you add some pork to the rice and beans, your meal will be even healthier.

_____

_____

_____

4. The boss does not hide her bad moods. Several times, I saw her walk by the reception desk without greeting her staff and then slamming her office door. The other day I heard her cursing at one of our friendliest clients.

_____

_____

5. Laura is a nutritionist. She enjoys grilling her food. Thus, all nutritionists like to grill their food.

_____

_____

_____

6. Chefs and prep cooks both work in restaurant kitchens, so their jobs mostly involve the same tasks.

_____

_____

7. Gourmet meals often cost more because the ingredients contained in the dishes are more expensive.

_____

_____

_____

8. Restaurant managers have the right to be frustrated because clients with reservations never show up on time.

_____

_____

Working with a search engine, do the following search, "TED Talks Mark Bittman What's wrong with what we eat?" Then click on "View Interactive Transcript." Peruse the transcript to gain a deeper understanding of the shortcomings of the American diet. You might choose to watch the video of Mr. Bittman's speech as well. After doing a careful reading of the transcript, write brief answers to the following questions about the content.

1. According to Bittman, what are some of the negative consequences of raising livestock?

   _____

   _____

   _____

2. What type of diet does Bittman recommend?

   _____

   _____

3. What is a "locavore"? What does Bittman say about how people ate one hundred years ago?

   _____

   _____

4. What point is Bittman making with his example of farm-raised salmon being shipped to US consumers from Chile?

   _____

   _____

5. Bittman argues, "To suggest that in the interests of personal and human health Americans eat 50 percent less meat – it's not enough of a cut, but it's a start." First, paraphrase the point Bittman is trying to make. Second, share your personal reaction to his point.

   _____

   _____

CHAPTER ESSAY ASSIGNMENT

What are the secrets to living a long and healthy life?

7 OBJECTIVE

Read, think, plan, and write an essay in response to the chapter essay assignment

Now that you have had the opportunity to read a number of articles and a textbook excerpt, you should have a deeper understanding of the discipline of nutrition and be prepared to respond to the chapter essay assignment.

Assignment: Write a two- to three-page essay on this topic or your own topic. Support your claims with evidence or examples drawn from what you have read in the chapter and other relevant readings from other sources. You can also support your claims with information you have learned in school and/or your personal life.

Be sure to include a clear thesis statement in your opening paragraph that focuses your essay around a central idea. When you are done, hand in your essay to your instructor. After you have received constructive feedback from your instructor, be sure to incorporate some of his or her suggestions into your second draft and submit the revised second draft to your instructor for further feedback on form and meaning.

FOCUS ON FORM

Editing for Faulty Argumentation

In the Trouble Spots in Writing section on page 289, you learned how to make sure that any arguments you put forth are logical and sound. Now let's put your skills into action. First, read the following paragraph on the essay question "Why Does Smoking Have Little Effect on Longevity?" Identify examples of weak arguments, cross them out, and list your rationale for eliminating them. When you are finished, compare your edits with those of your partner.

Everybody knows that the dangers of smoking are exaggerated. You hear people all the time laughing off these reports relating premature death to the habit of smoking. Because we smokers know that these reports are not accurate, we cannot believe that they should be believed. Let's face it. Like kissing someone you really like or eating fresh strawberries off the vine, smoking gives people pleasure. If we don't pick on others for enjoying other pleasurable activities, why should smokers be the target of our disdain? My grandfather has smoked a pack of cigarettes a day his whole life and he is 91. Face the facts. You can enjoy the habit of smoking and live a long life. Just don't pay attention to all of those exaggerated reports.

It's Your Turn!

Now that you have had a chance to practice editing for weak argumentation, take a look at your chapter essay and review it with new eyes. Pay close attention to how well you present and back up your arguments.

CHAPTER DEBATE OPTION

Is the quality of your health over a lifetime more influenced by your genetic makeup or by the lifestyle choices you make?

This chapter's debate topic is related to your chapter essay assignment. Refer to Appendix 8, page 455, for detailed guidelines on how to set up and participate in a formal debate.

8 Nursing

Learning Objectives

IN THIS CHAPTER, YOU WILL LEARN TO . . .

1 Read in the field of nursing

2 Understand and use key terms in nursing

3 Identify and read various genres of writing

4 Recognize and use patterns of organization to make sense of information

5 Use appropriate patterns of organization to convey information

6 Use the conventions of academic English for writing assignments

7 Read, think, plan, and write an essay in response to the chapter essay assignment

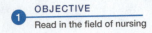

Introduction to the Field of Nursing

With the increasing shortage of nurses in major hospitals throughout the United States, nursing has become a highly sought-after profession. Typically, women pursue nursing as a career, but now men are realizing that nursing could be financially rewarding for them and bring job satisfaction. As you know, nurses provide care for sick individuals, sometimes families, and even communities. A registered nurse's purpose is to educate individuals on how to lead a healthy life, to prevent people from getting sick, to help patients regain health and proper function, and to provide care for those who are terminally ill. Not only do nurses administer medication to their patients but they also encourage sick individuals to keep a positive attitude and help to enhance their quality of life. Registered nurses provide care for their patients in homes, hospitals, physicians' clinics, extended-care facilities, and hospice settings.

While the focus of this chapter is on the discipline of nursing, the readings cover several subtopics. These include the nation wide search for male nurses, the qualities of a good nurse, and an overview of the nursing process. All of these readings will give you an appreciation for registered nurses and the work they perform.

CHAPTER ESSAY QUESTION

What are the most important qualities of an excellent nurse?

Quick Free-Write! Take out a piece of paper, and write for ten minutes without stopping about what you already know about the theme of the chapter essay question.

As you read through this chapter, keep in mind this essay question and consider how you might incorporate multiple perspectives on the issue into your writing. Chapter essays will be due when your class completes the chapter.

Your Option: Once you have worked your way through the chapter readings, you are welcome to narrow down the topics covered and compose your own chapter essay question.

Previewing Nursing

Read the following questions and discuss them with your classmates. As you answer the questions, consider your personal experience and knowledge of nursing in general.

1. Do you have a family member who needs in-home nursing care? If yes, how do you and your family members cope with the challenge of helping care for this individual? Be specific.

2. How long would you be willing to house and care for a relative who no longer can take care of him- or herself? How comfortable would you be allowing a professional nurse to manage critical decisions regarding your relative's lifestyle choices? What would be some of your concerns about trusting a nurse? What percentage of your monthly income would you allocate for subsidizing this relative's nursing expenses?

3. The average life expectancy of Americans has increased significantly due to the many advances in public hygiene, nutrition, and medical technology. How many years do you think the twenty-first-century American citizen can live self-sufficiently in relatively good health? At what age do you believe a senior citizen could become a liability to society? Explain.

4. Senior citizens living into their eighties, nineties, and beyond pose a great challenge to the nursing profession. In what ways can the field of nursing rise to the occasion and meet the growing needs of America's aging population? Discuss the role the government can play in producing sufficient nursing graduates to deal with this demographic change.

After you have discussed the preview questions with your classmates, post your responses to two of them on **The Wall**. Review the postings on The Wall and respond to at least two of your classmates' postings that grab your interest. Remember the guidelines for The Wall etiquette (see p. 35)!

Key Terms in Nursing

Take a moment to think about the discipline of Nursing as you complete the following two exercises.

EXERCISE 8.1   **Brainstorming Vocabulary**

Directions: What associated words come to mind when you think of the world of nursing? Work with a partner and write down as many related words as you can think of in a period of five minutes.

EXERCISE 8.2   **Creating Original Sentences**

Directions: Choose five of the words from your brainstorm list, and use them to write complete and meaningful sentences.

1. _____

2. _____

3. _____

4. _____

5. _____

A **synonym** is a word used to express a similar meaning to another word. An **antonym** is a word that conveys the opposite meaning of another word.

Each discipline has its own jargon and technical terms, and nursing is no exception. A student majoring in nursing will need to understand and use such terms as *care*, *critical*, *emergency*, and *diagnosis* in both spoken and written forms. Registered nurses use these terms when they communicate with doctors and other health professionals.

In addition, understanding how to work with synonyms and antonyms for these and other discipline-specific words is a useful skill, especially when you are writing a summary of a text and trying to paraphrase some of the key ideas and pieces of information contained in the original source. The following exercise will enable you to learn some key terms in the discipline of nursing and practice using synonyms and antonyms for them.

EXERCISE 8.3 Discipline-specific Vocabulary: Fishing for Synonyms and Antonyms

Directions: Read the following ten (10) discipline-specific words culled from the readings in this chapter and shown in the context of the sentences in which they appeared. In the space provided after each sentence, write a synonym or antonym for the highlighted term, as directed.

Discipline-specific Word Bank*

caring	medications	empathy
critical	humane	nurture
emergency	healthcare	disease
trauma		

* The term healthcare needs to be moved down to a separate line to avoid confusion.

1. "This is not about gender," said Thom Schwarz, a registered nurse and editorial director of *The American Journal of Nursing*. "It's about **caring**." (Selection 1, p. 304, para. 5)

   An antonym for **caring** is _____.

2. "Specialties most in demand include **critical** care, preoperative care and emergency services." (Selection 1, p. 305, para. 6)

   A synonym for **critical** is _____.

3. "Specialties most in demand include critical care, preoperative care and **emergency** services." (Selection 1, p. 305, para. 6)

   A synonym for **emergency** is _____.

4. "But a nurse comes across people who are dealing with **trauma**—both physically and mentally!" (Selection 2, p. 311, para. 4)

   A synonym for **trauma** is _____.

5. "Firmness too, is essential in the tone when it comes to instructing the patient about advised **medications** and exercises." (Selection 2, p. 311, para. 7)

   A synonym for **medications** is _____.

6. "Doing something just because it is your job, and doing something because it is your **humane** duty defines how passionate you are towards your profession." (Selection 2, p. 312, para. 12)

   A synonym for **humane** is _____.

7. "These days, nursing is one of the most sought-after careers. A nurse is an integral part of the **healthcare** profession." (Selection 2, p. 312, para. 13)

   A synonym for **healthcare** is _____.

8. "It involves sensitivity, creativity, **empathy**, and the ability to adapt care—either to meet a patient's unique needs or in the face of uncertainty." (Selection 3, p. 333, para. 2)

   An antonym for **empathy** is _____.

9. "This fits with the holistic idea that people have innate abilities for growth and self-healing and that the nurse's role is to **nurture** and support those abilities." (Selection 3, p. 333, para. 3)

   An antonym for **nurture** is _____.

10. "Although definitions and theories vary, most agree that even though nurses care for patients with health problems, nursing is not limited to **disease** processes and that nursing concerns are different from medical concerns." (Selection 3, p. 334, para. 6)

    An antonym for **disease** is _____.

SUCCESS IN READING

Recognizing and Reading a Diversity of Genres

It is critical before beginning to read a text that you are aware of both the source and genre of the text you are about to read. Embarking on a given text without knowing its genre is like turning the ignition of a transportation vehicle with no knowledge of whether you are driving a plane, a boat, or a bus! What follows is a list of text genres you will most likely encounter in college. Notice that there is a brief description of each genre type and some strategies on how best to approach these as a reader.

Genres in Reading

A **newspaper, magazine, or online article** reports on a topic or an event and is mostly informational. Readers first must understand the general theme, context, and topic area of a news article before trying to make sense of the details. Consider how the writer's choice of subtopics and examples keys you into his or her bias(es).

OBJECTIVE

3 Identify and read various genres of writing

A **newspaper editorial** is an opinion column written with the goal of persuading the reader to agree with a certain point of view. Readers should first try to understand the author's general position on the topic being discussed and then try to analyze how successfully the author proves his or her argument(s).

A **textbook** contains discipline-specific academic content. Textbook chapters are usually assigned for specific college courses. The content of a textbook chapter often reinforces material discussed in class, so the more active a learner you are during your course lectures, the easier it will be to work with the textbook readings. In addition, the more active a reader you are, the better you will understand lectures. Good highlighting skills are essential in pulling out key terms and concepts.

A **memoir** is a type of autobiographical writing. It is important to understand the general context when reading a memoir. Is this a famous person you are interested in learning about, or is it someone who has had a life experience that you would like to know more about? Pay close attention to the memoirist's life perspectives and to key turning points in his or her life experience from which you can learn.

An **interview** is a written version of a question-and-answer session. Often famous people or experts in a particular field are interviewed in magazines and newspapers. As in reading a memoir, the key is to try to understand the interviewed person's perspective and some of the main points he or she is trying to make. If you have some background knowledge on this person, it will make it much easier to connect with what he or she has to say.

A **poem** is a literary work often written in metrical form. The key is to pay close attention to symbolic meaning and to the author's choice of words. Remember that the meaning of a poem is open to subjective interpretation. (Depending on their background knowledge and experience, different readers may interpret the same poem differently.)

A **newspaper or magazine letter to the editor** is a response from a newspaper reader to an editorial. First, make sure you have a grasp of the topic the reader is responding to. Then consider his or her perspective, your point of view, and how other readers' viewpoints may vary.

An **online forum** is a place where Internet readers often share their opinions on a topic. Again, as is the case with letters to the editor, some knowledge of the topic, policy, and/or article that is being discussed goes a long way.

A **scene from a play** is an excerpt from a theater script. Remember, you are reading direct speech in this genre. Pay attention to conversational style, as it often keys you in to the characters' emotional state and how they interrelate with other characters. Notice deviations from standard language (such as regional dialects, slang, or idiomatic expressions).

In an **advice column**, experts offer their advice to readers' questions. The advice columnist's language is usually coaxing and reassuring, as it is his or her goal to guide readers through difficult situations. Focus mostly on the main points of advice offered. Think about alternative advice the writer could have offered.

A **novel** is a work of fiction and can vary in length. In first entering a novel, consider the setting (time and location), characters, plot, and the voice of the narrator.

An **official government document** is often replete with legalese (legal terms) and the tone is usually authoritative. You may have to read very carefully, line by line as these texts are often written in a formal, somewhat inaccessible manner.

An **Internet blog** is a Web site designed by an individual with or without qualifications in a specific field, with the goal of moderating an Internet chat forum. A good reader using critical-thinking skills can distinguish between an incoherent piece of writing (one that often contains basic grammar and spelling errors) and a well-written opinion. Just because a piece of writing appears online does not mean that a reader should accept it as an expert opinion. However, this does not mean that readers should devalue amateur writing. On the contrary, the beauty of most blogs is that they offer readers and writers the opportunity to share perspectives with one another in an informal forum.

EXERCISE 8.4   Connecting Genres and Disciplines

Directions: All of the disciplines covered in this text are listed below. Your task is to write the types of genres a college student is likely to read within a specific discipline. Work in pairs and compare your answers with those of your classmates. The first item is done for you.

Discipline	Genre
Psychology	Textbook reading, advice column, Internet blog
Criminal Justice	
Environmental Science	
Literature	
Education	
Health and Nutrition	
Nursing	
Business	
Sociology	

Men Are Much in the Sights of Recruiters in Nursing

Pre-Reading Questions

Answer the following questions before exploring the text:

1. When you hear the word *nurse*, what kind of image do you conjure up in your mind? Describe a nurse's physical appearance to your peers.

2. Do you believe that only women are capable of providing patient care as a nurse? If you do, discuss why male nurses may not be as efficient and caring as female nurses. If not, explain your thinking.

3. Despite a severe nursing shortage in this country, the idea that men also can pursue nursing as a rewarding career has not caught on. In your opinion, what role do you think the government and educational institutions can play in encouraging men to pursue nursing as a profession?

Eye on Vocabulary

Skim through the reading and look for the following key vocabulary terms in bold. Working with a partner, examine the words in context and try to guess the meaning of each. Then look them up in a dictionary. Keep in mind that many words have multiple meanings. Write the definition that best fits the word's context in the following article.

Word	Your definition	Dictionary definition
1. recruitment (n.)		
2. shortage (n.)		
3. anesthesia (n.)		
4. humanistic (adj.)		

Men Are Much in the Sights of Recruiters in Nursing

by Eve Tahmincioglu, the *New York Times*

April 13, 2003

1   On an episode of NBC's hospital spoof "Scrubs," a female doctor falls for a fellow medical staffer but backs away when she finds out he is a male nurse—or, as she calls him, a "murse." The episode, which was shown in

January, prompted the president of the American Nurses Association, Barbara A. Blakeney, to write a letter to the show's producer saying it "tastelessly makes fun of men who choose to become nurses" and may "damage nurse-**recruitment** efforts as a result."

2   With the nursing **shortage** in New York and around the country reaching severe proportions, even sitcoms are not spared the wrath of the health care industry. The "Scrubs" episode and movies like "Meet the Parents"—in which a male nurse is begged by his future father-in-law, played by Robert De Niro, to become a doctor—are especially troubling to health care providers. They are pinning their hopes of easing the staffing shortage on the single demographic group with the sheer numbers to make a difference: men.

3   The industry has stepped up efforts to recruit men, concentrating on those with a background in medicine, like paramedics and orderlies, but also aiming at areas like firefighting, the military, Wall Street and even the tattered dot-com industry.

4   Gary Liu, 31, is one of their prizes. Mr. Liu got a business degree from Baruch College and went to work for a computer company, but he felt unfulfilled and fretted about job security. Six months later, he left for a position as a patient advocate at a New York hospital. He soon decided to go into nursing for "the financial rewards and to help people," he said. Last summer, he was hired as a night nurse in the transplant unit of New York University Medical Center. "I'm often asked why I didn't become a doctor," he said. "I don't have to defend myself. I'm happy with my choice."

5   The potential for that kind of job satisfaction is the message that the health care industry is trying to get across to other men. "This is not about gender," said Thom Schwarz, a registered nurse and editorial director of *The American Journal of Nursing*. "It's about **caring**."And about money and job stability. At a time when most professions are stingy with both, nursing is bucking the trend. Nurses in the New York metropolitan area start at $50,000 to $70,000 a year, and in specialties like anesthesiology they make up to $100,000, according to Timothy Lehey, program

director of the nurse **anesthesia** program at the Columbia University School of Nursing. To lure workers, some health care operations are offering signing bonuses of up to $5,000, tuition assistance, day care and flexible hours.

6   Nurses can pick and choose their place of employment. Virtually every hospital, nursing home and home-health agency in the greater New York area has a shortage, varying from 4 percent to 14 percent. Among the areas most in need of hospital nurses are the Bronx and Staten Island, and Westchester, Dutchess, Orange and Ulster Counties, according to the Greater New York Hospital Association. Specialties most in demand include **critical** care, preoperative care and **emergency** services.

7   The need for nurses is unlikely to let up any time soon, given the growing health care needs of aging baby boomers. By 2020, the national nursing shortage will more than triple, to 400,000 openings from 126,000 today, the Bureau of Labor Statistics forecasts. In New York State, the shortage is expected to reach 17,000 nurses by 2005 and double that by 2015, according to a study by the state's Education Department.

8   To help narrow the gap, the industry is going after men, who make up a mere 5.4 percent of the nation's 2.7 million registered nurses and 4 percent of those in the New York metropolitan area. In February, Johnson & Johnson, the pharmaceutical and medical-devices company based in New Brunswick, N.J., featured men in a $20 million public service campaign to promote nursing. "Nursing has slipped from the radar screen for a lot of women who are pursuing other careers, so we thought, 'Why not look at all options, including men?'" said David Swearingen, a Johnson & Johnson spokesman. "They provide a promising audience."

9   And an increasingly receptive one. "It's becoming more acceptable for men to go into nursing because society's values are changing, making it more acceptable for men to have feelings and do **humanistic** kinds of work," said Kathleen Ames, director of nurse recruitment for New York University Medical Center, where 7.4 percent of the nursing staff are men. The pay helps. The medical center starts nurses at $60,000 and offers them free tuition at New York University, health benefits, 30 days of paid holidays and vacation, and a contribution equal to 6 percent of their salaries to their 403(b) plans, the nonprofit equivalent of a 401(k).

10   Men can be especially useful as nurses because of the physical strength required to lift patients and move medical equipment. Michael Cullen, a retired police officer who is a nurse with the Visiting Nurse Service of New York, is sometimes called "boostie boy" because he so often helps move heavy patients.

11   After 21 years on the Nassau County police force, Mr. Cullen, 55, had no qualms about going back to school and becoming a nurse. He loves the work, despite the occasional double take he gets. "I've had patients ask me if I'm gay," said Mr. Cullen, who is married with two grown children. "And sometimes the older men get disappointed when they see me. They say, 'I was hoping for a young, pretty girl.' But many are so sick, they couldn't care less."

12   The Visiting Nurse Service says former police officers like Mr. Cullen, as well as former soldiers and firefighters, are ideal nursing candidates not only for their strength but also for their long experience in thinking

on their feet. Jobs start at $60,000 a year, compared with $45,000 five years ago, plus a signing bonus of $3,000.

13   Becoming a nurse requires a two-year associate's degree or a bachelor's degree in nursing, though some nursing schools in the New York area offer accelerated programs. Nursing school grants are hard to come by, but low-interest loans are readily available, educators say. Students can often get hospitals or other potential employers to pay some of the tuition in return for a pledge to work for them for a year or more after graduation.

14   Of course, nursing is not for the squeamish or those averse to hard work. Many nurses put in 50 or even 60 hours a week, according to the American Nurse Association. But Carl Ankrah, 36, of the Bronx, is ready for the challenge. In 2001, Mr. Ankrah got a degree in hotel management, but the industry fell on hard times after Sept. 11. The real growth industry, he decided, was health care. He is now a first-year nursing student at the College of New Rochelle's School of Nursing. At times, he has wondered if he made the wrong choice—but not for long. "In a couple of classes where I was only one of two men, it hit me, 'What am I doing in the midst of all these ladies?'" he said. "But I said to myself, 'This is not a gender profession. It's a profession of people willing to sacrifice themselves and help people.'"

Thinking about the Reading

After doing a close reading of the article, write brief answers to the following questions. You will be asked to discuss your answers with your classmates.

1. Why is the episode of NBC's hospital spoof *Scrubs* mentioned at the beginning of the article?

   _____

   _____

2. In her letter to the producer of *Scrubs*, Barbara Blakeney, president of the American Nurses Association, states that the show "tastelessly makes fun of men who choose to become nurses" and may "damage nurse-recruitment efforts as a result." What can be inferred from Blakeney's statement?

   _____

   _____

3. Thom Schwarz, a registered nurse and editorial director of *The American Journal of Nursing*, points out that "This is not about gender. It's about caring." What logical conclusion can be drawn about people's general attitude toward the nursing profession?

   _____

   _____

Reading Comprehension Check

_____ **1.** As used in the sentence, "On an episode of NBC's hospital spoof 'Scrubs,' a female doctor falls for a fellow medical staffer but **backs away** when she finds out he is a male nurse—or, as she calls him, a 'murse,'" the phrase *backs away* means

a. walks backward.　　　　c. withdraws.

b. pursues aggressively.　　d. considers seriously.

_____ **2.** Which of the following sentences is the best statement of the main idea of the article?

a. Male nurses are usually not as competent as their female counterparts.

b. Most hospitals are seriously considering hiring female nurses from overseas.

c. The nursing industry is making conscious efforts to recruit men as nurses.

d. Recruiters are not interested in hiring men for nursing jobs.

_____ **3.** "With the nursing shortage in New York and around the country reaching severe proportions, even sitcoms are not spared the **wrath** of the health care industry." In this sentence, the meaning of the word *wrath* is

a. praise.　　　　　c. criticism.

b. anger.　　　　　d. comments.

_____ **4.** "Mr. Liu got a business degree from Baruch College and went to work for a computer company, but he felt unfulfilled and **fretted** about job security." In this sentence, what does the word *fretted* mean?

a. unconcerned　　　c. satisfied

b. agitated　　　　　d. worried

_____ **5.** "Of course, nursing is not for the **squeamish** or those averse to hard work." In the above context, the word *squeamish* is opposite in meaning to

a. bold.　　　　　c. afraid.

b. nervous.　　　　d. disgusted.

_____ **6.** The example of nurses making $50,000 to $70,000 and, in some cases, as much as $100,000 is used to support the fact that

a. in general, nurses are poorly compensated.

b. nursing as a career can provide financial stability.

c. there is no job stability in the nursing industry.

d. only male nurses can make as much as $100,000 a year.

_____ **7.** "To lure workers, some health care operations are offering signing bonuses of up to $5,000, tuition assistance, day care and flexible hours." A logical conclusion that can be drawn from the above statement is that

a. the demand for registered nurses is dwindling.

b. some healthcare operations have huge surpluses.

c. nurses are in great demand.

d. the number of registered nurses far exceeds the number of jobs available.

_____ 8. "The need for nurses is unlikely to let up any time soon, given the growing health care needs of aging baby boomers. By 2020, the national nursing shortage will more than triple, to 400,000 openings from 126,000 today, the Bureau of Labor Statistics forecasts." It can be inferred from this passage that

a. in 2020, the demand for registered nurses in the country will be much less than today.

b. most registered nurses will retire by 2020.

c. most nursing programs will not be able to produce enough nursing graduates to meet future demand.

d. baby boomers will not need health care by 2020.

_____ 9. Mr. Cullen, a male nurse, says, "And sometimes the older men get disappointed when they see me. They say, 'I was hoping for a young, pretty girl.' But many are so sick, they couldn't care less." Based on this statement, which of the following is a logical conclusion?

a. Older men do not care about the gender of their nurses.

b. Some older men prefer to be treated by attractive female nurses.

c. Mr. Cullen couldn't care less about older male patients.

d. Only those older men who are seriously ill want to be treated by young female nurses.

_____ 10. Which of the following statements gives a clear indication that nursing is a challenging profession?

a. Jobs start at $60,000 a year, compared with $45,000 five years ago, plus a signing bonus of $3,000.

b. The medical center starts nurses at $60,000 and offers them free tuition at New York University, health benefits, 30 days of paid holidays and vacation, and a contribution equal to 6 percent of their salaries to their 403(b) plans, the nonprofit equivalent of a 401(k).

c. Nurses can pick and choose their place of employment.

d. Nursing is not for the squeamish or those averse to hard work.

THEMATIC LINKS

If you want to learn more about the topic of male nurses, type the following words into your browser and explore the two sites that come up:

1. Male Nurses Are on the Rise Healthline

2. What It's Like to Be a Male Nurse Everyday Health

Writing Without BOUNDARIES

There Are No Checkpoints!

"I think one's feelings waste themselves in words; they ought all to be distilled into actions which bring results."

—FLORENCE NIGHTINGALE

Read the quote above and respond to Florence Nightingale's idea in any way you want. Write in your notebook for ten minutes without stopping. For this activity, it is important that you focus on ideas, not words. In other words, this will be an exercise in focusing on content and not getting hung up on word choice and grammar errors. You may wish to read what you have written out loud in front of your classmates and instructor.

READING

Selection 2

Online article

Qualities of a Good Nurse

Pre-Reading Questions

Answer the following questions before exploring the text:

1. In your opinion, what are the qualities of a good nurse? You may base your answer on a personal experience you have had dealing with a nurse.

2. Do you think nurses are the most responsible and reliable people in hospitals? Support your answer with specific examples.

3. Do you think that nursing is "just" a profession, or do you believe that it is a unique profession? If you think it is unique, what separates nursing from other professions? Give specific reasons to support your answer.

Eye on Vocabulary

Working with a partner, scan the reading and find the following key vocabulary terms in bold. Then look up the words in a dictionary. Keep in mind that many words have multiple meanings. Write the definition that best fits the word's context in the article.

Word	Your definition	Dictionary definition
1. devoted (adj.)		
2. soothe (v.)		
3. noble (adj.)		
4. inherent (adj.)		

Qualities of a Good Nurse

by Reshma Jirage

Part 1

1   A nurse is counted among the most responsible and dependable individuals in a hospital. If you want to make a career in this **devoted** profession, then you should know about the qualities that a good nurse must possess.

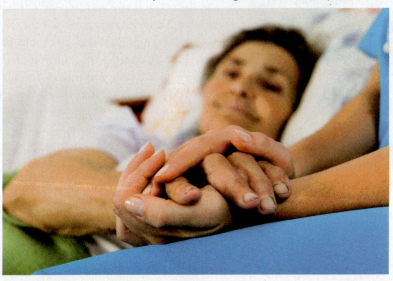

*I pray I do my part to lift each downcast spirit, and to **soothe** each heavy heart. May my touch bring reassurance, may my voice be soothing too. May my gentle care remind them of the love they have in you.*

—"A Nurse's Prayer," Author Unknown

2   To be a part of a **noble** profession such as nursing, is a matter of pride and achievement in itself. Though people may use the term "nurse" nonchalantly, only those who have seen a nurse's life would understand the honor and respect that goes into this profession. Nursing isn't merely a profession, or a job that you need to perform during your shift timings. It is a responsibility, a behavioral conditioning, an approach towards people, and a dedication towards healing others. To summarize the essence of this profession, it is not about the qualities that you can acquire to become a nurse, it is about the **inherent** qualities that you are born with, that will make you a great nurse.

Qualities that Define a Good Nurse

3   Before you choose to be a nurse, it is very important for you to understand who you are as an individual. If I say that anybody can be a good nurse, I would be lying! The reason why I say so is because this profession is extremely demanding, both physically and mentally. Physical pressures include dealing with emergency cases, on-call duties, extended working hours, and so on. Mentally, this job would need you to deal with the emotional situations of the patients and their families. Giving them constant moral support, aiding their needs to be heard and comforted, being an advocate of the patient in front of the doctor, and so on are integral duties

of a good nurse. All this requires the aspirant to be compassionate, mentally composed, physically strong, and professionally dedicated. Among the other qualities that an ideal nurse should have, the aforementioned qualities can only be found in a person naturally, and cannot be acquired forcefully.

Kind and Compassionate

4   We all tend to be kind and compassionate towards others in our daily lives. The majority of people that we meet are those at work and social gatherings, but a nurse comes across people who are dealing with **trauma**— both physically and mentally! These people are distressed and are looking for comfort and healing. It is easy to deal with healthy people, but if you are surrounded with patients who need your assistance, then it is important for you to be kind and compassionate towards them. While most of us might get frustrated after a point, a nurse is the one who understands their patients' miseries and comforts them even in the darkest hour. All this cannot be done without compassion being a major essence of your character.

Physical Endurance

5   Being a nurse is not a 9 to 5 desk job. One needs to be on one's toes, aiding both doctors and patients. Stressful situations are encountered almost everyday. In case of emergencies, immediate assistance is required. While the doctor examines and treats the patient, it is the nurse's duty to follow up according to the doctor's instructions. A normal phenomenon in this career is on-call duties and extended shifts when there are less staff. Therefore, it is important to be physically active and strong.

Mental Endurance

6   A nurse is a caregiver who acts as a source of connection between the doctor, patient, and the patient's family. There are various queries that the patient and his or her family members might have. Not only this, but in case of serious illnesses there will be issues like anger, frustration, pain, and agony, mainly from the patient's end, to address. On the other hand, there will also be the mental pressure to deal with the patient calmly through all the chaos, thereby, making sure that the doctor's instructions are being followed. Therefore, mental stability is a necessity in this profession.

Excellent Communication Skills

7   As mentioned earlier, a nurse is a caregiver, and it is not possible to provide complete care for a person if there is a lack of proper communication. When it comes to communication, especially in **healthcare**, it is about more than talking to a patient. One needs to cater to both his or her physical and emotional needs. The talking needs to be soft and polite, making the patient feel at ease. Firmness, too, is essential in the tone when it comes to instructing the patient about advised **medications** and exercises.

8   Another important aspect in communication is to be a good listener, and it goes beyond listening to the needs of the patient! It involves forming a bond of mutual trust and reliance. When a person goes through an illness or a trauma, it is usually accompanied by loneliness, frustration, and the need to be heard. During this phase, it is a nurse who can act as a caregiver and confidant, which is impossible without the ability to communicate well.

HALFWAY ROAD STOP

Get into a small group and answer the two questions that follow.

1. What have you learned from the article so far?

2. Try to predict what may be coming in the second half of the article.

Part 2

Constant Urge to Learn

9   A lot has changed from the time when Florence Nightingale founded modern nursing. With the continuous discovery of new illnesses, medicines, and developments in healthcare technology, professionals need to update and adapt themselves continuously to the changing trends. This cannot be done successfully if there is no impulse to learn.

Alert and Observant

10   It is mandatory for the aspirant to be alert and observant, considering the demands involved in the profession. Observing the unspoken needs of the patient, providing him or her with emergency care and assistance, taking charge of the situation when the doctor is not present are a part and parcel of the job. Without being alert and observant, a nurse would not be able to justify the given responsibilities and would lose the trust that the patient and the doctor has in him or her. This is because any kind of delay in taking the required action due to indecisiveness could prove to be fatal for the patient in an emergency situation.

Adaptable to Change

11   When I say change, I mean the dynamic nature of the working environment in the healthcare sector. Each day is different from the other with new patients, each varying from the previous ones. Every patient has different needs, and there are different ways to handle them. Which is why, a nurse needs to be flexible when it comes to adapting to changes, be it in the work schedule or simply in the way he or she deals with the patients.

Willingness to Provide a Healing Touch

12   This quality defines the difference between a nurse and a great nurse. Doing something just because it is your job or doing the same thing because it is your **humane** duty defines how passionate you are towards your profession. It is only if you have this quality that you will enjoy serving others, whether it is during your duty hours or if you have been called on duty in the middle of the night. This career is satisfying only if the need to comfort others is more than the need to remain in your comfort zone.

13   These days, nursing is one of the most sought-after careers. A nurse is an integral part of the healthcare profession. There are a number of institutes all over the world that offer different courses in nursing. This article is an attempt to highlight the importance of the personal qualities over a degree and a qualification, which undoubtedly are equally important. However, the aspirant should understand that nursing is not just a great way of making money, it is a profession that demands skills, hard work, and devotion.

Thinking about the Reading

After doing a close reading of the article, write your answers to the following questions. You may be asked to discuss your answers with your classmates.

1. The article begins with a nurse's prayer. What can be inferred from the prayer about the nursing profession?

   _____

   _____

2. According to the article, a lot has changed in the nursing field since Florence Nightingale first founded modern nursing. Discuss the changes and tell what a modern-day nurse needs to do to keep herself abreast of the changes.

   _____

   _____

3. Why is it important for a nurse to always be alert and observant and have the doctor and the patient trust her?

   _____

   _____

Reading Comprehension Check

_____ 1. The author's main idea is that
   a. an aspiring nurse can acquire the qualities of a good nurse.
   b. a nurse is a most respectable and dependable individual.
   c. an aspiring nurse should possess the inborn qualities of a good nurse.
   d. anyone can acquire the qualities of a good nurse easily.

_____ 2. "If you want to make a career in this devoted profession, then you should know about the qualities that a good nurse must **possess.**" In this sentence, the word *possess* can be replaced with
   a. surrender.   c. lack.
   b. learn.   d. own.

_____ 3. "It is **mandatory** for the aspirant to be alert and observant, considering the demands involved in the profession." In this context, the word *mandatory* is opposite in meaning to
   a. compulsory.   c. necessary.
   b. optional.   d. required.

_____ 4. In paragraphs 7 and 8, the author discusses
   a. the difference between an efficient nurse and a careless nurse.
   b. the difference between a difficult patient and an easy patient.
   c. the importance of a nurse's communication abilities.
   d. the consequences of a nurse's excellent communication abilities.

_____ 5. "These days, nursing is one of the most **sought-after** careers." As used in the sentence above, the phrase *sought-after* means

    a. pursued.   c. ignored.

    b. avoided.   d. overlooked.

_____ 6. According to the reading, what quality defines a great nurse?

    a. being willing to put others' needs before one's own comfort

    b. being willing to go on duty in the middle of the night

    c. remaining relaxed and unhurried at all times

    d. advocating the doctor's viewpoints articulately when communicating with patients

_____ 7. According to the reading, _____ requires excellent communication skills.

    a. dealing with trauma

    b. mental endurance

    c. being able to listen

    d. proper caregiving

_____ 8. Which of the following statements regarding the reading content is *false*?

    a. A nurse needs to be able to adapt to change.

    b. Nurses are not burdened with the responsibility of decision making.

    c. A nurse should not fail to follow up on the doctor's instructions.

    d. A nurse acts as a link between patients and their families.

_____ 9. In paragraph 2, we can infer from the context that the word *noble* means

    a. aristocratic, upper-class, prosperous.

    b. having high morals or honorable principles.

    c. magnificent, superior, impressive.

    d. a metal that doesn't corrode.

_____ 10. In addition to being a profession, nursing is described as being all of the following *except*

    a. a time saver.

    b. a behavioral conditioning.

    c. a dedication to heal others.

    d. a responsibility.

THEMATIC LINKS

If you want to learn more about the topic of pursuing a career in nursing, type the following words into your browser and explore the two sites that come up:

1. Is the Nursing Profession Right for You? Nurses Without Borders

2. What Makes a Good Nurse? 6 Key Traits

Patterns of Organization

4   OBJECTIVE

Recognize and use patterns of
organization to make sense of
information

Clear, logical, organized, and effective communication is important both for the author and the reader. Depending on the purpose of an article or essay, authors structure information differently to communicate with their readers. Good readers seek out these patterns of organization to make sense of the information. When they are unable to do so, communication between the author and the reader can break down, so effective communication begins with an organized set of ideas that follows a consistent pattern.

As a reader, you should familiarize yourself with how authors have structured their texts so you can understand their main ideas and supporting details. Recognizing authors' main ideas and purposes for writing can help you determine the specific patterns of organization they are using. Pay attention to how authors use different transition words to indicate different patterns of organization. (See Chapter 6, p. 247, for a chart showing transitions, the patterns they are commonly used with, and information on using transitions in your writing. Also see Appendix 5: Transitions and Patterns of Organization on page 445.)

Identifying the Pattern of Organization

To identify the overall pattern of organization a writer is using, do the following:

- Identify the topic and the main idea
- Establish the author's purpose
- Identify the details supporting the main idea
- Look for transitional words or phrases associated with specific patterns
- Analyze how the ideas are related to each other

This section introduces seven organizational patterns commonly used in textbooks: *chronological order/process*, *listing*, *definition*, *illustration and example*, *comparison and contrast*, *cause and effect,* and *classification.* You will have the opportunity to practice identifying each of the patterns as we examine them.

Chronological Order/Process

In the **chronological order/process organizational pattern**, information is arranged in the order in which events occurred (e.g., a historian recounts the events leading up to the War in Vietnam) or the order in which actions should occur in order to complete a process (such as fix a flat tire, bake a cake, or set up an IV drip). Refer to Appendix 5 (p. 445): Transitions and Patterns of Organization for a detailed list of transition words that indicate the chronological order and process patterns of organization.

Chronological Order

When you read a passage that uses the chronological order organizational pattern, pay special attention to the order in which the information is presented and look out for transition words that indicate time (*after*, *before*, *during*, *later*, *last*, *first*, *second*, *then*, *next*, *finally*, etc.). Let's read the following paragraph from Selection 1, "Men Are Much in the Sights of Recruiters in Nursing" (p. 304, para. 4), to understand this type of organizational pattern.

Gary Liu, 31, is one of their prizes. Mr. Liu got a business degree from Baruch College and went to work for a computer company, but he felt unfulfilled and fretted about job security. Six months later, he left for a position as a patient advocate at a New York hospital. He soon decided to go into nursing for "the financial rewards and to help people," he said. Last summer, he was hired as a night nurse in the transplant unit of New York University Medical Center. "I'm often asked why I didn't become a doctor," he said. "I don't have to defend myself. I'm happy with my choice."

You will notice that the topic of the passage is *Gary Liu's progress toward becoming a nurse*. Notice the transitions related to time, which have been highlighted, and indicate how Liu went from completing a degree in business and working at a computer firm to recognizing this was unfulfilling and taking steps that led to his new job in a transplant unit. As mentioned earlier, authors use chronological order when they want to show the sequence of events in reference to time.

Process

The **process pattern of organization** is similar to chronological order: the only difference is that instead of describing the order in which the *events occurred over a period of time*, the author describes the order in which *different steps occur in a process*. For example, in a nursing textbook, the author may describe how to give an injection to a patient or give directions for installing medical equipment, and in each case, it is important that the steps be performed in the order listed. Some of the transition words that indicate the process pattern of organization are *first*, *then*, and *after that*. Read the following paragraph to understand how the author uses the process pattern of organization.

Injections into muscle tissue (IM injections) are absorbed more quickly than subcutaneous injections because of the greater blood supply to the body muscles. Muscles can also take a larger volume of fluid without discomfort than subcutaneous tissues can, although the amount varies somewhat, depending on muscle size, muscle condition, and the site used. An adult with well-developed muscles can usually safely tolerate up to 4 mL of medication in the gluteus medius and gluteus maximus muscles. A major consideration in the administration of IM injections is the selection of a safe site located away from large blood vessels, nerves, and bone. Several body sites can be used for IM injections. See procedure 29-3A for administering IM injections.

Part A: Intramuscular Injection
Interventions
1. Check the medication order for accuracy.
2. Prepare the medication from the vial or ampule.
3. Identify the client, and assist the client to a comfortable position.
4. Select, locate, and clean the site.
5. Prepare the syringe for injection.
6. Inject the medication using a Z-track technique.

7. Withdraw the needle and then release hand that has been holding skin laterally.
8. Dispose of supplies appropriately.
9. Document all relevant information.
10. Assess effectiveness of the medication at the time it is expected to act.

—From Ramont and Niedringhaus, *Fundamental Nursing Care,* p. 657

Notice how the author describes the process of giving IM injections step by step. In addition, the steps are numbered, as the order in which the steps occur is important: for example, a nurse should not prepare a syringe for injection before completing steps 1–4. Using the process pattern of organization here, registered nurses can easily follow the steps and learn to safely administer IM injections to patients.

Listing (Also Known as Addition)

The **listing pattern of organization** arranges information in a list, and, unlike process or chronological order, information is arranged in no specific order. For example, the author may show the different ways that computers are used in the field of medicine. Keep in mind that the listing pattern of organization often uses transitional words such as *in addition*, *also*, and *furthermore* and/or letters or numbers that indicate items. Here is paragraph 11 (p. 335) from Selection 3, "Overview of Nursing Process":

Nursing is concerned with the whole process, ill or well. Nurses support ill people and help them to (a) solve or reduce their health problems and (b) adapt to and accept problems that cannot be treated. They help those who are terminally ill to achieve a peaceful death. For well people, nurses aim to prevent illness and promote wellness. This may involve a variety of activities, such as role modeling a healthy lifestyle; being an advocate for community environmental changes; or teaching self-care strategies, decision making, and problem solving.

If you take a closer look at the passage, you will notice that the topic is the *role of nurses*. The author lists two ways nurses help ill people, using letters, and then notes ways they help the terminally ill and promote wellness in healthy people. It should be noted that there is no particular order in which this information should be presented; the author is listing various types of nursing roles.

EXERCISE 8.5 Identifying Time Order/Process/Listing

Directions: Read the following passages, and for each one identify the topic, make a list of the events described, and note the pattern of organization.

Passage 1

The first training for practical nurses was at the Young Women's Christian Association (YWCA) in New York City in 1892. The following year this became the Ballard School. The program of study was 3 months long, and the participants studied special techniques for caring for the sick as well as a variety of homemaking techniques. Much of the care during this time was done in the client's home, making the licensed practical nurse (LPN) a home health or visiting nurse. Eleven years later, a second school, the Thompson Practical Nursing School, was established.

In 1914, the state legislature in Mississippi passed the first laws governing the practice of practical nurses. Other states were slow to follow. By 1940, only six states had passed such laws. In 1955, the state board test pool of the NLN Education Committee established the procedures for testing graduates of approved practical/vocational education programs in all states. Graduates who passed the examination became LPNs or, in California and Texas, licensed vocational nurses (LVNs). Each state set its own passing score.

Today, a graduate of an approved LPN/LVN training program is eligible to take the National Council Licensure Examination for Practical Nursing (NCLEX-PN).

—From Ramont and Niedringhaus, *Fundamental Nursing Care*, p. 9

1. What is the topic of the passage?

_____

2. What sequence of events is presented?

_____

_____

_____

_____

_____

3. Highlight the transitions that indicate the pattern of organization used.

4. What pattern is being used?

_____

Passage 2

The procedures provided in this book give you some of the basic skills you will need to provide excellent client care. Procedures should always begin with an initial set of actions that ensure a safe, efficient, and caring environment. These actions will become second nature to you as you continue your nursing training. Icons will be used to represent this initial set of actions at the start of each procedure. In some instances, an action may be optional. However, most are not. The icons are a reminder to do these basic, important interventions in nursing care:

1. Check the physician's order.

2. Gather the necessary equipment.

3. Introduce yourself to the client.

4. Identify the client (check the client's wristband against the chart).

5. Provide privacy as needed (close the curtain).

6. Explain the procedure.

7. Wash your hands. Hand hygiene is the single most effective way to prevent disease transmission.

8. Don gloves as needed.

—From Ramont and Niedringhaus, *Fundamental Nursing Care,* p. 76

1. What is the topic of the passage?

_____

2. How many steps need to be taken to provide good client care?

_____

3. Highlight the transitions and/or other clues that indicate the pattern of organization used.

4. What pattern is being used?

_____

Definition

In the **definition organizational pattern**, authors provide explanations of the meanings of terms they use and provide examples and/or analogies that illustrate what they are and sometimes what they are not. This pattern is common in most science-based text books such as those used in biology, nursing, and chemistry. Authors use this pattern of organization to introduce a term and help the reader understand what it means and how it is different from others. In textbooks, terms being defined are usually bolded or italicized. Definitions can also be provided in parentheses immediately after a bolded word, set off in dashes, or indicated by words like *means, refers to, involves, is called,* and so on. (Refer to Appendix 5: Transitions and Patterns of Organization for a detailed list of transition words that indicate the definition pattern of organization.)

In the following paragraph from Selection 3, "Overview of Nursing Process" (para.3, p. 333), taken from a nursing textbook, the author is defining the term *nursing,* and the table that follows shows how she uses the definition organizational pattern to do so.

Florence Nightingale (1820–1910), the first nurse theorist, said that what nurses do "is to put the patient in the best condition for nature to act upon him." This fits with the holistic idea that people have innate abilities for growth and self-healing and that the nurse's role is to nurture and support those abilities. The American Nurses Association (ANA), the professional organization for U.S. Nurses, defines nursing this way:

Nursing is the protection, promotion, and optimization of health and abilities, prevention of illness and injury, alleviation of suffering through the diagnosis, and treatment of human response, and advocacy in the care of individuals, families, communities, and populations (ANA, 2004, p. 7).

Term	Definitions
Nursing	1. Florence Nightingale said that what nurses do "is to put the patient in the best condition for nature to act upon him."
	2. The author says that Florence Nightingale's definition "fits with the holistic idea that people have innate abilities for growth and self-healing and that the nurse's role is to nurture and support those abilities."
	3. The American Nurses Association defines nursing as "protection, promotion, and optimization of health and abilities, prevention of illness and injury, alleviation of suffering through the diagnosis, and treatment of human response, and advocacy in the care of individuals, families, communities, and populations."

Clearly the term *nursing* is quite complex and covers many types of activity. The author of this reading wants to provide students with a working definition of the term, which will help them understand what the job requires and how they should approach it. She does this by providing a definition from Florence Nightingale, the founder of modern nursing, connecting it to current ideas about healing and nurses' roles, and then providing a current definition from the ANA.

When you read passages that use the definition organizational pattern, ask what terms are being defined. Identifying the terms will help you understand the author's purpose as well. Now that you have seen one example of the definition organizational pattern, let's do an exercise to make sure you understand how authors use this thought pattern.

EXERCISE **8.6**   Identifying Definitions

Directions: Read the following passages, identify the terms being discussed, and then define them.

Passage 1

For more than 30 years, nursing has been concerned with the cultural differences among clients. In the early years, culture was equated with ethnicity. Ethnicity was identified by a code on the client's chart or on the addressograph plate. As the profession became aware of the need to provide for the client holistically, the words cultural awareness (knowing about the similarities and differences among cultures) crept into the professional vocabulary. The goal of cultural awareness was to end prejudice and discrimination. In fact, though, awareness often resulted in a focus on differences, without providing the nurse with the tools to meet the culturally related needs of the client.

—From Ramont and Niedringhaus, *Fundamental Nursing Care,* p. 17

1. Highlight the transitions and/or other clues that indicate a definition is being provided.

2. What term is being defined?

3. What definition is provided?

_____

Passage 2

   One pitfall in communicating with a person from a different culture is ethnocentrism. **Ethnocentrism** means interpreting the beliefs and behavior of others in terms of one's own cultural values and traditions. It assumes that one's own culture is superior. It is difficult to avoid the tendency toward ethnocentrism. Nurses, though, must be extra diligent to avoid stereotypes (oversimplified conceptions, opinions, or beliefs about some aspects of a group of people). Individuals vary greatly within any ethnic group, just as children vary within one family. The nurse must look for ways to care for each client as a unique person, regardless of category.

—From Ramont and Niedringhaus, _Fundamental Nursing Care,_ 2e, p. 17

1. Highlight the transitions and/or other clues that indicate a definition is being provided.

2. What is the first term that is defined?

_____

3. What definition is provided?

_____

_____

4. What term is the second term that is defined?

_____

5. What definition is provided?

_____

Illustration and Example

When we do not understand a complex phenomenon, an abstract concept, or a difficult term, we often ask, "Can you give me an example?" Research in artificial intelligence shows that we retain information more easily when we are given appropriate examples of a key concept. Successful teachers, and textbook authors, are aware of this aspect of human nature and use the illustration/example organizational pattern to introduce main ideas or key concepts to students.

   Examples are especially helpful when the subject matter is unfamiliar to the reader. This pattern of organization is indicated by transition words such as _for example, as an example_, and _for instance._ (Refer to Appendix 5: Transitions and Patterns of Organization for a detailed list of transition words that indicate the illustration and example pattern of organization.)

   Let's look at the following paragraphs (10–12, p. 305) from Selection 1, "Men Are Much in Sight of Recruiters in Nursing" to understand the illustration/example pattern of organization more clearly.

Men can be especially useful as nurses because of the physical strength required to lift patients and move medical equipment. Michael Cullen, a retired police officer who is a nurse with the Visiting Nurse Service of New York, is sometimes called "boostie boy" because he so often helps move heavy patients.

After 21 years on the Nassau County police force, Mr. Cullen, 55, had no qualms about going back to school and becoming a nurse. He loves the work, despite the occasional double take he gets. "I've had patients ask me if I'm gay," said Mr. Cullen, who is married with two grown children. "And sometimes the older men get disappointed when they see me. They say, 'I was hoping for a young, pretty girl.' But many are so sick, they couldn't care less."

The Visiting Nurse Service says former police officers like Mr. Cullen, as well as former soldiers and firefighters, are ideal nursing candidates not only for their strength but also for their long experience in thinking on their feet. Jobs start at $60,000 a year, compared with $45,000 five years ago, plus a signing bonus of $3,000.

As you can see, in the above paragraphs, the main idea is that *men are especially useful as nurses*, and the author uses Michael Cullen as an example of why this is true, noting that retired police officers, firefighters, and soldiers are particularly useful because of their physical strength and experience in thinking fast in difficult situations.

EXERCISE 8.7   Identifying Examples

Directions: Read the following passages carefully, underline the main idea, and list the examples the author provides to support the main idea in each.

Passage 1

Autonomy refers to the right to make one's own decisions. Nurses who follow this principle recognize that each client is unique, has the right to be what that person is, and has the right to choose personal goals.

Honoring the principles of autonomy means that the nurse respects a client's right to make decisions even when those choices seem not to be in the client's best interest. It also means treating others with consideration. In a healthcare setting, this principle is violated, for example, when a nurse disregards a client's report of the severity of his or her pain.

—From Ramont and Niedringhaus, *Fundamental Nursing Care,* p. 39

1. Highlight the transitions and/or other clues that indicate an example(s) is being provided.

2. List the example(s) provided by the author:

_____

_____

_____

Passage 2

Values are freely chosen, enduring beliefs or attitudes about the worth of a person, object, idea, or action. Values are important because they influence decisions and actions. Values are often taken for granted. In the same way that people are not aware of their breathing, they usually do not think about their values; they simply accept them and act on them. The word *values* usually brings to mind things such as honesty, fairness, friendship, safety, or family unity. Of course, not all values are moral values. For example, some people hold money, work, power, and politics as values in their lives.

—From Ramont and Niedringhaus, *Fundamental Nursing Care*, pp. 37–38

3. Highlight the transitions and/or other clues that indicate an example(s) is being provided.

4. List the example(s) provided by the author:

_____

Comparison and Contrast

When authors want to show how two things—objects, ideas, people, places, theories, and so on—are similar (comparison) or different (contrast), they use the **comparison and contrast organizational pattern**. When comparing two items, authors focus on their similar features. Some transition words that indicate a comparison is being made are *similarly*, *likewise*, and *in comparison*. When contrasting objects, they focus on their different characteristics, using transitions like *in contrast*, *on the contrary*, *but*, and *on the other hand*. (Refer to Appendix 5: Transitions and Patterns of Organization for a detailed list of transition words that indicate the comparison/contrast pattern of organization.)

Depending on their purpose, authors may focus only on the similarities or differences between two subjects, or they may focus on both the similarities and differences between them. Let's look at an example from Selection 2, "Qualities of a Good Nurse" (para. 4, p. 311), to understand the comparison and contrast organizational pattern clearly.

We all tend to be kind and compassionate towards others in our daily lives. The majority of people that we meet are those at work and social gatherings, but a nurse comes across people who are dealing with trauma— both physically and mentally! These people are distressed and are looking for comfort and healing. It is easy to deal with healthy people, but if you are surrounded with patients who need your assistance, then it is important for you to be kind and compassionate towards them. While most of us might get frustrated after a point, a nurse is the one who understands their miseries and comforts them even in the darkest hour. All this cannot be done without compassion being a major essence of your character.

In this paragraph, the author is making the point that a high degree of compassion is crucial if someone is to be a good nurse. She contrasts the kindness and compassion of most people to others in their daily life to the greater depth of compassion needed by nurses, who deal with people who are both physically and mentally traumatized and in need of comfort and healing.

	People	**Nurses**
Differences (contrast)	Kind and compassionate at work and in social settings toward healthy people	Compassionate for those dealing with physical and mental trauma who are looking for comfort and healing
Differences (contrast)	Get frustrated with helping others after a certain point	Understand the miseries of their patients and comfort them even in their darkest hour

Now that you understand the comparison and contrast organizational pattern, complete the following exercise.

EXERCISE 8.8   Identifying Comparison and/or Contrast

Directions: Read the following passages and point out the similarities and differences between the two things being compared and contrasted.

Passage 1

Women are not the sole providers of nursing services. The first nursing school in the world was started in India in about 250 B.C. Only men were considered to be "pure" enough to fulfill the role of nurse at that time. In Jesus's parable in the New Testament, the good Samaritan paid an innkeeper to provide care for the injured man. Paying a man to provide nursing care was fairly common. During the Crusades, several orders of knights provided nursing care to their sick and injured comrades and also built hospitals. The organization and management of their hospitals set a standard for the administration of hospitals throughout Europe at that time. St. Camillus de Lellis started out as a soldier and later turned to nursing. He started the sign of the Red Cross and developed the first ambulance service.

In 1876, only three years after the first U.S. nurse received her diploma from New England Hospital for Women and Children, the Alexian brothers opened their first hospital in the United States and a school to educate men in nursing.

During the years from the Civil War to the Korean War, men were not permitted to serve as nurses in the military. Today, men have resumed their historical place in the profession. As the history of nursing continues to be written, men and women will work side by side.

—From Ramont and Niedringhaus, *Fundamental Nursing Care*, 2e, pp. 8–9

1. What are being compared and contrasted?

2. What is the similarity between male and female nurses?

_____

3. Highlight the transitions and/or other clues that indicate comparisons and contrasts are being provided.

4. What are the differences between male and female nurses?

_____

_____

_____

_____

Passage 2

One of the first questions that should be asked in any healthcare situation is "What language do you normally use to communicate?" Even though a client may understand English in a casual conversation, he or she may not be able to communicate on the technical level required during a health interview. Healthcare workers need to be aware of the dominant language of an area, as well as problems that may be caused by particular dialects. Clients from Mexico may speak 1 of more than 50 dialects. People from the Philippines may speak 1 of 87. The dialect may pose a communication barrier even if a nurse speaks the same language. Dialect differences increase the difficulty of obtaining accurate information.

Many times much more is learned from what is not said than from what is said. Nonverbal communication is vital to communicating with clients, but here cultural variations can have a big impact. For example, in Western cultures, people are expected to make eye contact during communication. In other cultures, Asian specifically, making eye contact is a demonstration of lack of respect.

Touch can convey much, but again, cultures differ on what they permit and accept. It is important for the nurse to be aware of the client's reaction to touch. During the first contact with a client, the nurse should ask permission to touch the client. When performing a procedure that involves touch, the nurse should fully explain the procedure before touching the client.

Facial expressions and hand gestures also have different meanings from one culture to another. For example, individuals of Jewish, Hispanic, and Italian heritage rarely smile because showing one's teeth can be viewed as a sign of aggression. A therapeutic relationship can be promoted or hampered by the nurse's understanding of transcultural communication.

—From Ramont and Niedringhaus, _Fundamental Nursing Care,_ 2e, p. 19

5. What are being compared and contrasted?

_____

6. What is the comparison?

_____

7. Highlight the transitions and/or other clues that indicate comparisons and contrasts are being provided.

8. What are the contrasts?

_____

_____

_____

_____

Cause and Effect

Authors use the **cause and effect organizational pattern** to demonstrate a causal relation between an event and its impact. Sometimes one cause has only one effect. Other times, one cause has several effects. Likewise, multiple causes may have only one effect, and sometimes several causes can have several effects. Look at the diagrams to understand the different types of causal relations between events and their impact.

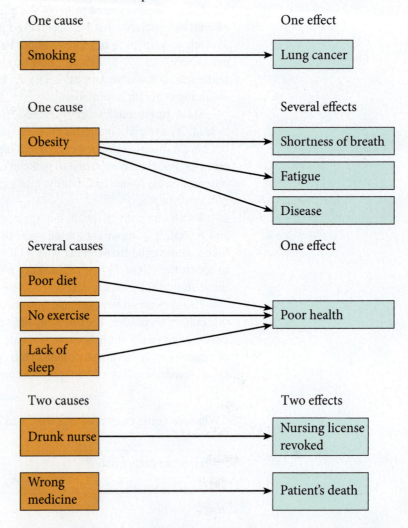

As you can see, the cause and effect relation is quite complex. In addition, just because two things occur close to each other, there is not necessarily a causal relation between them; it could be that two events happened at the same time but were not connected to each other. You will need to read a passage carefully and determine exactly what cause(s) is producing what effect(s) and whether the author has provided enough evidence to support the connections he or she makes. As with the other patterns of organization, it will help if you recognize the transition words that indicate the cause and effect pattern of organization, such as *for this reason, as a result, because,* and *consequently.*

The following paragraphs from Selection 1, "Men Are Much in the Sights of Recruiters in Nursing" (para. 7, p. 305), will help you understand the cause and effect organizational pattern.

> The need for nurses is unlikely to let up any time soon, given the growing health care needs of aging baby boomers. By 2020, the national nursing shortage will more than triple, to 400,000 openings from 126,000 today, the Bureau of Labor Statistics forecasts. In New York State, the shortage is expected to reach 17,000 nurses by 2005 and double that by 2015, according to a study by the state's Education Department.
>
> To help narrow the gap, the industry is going after men, who make up a mere 5.4 percent of the nation's 2.7 million registered nurses and 4 percent of those in the New York metropolitan area. In February, Johnson & Johnson, the pharmaceutical and medical-devices company based in New Brunswick, N.J., featured men in a $20 million public service campaign to promote nursing. "Nursing has slipped from the radar screen for a lot of women who are pursuing other careers, so we thought, 'Why not look at all options, including men?'" said David Swearingen, a Johnson & Johnson spokesman. "They provide a promising audience."

This passage explains why there is a need for more nurses and how this need has caused the industry to start actively recruiting men. The cause and effect relationship established in the passage can be diagrammed as shown here.

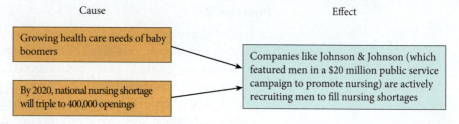

By now you should have an understanding of the cause and effect organizational pattern. Let's do an exercise to further solidify what you have learned.

EXERCISE 8.9 Identifying Cause(s) and Effect(s)

Directions: Read each of the following passages carefully and answer the questions that follow to show your understanding of the cause and effect relationship.

Passage 1

Answers to essay, short-answer, and calculation questions will need to be extracted from your memory. Read the question carefully to determine what is being asked. Some students find it helpful to develop a brief outline before beginning an essay question. Check with the instructor to see if this can be written on the test paper or if you are permitted to use an additional sheet. The outline can help you organize your thoughts and can serve as a checkpoint that all important information was included. Usually, a number of key introductory words appear in essay questions. Look for these words, and do only what is required of you. Many low grades are caused by ignoring these key words.

Calculation questions are particularly troubling for many students who have convinced themselves that they cannot do math. Although math may be difficult, it is a necessary skill for a nurse. With extra practice, calculations are possible to learn. Several methods are used to do calculations.

It is important to show your work on calculations. If you are unable to arrive at the correct answer, your instructor can review your work and will be able to tell you where you went wrong. Memorizing formulas and frequently used conversions will make calculations on tests and in the clinical area much easier.

—From Ramont and Niedringhaus, *Fundamental Nursing Care*, p. 6

1. What are the causes of answering test questions successfully?

_____

_____

_____

_____

2. What are the effects?

_____

_____

Passage 2

Good communication is also important because customer service has become an important part of health care. Health care is a service industry, and clients are increasingly aware consumers. Clients frequently research their disease and the available treatments. When they come for a consultation, they expect to be given all the appropriate information. If information is not given to their satisfaction, they may look elsewhere for care. They may change doctors or refuse to allow a particular healthcare professional to administer treatment to them. Taking time to communicate effectively on first contact is not wasting time. In fact, it may save time, because corrections will not have to be made. Further, a well-informed client is likely to be more willing to participate in the treatment plan than one who is not well informed.

—From Ramont and Niedringhaus, *Fundamental Nursing Care,* p. 20

3. Highlight the transitions and/or other clues that indicate causes and/or effects are being provided.

4. Make a list of causes and their effects based on the information provided in this passage in the table below.

Cause	Effect

Classification

Authors use the **classification organizational pattern** to sort ideas into categories according to their characteristics. These characteristics are chosen on the basis of their similarities. For example, a nursing textbook may describe the different types of drugs by their function and the reaction expected in a patient. Authors use this pattern to make a complicated topic easier to understand and/or to analyze it.

An effective way to understand content organized by the classification pattern is to determine how the topic is divided (what criteria the author used) and what his or her purpose was for breaking the topic into parts. If you can see how the different characteristics are categorized, you are more likely to understand and remember the important parts of the topic. Paying attention to transition words such as *this type, this group*, or *these varieties* will help you to identify when an author is classifying a topic.

Read the following paragraph from Selection 3, "Overview of Nursing Process" (para. 8, p. 335), and pay special attention to how the topic is divided into different categories.

An infinite variety of possible human responses occurs at all levels: cells, organs, systems, interpersonal, cultural, and so on. The stressors that cause health problems are often diseases or microorganisms, but they can also be:

- Environmental—e.g., too much exposure to the sun produces a sunburn.
- Interpersonal—e.g., adapting to parenthood causes stress after a baby is born.
- Spiritual—e.g., guilt about falling away from one's religion may lead to depression.

As you can see, the topic of the passage is *the infinite variety of possible human responses*, which has three categories that are provided in the bulleted list. Notice that all of these categories are chosen on the basis of their similarities; that is, they are all types of stressors that can cause health problems.

Now that you understand how writers use the classification organizational pattern, do the following exercise. Look for the main categories; some of these may have subtopics.

EXERCISE 8.10   Identifying Classification

Directions: Read the following passages carefully. Then find the topic of each passage and the different categories into which the topic is divided.

Passage 1

Nurses learn general concepts about transcultural nursing and specific facts about various cultures so that we can provide ethical and effective care to all our clients. We must understand how ideas from other cultures agree with or differ from our own. We must be sensitive to issues of race, gender, sexual orientation, social class, and economic situation in our everyday work. A cultural assessment has four basic elements. These data can be collected by the LPN/LVN.

1. The cultural identity of the client. How does the client identify himself or herself culturally? Does the client feel closer to the native culture or to the host culture? What is the client's language preference?

2. The cultural factors related to the client's psychosocial environment. What stressors are there in the local environment? What role does religion play in the individual's life? What kind of support system does the client have?

3. The cultural elements of the relationship between the healthcare provider and the client. What kind of experiences has the client had with healthcare providers, either now or in the past? (The nurse should also consider what differences exist between the provider's and the client's culture and social status. These differences are important in communicating and in negotiating an appropriate relationship.)

4. The cultural explanation of the client's illness. What is the client's cultural explanation of the illness? What idioms does the client use to describe it? (For example, the client may say she is suffering from *ataque de nervios*— an attack of the nerves. This is a syndrome in Hispanic cultures that closely resembles anxiety and depressive disorders.) Is there a name or category used by the client's family or community to identify the condition? In order for care to be client centered, no matter what culture the client is, the nurse has to elicit specific information from the client and use it to organize strategies for care.

When performing the cultural assessment, the nurse needs to consider many of the cultural domains that were mentioned earlier.

—*Fundamental Nursing Care*, pp. 21–22

1. What is the topic?

_____

2. How many categories is the topic divided into?

_____

3. Highlight the transitions and/or other clues that indicate categories are being provided.

4. What are those categories?

_____

_____

_____

Passage 2

Larry Purnell and B. J. Paulanka (1998) developed a model for cultural competence that describes 12 domains of culture. This assessment tool identifies ethno cultural attributes of an individual, family, or group. Box A provides a list of these domains.

Box A

Twelve Domains of Culture
 1. Overview, inhabited localities, and topography
 2. Communication
 3. Family roles and organization
 4. Workforce issues
 5. Biocultural ecology
 6. High-risk health behaviors
 7. Nutrition
 8. Pregnancy and childbearing practices
 9. Death rituals
10. Spirituality
11. Healthcare practices
12. Healthcare practitioners

In everyday practice as a practical or vocational nurse, you will need to be aware of these domains. You will develop knowledge of different cultures, especially those in the area where you live and work. This should include becoming familiar with the part of the world where those cultures were established and the heritage of the people. It is also important for you to realize that individuals within a particular culture may have characteristics that don't "fit" their group. It is important not to generalize and stereotype a member of a group (Purnell & Paulanka, 1998).

—From Ramont and Niedringhaus, _Fundamental Nursing Care,_ 2e, p. 18

1. What is the topic of the passage?

_____

2. Highlight the transitions and/or other clues that indicate categories are being provided.

3. The topic is divided into twelve parts. What are they?

_____

_____

_____

_____

READING

Selection 3

Textbook excerpt

Overview of Nursing Process

Pre-Reading Questions

Answer the following questions before exploring the text:

1. What, in your opinion, are some of the responsibilities of a registered nurse? Be specific.

2. Most people assume that a nurse is almost always a woman. Do you think women are superior to men in terms of taking care of patients, or do you believe men can be as good as women when it comes to giving patient care? Why, or why not?

3. Florence Nightingale, one of the most dedicated nurses, once said that what nurses do "is to put the patient in the best condition for nature to act upon him." Discuss what she meant by that.

Overview of Nursing Process

by Judith Wilkinson

What Is Nursing?

1   A broad understanding of nursing will help you to understand the nursing process and how it fits into the way you think and practice as a nurse. Nursing has the following unique combination of characteristics. It is:

- A blend of art and science
- Applied within the context of interpersonal relationships
- Done for the purpose of promoting wellness, preventing illness, and restoring health
- Used when caring for individuals, families, and communities

The Art of Nursing

2   Think about the difference between a painting you might make and one you would find hanging in an art gallery. Now apply that to nursing. It should be assumed that you will have the theoretical knowledge and technical skills to provide safe nursing care. However, nursing art goes beyond this. It involves sensitivity, creativity, **empathy**, and the ability to adapt care—either to meet a patient's unique needs or in the face of uncertainty (Finfgeld Connett, 2008), and it includes the ability to

1. Develop meaningful connections with clients
2. Grasp the meaning in client encounters.
3. Perform nursing activities skillfully.
4. Use rational thinking to choose appropriate courses of action.
5. Conduct one's nursing practice ethically (Johnson, 1994)

FIGURE A

Overview of the Interconnected Phases of the Nursing Process

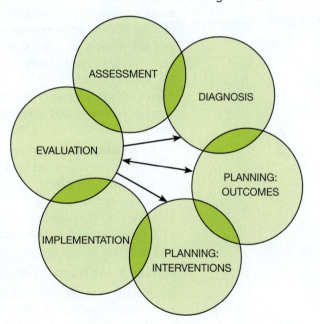

Defining Nursing

3   Florence Nightingale (1820–1910), the first nurse theorist, said that what nurses do "is to put the patient in the best condition for nature to act upon him." This fits with the holistic idea that people have innate abilities for growth and self-healing and that the nurse's role is to **nurture** and support those abilities. The American Nurses Association (ANA), the professional organization for U.S. Nurses, defines nursing this way:

> Nursing is the protection, promotion, and optimization of health and abilities, prevention of illness and injury, alleviation of suffering through the diagnosis, and treatment of human response, and advocacy in the care of individuals, families, communities, and populations (ANA, 2004, p. 7).

4   The ANA Social Policy Statement describes six essential features of contemporary nursing practice (2003). Nurses:

1. Do not focus only on problems—they consider a range of human experiences.
2. Integrate patients' subjective experience with objective data.
3. Use critical thinking to apply scientific knowledge to diagnosis and treatment processes.
4. Provide a caring relationship that facilitates health and healing.
5. Advance professional nursing knowledge through scholarly inquiry.
6. Influence social and public policy to promote social justice.

Nursing Theory

5   Nursing theory offers a way of looking at the discipline in clear, explicit terms that can be communicated to others. Theories help to explain the unique place of nursing in the interdisciplinary team. They are based on the theorist's values and assumptions about health, patients, nursing, and the environment. Each theory describes those concepts and explains how they are related. Think of a theory as a lens through which to view nursing and patients: the color and shape of the lens affect what you see. That is why there are so many definitions of nursing and why your theory of nursing affects your use of the nursing process.

6   Although definitions and theories vary, most agree that even though nurses care for patients with health problems, nursing is not limited to **disease** processes and that nursing concerns are different from medical concerns. Overall, nursing theories (models) describe nursing as:

- An art and a science with its own evolving, scientific body of knowledge
- Holistic, or concerned with the client's physical psychosocial,cultural, and spiritual needs
- Involving caring
- Occurring in a variety of settings
- Concerned with health promotion, disease prevention, and care during illness

Nurses Treat Human Responses

7   Nurses view patients holistically, so they are concerned with human responses—reactions to an event or stressor such as disease or injury. Nurses diagnose, treat, and prevent patient responses to diseases rather than the disease itself. For example, if a patient has diabetes, the nurse would be concerned about the patient's lack of knowledge about diet and possible loss of self-esteem; the primary care provider would prescribe insulin to treat high blood sugar. Reactions (responses) may be biological, social, and spiritual.

> **Example:** Consider the following possible patient responses to a heart attack:
> Physical response: Pain
> Psychological response: Fear
> Sociological response: Returning to work before she is well
> Spiritual response: Praying

8   An infinite variety of possible human responses occurs at all levels: cells, organs, systems, interpersonal, cultural, and so on. The stressors that cause health problems are often diseases or microorganisms, but they can also be:

- Environmental—e.g., too much exposure to the sun produces a sunburn.
- Interpersonal—e.g., adapting to parenthood causes stress after a baby is born.
- Spiritual—e.g., guilt about falling away from one's religion may lead to depression.

Interdisciplinary Practice

9   Increasingly, healthcare is delivered by multidisciplinary teams. This is also referred to as collaborative practice and interdisciplinary practice. This means that nurses, physicians, and other professionals work together to plan and provide patient care. This does not mean that nurses must become invisible; each discipline retains its identity even as they collaborate.

10   Although some functions may be shared, nursing is different from medicine. Physicians focus on diagnosis and treatment of disease; nurses focus on giving care during the cure. This is sometimes referred to as curing versus caring. Caring in this sense refers to the activities that nurses perform in taking care of patients, not the subjective feeling of caring about patients. That feeling may, of course, be involved, but it does not necessarily differentiate nursing from medicine. Table 1.1 summarizes the differences between nursing and medicine.

Table 1.1 Comparison of Nursing and Medicine

Medical Focus	Nursing Focus
1. Diagnose and treat disease. 2. Cure disease. 3. Focus on pathophysiology and biological, physical effects. 4. Teach patients about the treatments for their disease or injury.	1. Diagnose, treat, and prevent human responses. 2. Care for the patient. 3. Take a holistic approach—consider the effects on the whole person (biological, psychosocial, cultural, spiritual). 4. Teach clients self-care strategies to increase independence in daily activities. 5. Promote wellness activities.

Nursing in Wellness and Illness

11   Nursing is concerned with the whole process, ill or well. Nurses support ill people and help them to (a) solve or reduce their health problems and (b) adapt to and accept problems that cannot be treated. They help those who are terminally ill to achieve a peaceful death. For well people, nurses aim to prevent illness and promote wellness. This may involve a variety of activities, such as role modeling a healthy lifestyle; being an advocate for community environmental changes; or teaching self-care strategies, decision making, and problem solving.

Thinking about the Reading

After doing a close reading of the article, write your answers to the following questions. You may be asked to discuss your answers with your classmates.

1. Why are interpersonal relationships mentioned as a characteristic of nursing?

   _____

   _____

2. Why does the author believe that nursing art goes beyond the theoretical knowledge and technical skills necessary to provide nursing care? Refer to the text to answer the question.

   _____

   _____

   _____

3. According to the essay, how do nurses support well people? Refer to the text to give specific examples.

   _____

   _____

Reading Comprehension Check

_____ 1. "It involves sensitivity, creativity, empathy, and the ability to **adapt** care—either to meet a patient's unique needs or in the face of uncertainty." In this context, the word *adapt* means

   a. to continue to practice the same thing.
   b. to make appropriate by modification.
   c. to decrease care.
   d. to increase care.

_____ 2. The overall pattern of organization in paragraph 2 is

   a. comparison and contrast.
   b. cause and effect.
   c. process.
   d. statement and clarification.

_____ 3. In paragraph 6, the overall pattern of organization is

   a. process.   c. definition.
   b. cause and effect.   d. listing.

_____ 4. The overall pattern of organization used in Table 1-1 is

   a. definition.   c. chronological order.
   b. cause and effect.   d. comparison and contrast.

_____ 5. The author uses the following pattern of organization in paragraph 10:

   a. example.   c. comparison and contrast.
   b. spatial order.   d. listing.

_____ **6.** Most nursing theories describe nursing as involving caring, occurring in a variety of settings, and _____.

    a. concerned with mechanical processes

    b. concerned with health promotion

    c. prescribing medication

    d. diagnosing disease

_____ **7.** According to one theory mentioned in the reading, nursing is different from medicine in that nurses provide caring, while physicians provide _____.

    a. curing   c. prescriptions

    b. confidence   d. compassion

_____ **8.** Which of the following statements about the reading content is _false_?

    a. A nurse's theory of nursing will affect his or her nursing process.

    b. Nurses are usually part of an interdisciplinary team of health care professionals.

    c. Nurses help people with fatal illness die peacefully.

    d. Nurses focus specifically on the physical complaints of their clients.

_____ **9.** In the reading, the word _holistic_ is used to mean

    a. advancing professional nursing knowledge through scholarly inquiry and scientific research.

    b. the theory of nursing rather than with the practice of medicine.

    c. diagnosing, treating, and preventing disease.

    d. a comprehensive approach to all of a client's needs (physical, mental, or spiritual).

_____ **10.** According to the reading, in addition to the diseases themselves, stressors that cause health problems can include _____, interpersonal, or spiritual factors.

    a. environmental   c. marital

    b. financial   d. educational

Think to Write

Now that you have completed three readings in this chapter on nursing, think about which of the three is most interesting to you. Write a paragraph response about this reading and post it to The Wall. You can also choose a reading that you like most and write a summary of it. You will submit your summary to your peers and instructor for feedback on both form (grammar) and content (ideas).

It's SHOWTIME!

Watching a video clip related to the chapter content can be an enriching experience. Go online and find a video link whose topic ties into one of the chapter readings (maximum length = ten minutes). After viewing the video clip, write a half-page summary of the video's key points. Post your personal reaction to the ideas in the clip (between 150 and 400 words) on The Wall.

WRITING

Choosing Patterns of Organization to Match Your Writing Assignment

OBJECTIVE

5 Use appropriate patterns of organization to convey information

As you learn to write academic essays, your professor will give you many writing assignments. Some may require you to compare and contrast two important people, others will ask you to define a term or concept, and yet others will need you to establish a causal relation between two things. As you learned earlier in this chapter, different patterns of organization use different transition words, which help to make the author's purpose clear to the reader. It is important that you familiarize yourself with the transitions associated with different patterns of organization, so that you can use them in your own writing to guide readers through your ideas.

EXERCISE 8.11 **Using Appropriate Patterns of Organization for Different Writing Assignments**

Directions: Imagine that you are an expert in the discipline of nursing, and you frequently write papers on topics related to the field. In the table below, write the pattern of organization that pertains to the topic and provide examples of transition words that are related to the pattern of organization. The first example is done for you.

Topic	Pattern of Organization	Transition Words
Define "segregation" and "discrimination" with respect to the profession of nursing.	Definition	it involves, it is called, it occurs when, it entails, it means, for example
Explain why "fidelity" is an important quality in a nurse.		
What are the differences between a customer and a patient?		
How does an impaired nurse affect the practice of nursing?		
Discuss why it is important for a registered nurse to learn about various cultures.		
Write a short biography of Florence Nightingale.		
Explain to a novice nurse how to administer an intramuscular injection.		

Topic	Pattern of Organization	Transition Words
Review client records for student and graduate nursing professionals.		
Discuss the relevance of facial expressions to a registered nurse.		
Explain to a patient how she should walk with a cane.		

EXERCISE 8.12 **Choosing Patterns to Match a Writing Assignment**

Directions: Choose two essay topics from the following list and write at least three paragraphs for each one. Be sure to use transition words that are appropriate for the patterns of organization you use.

1. What are the differences between a customer and a patient?

2. Write a short biography of Florence Nightingale.

3. Discuss why it is important for a registered nurse to learn about various cultures.

4. Discuss the relevance of facial expressions to a registered nurse.

5. How does a nurse help a patient recover from an illness?

6. How does an impaired nurse affect the practice of nursing?

TROUBLE SPOTS IN WRITING

OBJECTIVE
6 Use the conventions of academic English for writing assignments

Formal Versus Informal Writing

Among other things, your success as a college student will depend on your ability to understand the difference between formal and informal writing. As you write academic essays for your professor, you will need to adhere to the linguistic conventions of North American academic written discourse.

While informal writing is acceptable in texting a friend or a family member, it is inappropriate to use contractions such as *can't* and *won't* in an academic essay. It is fine if you are a fiction writer and one of the characters in your novel uses slang and idiomatic expressions. However, your writing professor will expect you to demonstrate a certain level of proficiency and sophistication as you write a response to an assigned reading. Clearly, your college career will be largely determined by how well you write and demonstrate your mastery of language.

EXERCISE 8.13   Distinguishing Between Formal and Informal Writing

Directions: The table below begins with an example of how to convert informal language into formal writing. Refer to this example as you provide your own examples of formal writing to replace the informal writing provided. You may work with a classmate to do this exercise. After you finish the exercise, share your examples with your classmates and professor.

Informal Writing	Formal Writing
I'm gonna drop this whole thing.	I will have to consider another alternative.
The study didn't really do much.	
You betcha the economy won't be better.	
The government ain't gonna give no dough for the program.	
These things can be used in all kinds of things.	
You've gotta see the numbers in Table 1.	
Whatcha gonna do to reduce global warming?	
This thing was made by Hoffman first.	
I need to really know what went down last night.	
It is gonna be really hard to make a final decision about the method we should use in the future.	

THEN & NOW

If you really want to understand an academic field, it is useful to get a sense of how the academic discipline has evolved over time. This feature gives you the opportunity to do just that.

Go online and do some research to gather information about two experts in the field of nursing: one from the past and another contemporary. You may learn about a prominent nurse from the past such as Florence Nightingale or Walt Whitman and a contemporary nurse such as Erin Murphy or Donna Howard. Fill out the table provided below with pertinent information about the two nurses.

Past Influential Expert	**Present Influential Expert**
Name	Name
Place of birth	Place of birth
Year of birth	Year of birth
Education	Education
What is s/he most famous for?	What is s/he most famous for?
Famous quote	Famous quote

After you fill out the table, discuss your findings with your classmates and learn from them about what they discovered on the Internet.

Working with a search engine, do the following search: "The Life of Florence Nightingale Reynolds Historical Library." Peruse the article to appreciate the great contributions of Florence Nightingale to the field of nursing. After doing a careful reading, write brief answers to the following questions about the content.

1. According to the article, Florence Nightingale's parents had great expectations for the "marriage and social life of their daughters." Discuss why she chose nursing as a profession in contradiction to her parents' expectations.

   _____

   _____

2. Why did medical historian Fielding Garrison call the period between the second half of the seventeenth century and the middle of the nineteenth century "the dark age of nursing"?

   _____

   _____

3. Why is Florence Nightingale most famously known for her work during the Crimean War?

   _____

   _____

   _____

CHAPTER ESSAY ASSIGNMENT

What are the most important qualities of an excellent nurse?

 7

OBJECTIVE

Read, think, plan, and write an essay in response to the chapter essay assignment

Now that you have had the opportunity to read a number of articles and a textbook excerpt, you should have a deeper understanding of the field of nursing and be prepared to compose your chapter essay assignment.

Assignment: Write a two- to three-page essay on this topic, or your own topic. Support your claims with evidence or examples drawn from what you have read in the chapter and other relevant readings from other sources. You can also support your claims from what you have learned in school and/or personally experienced

Be sure to include a clear thesis statement in your opening paragraph. After you have received constructive feedback from your instructor, be sure to incorporate some of his or her suggestions into your second draft and submit it for further feedback on form and meaning.

| FOCUS ON FORM | # Informal Versus Formal Writing |

In this chapter, we discussed distinguishing between informal and formal writing. Let's put your newly acquired skills into action! First, read the following paragraph and find examples of informal writing. After that, revise the passage to make it more formal, and rewrite it below. When you are done, compare your version with that of a classmate.

> I'm gonna talk about nurses who take drugs. About 10–15% of registered nurses are kicking the habit of smoking pot. You betcha they won't be able to quit cold turkey without support. Clearly, the government ain't gonna give no dough for the rehabilitation program. You've gotta see the scary numbers in Table 1. It shows that it is gonna be crazy hard for nurses to quit taking drugs and go back to work.

_____

_____

_____

_____

_____

_____

_____

It's Your Turn!

Now that you have had a chance to identify instances of informal writing and rewrite them to adhere to the linguistic conventions of formal writing, review the essay you wrote for the chapter essay assignment and look for examples of informal writing. After locating all instances of informal writing, rewrite the sentences to conform to the rules of formal writing.

CHAPTER DEBATE OPTION

What are the most important qualities of an excellent nurse?

This chapter's debate topic is the same as your chapter essay assignment. Refer to Appendix 8, page 455, for detailed guidelines on how to set up and participate in a formal debate.

9 Business

Learning Objectives

IN THIS CHAPTER, YOU WILL LEARN TO . . .

1 Read in the field of business

2 Understand and use key terms in business

3 Differentiate between facts and opinions

4 Correctly use MLA format

5 Use punctuation rules appropriately

6 Read, think, plan, and write an essay in response to the chapter essay assignment

Introduction to the Field of Business

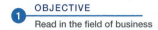

There are businesses of all different sizes, from giant corporations such as IBM, Google, and Apple to local mom-and-pop stores to small online start-up companies. Regardless of their size, resources, annual revenue, or the kinds of products and services they offer, these businesses have one thing in common—they all offer either products or services to earn money. All of these businesses try to keep their overheads as low as possible to maximize profits. To reach this goal, some businesses—whether small or big—do not hesitate to manipulate the consumer, as they have a vested interest in selling their products and services.

This chapter introduces the discipline of business. The main theme, however, is whether business and ethics can coexist. Selection 1 focuses on the issue of businesses lowering their moral standards to compete with each other and how this eventually hurts the companies, their shareholders, and employees. Selection 2 examines why Facebook, a social media juggernaut, should follow ethical standards like any other company. Finally, Selection 3, a textbook reading, questions if Fair Trade programs designed to support farmers are really fair. After reading these selections, you will understand that while business ethics and social responsibility may coexist in principle, the reality can be different.

CHAPTER ESSAY QUESTION

Can business and ethics coexist?

Quick Free-Write! Take out a piece of paper, and write for ten minutes without stopping about what you already know about the theme of the chapter essay question.

As you read through the chapter, keep in mind the essay question and consider how you will incorporate multiple perspectives on the issue into your paper. Chapter essays will be due when your class completes the chapter.

Your Option: Once you have worked your way through the chapter readings, you are welcome to narrow down the topics covered and compose your own chapter essay question.

Previewing Business

Read the following questions and discuss them with your classmates. As you answer the questions, consider your personal experience and knowledge of business.

1. Many people believe that there is "no heart in business." This brings up the debate as to whether business and ethics can coexist. Express your opinion on this topic and share some examples based on your personal experience.

2. Millions of Americans share the dream of starting a business. Do you believe that working for yourself offers a better life than working for a company or an organization? Discuss the advantages and disadvantages of entrepreneurship as opposed to simply being an employee.

3. More and more American companies are hiring employees in foreign countries to maximize profits. Critics argue that this trend, called outsourcing, hurts the local economy and deprives the American people of employment opportunities. Do you think that the government should mandate that corporations solely hire domestically, or should corporations have the freedom to act as they please?

4. Some people are concerned that the United States of America is losing its edge as a world economic leader. They worry that rising powers such as China and the European Union (EU) are a threat to America's supremacy as a leader in science and technology. Discuss what the United States must do to maintain its leadership in the world.

5. Mihaly Csikszentmihalyi, a famous Hungarian psychologist, once said, "A business is successful to the extent that it provides a product or service that contributes to happiness in all of its forms." Discuss whether the principal goal of business should be to enhance the quality of life for all. Name a few socially responsible companies that are working toward this goal. Can you think of some whose attitudes appear to be heartless? Do you think that envisioning a world where all businesses contribute to our overall happiness is far-fetched? Explain.

After discussing the preview questions with your classmates, post your responses to two of them on The Wall. Peruse The Wall and respond to at least two of your classmates' responses that pique your interest.

OBJECTIVE
②
Understand and use key terms in business

Key Terms in Business

Take a moment to think about the discipline of business as you complete the following two exercises.

EXERCISE 9.1 Brainstorming Vocabulary

What associated words come to mind when you think of the world of business? Work with a partner and write down as many related words as you can think of in a period of five minutes.

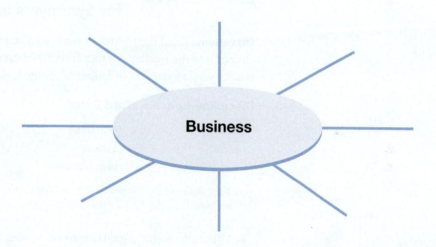

EXERCISE 9.2 Creating Original Sentences

Directions: Choose five of the words from your brainstorm list, and use them to write complete and meaningful sentences.

1. _____

2. _____

3. _____

4. _____

5. _____

One of the most effective ways to build your academic vocabulary is to study key terms that are connected thematically. When you take your 100-level credit-bearing content courses, it will be critical that you have a strong vocabulary base in the academic subjects you are studying, so it is important for you to learn key terms that are pertinent to the academic discipline you choose to study. As the focus of this chapter is business, you will need to learn and apply such terms as *profit, supply,* and *economy* in your speech and writing.

In addition, understanding how to work with synonyms and antonyms is a useful skill, especially when you are writing a summary of a text and/or trying to paraphrase some of the key ideas and pieces of information contained in an original source. The following exercise will enable you to learn some key terms in the discipline of business and practice using synonyms and antonyms for them.

> A **synonym** is a word used to express a similar meaning to another word. An **antonym** is a word that conveys the opposite meaning of another word.

EXERCISE 9.3 Discipline-specific Vocabulary: Fishing for Synonyms and Antonyms

Directions: Read the following ten (10) discipline-specific words in context culled from the readings in this chapter. In the space provided after each sentence, write a synonym or antonym for the highlighted term, as directed.

Discipline-specific Word Bank*

moral	practices	supply	economy
profit	ethical	production	incentive
negotiating	regulations		

* These discipline-specific words are shown in bold green the first time they appear in the chapter readings.

1. "Recently major organizations have been lumped with hefty fines for questionable **moral** practices." (Selection 1, p. 350, para. 1)

   An antonym for *moral* is _____.

2. "While businesses compete for **profit**, the boundaries between right and wrong become blurred and people's ethical frame of reference shifts." (Selection 1, p. 351, para. 2)

   A synonym for *profit* is _____.

3. "They, in turn, need to teach not just right vs. wrong, but a way of **negotiating** ethical dilemmas so that their followers always act with integrity." (Selection 1, p. 351, para. 3)

   An antonym for *negotiating* is _____.

4. "She argued that the company and other social media sites regularly engage in research, and that the **practice** is thus acceptable." (Selection 1, p. 356, para. 1)

   A synonym for *practice* is _____.

5. "Social media companies can now strengthen users' trust by agreeing to follow **ethical** standards." (Selection 2, p. 356, para. 3)

   An antonym for *ethical* is _____.

6. "At present, researchers at almost all universities and pharmaceutical and biotech companies have agreed to follow the federal **regulations** governing research as a standard in conducting experiments on human beings." (Selection 2, p. 357, para. 6)

 An antonym for *regulations* is _____.

7. "More than 40 percent of the world's **supply** of cacao beans comes from small farms scattered throughout the West African nation of Ivory Coast, which may ship as much as 47,000 tons per month to the United States." (Selection 3, p. 367, para. 1)

 An antonym for *supply* is _____.

8. "According to reports issued at the end of the 1990s by the United Nations Children's Fund and the U.S. State Department, much of the labor involved in Ivory Coast cocoa **production** is performed by children, chiefly boys ranging in age from 12 to 16. (Selection 3, p. 367, para. 1)

 A synonym for *production* is _____.

9. "One-third of the country's **economy** is based on cocoa exports, and the Ivory Coast is heavily dependent on world market prices for cocoa." (Selection 3, p. 368, para 2)

 A synonym for *economy* is _____.

10. "What **incentive** encourages importers, manufacturers, and distributors not only to adopt FLO-Transfair standards but to bear the costs of subsidizing overseas producers? (Selection 3, p. 368, para. 5)

 A synonym for *incentive* is _____.

READING

Selection 1

Magazine article

Business Leaders Beware: **Ethical** *Drift Makes Standards Slip*

Pre-Reading Questions

Answer the following questions before exploring the text:

1. In your opinion, is it possible for an honest person to become a business leader? Why, or why not?

2. Some believe that shrewdness and immorality are necessary traits for successful business people. Do you agree or disagree with this view? Explain.

3. Can you think of a company that lied and broke the law to make a profit? Give specific examples to describe this company.

4. Can you think of a company that lives up to ethical standards? Give specific examples to describe this company.

Eye on Vocabulary

It may be helpful to focus on the meaning of some key words in the article before you read. Skim through the reading and look for the following key vocabulary terms in bold. Working with a partner, examine the words in context and try to guess the meaning of each. Then look up the words in a dictionary. Keep in mind that many words have multiple meanings. Write the definition that best fits the word's context in the article.

Word	Your definition	Dictionary definition
1. scandals (n.)		
2. dubious (adj.)		
3. legislation (n.)		
4. loophole (n.)		

Business Leaders Beware: Ethical Drift Makes Standards Slip

by Sebastian Bailey

1   Business ethics have certainly been in the spotlight over the last couple of years—with **scandals** involving Libor-fixing (Libor stands for London Inter-Bank Offer Rate and refers to the standard interest rate for loans between financial institutions), failing to prevent money laundering, and breaking the rules around defaulted mortgages to name a few. Recently

major organizations have been lumped with hefty fines for questionable **moral practices**. Are **dubious** morals inevitable for successful business?

2   In his recent paper on ethical reasoning, eminent psychologist Robert Sternberg suggests that organizations suffer from ethical drift—a gradual, unconscious lowering of moral standards. While businesses compete for **profit**, the boundaries between right and wrong become blurred and people's ethical frame of reference shifts. Human biases like being unrealistically optimistic about an outcome, believing ourselves to be all-powerful, all-knowing and invincible, and the tendency to justify our own behavior no matter how morally hollow (finessing my expenses is OK because I pay for lots of things which I forget about) means that few people recognize the problem, let alone know how to tackle it.

3   Rules and **legislation** aren't the answer—there's always a **loophole** to be found and the focus becomes navigating the system, rather than doing what's right. Instead we need leaders with a strong moral compass. They, in turn, need to teach not just right vs. wrong, but a way of **negotiating** ethical dilemmas so that their followers always act with integrity.

4   Sternberg suggests that to behave ethically, you have to first go through a series of stages of reasoning:

1. **Recognize that there's an event to react to, that it has an ethical dimension and that it's serious enough to require an ethical response.** Ethical drift means that questionable behavior is simply the norm and therefore not questioned at all. One leader I know who has a huge amount of integrity asks the question, 'If this situation was printed on the front page of the *New York Post* or the UK's *Sun*, would you be comfortable with it?'

2. **Take responsibility for generating an ethical solution.** Even if employees recognize there's a moral issue at stake, the typical response is "it's none of my business." We assume that if it's OK with the boss, it's OK with us. With all the other competing priorities—revenue, profit, quality, customer service, team engagement—ethical decision making can be demoted to a footnote.

3. **Figure out what ethical rules apply.** What are the principles that apply here? Organizations often develop values statements or charters to support leaders in making these decisions. Johnson & Johnson, who frequently top the charts in terms of being a reputable brand, constantly refer to their Credo.

4. **Decide how to apply those abstract rules to the situation in order to suggest a concrete solution.** This is where it gets interesting as it involves managerial judgment. It's also perhaps the hardest step, as values statements and credos can quickly become inane platitudes plastered on mouse mats and canteen posters. Instead leaders and managers have to judge the dilemma. In one values project I worked on with a global consultancy we set up dilemmas that the leaders had to resolve. Two of the values were, and I'm paraphrasing here, "Caring for people" and "Delighting clients."No one would disagree with either. We then collected real situations where these values collided. One dilemma was: "You are working on one of the firm's most important clients. On Friday afternoon,

the CEO unexpectedly calls an emergency board meeting on a Sunday morning. The lead consultant is the only person with the knowledge to effectively put together the papers for the board meeting. The lead consultant is the best man at a wedding on Saturday. What do you do?" A second dilemma involved the discovery that a consultancy project had run a significantly negative ROI (return on investment) for the client! What's the appropriate course of action here? It was in these conversations that the values and the practice of ethical decision making came to life.

5. **Prepare for the repercussions.** There's no shortage of whistle-blowers who've been ostracized, ridiculed or even attacked. Look at Greg Smith, the former Goldman Sachs employee who famously penned a *New York Times* article branding the organization's culture "toxic" and "morally bankrupt." Goldman Sachs investigated his claim and responded by revealing that he was "off the charts unrealistic" about his own ability.

6. **Act.** Of course, for all the chaste codes of conduct, being good is a lot harder in practice than in theory. Leaders need to take an approach of doing well by doing good, otherwise the ethical drift shows little sign of slowing.

Thinking about the Reading

After doing a close reading of the article, write your answers to the following questions. When you have written all of your answers, discuss them with your classmates.

1. The author asks, "Are dubious morals inevitable for successful business?" Answer the question from your own experience.

_____

_____

2. Why does the psychologist Robert Sternberg suggest that "organizations suffer from ethical drift—a gradual, unconscious lowering of moral standards"? Refer to the passage to answer the question.

_____

_____

_____

3. Sternberg suggests that a corporation needs to go through six stages of reasoning to make sure it behaves ethically. Which stages are most important to you and why? Explain.

_____

_____

Reading Comprehension Check

_____ 1. "Recently major organizations have been lumped with **hefty** fines for questionable moral practices." The word _hefty_ in the above context is opposite in meaning to _____.

    a. large   c. light
    b. heavy   d. big

_____ 2. The main idea of the article is that

    a. business leaders must behave ethically so that their followers will act with integrity.
    b. business leaders cannot be expected to be role models because they have to make tough decisions in a competitive world.
    c. leaders do not need to teach their subordinates right versus wrong.
    d. leaders must do a lot of good to become role models for their industries.

_____ 3. The author mentions examples of "scandals involving Libor-fixing, failing to prevent money laundering, and breaking the rules around defaulted mortgages" to establish which of the following?

    a. Many businesses have behaved ethically in the last two years.
    b. Many businesses have not acted ethically in the last two years.
    c. Many business leaders have taught employees right versus wrong.
    d. Many business leaders make ethically sound decisions.

_____ 4. It can be inferred from Greg Smith's example that

    a. whistle-blowers can be rewarded by those they expose.
    b. whistle-blowers are favored by most business leaders.
    c. whistle-blowers are appreciated by most businesses.
    d. whistle-blowers can be ostracized by the company's they work for.

_____ 5. According to the author, why are ethical rules crucially important?

    a. They can help business leaders find loopholes in the law and avoid punishment.
    b. They come in handy when a company is trying to cover up a scandal.
    c. When faced with an ethical dilemma, they help a company find a moral solution.
    d. Ethical rules can cause business leaders to make unsound decisions when faced with a crisis.

_____ 6. According to Bailey, the term _ethical drift_ most nearly means

    a. a slow, unwitting relaxation of strict moral standards of behavior.
    b. adopting dubious morals that are necessary for conducting business.
    c. deciding on rules and legislation regarding morals in business dealings.
    d. a constantly changing perspective on the process of negotiating ethical dilemmas.

_____ **7.** In paragraph 3, the phrase "a strong moral compass" most nearly means

     a. the ability to apply abstract rules to a concrete solution in the business world.

     b. the ability to find a way out of a business loophole.

     c. the ability to navigate the system of rules and legislation with ease.

     d. the ability to judge between right and wrong and act with integrity.

_____ **8.** Applying rules to a situation in order to arrive at a solution involves

     a. managerial judgment.

     b. working through stages of reasoning.

     c. ethical drift.

     d. a loophole.

_____ **9.** According to the reading, if not applied to real situations, values statements and credos can quickly become

     a. loopholes.

     b. ethical rules.

     c. inane platitudes.

     d. questionable moral practices.

_____ **10.** In paragraph 2, which of the following is *not* mentioned as an example of human bias?

     a. believing that the customer is always right

     b. believing oneself to be all-powerful

     c. defending one's questionable moral behavior

     d. being overly optimistic

THEMATIC LINKS

If you want to learn more about the topic of business leaders and ethics, type the following words into your browser and explore the two sites that come up:

  1. The Decline of Ethical Behavior in Business Quality Digest

  2. A Tale of Two CEOs: Elizabeth Holmes and Martin Shkreli

Writing Without BOUNDARIES

There Are No Checkpoints!

"To give real service you must add something which cannot be bought or measured with money, and that is sincerity and integrity."

—Douglas Adams

Read the quote above and respond to Adams's idea in any way you want. Write in your notebook for ten minutes without stopping. For this activity, it is important that you focus on ideas, not words. This is an exercise in focusing on content and not getting hung up on word choice and grammar errors. You may wish to read what you have written out loud in front of your classmates and instructor.

Selection 2

Huffington Post/
Online article

Why Facebook Should Follow Ethical Standards—
Like Everybody Else

Pre-Reading Questions

Answer the following questions before exploring the text:

1. Do you believe that Facebook has the right to collect its users' data without their knowledge and consent for research purposes? Why, or why not?

2. In your opinion, can the information you receive from social media affect your mood? Explain.

3. Discuss why it is important for social media companies to follow ethical standards when conducting research on human subjects.

Eye on Vocabulary

It may be helpful to focus on the meaning of some key words in the article before you read. Skim through the reading and look for the following key vocabulary terms in bold. Working with a partner, examine the words in context and try to guess the meaning of each. Then look up the words in a dictionary. Keep in mind that many words have multiple meanings. Write the definition that best fits the word's context in the article.

Word	Your definition	Dictionary definition
1. controversial (adj.)		
2. trust (n.)		
3. ethical (adj.)		
4. consumers (n.)		

Why Facebook Should Follow Ethical Standards—Like Everybody Else

By Robert Klitzman, Professor of Psychiatry and Director of the Masters of Bioethics Program, Columbia University and author of the book Am I My Genes? Confronting Fate and Family Secrets in the Age of Genetic Testing

Posted: 07/07/2014 2:51 pm EDT Updated: 09/06/2014 5:59 am EDT

Part 1

1   On July 2, 2014, Facebook's Chief Operating Officer, Sheryl Sandberg, defended the company's recent **controversial** experiment, which manipulated users' newsfeeds to change their moods. But in so doing, she raised more concerns than she answered. She argued that the company and other social media sites regularly engage in research, and that the practice is thus acceptable. Facebook defenders say that the company could instead simply conduct its experiments secretly and not publish the results.

2   But past errors do not justify future ones.

3   Social science can help us all, but depends on **trust**—which can be fragile. Social media companies can now strengthen users' trust by agreeing to follow **ethical** standards.

4   The company seeks to portray all of its experiments as utterly benign, but that may not always be the case. Playing with people's emotions is very different than asking them how, for instance, they might vote in an upcoming election. Research suggests that the information individuals receive through social media can significantly affect their moods. Altered mood can in turn affect drug use, weight and appetite, school and work performance, and suicidal thoughts. Depressed teens can be very fragile. It may not take a lot to push them more than one would like. Facebook has apparently conducted hundreds of experiments. We simply don't know how far these studies have gone—whether any have tried manipulating users' moods over a longer period.

5   Facebook's researchers at first said that the subjects in its experiment, conducted in 2012, consented when they signed up for Facebook; but it turns out that the company only mentioned the possibility of research in its data use agreement afterwards. The current agreement may not necessarily be sufficient either, however, depending on the experiment.

Get into a small group and answer the two questions that follow.

1. What have you learned from this article so far?

2. What do you predict may be coming in the second half of the article?

Part 2

6   At present, researchers at almost all universities and pharmaceutical and biotech companies have agreed to follow the federal **regulations** governing research as a standard in conducting experiments on human beings. We do not allow pharmaceutical or automobile companies to alter their products on their own and then see whether any **consumers** get hurt. Internet companies—which regularly conduct studies on us all—do not follow accepted ethical standards of research, and have never publicly made any effort to do so. But they should.

7   Facebook says its employees review its own studies, but it has nowhere indicated what criteria they use. We don't know, for instance, if they have ever rejected or altered experiments because these were too unethical, and if so, what types of studies? Moreover, these employees have a conflict of interest in assessing their own company's experiments. Federal regulations require that institutions conducting experiments have research ethics committees, known as Institutional Review boards (or IRBs) review all studies, following clear ethical guidelines. These boards must, for instance, have an unaffiliated member, to try to avoid conflicts of interest.

8   Much of the company's research will no doubt be minimal risk and judged to be ethical and unproblematic. But standard practice is not to allow researchers to make these determinations about their own studies. At times, egregious violations have occurred when social scientists and other researchers have done so. In the Stanford prison experiment, for instance, the psychologist Philip Zimbardo randomly assigned students to play the roles of "guards" and "prisoners" in a mock penitentiary. He assumed the study would be minimal risk. But the guards soon began physically abusing the prisoners.

9   Social media company researchers are presumably trained social scientists—psychologists, sociologists and anthropologists. These fields all have established codes of professional ethical standards and conduct that should be followed, and that include stipulations that researchers obtain appropriate informed consent.

10   It is not clear that Facebook broke the law—the regulations apply technically to federal-funded research but have been universally adopted by researchers as the standard. Facebook should agree to follow these guidelines as well. Doing so need not be onerous. The company could simply submit its studies to an established independent IRB for review. Facebook could also, for instance, not include children in mood-manipulation experiments, which could easily be done, since users' indicate their age.

11   Much more discussion about these areas is essential. Indeed, the British government is now investigating the company's experiment. I don't think our federal government needs to get involved.

12   But all of us elsewhere—whether we use Facebook or not—deserve a bit more. Isn't our trust worth it?

Thinking about the Reading

After doing a close reading of the article, write your answers to the following questions. When you are done, discuss your answers with your classmates.

1. Sheryl Sandberg argues that the practice of social media companies engaging in research involving their users is quite acceptable. Do you agree or disagree with this statement? Explain your position.

2. Do you believe that Facebook should follow ethical standards when conducting research on its users? Why, or why not?

3. The author argues that Facebook should not include children in its mood-manipulation experiments. Do you agree with the author's claim? Why, or why not?

Reading Comprehension Check

_____ 1. "On July 2, 2014, Facebook's Chief Operating Officer, Sheryl Sandberg, defended the company's recent controversial experiment, which **manipulated** users' newsfeeds to change their moods." The meaning of the word *manipulated* in the above context is which of the following?

  a. changed for a particular purpose
  b. maintained for a specific reason
  c. maintained the integrity of users
  d. respected users' right to privacy

_____ 2. The author's main idea is that

  a. Facebook is not responsible for its users' moods.
  b. Facebook should not follow ethical standards.
  c. Facebook must adhere to ethical standards.
  d. Facebook should manipulate users' data.

_____ 3. The author's purpose is to

  a. inform the reader that Facebook does not follow ethical standards.
  b. entertain the reader by telling humorous stories about Facebook.
  c. instruct the reader on how to upload images and videos to Facebook.
  d. convince the reader that Facebook ought to follow ethical standards.

_____ 4. Why is the Stanford prison experiment mentioned?

  a. to prove that most social scientists are ethical
  b. to verify the fact that Facebook follows ethical standards
  c. to refute the claim that some researchers are unethical
  d. to support the fact that some social scientists can be unethical

_____ 5. Which of the following statements is *not* a fact?

  a. Social media companies collect their users' information to do research.
  b. Sandberg believes that Facebook is not wrong in engaging in research.

   c. It is ethical for a social media company to do research on its users.

   d. The British government is now investigating Facebook's experiment.

_____ **6.** Which of the following statements about the content of this article is *true*?

   a. Facebook clearly broke the law by conducting its research on users without informed consent.

   b. Facebook's practice of asking its own employees to evaluate the company's experiments constitutes a conflict of interest.

   c. Automobile manufacturers can legally alter their products, and then see whether any consumers get hurt as a result.

   d. The general public knows all of the details of Facebook's research experiments because Facebook has willingly disclosed them.

_____ **7.** The author concludes that Facebook should

   a. agree to follow the same guidelines other researchers already follow.

   b. continue to conduct its experiments without full disclosure.

   c. interpret its users trust to mean that users don't mind participating in all types of research.

   d. conduct an experiment that is similar to the Stanford prison experiment.

_____ **8.** Which of the following is a specific example of a problematic Facebook research experiment mentioned in this article?

   a. the Stanford prison experiment

   b. controlling newsfeed content in an attempt to change users' moods

   c. pharmaceutical companies changing their products to see what consequences result

   d. keeping track of how many friends people add to their Facebook accounts in the course of one year

_____ **9.** According to the article, how could the mental states of depressed teens be affected by Facebook research?

   a. Manipulating the information teens receive through Facebook can affect their mood to the point of triggering suicidal thoughts.

   b. Sending teens smiley faces and other cheerful emoticons could result in markedly improved moods and a more hopeful outlook.

   c. Sending teens information about political issues and upcoming elections could inspire them to volunteer for a worthwhile cause and begin helping others.

   d. Sending teens false information about pharmaceuticals and automobiles could cause them to suffer severe consequences, such as overdoses and car accidents.

_____ **10.** According to the article, Facebook does not

   a. attempt to manipulate users' moods.

   b. review their own research studies.

   c. conduct any research without disclosing it to users.

   d. follow accepted ethical standards of research.

THEMATIC LINKS

If you want to learn more about the topic of Facebook and ethics, type the following words into your browser and explore the two sites that come up:

1. Facebook Study Sparks Soul-Searching Wall Street Journal

2. Social media research raises privacy and ethics issues USA Today

**READING
SKILL FOCUS**

③ OBJECTIVE
Differentiate between facts
and opinions

Facts Versus Opinions

A **fact** is a statement about something that is a true piece of information. In other words, a fact can be verified with evidence. If a statement cannot be proven to be true, it is safe to state that it is not a fact. In contrast, an **opinion** is a view, belief, or judgment about something; that is, an opinion is what someone thinks about a particular topic or person, his or her subjective view of a topic. It is important to note that an opinion may or may not be substantiated with evidence. As a college student, you will need to differentiate between facts and opinions when you read.

In general, when writing *objectively*, an author conveys only facts to the reader without including her or his biases or opinions. However, when writing *subjectively*, authors include their personal beliefs and opinions. Keep in mind, though, that subjective writing may also include facts; good writers use evidence to support their opinions. When you read an article, think critically to determine the following:

- Has the author simply provided facts to inform the reader about a topic?
- Is the author purely expressing her or his opinion on a topic?
- Is the author stating an opinion that is substantiated with evidence?

In many instances, the question of whether a sentence is made up of facts or opinions may seem clear cut. Examples 1 and 2 on the following page, which are taken from Selection 1, "Business Leaders Beware: Ethical Drift Makes Standards Slip," are cases in point.

1. *Fact:* Recently major organizations have been lumped with hefty fines for questionable moral practices.
2. *Opinion:* We need leaders with a strong moral compass.

Example 1 is a recognized truth and an observable fact. Example 2 is a judgment and a clear statement of opinion.

So why should you spend your valuable time on this Skill Focus area? The answer is that the line between fact and opinion can get tricky in particular contexts, as seen in Examples 3 and 4 below, from Selection 2, "Why Facebook Should Follow Ethical Standards—Like Everybody Else" (p. 355).

3. She argued that the company and other social media sites regularly engage in research, and that the practice is thus acceptable.
4. It is not clear that Facebook broke the law.

What may seem like an opinion (Cheryl's Sandberg's view that the practice of engaging in research is acceptable) in Example 3 is actually a fact, as the sentence simply reports that she put forth an argument. What may seem like a fact in Example 4 (about the question of Facebook breaking the law) is an opinion as it is a personal judgment made by the authors not a legal professional.

Facts

"Don't trust half of what you hear and less of what you read."

While this statement might seem overly skeptical, good readers think critically about what they read and do not trust claims that are not well supported. Just because you see it in print, it does not mean that it is true! A fact is a provable claim, that is, a statement that is verifiable, as in the following example from Selection 1 (p. 351).

In one values project I worked on with a global consultancy we set up dilemmas that the leaders had to resolve.

This is a *stated fact.* It may or may not be true, but it is provable. Stated facts can go in two directions. If the above fact is shown to be true about the project the writer conducted with the global consultancy, then it is a *substantiated fact,* because it has been fact-checked and supported. If the information can be disproved, then it is a *false statement of fact* (see the following diagram).

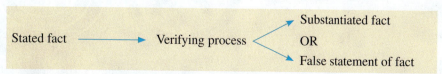

Stated fact ⟶ Verifying process ⟨ Substantiated fact OR False statement of fact

Opinions

An *opinion* is a personal belief or judgment that is not provable. The following examples are taken from Selection 2, paragraph 12 (p. 357):

> 1. But all of us elsewhere—whether we use Facebook or not—deserve a bit more.
> 2. I don't think our federal government needs to get involved.

It is important to make a distinction between *well-supported opinions* based on plausible evidence and valid reasons and *poorly supported opinions* that seem to contradict known facts. That is to say, a *set of facts* can be used to support, or back up, an opinion.

Let's look at the following examples from Selection 2, paragraph 4 (p. 356), to understand this.

> The company [Facebook] seeks to portray all of its experiments as utterly benign, but that may not always be the case.

Alone, this is a poorly substantiated opinion because there is no evidence to prove that Facebook's experiments are harmful. However, the author goes on to say,

> Playing with people's emotions is very different than asking them how, for instance, they might vote in an upcoming election. Research suggests that the information individuals receive through social media can significantly affect their moods. Altered mood can in turn affect drug use, weight and appetite, school and work performance, and suicidal thoughts. Depressed teens can be very fragile.

In these sentences, the author provides reasons to support his statement and indicates that research suggests information received through social media can affect mood with detrimental effects.

EXERCISE 9.4 **Generating Support for an Opinion**

Directions: What types of facts might support the opinion below? Make a short list with a partner.

> **Opinion:** Apple's iWatch is better than Samsung's Galaxy Gear.
> **Supporting facts**

_____

_____

_____

_____

_____

Differentiating Between Fact and Opinion

How can you tell when you are reading a fact rather than an opinion? Consider the author's purpose in writing the piece you are reading. Is the author simply providing information about a topic, or is she or he trying to persuade the reader about a particular argument or set of arguments? Compare the two paragraphs below:

Passage 1

Apple's launch of iPhone 6 and iPhone 6 Plus in China was delayed because of China's refusal to allow Apple to collect information about the Chinese users. Apple usually collects information about the location and preferences of its iPhone users for marketing purposes, but China was adamant that Apple abandon its practice of collecting user data. It was only after Apple agreed not to collect information from its Chinese users that China gave it permission to sell iPhone 6 and iPhone 6 Plus to the Chinese people.

Passage 2

China's decision to delay the launch of iPhone 6 and iPhone 6 Plus until Apple agrees not to collect information about the Chinese users is unfortunate and unethical. Apple is a great American company, and it has the right to sell its amazing products wherever it wants. China cannot go on harassing an iconic company like Apple and have its own way. We live in the Information Age, and individuals and companies ought to have the ability to transfer Information freely.

How does the author's purpose differ from Passage 1 to Passage 2? Which paragraph is more factual? Which is more opinion based? Clearly, the first paragraph is more objective and fact based, and the author's purpose is to provide information. The second is subjective, contains strong opinions, and is trying to persuade the reader to agree with the writer's point of view.

Of course, not all readings are purely fact or purely opinion. It is often the case that an author uses a set of facts to back up an opinion. Read Passage 3, and underline any sentences that offer an opinion.

Passage 3

Apple's practice of collecting information from its users is actually helpful in some cases. When an iPhone is lost, Apple can easily track it down, alert the police, and they can find the phone and return it to its rightful owner. Also, by keeping track of a user's buying history, Apple can recommend songs, movies, and books that the user likes. I believe Apple is not unethical at all in monitoring user data.

Consider the opinion(s) put forth by the writer. What facts are used to support this viewpoint?

Signs of an Author's Point of View

There are certain words and phrases that signal that a judgment, belief, or interpretation is being offered by an author, such as those shown below.

Presentation of Opinion: Signal Phrases	
In my opinion …	This suggests …
One possibility is …	In my view …
Maybe it is the case …	It seems likely …
I believe/I think …	One idea is that …

You should also look for descriptive adjectives that specify value judgments.

Presentation of Opinion: Descriptive Words		
best	effective	successful
better	greater	useful
boring	impressive	wasteful
dishonest	nicer	worst
disastrous	stimulating	

Pay attention to key words that express uncertainty, such as those listed below.

Key Words that Express Uncertainty		
doubt	might	seem
maybe	perhaps	possibly

Considering Genre When Distinguishing Facts from Opinions

Different genres of writing tend to rely more or less heavily on facts and opinions depending on their purpose.

1. Texts that are primarily fact based include the following:

   • *News reports* in the form of magazine or newspaper articles are mostly factual (even though these facts are not always substantiated, and bias can play a role in which "facts" get reported).
   • *Textbook readings* are predominantly fact focused, as the purpose is to inform; however, they also contain opinions that may or may or may not be substantiated with facts. Read carefully!
   • *Statistical data* is factual (as numerical claims are verifiable). Keep in mind that different people may interpret the same information differently and statistics can be used to mislead as well as to inform.

2. Texts that are more often opinion based include the following:

   • *Newspaper or magazine editorials* are, by definition, someone's opinion on an issue.
   • *Letters from readers to newspapers and magazines* are usually readers' responses to articles they have read.
   • *Internet blogs* allow members to share their opinions online.
   • *Quoted speech within newspaper and magazine articles* often offers a diversity of perspectives on the topic featured in the article. The journalistic tone may be neutral, but interviewed sources share their viewpoints.

EXERCISE 9.5 Identifying Opinions and the Facts that Support Them

Directions: In the following short paragraphs, underline sentences that contain an opinion. Discuss with a partner what kind of factual support is offered, if any, to back up the opinion. What kind of factual evidence is **not given** that could be used to support the view(s) of the writer?

Passage 1

Prospective job seekers lie too often on their resumes! They often do this believing that they will not get caught. In cases, where these inaccuracies slip past the human resources department, there is always the chance that the job seeker's lies will be exposed during the interview itself. Many companies are now getting stricter in their resume review process. Some now ask for verification letters to back up claims made on resumes.

—Internet Blog

1. **Factual support for offered opinion:** (If not given, what kind of factual details would support such a view?)

_____

_____

Passage 2

Your energy, positive or negative, is contagious. Both in person and on-line, you'll spend as much time with your colleagues as you spend with family and friends. Personal demeanor is therefore a vital element of workforce harmony. No one expects (or wants) you to be artificially upbeat and bubbly every second of the day, but one negative personality can make an entire office miserable and unproductive. Every person in a company has a responsibility to contribute to a positive, productive work environment.

—From Bovee & Thill, *Business in Action.* 7e, p. 20

2. **Factual support for offered opinion:** (If not given, what kind of factual details would support such a view?)

_____

_____

_____

_____

Passage 3

One of the clearest examples of workplace discrimination is the gender pay gap, the difference between what women and men earn. Study after study points to the fact that women have not closed this gap, despite numerous legislative efforts aimed at doing just that. For example, at all levels of education, women in the United States earn about 75 to 80 percent of what men do.

—*Internet Blog*

3. **Factual support for offered opinion:** (If not given, what kind of factual details would support such a view?)

_____

_____

Passage 4

Paid sick leave should not only apply when an employee is ill but should include time off when an employee needs to take care of a sick family member. How can a single parent go to work when her or his child has 103° fever? How can an employer expect a member of staff to come to work when his elderly parent collapsed on the stairwell the night before?

The debate on family leave policy has reached the assembly floor in several state senates, but passage of such worthy legislation has been slow. The California State Assembly was the first to pass a family leave bill in 2002. Yet by 2015, only two other states had enacted similar policies into law.

Legislators and business leaders lobbying against family leave bills should consider the choice parents have to make when they get a call from their child's school letting them know their son or daughter is sick. In the many states without a family leave policy in place, the current choice is to either lose pay or to lose their jobs.

4. **Factual support for offered opinion:** (If not given, what kind of factual details would support such a view?)

_____

_____

_____

READING

Selection 3

Textbook Excerpt

Understanding Business Ethics and Social Responsibility: Is Fair Trade Really Fair?

Pre-Reading Questions

1. Some people believe that the term *business ethics* is an oxymoron. In other words, they think that business and ethics cannot exist together. Do you agree or disagree with the statement? Support your answer with examples from your own experience or that of someone you know.

2. When you purchase a product, do you consider whether or not the company that produced it is socially responsible? Why, or why not?

3. Can you think of a company that you believe makes money by exploiting its workers and a company that is socially responsible? Give specific examples to support your answers.

Understanding Business Ethics and Social Responsibility: Is Fair Trade Really Fair?

by Ebert & Griffin

1   Do you know where chocolate comes from? It comes from cocoa, which is produced by roasting and grinding the almond-sized beans that grow (in pods) on cacao trees. More than 40 percent of the world's **supply** of cacao beans comes from small farms scattered throughout the West African nation of Ivory Coast, which may ship as much as 47,000 tons per month to the United States. According to reports issued at the end of the 1990s by the United Nations Children's Fund and the U.S. State Department, much of the labor involved in Ivory Coast cocoa **production** is performed by

children, chiefly boys ranging in age from 12 to 16. Most of them have been tricked or sold into forced labor by destitute parents unable to feed them.

2   How did enslaving children become "business as usual" in the Ivory Coast cocoa industry? One-third of the country's **economy** is based on cocoa exports, and the Ivory Coast is heavily dependent on world market prices for cocoa. Unfortunately, cocoa is an extremely unstable commodity—global prices fluctuate significantly. Because of this instability, profitability depends on prices over which farmers have no control. This problem is compounded by unpredictable natural conditions, such as drought, over which they also have no control. To improve their chances of making a profit, cocoa farmers look for ways to cut costs, and the use of slave labor is the most effective money-saving measure.

3   This is where the idea of "fair trade" comes in. *Fair trade* refers to programs designed to ensure that export-dependent farmers in developing countries receive fair prices for their crops. Several such programs are sponsored by Fairtrade Labeling Organizations (FLO) International, a global nonprofit network of fair-trade groups headquartered in Germany. FLO partners with cooperatives representing cocoa producers in Africa and Latin America to establish certain standards, not only for the producers' products but for their operations and socially relevant policies (such as enforcing anti-child-labor laws and providing education and healthcare services). In return, FLO guarantees producers a "Fairtrade Minimum Price" for their products. Since 2007, FLO has guaranteed cocoa farmers a price of $1750 per ton. If the market price falls below that level, FLO ensures farmers that they will make up the difference. If the market price tops $1750, FLO pays producers a premium of $150 per ton.

4   Where does the money come from? The cost is borne by the importers, manufacturers, and distributors who buy and sell cocoa from FLO-certified producers. These companies are in turn monitored by a network of FLO-owned organizations called TransFair, which ensures that FLO-criteria are met and that FLO-certified producers receive the fair prices guaranteed by FLO.

5   What **incentive** encourages importers, manufacturers, and distributors not only to adopt FLO-Transfair standards but to bear the costs of subsidizing overseas producers? They get the right to promote their chocolate products

not only as "fair trade" but, often, as organic products as well—both of which categories typically command premium retail prices. In fact, organic fair-trade chocolate products are priced in the same range as luxury chocolates, but consumers appear to be willing to pay the relatively high asking prices—not only for organic products but for all kinds of chocolate products bearing the "Fair Trade Certified" label. TransFair U.S. chief executive Paul Rice explains that when consumers know they're supporting programs to empower farmers in developing countries, sellers and resellers can charge "dramatically higher prices, often two or three times higher." Consumers, he says, "put their money where their mouth is and pay a little more."

6   A 3.5-ounce candy bar labeled "organic fair trade" may sell for $3.49 compared to about $1.50 for one that's not. Why so much? Because the fair-trade candy bar, says TransFair U.S. spokesperson Nicole Chettero, still occupies a niche market. She predicts, however, that, "as the demand and volume of Fair Trade-certified products increase, the market will work itself out … Retailers will naturally start to drop prices to remain competitive." Ultimately, she concludes, "there is no reason why fair-trade [products] should cost astronomically more than traditional products."

7   Some critics of fair-trade practices and prices agree in principle but contend that consumers don't need to be paying such excessive prices even under current market conditions. They point out that, according to TransFair's own data, cocoa farmers get only 3 cents of the $3.49 that a socially conscious consumer pays for a Fair Trade-certified candy bar. "Farmers often receive very little," reports consumer researcher Lawrence Solomon. "Often fair trade is sold at a premium," he charges, "but the entire premium goes to the middlemen."

8   Critics like Solomon suggest that sellers of fair-trade products are taking advantage of consumers who are socially but not particularly price conscious. They point out that if sellers priced that $3.49 candy bar at $2.49, farmers would still be entitled to 3 cents. The price, they allege, is inflated to $3.49 simply because there's a small segment of the market willing to pay it (while farmers still get only 3 cents). Fair-trade programs, advises English economist Tim Harford, "make a promise that the producers will get a good deal. They do not promise that the consumer will get a good deal. That's up to you as a savvy shopper."

Thinking about the Reading

1. What are the trade-offs in the fair-trade process? Do you think fair trade promotes fair trade-offs? Why or why not?

_____

_____

2. Do you pay attention to fair-trade products in your own purchasing behavior? For what kinds of products might you be willing to pay a premium price to help those who produce the ingredients?

_____

_____

3. Under what circumstances might fair trade actually cause harm? To whom? At what point would fair-trade trade-offs no longer be acceptable?

_____

_____

Reading Comprehension Check

_____ **1.** "Most of them have been tricked or sold into forced labor by **destitute** parents unable to feed them." In the above sentence, the word *destitute* means

a. exceptionally kind.

b. extremely affluent.

c. extremely poor.

d. extremely frugal.

_____ **2.** Which of the following is the main idea of the passage?

a. Fair Trade programs ensure that the consumer gets a good deal.

b. Fair Trade programs that are designed to protect farmers are unfair to consumers.

c. Fair Trade programs benefit consumers because they pay a premium price.

d. Fair Trade programs protect farmers that produce cocoa in Ivory Coast.

_____ **3.** Which of the following statements is a fact?

a. Parents who sold their children into forced labor must be punished.

b. The consumer should not have to pay a premium price for chocolate.

c. The farmers in Ivory Coast must be prosecuted for hiring children.

d. Most of the laborers involved in Ivory Coast cocoa production are children.

_____ **4.** Which of the following statements is an opinion?

a. Using children for slave labor is wrong and should be prohibited.

b. Forty percent of the world's supply of cacao beans comes from Ivory Coast.

c. The boys involved in Ivory Coast cocoa production range from 12 to 16.

d. Ivory Coast farmers get only 3 cents or $.03. of the $3.49 for a candy bar.

_____ **5.** Which of the following statements is not a fact?

a. Cocoa farmers use slave labor to cut costs and make a profit.

b. One-third of Ivory Coast's economy is based on cocoa exports.

c. Consumers ought not to pay a premium price for cocoa products.

d. FLO pays cocoa producers a premium of $150 per ton.

_____ **6.** In the context of this article, the term *fair trade* most nearly refers to

    a. allowing Ivory Coast to overcharge for cacao beans in exchange for the United States being allowed to inflate its sugar prices.

    b. the practice of selling children into farm labor in exchange for an adequate supply of cacao beans.

    c. monitoring the quality of chocolate produced outside of the United States.

    d. ensuring that farmers in developing countries get paid fairly for their products.

_____ **7.** According to the reading selection, what is TransFair?

    a. a network of organizations that ensures that cocoa farmers who have been approved will continue to receive fair prices for their crops

    b. a nonprofit organization that monitors the enforcement of child labor laws and provides education and health care

    c. a concert put on annually to raise funds for children exploited by Ivory Coast's cocoa industry

    d. the brand name of a type of chocolate product that is priced in the same range as luxury chocolates

_____ **8.** In paragraph 6, the phrase *niche market* means

    a. a specialized subsection of the usual market for a product.

    b. any supermarket or store that sells fair trade products.

    c. a neighborhood "corner store."

    d. a highly priced version of a regular product.

_____ **9.** According to the reading, what type of consumer pays premium prices for fair-trade candy bars?

    a. wealthy and middle-aged

    b. image conscious

    c. socially conscious

    d. college age

_____ **10.** Which of the following statements about the article content is *false*?

    a. A farmer gets only 3 cents per fair-trade candy bar, whether it is priced at $3.49 or at $2.49.

    b. Parents in Ivory Coast are forced into labor in the cocoa production industry so that struggling cocoa farmers can cut costs and increase profits.

    c. Sellers of fair-trade products might be taking advantage of naïve consumers by overpricing products.

    d. Chocolate is made from cocoa, which in turn is made from ground and roasted cacao beans.

THEMATIC LINKS

If you want to learn more about the topic of fair trade, type the following words into your browser and explore the two sites that come up:

1. Start Drinking Fair Trade Coffee Huffington Post

2. Fairtrade: Is it really fair? Independent

Think to Write

Now that you have completed three readings in this chapter on business, think about which of the three is most interesting to you. Write a paragraph response about this reading and post it to The Wall.

It's SHOWTIME!

Watching a video clip related to the chapter content can be an enriching experience. Go online and find a video link whose topic ties into one of the chapter readings (maximum length = ten minutes). After viewing the video clip, write a half-page summary of the video's key points. Post your personal reaction to the ideas in the clip (between 150 and 400 words) on The Wall.

WRITING
SKILL FOCUS

MLA Documentation Style for the Humanities

OBJECTIVE

4

Correctly using MLA format

When you write academic essays and research papers for humanities courses, you will often be required to follow the Modern Language Association (MLA) documentation style, which consists of a system of in-text citations that reference complete source information provided at the end of the paper in a Works Cited page. You can find detailed information about MLA in the *MLA Handbook for Writers of Research Papers*, 7th edition, by accessing the MLA site at www.mla.org; by purchasing a good handbook; or by visiting the Purdue University Online Writing Lab (OWL) at http://owl.english.purdue.edu.

We will not get into much detail here, as there are so many other resources available, but we will cover some of the most important basics.

Formatting Your Paper

Different disciplines have different formatting requirements, so if you are writing a paper for a biology course, another for a history course, and third for an

English course, the formatting requirements will be different for each. It is best for you to ask your instructors what they require for their specific courses.

For English and language courses, adhere to the format recommended by the MLA as follows:

1. Use plain white 8½ × 11-inch paper and black ink for typed or computer-printed papers, and type or print only on one side of the paper.
2. Use a 12-point font that is easy to read (e.g., Times New Roman).
3. Leave 1-inch margins on all four sides of the paper.
4. Double-space each line of typing (leave a blank line between two lines).
5. Indent the first line of each paragraph five spaces.
6. Do not justify the right margin.
7. Put the title of the paper in the center of the page. Do not underline, bold, or put quotation marks around the title.
8. In the top left corner of the first page of your paper, put your full name, your instructor's name, the course number, and the date you turn in your assignment. Write the date in this order without punctuation: *day month year*.
9. Put your last name and the page number in the upper-right corner of all pages. Use Arabic numerals (1, 2, and 3), and do not put a period or a comma after the number or enclose it in parentheses. If your instructor requires a separate title page, do not number it.

Citing Your Sources

When you borrow information from a scholar or a researcher, you must cite the source. In other words, you must tell the reader where the information came from. There are two ways you cite your sources:

1. **In-Text Citation:** You include a short reference to the source you are using in the body of your paper, immediately after the material you are quoting or paraphrasing.
2. **Works Cited Page:** At the end of your paper, you provide an alphabetized list of all of your sources, which provides the detailed information a reader would need to access the source themselves.

In-Text Citation

In-text citations are placed immediately after quotations or paraphrased information at the end of the sentence and before the period. The primary purpose of an in-text citation is to refer the reader to the Works Cited list at the end of the paper. Keep your in-text citations as short as possible. They should contain just enough information for the reader to find the full reference in the Works Cited list.

Here are some common types of in-text citations:

1. **Author is mentioned in the text:** If you refer to the author in your text, do not repeat the author's name in your citation, but just include the page number in parentheses before the closing period.

> According to Ebert and Griffin, "Since 2007, FLO has guaranteed cocoa farmers a price of $1750 per ton" (122).

2. **Author is not mentioned in the text:** If you do not name the author in your text, include the author name and page number in parentheses before the closing period.

> Apparently, "FLO has guaranteed cocoa farmers a price of $1,750 per ton" (Ebert and Griffin 122).

3. **Two or three authors:** If you use information from a paper written by two or three authors, give all their names in parentheses if you do not name them in your sentence.

> (Ball, Call, and Hall 123).

4. **Four or more authors:** If you use information from a paper written by four or more authors, only use the first author's last name and put *et al.* (Latin abbreviation of *et alii*, "and others") in parentheses.

> (Johnson et al. 445).

5. **A one-page article:** Do not include a page number in your in-text citation if the article you are using information from is only one page long.

> (Dowson).

6. **Two different works by the same author:** When you use information from two different works by the same author, include a shortened version of the title of each work. For example, if you referred to *Stocks and Bonds* and *Personal Finance* written by O'Neil, cite the two works as follows:

> (O'Neil, Stocks 65).   (O'Neil, Personal 89).

7. **Author unknown:** If you do not know the author's name, use the title, or a shortened version if it is long, in quotation marks in the parenthetical citation.

> ("Intelligent" 425).

8. **Encyclopedia article:** If you use information from an encyclopedia article, include the author's name in the parenthetical citation. If you do not know the author's name, just use the article's title, or a shortened version of it, in quotation marks in the citation.

(Marston).   ("Global Markets").

9. **Electronic Source:** If your information comes from an electronic source, cite the source as you do for print sources. Do not use a page number, as most online sources are not paginated.

(Johnson "Correction").

Works Cited Page

The **Works Cited list** appears as a separate page at the end of your essay and lists full source information for everything you have cited. It should have the same margins as the rest of the essay, be double-spaced, and include your last name and the page number top right. Center the title "Works Cited," and do not use bold, italics, or underlining with it. List your sources in alphabetical order by last name of the author, or if there is no author, the first word of the source's title. Indent the second and subsequent lines of an entry to create a hanging indent.

Here is some basic information on how to format entries:

1. **Books**
   - **One author:** Put the last name of the author first, followed by a comma, the first name, and a period. Place the title in italics followed by a period. (Use a semicolon between a title and subtitle.) Provide the city of publication followed by a colon, the name of the publisher, a comma, the year of publication, and a period. Finally, indicate the medium of publication followed by a period.

Graham, Benjamin. *The Intelligent Investor: The Classic Text on Value Investing.*

New York: Harper, 2010. Print.

   - **Two or three authors:** Put the full name of the first author in reverse order (last name first), and write all other names in normal order. Put a comma after the last name of the first author and between authors.

> Lane, Carry, Randal Lane, and Jeff Montgomery. *Investing in the Stock Market: A Beginner's Guide.* Boston: Pearson, 2013. Print.

- **Four or more authors:** If there are four or more authors, use the full name of the first author in reverse order, put a comma after the last name, and use the Latin abbreviation et al. ("and others").

> Johnson, et al. *Understanding the Workings of the Stock Market.* Houston: Hunt, 2013. Print.

- **More than one edition:** Put the number of the edition and the abbreviation ed. (2nd ed., 3rd ed., etc.) after the title, and put a period.

> O'Neil, William. *How to Make Money in Stocks: A Winning System in Good Times or Bad.* 4th ed. New York: McGraw Hill, 2009. Print.

- **Two different works by the same author:** When you refer to two different works by the same author, put the author's full name in reverse order for the first work. For all other works by the same author, type three hyphens instead of the name and list the works in alphabetical order.

> Graham, Benjamin. *The Intelligent Investor: The Classic Text on Value Investing.* New York: Harper, 2010. Print.
>
> —. *Security Analysis: Principles and Techniques.* New York: McGraw Hill, 2002. Print.

2. Articles

- **Magazine article:** Put the last name of the author first, followed by a comma, the first name, and a period. Place the title of the article in quotation marks with a period within the closing quotation mark, and italicize the name of the magazine and follow it with a period. Then provide the date as shown in the examples below (notice how the month, year, and page numbers are listed differently in the first one, a monthly magazine, from the second one, which is a weekly magazine).

> Koroski, Paul. "The Rise of the Chinese Dragon." *The Economist* Sep. 2014: 5. Print.
>
> Gordon, Amy. "The Rise and Fall of a Russian Tycoon." *Time* 8 Aug. 2013: 13–17. Print.

- **Newspaper article:** If you refer to a newspaper article, cite the source as follows:

> Friedman, Morgan. "As Global Economy Falters: Vietnam Weathers the Storm." *The New York Times* 22 Feb. 2015 B5.

(Notice that this article appeared on page 5 of the Business section of the newspaper.)

- **Online article:** When you cite an online source, list your references as follows:

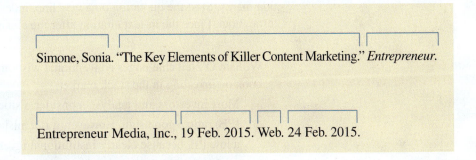

> Simone, Sonia. "The Key Elements of Killer Content Marketing." *Entrepreneur.*
>
> Entrepreneur Media, Inc., 19 Feb. 2015. Web. 24 Feb. 2015.

Integrating Quotations

Whenever you quote or paraphrase somebody's words in your academic work, you have to include an in-text citation. If you give the author's last name in the sentence, provide the page number where you found the original quote in parentheses at the end of your sentence. Look at the following examples:

Direct Quote

> As Buffett says, "You want to be greedy when others are fearful. You want to be fearful when others are greedy. It's that simple" (186).

Indirect Quote

> Buffett suggests that intelligent investors buy stocks when others are selling because of fear and sell when there is a buying frenzy (186).

Notice that the parenthetical citation goes outside the quotation mark and inside the period that ends the sentence in the first example and before the period in the second example. When you do not include the author's name in the sentence, place it in parentheses with the page number as shown below.

> The directors of Enron, an energy giant, were prosecuted for lying to the shareholders that the company was profitable (Adams 88).

Partial Quote: Sometimes you may insert your reference in the middle of the sentence to indicate that one part of the sentence is quoted (indirect quote) and the other part is written by you.

> Although the directors of Enron, the energy giant, were prosecuted for lying to the shareholders that the company was profitable (Adams 88), most employees lost their lifetime savings when Enron's stock crashed and was finally delisted.

Block Quotations: If you use a quote that is more than four lines of prose or three lines of poetry, place the quote in a block of text and do not use quotation marks. Start the quotation on a new line, indent one inch, and double-space throughout. Place the in-text citation after the closing period.

> William O'Neil challenges conventional wisdom in his groundbreaking book on investing in the stock market:
>
>> Most investors and analysts consider a stock's low price-to-earnings (PE) ratio a good sign. However, it is a mistake to invest in stocks with a low PE, because clearly institutional investors are not willing to bid up the stock and drive the price high. I challenge this common notion and claim that a low PE actually reflects investors' low confidence in the company's future prospects. In the second chapter, I argue that intelligent investors should buy stocks with a high PE. The logic here is that savvy investors have such high confidence in the company's bright prospects that they are willing to pay the multiples. (23)

TROUBLE SPOTS IN WRITING

Punctuation Issues

OBJECTIVE

5

Use punctuation rules appropriately

When you write an essay, your word choice may be good, and your grammar may be correct. However, if you do not use punctuation rules appropriately, the reader may have a difficult time understanding your intended meaning. This section will discuss some of the most frequently used punctuation marks in academic writing.

Using a Comma [,]

A *comma* is a punctuation mark that serves many purposes in writing, such as linking two complete ideas, separating items in a series, and separating adjectives in a sequence. It is the most frequently used punctuation mark in writing, but it is also most commonly misused. It should be noted that in the academic community and other formal contexts such as communication in business, commas are mandatory. Therefore, you need to learn how to use them appropriately so as not to confuse the reader. Keep in mind that readers find inappropriate commas both confusing and disruptive! Here are some of the most common ways to use commas:

1. **To join sentences:** Use a comma when you connect two complete sentences with a coordinating conjunction such as *for*, *and*, *nor*, *but*, *or*, *yet*, and *so* (use the mnemonic FANBOYS to remember these).

   > Apple is confident that its iWatch will be popular, but some analysts believe that it will not be a commercial success.

2. **After a subordinator:** Use a comma when you begin a sentence with a subordinator such as *although*, *even though*, *if*, or *whereas*. Remember that a comma is used to separate a dependent (subordinate) clause from an independent clause.

   > Although most experts believe that Jack Ma is a genius entrepreneur, some think that he is not as sharp as Tesla's CEO, Elon Musk.

3. **After transitional expressions:** Place a comma after transitional expressions such as *on the other hand*, or *for example*.

   > On the other hand, Google Watch was a commercial failure.

4. **After conjunctive adverbs:** Use a comma when you begin a sentence with a conjunctive adverb such as *however*, *therefore*, or *moreover*.

   > However, Steve Jobs did not live to witness the fate of iWatch.

5. **After introductory phrases:** Add a comma after introductory phrases to make it easier for the reader to read the sentence.

Refusing to answer the analyst's question, the arrogant CEO left the conference room.

6. To set off nonrestrictive modifiers: When you use a nonrestrictive modifier to provide additional information about nouns and verbs, set it off with commas so that the reader knows that the information is helpful but not necessary.

The iPod, invented by Apple, revolutionized the way people used to listen to music.

7. To separate items in a series: When you write several items in a series, separate them with commas.

Most corporations are required by law to offer their employees medical benefits, stock options, and retirement contributions.

8. To separate coordinate adjectives: When you use a pair of coordinate adjectives, separate them with commas to show that they equally modify the noun.

The Board of Directors came up with a quick, simple solution to address the shareholders' concerns.

9. To set off dates, numbers, addresses, place names, and people's titles:
- **Dates:** Put a comma between the day of the week, the date, and the year.

I ordered a laptop from Amazon on Monday, January 21, 2015, and it arrived on Wednesday, January 23.

Keep in mind that you do not need a comma when a date comes before the month and the year (5 July 2013) or when only month and year (February 2015) or month and day (April 10) are mentioned.
- **Numbers:** Use a comma to create groups of three from the right to make it easier for the reader to read the numbers.

The electric car manufacturer announced that in the Year 2014 it sold electric vehicles worth $3,540,000.

- **Addresses and place names:** If your sentence contains an address, place commas between everything except the state and zip code.

  Apple's corporate headquarters are located at 1 Infinite Loop, Cupertino, CA 95014.

- **People's names and titles:** Put a comma before and after a title when it follows a person's full name.

  Elon Musk, CEO, announced that Tesla Motors would be profitable by the Year 2020.

  When you give a person's last name first, put a comma before the first name (Cook, Tim).

10. **To introduce and conclude quotations:** When you introduce or conclude a quotation, use commas to help the reader differentiate between the quotation and your explanation.

    At the Annual Meeting, the CEO stated, "We will launch the most aggressive marketing campaign ever, and we will destroy our competitors within a year."

    "Wall Street has a tendency to reward overvalued stocks and punish companies with solid fundamentals," the CEO stated.

Using a Semicolon [;]

A *semicolon* is a punctuation mark that helps the reader make connections between equally strong and related clauses. Semicolons can be used in the following ways:

1. **Before sentence connectors:** Put a semicolon before a sentence connector (a conjunctive adverb). Notice how a comma is used after the sentence connector.

   Wall Street is usually seen as a quick way to make money; however, trading stocks without understanding the workings of a stock market is quite dangerous.

2. **To join main clauses:** Use a semicolon to connect two related main clauses not joined by a coordinating conjunction.

   The demand for recycled paper is extremely high; businesses alone use thousands of tons of recycled paper every year.

3. **To break longer sequences into parts:** Use a semicolon to break longer sequences into parts to help the reader separate them.

> Many economists have opined that capital gains should not be taxed (Rothman, 2014; Lane, 2005; Rochford, 2003).

4. **To separate a long list of items:** Use a semicolon when you have a long list of items or are using numerous commas in a sentence.

> Among others, some of the most important qualities of a successful entrepreneur include finding an existing gap in the market; taking calculated risks; having a clear vision for the future of the enterprise; and being able to communicate effectively with the employees.

Using a Colon [:]

A *colon* is most often used to indicate that examples, a list, or a quotation are to follow that will clarify what the writer is saying. A colon is usually placed at the end of a complete sentence, and the following text begins with a lowercase letter. Colons can be used in the following ways.

1. To introduce examples, lists, and quotations
   - **Colons and examples:** A colon usually follows a statement, and the rest of the sentence illustrates that statement.

     > The new CEO has only one priority: increase shareholder value.

   - **Colons and lists:** A colon can also introduce a list of items after a complete sentence.

     > The Board of Directors approved three items at the company's Annual Meeting: share buyback, stock options, and dividend payout.

   - **Colons and quotations:** A colon can introduce a quotation after a complete sentence.

     > The president of the start-up spoke enthusiastically at the conference: "Our company will become a force to reckon with."

2. To separate titles from subtitles

> *How to Invest in the Stock Market: A Beginner's Guide*
> *Your Retirement: Preparing for the Rainy Days*

Using Apostrophes [']

Apostrophes are used with words to indicate possession or the omission of letters.

1. **To show possession:** Notice in the examples below how the apostrophe is used differently with a singular and a plural noun.

> The director's report surprised the analysts. (only one director)
>
> The directors' report surprised the analysts. (more than one director)

2. **To indicate the omission of letters in contractions:** People often use contractions in their daily speech (*can't, won't, didn't*), and apostrophes indicate where letters have been omitted in words when they are written down. It is usually best to avoid using contractions in academic writing, except in dialogue. It is also easy to confuse contractions with possessive personal pronouns, so check your spelling carefully.

Using Quotation Marks [" "]

Quotation marks are used to tell the reader who said what. In academic work, the reader expects you to use quotation marks appropriately.

1. **Direct Quotations:** Use double quotation marks (" ") before and after a quotation to differentiate between what you said and what someone else said. Notice how the period is placed before the closing quotation mark in the direct quote below:

> The Security and Exchange president maintains that "suspicious trading activities will be investigated and those guilty of illegal transactions will be brought to justice."

2. **Indirect Quotations:** Do not use quotation marks when you paraphrase someone else's words.

> A Forgan Spangli analyst predicts that the stock market is due for a major correction.

3. **Punctuating Quotations Correctly:** Follow these rules when you use quotation marks with other punctuation marks.
   - Always place commas and periods inside the quotation marks.

> "I want you to finish this project in two weeks," the CEO said.

- Place colons and semicolons outside the quotation marks.

> The billionaire entrepreneur argued that he did not misrepresent the truth in his autobiography"; his assertion, to me, was totally unconvincing.

- If the quotation is a question or an exclamation, always put the question mark or exclamation point inside the closing quotation mark.

> The aggressive businessman kept asking me, "Will you sign the contract or not?"
> The CEO proudly announced to the analysts, "We sold 35 million iPods this quarter!"

4. **Single Quotation Marks:** Use single quotation marks when you put a quote within a quote.

> "We couldn't beat earning estimate," the vice-president said. "The president specifically said to me, 'Miss one more earning estimate and you are fired!' So now what do I do?"

5. **To indicate titles of short works:** Use quotation marks for titles of short stories, articles, book chapters, and essays.

> "CANSLIM" is a chapter from a well-known book written by Bill O'Neil.
>
> "How I Made Millions Trading Penny Stocks" is an essay by Pat Cash.

Using End Punctuation

Use **end punctuation** such as a period, question mark, or exclamation point to mark the boundaries between two sentences. In speech, people do it by changing pitch or by pausing between two complete ideas. In writing, you must use end punctuation to help the reader understand where one idea ends and where another begins.

1. **Periods [.]:** End all sentences that are statements with periods to indicate to the reader that you have finished a complete idea.

> The Board of Directors unanimously approved the appointment of the new president of the solar company.

2. **Question Marks [?]:** Always end a direct question with a question mark, even when it is quoted.

> Why does a publically traded company's stock skyrocket suddenly?
>
> A famous financial advisor asked, "Why does a publically traded company's stock skyrocket suddenly?"

3. **Exclamation Points [!]:** Use an exclamation point to end emphatic statements such as commands and warnings. Keep in mind that exclamation points are more common in public contexts than they are in academic writing.

> Display all of our hot products at eye level in the store!

Using Parentheses [( )]

Use **parentheses** to enclose a word, sentence, or clause that explains or provides examples that amplify what is being said. Readers see whatever is between parentheses as an aside.

> When you sign up for Umba International Calling Plan and refer us to four friends or family members, you will get one month of free service (like one million other happy customers).
>
> Your friends and family members can call you for free (and speak for as long as they like) as long as they use Zumbi as their long distance carrier.

Using Hyphens [–]

Use a **hyphen** in the following ways:

1. **To indicate a compound word:** Use the hyphen between two words to indicate a compound word.

> a well-designed product
> the vice-president of our company
> twentieth-century technology

2. **To indicate a common root for prefixes:** Use the hyphen when you have two or more prefixes in the same sentence.

> The company is having trouble selling its first-, second-, and third-tier perfume brands.

Using Dashes [––]

A **dash** marks an interruption or break in text. Make a dash with two hyphens (––) and do not leave any space before, between, or after it. Dashes can be used in the following ways:

1. **To introduce a series:** Use dashes to set off introductory and concluding series of information.

> Steve Jobs, Jeff Bezos, and Elon Musk––they are my favorite entrepreneurs.
>
> I am especially fascinated by Jeff Bezos––his leadership abilities, his phenomenal success as CEO of Amazon.com, and his emphasis on customer care.

2. **To add emphasis**

> Only two stocks in my portfolio––the two I did not care much about––survived the bloodbath today.

3. **To indicate a hesitation or pause**

> I thought––well––maybe I was mistaken, but I thought you were my broker.

Using Ellipses [. . .]

Ellipses are three spaced periods or points that are used to indicate that part of a quotation has been omitted.

> "An entrepreneur . . . takes calculated risks that may pay off in the long run. . . ."

When using an ellipsis, be sure to leave a space before and after each period. Notice that when the ellipsis comes at the end of the sentence, four periods are used; the first period immediately follows the last word of the quote.

By no means is the above list an exhaustive discussion of punctuation marks. There are many style guides that can provide detailed explanations of punctuation use that you can refer to.

EXERCISE 9.6   Using Punctuation Marks

Directions: The following passages are missing punctuation marks. Read them carefully and add appropriate punctuation marks such as commas, semicolons, periods, and question marks where they are needed.

Passage 1

Most American corporations provide their employees with e-mail accounts and free Internet access but these companies are concerned about their employees abusing these privileges and monitor their Internet use Although most corporations admit that they constantly monitor their employees e-mail and Internet use, their employees are usually not aware that their e-mails are being read by unintended readers. In fact companies have many reasons for constant surveillance of Internet use for example they are concerned about keeping company information confidential or they may be wary of some employees using e-mail and the Internet for sexual harassment. In addition employees using the Internet during their work hours excessively may affect productivity. Research has indicated that almost 90% of employees surf the Internet for personal reasons thus prompting many corporations to prohibit personal and fruitless e-mail, such as dirty jokes, and to limit Internet access.

Passage 2

Steve Jobs co-founder and CEO of Apple was born on February 24 1955 in San Francisco California. His parents gave him up for adoption because his mother's parents did not approve of her marriage with his Syrian father he was adopted and raised by Paul Jobs and Clara Jobs. When asked about his adoptive parents Steve Jobs said that they were my parents, 1,000% He co-founded Apple Inc with Steve Wozniak and conceived products that are admired by people around the world. He was a marketing genius who knew how to promote Apple products. However he died prematurely of pancreatic cancer leaving behind a legacy of innovation and disruptive technology before he succumbed to his disease, Jobs designed futuristic corporate headquarters which are located at 1 Infinite Loop, Cupertino CA 95014.

THEN & NOW

Go online and do some research to gather information about two experts in the field of business: one from the past and another contemporary. For example, learn about a prominent entrepreneur from the past such as Thomas Edison or Alexander Graham Bell, and a contemporary entrepreneur such as Mark Zuckerberg or Jack Ma. Fill out the table provided below with pertinent information about the two entrepreneurs.

Past Influential Entrepreneur	Present Influential Entrepreneur
Place of birth	Place of birth
Year of birth	Year of birth
Education	Education
What are they most famous for?	What are they most famous for?
Famous quote	Famous quote

After you fill out the table, discuss your findings with your classmates and learn from them about what they discovered on the Internet.

Working with a search engine, do the following search: "Enron, Ethics, and Today's Corporate Values." Read Ken Silverstein's article carefully to learn about the role of ethics in business. After doing a careful reading, write brief answers to the following questions about the article.

1. Justin Schultz, a corporate psychologist in Denver, believes that "Just as character matters in people, it matters in organizations." How and why do you think character matters in corporations? Explain.

   _____

   _____

2. Why does Silverstein believe that "a clear-cut mission and a corporate code of ethics is crucial" for businesses to survive and operate in an ethical manner?

   _____

   _____

   _____

3. Richard Rudden, managing partner at Target Rock Advisors in New York State, says, "Ethics and integrity are at the core of sustainable long-term success. Without them, no strategy can work and, as Enron has demonstrated, enterprises will fail. That's despite having some of the 'smartest' guys in the room." Discuss how it is possible for an enterprise to collapse despite having really smart guys.

   _____

   _____

CHAPTER ESSAY ASSIGNMENT

Can business and ethics coexist?

 OBJECTIVE
6
Read, think, plan, and write an essay in response to the chapter essay assignment

Now that you have had the opportunity to read a number of articles and a text-book excerpt, you should have a deeper understanding of the topic of business ethics, and be prepared to compose your chapter essay assignment.

Assignment: Write a two- to three-page essay on this topic, or your own topic. Support your claims with evidence or examples drawn from what you have read in the chapter and other relevant readings from other sources. You can also support your claims with information you have learned in school and/or personally experienced.

Be sure to include a clear thesis statement in your opening paragraph. After you have received constructive feedback from your instructor, be sure to incorporate some of his or her suggestions into your second draft and submit it for further feedback on form and meaning.

FOCUS ON FORM

Using Punctuation Correctly

In the Trouble Spots in Writing section of this chapter, you learned how to use punctuation appropriately. Let's put your newly acquired skills into action. The following paragraph was written by a student who was pressed for time and did not pay close attention to punctuation issues. Your task is to identify where there are punctuation issues and then to revise accordingly. Remember to use commas, apostrophes, question marks, periods, and quotation marks when necessary. When you are done, compare your paragraph with that of a classmate.

Five of the worlds largest banks Barclays, JP Morgan Chase UBS Group, Royal Bank of Scotland Group and Citigroup have pleaded guilty to manipulating international interest and foreign currency exchange rates they have agreed to pay $5 billion in fines to settle charges made by the Justice Department Critics say that this unethical practice is quite common in the financial markets and the Justice Department has failed to bring the offenders to justice Senator Elizabeth Warren D-Mass said in an e-mail Thats not accountability for Wall Street Its business as usual and it stinks the real question to ask is this is this just a slap on the wrist or have the big fish finally been brought to justice

It's Your Turn!

Now that you have had a chance to identify punctuation issues and practice editing for punctuation, review the essay you wrote for the chapter essay assignment and look for missing commas, semicolons, colons, apostrophes, quotations marks, end punctuation (periods, question marks, and exclamation points), parentheses, hyphens, dashes, or ellipses.

CHAPTER DEBATE

Can business and ethics coexist?

This chapter's debate topic is related to your chapter essay assignment. Refer to Appendix 8, page 455, for detailed guidelines on how to take a position on a controversial issue and argue for and against the view.

10 Sociology

Learning Objectives

IN THIS CHAPTER, YOU WILL LEARN TO . . .

1 Read in the field of sociology

2 Understand and use key terms in sociology

3 Locate and evaluate evidence in text

4 Develop effective strategies for answering multiple-choice questions

5 Ensure your paragraphs are cohesive and coherent

6 Solve writer's block

7 Read, think, plan, and write an essay in response to the chapter essay assignment

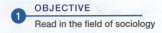

Introduction to the Field of Sociology

Sociology is the study of human behavior in society, including the study of the organization, institutions, and development of human society. Human behavior is quite complex, so sociologists study various aspects of it, such as race and ethnicity, gender and age, families, education and religion, and environment and urbanization. Sociologists want to know how groups influence people, especially how people are influenced by their society.

The chapter readings focus primarily on gender issues. You will read a book excerpt on how males and females sometimes misunderstand each other in conversation. Another reading deals with the factors that are causing boys to fall behind girls in educational achievement. The third selection explores a host of variables that lead many married couples to get divorced. Through exposure to multiple perspectives on these issues in sociology, you will be better positioned to add your own voice to the larger discussion.

CHAPTER ESSAY QUESTION

Aside from physiological differences, are men and women truly different in any significant ways?

Quick Free-Write! Take out a piece of paper, and write for ten minutes without stopping about what you already know about the theme of the chapter essay question.

Option: Once you have worked your way through the chapter readings, you are welcome to narrow down the topics covered and compose your own chapter essay question.

Previewing Sociology

Read the following questions and discuss them with your classmates. As you answer the questions, consider your personal experience and knowledge of sociology in general.

1. Imagine a world without cell phone communication. You wouldn't have to go too far back in time to experience this reality. Thirty years ago, cell phones, texting, Skype, Facebook, and other forms of social media were not part of people's lives. How have cell phones, texting, and social media changed the way people communicate?

2. How are men and women different? What stereotypes do we hold of typical male behavior and of typical female behavior? How have gender roles in society changed in the last fifty years?

3. In what ways do wealthy people behave differently from poorer people? Share some examples.

4. Why do teenagers often have trouble relating to their parents? What factors may lead to miscommunication between parents and their teen children?

5. How do people choose their life mate? How can someone really know if another person is *the* one he or she wants to spend the rest of his or her life with? What factors might play a role in making this determination?

After discussing the preview questions with your classmates, post your responses to two of them on The Wall. Peruse The Wall and respond to at least two of your classmates' responses that pique your interest.

OBJECTIVE

2

Understand and use key terms in sociology

Key Terms in Sociology

Take a moment to think about the discipline of sociology as you complete the following two exercises.

EXERCISE **10.1** Brainstorming Vocabulary

Directions: What associated words come to mind when you think of the world of sociology? Work with a partner and write down as many related words as you can think of in a period of five minutes.

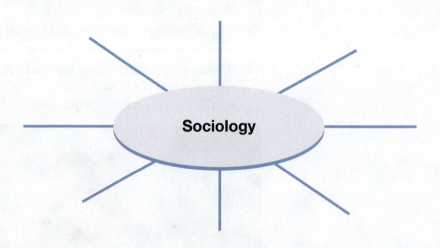

EXERCISE **10.2** Creating Original Sentences

Directions: Choose five of the words from your brainstorm list, and use them to write complete and meaningful sentences.

1. _____

2. _____

3. _____

4. _____

5. _____

A **synonym** is a word used to express a similar meaning to another word. An **antonym** is a word that conveys the opposite meaning of another word.

One of the most efficient ways to acquire academic vocabulary is to study key terms that are thematically connected. As you begin your college-level studies, it is critical that you internalize vocabulary terms that relate to the academic disciplines that make up most 100-level content courses. For example, a student taking an introduction to sociology course should be able to apply such terms as *individualistic, segregating*, and *dominate* in both spoken and written forms.

As in previous chapters, here you will practice finding appropriate synonyms and antonyms for those terms and others. Understanding how to work with synonyms and antonyms is a useful skill, especially when you are writing a summary of a text and trying to paraphrase some of the key ideas and pieces of information contained in the original source.

EXERCISE **10.3** Discipline-specific Vocabulary: Fishing for Synonyms and Antonyms

Directions: Read the following ten (10) discipline-specific words culled from the readings in this chapter and shown in the context of the sentences in which they appeared. In the space provided after each sentence, write a synonym or antonym for the highlighted term, as directed.

Discipline-specific Word Bank*

point of view	gender gap
preference	patriarchy
relationships	dominate
assumptions	individualistic
segregating	stigma

* The first time these discipline-specific words appear in the chapter, they are shown in bold green.

1. "From her **point of view**, she had shown concern for her husband's wishes, but he had shown no concern for hers." (Selection 1, p. 403, para. 1)

    A synonym for *point of view* is _____.

2. "The wife, I explained, was annoyed not because she had not gotten her way, but because her **preference** had not been considered." (Selection 1, p. 403, para. 1)

    An antonym for *preference* is _____.

3. "**Relationships** are sometimes threatened by psychological problems, true failures of love and caring, genuine selfishness, and real effects of political and economic inequity." (Selection 1, p. 403, para. 3)

    A synonym for *relationships* is _____.

4. "But there are also innumerable situations in which groundless allegations of these failings are made, simply because partners are expressing their thoughts and feelings, and their **assumptions** about how to communicate, in different ways." (Selection 1, p. 403, para. 3)

    A synonym for *assumptions* is _____.

5. "To what factors might those who advocate **segregating** boys and girls point to defend this policy idea?" (Selection 2, p. 406, Intro. Q 3)

An antonym for *segregating* is _____

6. "Even in the United States, many people still associate the educational '**gender gap**' with girls left behind in math." (Selection 2, p. 407, para. 1)

An antonym for *gender gap* is _____.

7. "Although **patriarchy** has weakened, most people still expect husbands to be older and taller than their wives and to have more important, better-paid jobs." (Selection 3, p. 420, para. 1)

An antonym for *patriarchy* is _____.

8. "She is quick to add that marriage could be healthful for women if husbands did not **dominate** wives and expect them to do almost all of the housework." (Selection 3, p. 420, para. 4)

A synonym for *dominate* is _____.

9. "We have become more **individualistic** and more concerned about personal happiness and earning income than about the well-being of our partners and children." (Selection 3, p. 420, para. 5, item 1 in list)

An antonym for *individualistic* is _____.

10. "Divorce no longer carries the powerful **stigma** it did several generations ago." (Selection 3, p. 421, para. 5, item 5 in the list)

A synonym for *stigma* is _____.

SUCCESS IN
READING

Finding and Evaluating Evidence in the Text

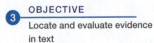

OBJECTIVE

3 Locate and evaluate evidence in text

Just as writers substantiate the claims they make with factual details, good readers are able to locate and evaluate different forms of evidence as they examine a given text. When reading, you are often expected to compare the ideas discussed in a text with your knowledge and experience of the world. However, one of the challenges in doing critical reading is being able to separate your own opinions, assumptions, and life experiences from those expressed by the author.

So, for example, if you are evaluating an essay on the death penalty in which the author argues against it, you cannot judge the article as weakly reasoned simply because you happen to hold the opposite viewpoint. At the same time, if you agree with the author that the death penalty is wrong, when discussing the merits of the author's support for his or her arguments, you cannot bring in your own supporting points to back up the author's arguments. You have to find evidence for any claims made by the author in the original text itself.

Evidence in support of an argument usually directly follows the argument. Factual evidence, or proof, comes in many forms. Some forms of evidence are statistical information, logically reasoned statements, informed opinions, or references to past research. Personal observation and experience can also serve as evidence.

One active reading method that can be very helpful is to put boxes around arguments you identify as you read and to highlight any evidence offered to support these arguments. You can draw an arrow connecting boxed arguments and highlighted supporting evidence, and label them accordingly (see example below). If you cannot find evidence for a claim made by an author, skim through the text again. It is easy to miss some details when you are doing a first read.

Example: Connecting Supporting Evidence with a Claim

While the stereotype of seniors is that they are fraught with health problems and can no longer live independently, a number of studies suggest otherwise. In 2010, only 16% of seniors reported they could not walk a quarter-mile by themselves, and fewer than one in twenty resided in a nursing home. Overall, only 26 percent of people over age seventy-five characterized their health as "fair" or "poor"; 74% consider their overall condition "good" or "excellent". In fact, the share of seniors reporting good or excellent health is going up (CDC, 2012, Schiller, et al, 2012).

—Adapted from *Sociology*, by John Macionis, 15th ed., p. 430

EXERCISE **10.4** Identifying Claims and Relevant Supporting Evidence

Directions: Read the following newspaper editorial. Box the arguments made and highlight the evidence cited in support of these claims. Using a pen, draw arrows connecting arguments and evidence, and label them. When you are finished, compare how the text now looks with that of a classmate's.

How TV Affects Your Children

Most kids plug into the world of television long before they enter school. According to the Kaiser Family Foundation (KFF):

- two-thirds of infants and toddlers watch a screen an average of 2 hours a day
- kids under age 6 watch an average of about 2 hours of screen media a day, primarily TV and videos or DVDs
- kids and teens 8 to 18 years spend nearly 4 hours a day in front of a TV screen and almost 2 additional hours on the computer (outside of school-work) and playing video games

The American Academy of Pediatrics (AAP) recommends that kids under 2 years old not watch *any* TV and that those older than 2 watch no more than 1 to 2 hours a day of quality programming.

The first 2 years of life are considered a critical time for brain development. TV and other electronic media can get in the way of exploring, playing, and interacting with parents and others, which encourages learning and healthy physical and social development.

As kids get older, too much screen time can interfere with activities such as being physically active, reading, doing homework, playing with friends, and spending time with family.

Of course, TV in moderation can be a good thing: Preschoolers can get help learning the alphabet on public television, grade schoolers can learn about wild-life on nature shows, and parents can keep up with current events on the evening news. No doubt about it—TV can be an excellent educator and entertainer.

But despite its advantages, too much television can be detrimental:

- Children who consistently spend more than 4 hours per day watching TV are more likely to be overweight.
- Kids who view violent acts are more likely to show aggressive behavior but also fear that the world is scary and that something bad will happen to them.
- TV characters often depict risky behaviors, such as smoking and drink-ing, and also reinforce gender-role and racial stereotypes.

Children's advocates are divided when it comes to solutions. Although many urge for more hours per week of educational programming, others assert that zero TV is the best solution. And some say it's better for parents to control the use of TV and to teach kids that it's for occasional entertainment, not for constant escapism.

That's why it's so important for you to monitor the content of TV programming and set viewing limits to ensure that your kids don't spend too much time parked in front of the TV.

—From http://kidshealth.org/parent/positive/family/tv_affects_child.html

Guidelines for Evaluating Supporting Evidence

The ability to locate supporting evidence for a given claim is one skill. Evaluating the evidence you find is another. In Chapter 7 (p. 289), we examined faulty argumentation from the writer's perspective. The focus was on trying to steer clear of some faulty paths in constructing a solid argument. As a reader, you need to put your critical lenses on and consider whether the evidence that is offered in a text is relevant and consistent with the claim this evidence is supporting.

One way to approach supporting evidence is to consider it guilty until proven innocent. That is, it is useful be skeptical of the relevance, validity, and sufficiency of supporting evidence until you have examined the given evidence in light of these three criteria.

- **Relevance of evidence.** Consider whether the evidence that is offered in a text relates directly to the claim. Evidence can be off-topic or may even contradict the claim it is aiming to support.
- **Validity of evidence.** Just because a writer offers factual supporting evidence does not mean that this information is valid and accurate. You need to consider if the writer is working with reliable sources and whether the facts he or she uses can be verified. In some cases, a writer may not offer source information at all, in which case, you may want to try to verify the facts yourself.
- **Sufficiency of evidence.** Is enough evidence offered to back up the claim? If the evidence is based on an individual case, for example, this evidence cannot be generalized to support a claim about a larger group. For instance, if the claim is that many students struggle in high school math classes, supporting evidence based on the example of the author's cousin's difficulty in math would not be sufficient evidence to prove this point. The author would need to cite well-researched studies or other verifiable facts to support his or her claim.

The following chart shows some examples of claims and their supporting evidence and explains what evidence in each case is questionable.

Examining Supporting Evidence for Relevance, Validity, and Sufficiency			
Claim	**Supporting Evidence**	**Issue with the Quality of Evidence**	**Explanation**
Many smokers have other addiction issues.	A recent study showed that smoking is related to more illnesses than previously believed.	Relevance: evidence is off-topic	The evidence focuses on the topic of "illnesses related to smoking" and does not bear on the topic of addiction.
Only children are more selfish, and have generally weaker characters than children with siblings.	In hundreds of studies during the past decades exploring sixteen character traits—including leadership, maturity, and social participation—only children scored just as well as children with siblings.	Relevance: evidence contradicts claim	The evidence presented—that only children scored equally to children with siblings on a character trait study—would lead one to believe that only children are not different in this area.
Racial profiling is extremely common among area police.	According to a middle school club newspaper in Dallas, 90 percent of suspects stopped by police for routine checks were nonwhite.	Validity: source of evidence questionable	The evidence comes from a middle-school newspaper. You should always pay attention to the source of information and evaluate the quality of supporting evidence provided. Check to see if the writer provided facts to support this statement.
Many parents do not feel comfortable leaving their toddler alone in his or her bedroom at night.	For example, my Uncle Joseph and Aunt Lila say that they can't sleep at night when they don't have their 2-year-old with them in bed.	Sufficiency: evidence is based on a single example	Single example evidence does not serve as evidence beyond the individual case. The fact that the author's aunt and uncle hold a certain belief doesn't tell us anything about the views other members of society hold.

EXERCISE 10.5 Evaluating Supporting Evidence

Directions: For each claim stated below, place a check mark in front of those statements that offer solid supporting evidence. If the statement does not back up the claim, explain why not.

1. Claim: Laws permitting physician-assisted suicide invite abuse.

    a. Critics point to surveys indicating that in most cases the conditions for physician-assisted suicide are not met.

    _____

    _____

    b. Physician-assisted suicide is highly regulated and only allowed in rare cases.

    _____

    _____

c. Most physicians acting on requests for assisted suicide do not consult with other doctors.

_____

_____

2. Sociologist William Julius Wilson studied a poor neighborhood in Chicago.
   Claim: The neighborhood has declined because there are no jobs.

   a. Wilson identified more than 800 businesses that had operated in 1950. Now, fewer than 100 remain.

   _____

   _____

   b. A number of major employers in the past, including Western Electric, closed their plant doors in the late 1960s.

   _____

   _____

   c. Wilson pointed to the broken-down infrastructure, including unstable bridges and worn-out public buses.

   _____

   _____

3. **Claim:** A sad fact of our political life is that many Americans do not vote.

   a. Americans spend a lot of their time watching sports on TV.

   _____

   _____

   b. In the 2000 presidential elections, only half the people eligible to vote went to the polls.

   _____

   _____

   c. My brother sometimes votes, but other times forgets to take care of his civic duty.

   _____

   _____

4. **Claim:** Today's sports stars are making more money than they deserve.

   a. Alex Rodriguez of the New York Yankees took home $32 million in 2011.

   _____

   _____

   b. Some Hollywood actors command over $50 million per film.

   _____

   _____

c. The average NFL football player salary is $1.9 million a year, while
the average salary for American workers is $45,000 a year.

_____

_____

Learning Implications

The ability to find evidence in a text is a valuable skill, and not just for lawyers.
Whether you are reviewing class readings for an exam, taking a multiple-choice
test, or doing research for an assigned paper, building the habit of locating and
evaluating evidence within a reading passage will make it much easier to follow
both the major and minor ideas contained in the text.

READING

Selection 1

Book Excerpt

You Just Don't Understand: Women and Men in Conversation

Pre-Reading Questions

Answer the following questions before exploring the text:

1. In what ways do men and women communicate differently? How can some
of these differences cause conflicts between the sexes?

2. Some people believe that as we move deeper into the twenty-first century,
the roles of men and women in American society have become nearly identical. Others argue that traditional male and female roles still exist. What is
your opinion about the male and female roles in modern society?

3. How best can men learn how to understand women and vice versa? Offer
some advice.

Eye on Vocabulary

Working with a partner, skim through the reading and find the following key
vocabulary terms in bold. Examine the words in context and try to guess the
meaning of each. Then look up the words in a dictionary. Keep in mind that
many words have multiple meanings. Write the definition that best fits the
word's context in the article.

Word(s)	Your definition	Dictionary definition
1. taken place (v.)		
2. proposes (v.)		
3. genuine (adj.)		
4. confront (v.)		

Adapted from *You Just Don't Understand: Women and Men in Conversation*

by Deborah Tannen (2004)

Deborah Tannen is a world-famous linguist who has studied the differences in male and female conversational styles. The following excerpt is from her best-selling book on this subject.

1   In an article I wrote for the *Washington Post*, I presented a conversation that had **taken place** between a couple in their car. The woman had asked, "Would you like to stop for a drink?" Her husband had answered truthfully, "No," and they hadn't stopped. He was later frustrated to learn that his wife was annoyed because she had wanted to stop for a drink. He wondered, "Why didn't she just say what she wanted? Why did she play games with me?" The wife, I explained, was annoyed not because she had not gotten her way, but because her **preference** had not been considered. From her **point of view**, she had shown concern for her husband's wishes, but he had shown no concern for hers.

2   A woman I'll call Diana often begins statements with "Let's." She might say, "Let's go out for brunch today," or "Let's clean up now, before we start lunch." This makes Nathan angry. He feels she is ordering him around, telling him what to do. Diana can't understand why he takes it that way. It is obvious to her that she is making suggestions, not demands. If he doesn't feel like doing what she **proposes**, all he has to do is say so.

3   Conversational style differences do not explain all the problems that arise in **relationships** between men and women. Relationships are sometimes threatened by psychological problems, true failures of love and caring, **genuine** selfishness, and real effects of political and economic inequity. But there are also innumerable situations in which groundless allegations of these failings are made, simply because partners are expressing their thoughts and feelings, and their **assumptions** about how to communicate, in different ways. If we can sort out differences based on conversational style, we will be in a better position to **confront** real conflicts of interest and to find a shared language in which to negotiate them.

Thinking about the Reading

After doing a close reading of the article, write your answers to the following questions. When you have written all of your answers, discuss your answers with your classmates.

1. In your understanding, if a friend says, "Let's park over there," would you consider this an order or a proposal? Explain.

   _____

   _____

2. Deborah Tannen believes that the best way for males and females to reduce conflict between themselves is to better understand how the opposite sex communicates. Do you think this type of understanding can solve relationship problems? Explain.

   _____

   _____

3. Tannen is indirectly making the claim that generally speaking men tend to be more direct in their speech and women more indirect. Do you agree with this claim? Can you think of any examples that either back up or contradict this idea?

   _____

   _____

Reading Comprehension Check

_____ 1. What caused the fight between the husband and wife in the first example?

    a. The husband was tired and frustrated.

    b. The couple misunderstood each other.

    c The husband wanted to stop for a coffee.

    d. The wife wanted an instant decision.

_____ 2. In the sentence, "Conversational style differences do not explain all the problems that **arise** in relationships between men and women," *arise* means _____.

    a. disappear   c. come up

    b. are highlighted   d. sink down

_____ 3. In the sentence, "But there are also **innumerable** situations in which groundless allegations of these failings are made, simply because partners are expressing their thoughts and feelings, and their assumptions about how to communicate, in different ways," the term *innumerable* could be replaced with _____.

    a. few   c. limited

    b. countable   d. many

_____ **4.** Tannen writes, "If we can **sort out** differences based on conversational style, we will be in a better position to confront real conflicts of interest and to find a shared language in which to negotiate them." In this context, the expression *sort out* means

    a. separate out.

    b. ignore.

    c. assemble.

    d. synthesize.

_____ **5.** In the example given in the second paragraph, why is Nathan upset?

    a. He wants to make all the decisions for the couple.

    b. Men don't like women making decisions.

    c. He feels he is being told what to do.

    d. He doesn't want to do any cleaning.

_____ **6.** Conversational style differences between men and women _____.

    a. result from psychological disorders in one or both partners

    b. result in true failures of love and caring

    c. are to blame for the most serious problems that arise in relationships

    d. can be examined in order to tackle conflicts of interest

_____ **7.** How does Nathan interpret Diana's use of *let's* to begin a statement?

    a. as an order   c. as a suggestion

    b. as indecisive   d. as a test

_____ **8.** What is a major result of couples expressing themselves in mismatched conversational styles?

    a. couples learning more about themselves and each other in the course of day-to-day conversational interaction

    b. allegations of psychological problems, failures of caring, and genuine selfishness

    c. quarreling about whether or not to stop for a drink

    d. separation or divorce

_____ **9.** According to the article, a good way to address conflicts between men and women in relationships is to

    a. use nonverbal techniques.

    b. find a shared language.

    c. match couples based on conversational style.

    d. teach men to converse like women and vice versa.

_____ **10.** In the example of the misunderstanding between the couple in the car, what did the woman want?

    a. She wanted to find out whether her husband would respond to her question honestly.

    b. She wanted to go straight home without stopping anywhere along the way.

    c. She wanted to get intoxicated and have her husband stay sober and drive her home safely.

    d. She wanted her husband to take her wishes about what to do into consideration.

THEMATIC LINKS

If you want to read more on the topic of gender differences in communication, type the following words into your browser and explore the two sites that come up:

1. He said, She said Monster

2. Communication Styles Make a Difference

Writing Without BOUNDARIES

There Are No Checkpoints!

"Single parents—both women and men—can play as critical a role as the traditional two-parent family, and gay and lesbian parents can, and do, raise happy, resilient children. When it comes to family life, form is not merely as important as content. Feeling loved and supported, nurtured and safe, is far more critical than the 'package' it comes in."

—Michael S. Kimmel, Guyland

Read the quote above and respond to Kimmel's idea in any way you want. Write in your notebook for ten minutes without stopping. For this activity, it is important that you focus on ideas, not words. In other words, this will be an exercise in focusing on content and not getting hung up on word choice and grammar errors. You may wish to read what you have written out loud in front of your classmates and instructor.

READING

Selection 2

Newspaper article

The Boys Have Fallen Behind

Pre-Reading Questions

Answer the following questions before exploring the text:

1. Thinking about your high school experience, compare how boys and girls behaved in the classroom. Describe any differences you noticed.

2. One hundred years ago, boys far surpassed girls in academic achievement. How did the social context of the times set boys up to be more successful than girls? How has the context changed today?

3. Some educators believe that girls and boys can be more successful students if they attend single-sex schools. To what factors might those who advocate **segregating** (separating) boys and girls point to defend this policy idea? Do the two sexes act differently when they are separated? How?

Eye on Vocabulary

Working with a partner, skim through the reading and find the following key vocabulary terms in bold. Examine the words in context and try to guess the meaning of each. Then look up the words in a dictionary. Keep in mind that many words have multiple meanings. Write the definition that best fits the word's context in the article.

Word	Your definition	Dictionary definition
1. associate (v.)		
2. skewed (adj.)		
3. evolved (v.)		
4. entice (v.)		

The Boys Have Fallen Behind

By Nicholas Kristof

March 27, 2010

Part 1

1   Around the globe, it's mostly girls who lack educational opportunities. Even in the United States, many people still **associate** the educational "**gender gap**" with girls left behind in math.

2   Yet these days, the opposite problem has sneaked up on us: In the United States and other Western countries alike, it is mostly boys who are faltering in school. The latest surveys show that American girls on average have roughly achieved parity with boys in math. Meanwhile, girls are well ahead of boys in verbal skills, and they just seem to try harder. The National Honor Society says that 64 percent of its members—outstanding high school students—are girls. Some colleges give special help to male applicants—yes, that's affirmative action for white males—to avoid **skewed** sex ratios.

3   A new report just issued by the Center on Education Policy, an independent research organization, confirms that boys have fallen behind in reading in every single state. It found, for example, that in elementary schools, about 79 percent of girls could read at a level deemed "proficient," compared with 72 percent of boys. Similar gaps were found in middle school and high school. In every state, in each of the three school levels, girls did better on average than boys. "The most pressing issue related to gender gaps is the lagging performance of boys in reading," the report said.

4   A sobering new book, *Why Boys Fail*, by Richard Whitmire, cites mountains of evidence to make the point:

- The average high school grade point average is 3.09 for girls and 2.86 for boys. Boys are almost twice as likely as girls to repeat a grade.
- Boys are twice as likely to get suspended as girls, and three times as likely to be expelled. Estimates of dropouts vary, but it seems that about one-quarter more boys drop out than girls.

- Among whites, women earn 57 percent of bachelor's degrees and 62 percent of master's degrees. Among blacks, the figures are 66 percent and 72 percent.
- In federal writing tests, 32 percent of girls are considered "proficient" or better. For boys, the figure is 16 percent.

5   There is one important exception: Boys still beat out girls at the very top of the curve, especially in math. In the high school class of 2009, a total of 297 students scored a perfect triple-800 on the S.A.T., 62 percent of them boys, according to Kathleen Steinberg of the College Board. And of the 10,052 who scored an 800 in the math section, 69 percent were boys.

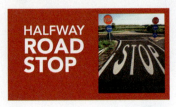

HALFWAY ROAD STOP

Get into a small group and answer the two questions that follow.

1. What have you learned from this editorial so far?
2. What do you predict may be coming in the second half of the editorial?

Part 2

6   Some say that the "boy problem" is just a problem for members of minorities. But *Why Boys Fail* says that at the end of high school, among white boys who have at least one parent who attended college, 23 percent score "below basic" in reading. Only 7 percent of their female counterparts score that low. Likewise, boys are also lagging in Scandinavia, Canada, Britain and throughout the industrialized world.

7   What is going on? Many theories have been proposed. Some people think that boys are hard-wired so that they learn more slowly, perhaps because they **evolved** to fight off wolves more than to raise their hands in classrooms. But that doesn't explain why boys have been sinking in recent decades.

8   Mr. Whitmire argues that the basic problem is an increased emphasis on verbal skills, often taught in sedate ways that bore boys. "The world has gotten more verbal," he writes. "Boys haven't." The upshot, he writes, is that boys get frustrated, act out, and learn to dislike school. "Poor reading skills snowball through the grades," he writes. "By fifth grade, a child at the bottom of the class reads only about 60,000 words a year in and out of school, compared to a child in the middle of the class who reads about 800,000 words a year."

9   Some educators say that one remedy may be to encourage lowbrow, adventure or even gross-out books that disproportionately appeal to boys. (I confess that I was a huge fan of the Hardy Boys, and then used them to **entice** my own kids into becoming avid readers as well.) Indeed, the more books make parents flinch, the more they seem to suck boys in. A Web site, guysread.com, offers useful lists of books to coax boys into reading, and they are helpfully sorted into categories like "ghosts," "boxers, wrestlers, ultimate fighters," and "at least one explosion."

10   At a time when men are still hugely overrepresented in Congress, on executive boards, and in the corridors of power, does it matter that boys are struggling in schools? Of course it does: our future depends on making the best use of human capital we can, whether it belongs to girls or boys. If that means nurturing boys with explosions, that's a price worth paying.

Thinking about the Reading

After doing a close reading of the article, write your answers to the following questions. When you have written all of your answers, discuss your answers with your classmates.

1. What does Kristof mean when he writes in the second paragraph, "Yet these days, the opposite problem has sneaked up on us"? What is this "opposite problem" he is referring to?

   _____

   _____

   _____

2. What are some theories mentioned in the article to explain why boys are falling behind? Which theory, if any, makes sense to you? Explain.

   _____

   _____

3. What solutions are offered to deal with this troubling gender gap issue?

   _____

   _____

Reading Comprehension Check

_____ 1. "Likewise, boys are also **lagging** in Scandinavia, Canada, Britain and throughout the industrialized world." The word *lagging* could be replaced by _____.

   a. speeding forward
   b. falling behind
   c. staying neutral
   d. getting tired

_____ 2. What is the main idea of the editorial?

   a. Many boys are lagging behind girls in their educational achievements.
   b. Boys and girls are not the same.
   c. Boys should be given more opportunity to read adventure books.
   d. Boys' lack of success reflects the gender gap in education.

_____ 3. When Kristof writes, "Indeed, the more books make parents flinch, the more they seem to suck boys in," we can infer that

   a. some parents do not have a high opinion of ghost stories and thrillers.
   b. it hurts parents to think that their children are not reading at all.
   c. most boys like to read the same things that their parents read.
   d. books parents do not like are often the ones boys enjoy reading.

_____ **4.** What does Richard Whitmore, the author of *Why Boys Fail*, believe is the cause of boys' lagging reading scores?

    a. They are easily frustrated and act out because they dislike school.

    b. Girls are becoming better readers, which makes boys look less successful.

    c. The problem is the American education system, as boys are doing well in other countries.

    d. The increasing emphasis on verbal skills taught in sedate ways leads boys to become frustrated and act out.

_____ **5.** What is Kristof's final point?

    a. We may have to use explosions to entice boys to read.

    b. It doesn't matter that much if boys fall behind in school.

    c. Whatever it takes to get boys to read is worth it.

    d. Boys should be encouraged to read classic literature.

_____ **6.** Which of the following statements about the content of this reading is *true*?

    a. The phenomenon of boys lagging behind girls in school is unique to the United States.

    b. The average high school grade point average for boys is 3.09.

    c. Boys do better than girls when it comes to who earns the highest SAT math scores.

    d. Boys have fallen behind girls in reading in nearly every state.

_____ **7.** How does the author say that he got his own children excited about reading?

    a. banned television from their home

    b. read fairy tales out loud to them at bedtime

    c. withheld their allowances if they did poorly in reading

    d. used the Hardy Boys adventure books

_____ **8.** In paragraph 8, the verb *snowball* most likely means

    a. decline steadily.

    b. increase rapidly.

    c. lessen the chances of success.

    d. create a chilling effect.

_____ **9.** According to the reading, boys in elementary school are likely to be interested in reading about all of the following except

    a. terrorist attacks.

    b. looking for ghosts in a haunted mansion.

    c. a biography of a famous boxer.

    d. starting a babysitting service.

_____ **10.** According to the author, we should care that boys are struggling in school because our future depends on

    a. having the best human resources available to us, male or female.

    b. keeping the balance of power in the workplace approximately equal between the sexes.

    c. boys becoming more verbal.

    d. males staying in charge of politics and business.

THEMATIC LINKS

If you want to read more on the topic of boys falling behind in school, type the following words into your browser and explore the two sites that come up:

1. Boy Trouble? Change for Boys' Educational Prospects Scholastic

2. The Gender Gap: Boys Lagging

READING SKILL FOCUS

OBJECTIVE

4

Develop effective strategies for answering multiple-choice questions

Effective Strategies for Answering Multiple-Choice Questions

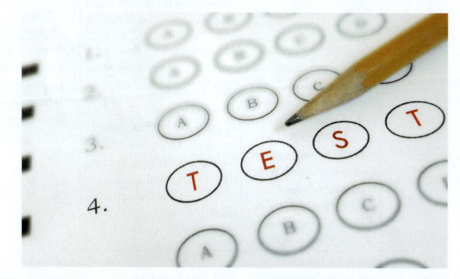

Most college-level reading exams, and many 100-level content class exams, include a set of reading passages, each followed by a set of multiple-choice questions. Thus, it is critical that you not only develop your academic reading ability but also sharpen your skills in multiple-choice test taking. In this section, we will focus on four key strategy areas, which can guide you toward greater success on these types of exams:

• Familiarize yourself with the most common question types.
• "Enter the text" before worrying about the questions.
• Find evidence to support your answer choice.
• Justify the incorrect answer options.

Become Familiar with the Most Common Question Types

As we are now in the final chapter of this textbook, you have already had a lot of practice with each of the most typical question types. However, it would be wise to review the most common question types and strategies for interacting with them.

Strategies for Answering Common Multiple-Choice Question Types			
Question Type	**Description**	**Strategy**	**Example Questions (based on chapter selections)**
Detail	These are the most common question types on most exams. Detail questions focus on specific facts contained in the reading passage that answer the *Who? What? Where? When? How?* and *Why?* of the reading.	*Review Chapter 4 Reading Skill Focus: Identifying Supporting Details, p.* 141. The answers to detail questions are usually directly stated in the text. Find the paragraph where this information is contained, and zero in on the correct fact.	• What caused the fight between the husband and wife in the first example in Selection 1? • Why do boys respond to a more verbally focused classroom? What do some educators point to as one remedy to the educational crisis many boys are facing?
Main Idea	These questions relate to "overall meaning" because they focus on the entire reading, not just one particular part of the text. When you are asked to find the main idea, ask yourself: What is the author's main point? What key idea do the major details of the text revolve around?	*Review Chapter 3 Reading Skill Focus: Identifying Main Idea, p.* 92. First, get a sense of the topic of the reading. Then, look for an answer choice that is not too specific (this would be a detail), but that covers the key point of the entire reading.	• What is the author's main point in the excerpt from *You Just Don't Understand: Women and Men in Conversation*? • What is the main idea of the article "The Boys Have Fallen Behind"?
Inference	Inference questions can be challenging because you have to "read between the lines" to find the correct answer. You can infer the author's intended meaning through paying close attention to the author's point of view, ideas, supporting evidence, and choice of words.	*Review Chapter 5 Reading Skill Focus: Making Inferences, p.* 181. One key to making accurate inferences is to read the text very carefully to gain a deeper understanding of the point of view the author takes toward his or her subject. Another key is to examine the details and think about what one general idea would encompass them all. Also, make sure to check that all the details are covered by the idea you infer.	• What can you infer from what Kristof says in paragraph 3 of the article "The Boys Have Fallen Behind"? • From what Tannen says about differences in male and female conversational styles, what can you infer that she will discuss in the body of her article?

Strategies for Answering Common Multiple-Choice Question Types			
Question Type	**Description**	**Strategy**	**Example Questions (based on chapter selections)**
Vocabulary in Context	Vocabulary questions ask you to define the meaning of particular terms used in a given reading. You may also be asked to provide or identify a synonym or antonym for the vocabulary term.	*Review Chapter 2 Reading Skill Focus: Determining Meaning from Context, p. 51.* You will need to zero in on how the word is being used in the context of the sentence, as many words have multiple meanings. Pay attention to context clues, prefixes, suffixes, and the word's connotation.	• "Likewise, boys are also **lagging** in Scandinavia, Canada, Britain and throughout the industrialized world." In the above sentence, what word could replace the word *lagging*? • In the sentence, "Conversational style differences do not explain all the problems that **arise** in relationships between men and women," what would be a synonym for *arise*?
Not/ Except	Not/Except questions are asking you which item in a list of multiple-choice options is *not* mentioned in the text.	You will need to carefully cross-check each of the items on the list to locate which was *not* mentioned in the text.	• All of the factors contributing to boys being not as academically successful as girls are mentioned in the second reading, *except …* • Which of the following conversational traits is *not* mentioned as causing communication breakdowns between men and women?

"Enter the Text"

Many anxious, multiple-choice test-taking students focus so much of their attention on the questions and answer options that they neglect the most important item in front of them . . . the reading passage itself! Before you worry about the specifics of the question set you are being asked to complete, you should first get a clear sense of the reading passage. "**Entering the text**" involves identifying the genre of the reading, the topic of the passage, and how the reading is organized. We can also call this process "getting the lay of the land." Examine the chart below, based on Selection 3, "Marriage, Divorce and Gender." This type of orientation will help you make a first connection with the text at hand.

Entering the Text "Marriage, Divorce and Gender"		
Genre	**Topic**	**Organization**
Textbook	Societal notions of marriage, divorce, and gender	The reading is divided into two sections. The first section focuses on the relationship between gender and marriage, and the second section deals with divorce in American society.

In Exercise 10.7 on p. 415, you will have the opportunity to work with a several short readings and fill out "entering the text" charts.

Find Evidence to Support Your Answer Choice

Non-evidence-based guessing on a multiple-choice question is like jumping off a plane without a parachute and betting on the small chance that you might land in a soft spot! It's simply not advisable. Instead, you will need to take the time to locate in the text the evidence required to answer a given question.

Where does this evidence search fit into the overall process of taking the test? Well, as stated earlier, you should do a first read of the passage to enter the text and get a lay of the land. If you do not feel like you fully understand it, you should take the time to do a second reading. After doing this, carefully read over question #1 and the answer options that follow it. Before rushing to answer, it is critical that you now go back to the text and locate the evidence you need to answer the question correctly. Some students wrongly believe that there is no reason to go back, if they have already read the passage one or two times. This could not be further from the truth. The only place to find the evidence you will need to choose the correct answer option is the reading itself. It's all right in front of you!

Justify the Incorrect Answer Options

An exercise that could prove helpful in narrowing down the four or five answer options and moving toward a correct multiple-choice response is to justify why each incorrect answer option is, in fact, incorrect. Let's illustrate this process of justification with the following short reading and multiple-choice question.

The Gender Gap

Will the glass ceiling crack open? Some think so. They point out that women who began their careers twenty or thirty years ago are now running major divisions within the largest companies, and from them, some will emerge as the new CEOs. Others reply that these optimists have been saying this same thing for years, that the glass ceiling continues to be so strong that most of these women they refer to have already reached their top positions.

We'll have to see what the future brings, but the growing number of women who are majoring in law and business is certainly a promising indication of positive change.

—Excerpted from *Mastering Sociology* by James Henslin, p. 289

_____ 1. What is the main idea of this passage?

    a. the glass ceiling

    b. Many women are now majoring in law and business.

    c. Some people believe that the new generation of women will crack the glass ceiling.

    d. Many CEOs are males making millions of dollars a year without working very hard for their salaries.

Multiple-Choice Justification

    a. *This is not the correct answer because* the answer option is too general. In fact, this is the topic of the passage, not the main idea.

    b. *This is not the correct answer because* this answer option is too specific and is a detail.

c. *This <u>is</u> the correct answer because* it sums up the main idea of the passage and all the details support it!

d. *This <u>is not</u> the correct answer because* this idea is not mentioned in the text.

There are a number of reasons why a multiple-choice answer is incorrect, and knowing those reasons can help you identify the correct answer. Here are some of the main ones:

List of Common Reasons a Multiple-Choice Option Is Incorrect

- Answer option is too specific
- Answer option is too general
- Answer option is not related to the topic
- Answer option is not mentioned in the text
- Answer option is factually inaccurate
- Answer option is the opposite of the correct response
- Answer option includes an inaccurate quantifier (e.g., the correct quantifier is "sometimes," but the answer option says "always" or "never"). The term *quantifier* refers to words that express how often/how much/how many, such as *always/never/ everyone/no one.*

EXERCISE 10.7 Practicing with Multiple-Choice Strategies

Directions: After reading the passage below, fill out the "entering the text" chart, then read the questions, underline whether each multiple-choice option *is* or *is not* correct, and justify (explain) your answer choice for each option. Be sure to highlight evidence that supports each of your answers.

Reading Passage 1

When immigrants from Japan arrived, they encountered spillover bigotry, a stereotype that lumped Asians together, depicting them as sneaky, lazy and untrustworthy. After Japan attacked Pearl Harbor in 1941, conditions grew worse for the 110,000 Japanese Americans who called the United States their home. U.S. authorities feared that Japan would invade the United States and that the Japanese Americans would fight on Japan's side. They also feared that Japanese Americans would sabotage military installations on the West Coast. Although no Japanese American had been involved in even a single act of sabotage, on February 19th, 1942, President Franklin D. Roosevelt ordered that everyone who was one-eighth Japanese or more be confined in detention centers (called "internment camps"). These people were charged with no crime, and they had no trials. Japanese ancestry was sufficient cause for being imprisoned.

—Excerpted from *Mastering Sociology*, by James Henslin, p. 256–257

Entering the Text		
Genre	**Topic**	**Organization**

_____ **1.** What is the main idea of this passage?

    a. There was a fear that Japanese Americans would commit acts of sabotage.

    b. Japanese Americans were discriminated against during the WWII period.

    c. Japanese Americans' experience

    d. Japanese Americans enjoyed special treatment during the WWII period.

Multiple-Choice Justification

    a. This is/is not the correct answer because _____

_____

    b. This is/is not the correct answer because _____

_____

    c. This is/is not the correct answer because _____

_____

    d. This is/is not the correct answer _____

_____

_____ **2.** We can infer from the passage that

    a. being detained in internment camps was a horrible experience for Japanese Americans.

    b. there was great support for these internment camps among Japanese Americans.

    c. many non-Japanese Americans were also put in these same internment camps.

    d. President Roosevelt protested before finally agreeing to detain Japanese Americans.

Multiple-Choice Justification

    a. This is/is not the correct answer because _____

_____

    b. This is/is not the correct answer because _____

_____

    c. This is/is not the correct answer because _____

_____

    d. This is/is not the correct answer because _____

_____

_____ **3.** The U.S. government's main fear was which of the following?

    a. Japanese Americans would attack large cities.

    b. Military installations would sabotage Japanese Americans.

    c. All Japanese Americans would work against our national interests.

    d. Some Japanese Americans would work against our national interests.

Multiple-Choice Justification

a. This is/is not the correct answer because _____

_____

b. This is/is not the correct answer because _____

_____

c. This is/is not the correct answer because _____

_____

d. This is/is not the correct answer because _____

_____

_____

Reading Passage 2

It is rare for social science research to make national news, but occasionally it does. This is what happened when researchers published their findings on 1,200 kindergarten children they had studied since they were a month old. They observed each child multiple times, both at home and at day care. They also videotaped and made detailed notes on how the children interacted with their mothers (National Institute of Child Health and Human Development 1999; Guensburg 2001).

What caught the media's attention? Children who spend more time in day care have weaker bonds with their mothers and are less affectionate to them. They are also less cooperative with others and more likely to fight and to be "mean." By the time they get to kindergarten, they are more likely to talk back to teachers and to disrupt the classroom. This holds true regardless of the quality of the day care, the family's social class, or whether the child is a girl or a boy (Belsky 2006). On the positive side, the children scored higher on language tests.

Are we producing a generation of "smart but mean" children? This is not an unreasonable question since the study was designed well and an even larger study of children in England has come up with similar findings (Belsky 2006). Some point out that the differences are slight between children who spend a lot of time in day care and those who spend less time. Others respond that there are 5 million children in day care, so slight differences can be significant for society (Statistical Abstract 2012; Table 566).

—Excerpted from *Mastering Sociology*, by James Henslin, p. 93

Entering a Text		
Genre	Topic	Organization

_____ **1.** What is the main idea of this passage?

   a. There are over five million children in day care.
   b. A number of studies have shown that children who have spent time in day care are more likely to have behavioral issues than those who spent more time at home with their mothers.
   c. Studies show that kids who spent time in day care are more cooperative and kind to others.
   d. Parents should not put their kids in day care.

Multiple-Choice Justification

   a. This is/is not the correct answer because _____

   _____

   b. This is/is not the correct answer because _____

   _____

   _____

   c. This is/is not the correct answer because _____

   _____

   d. This is/is not the correct answer because _____

   _____

_____ **2.** Which effects on children's behavior are mentioned in the text?

   a. more crying and screaming
   b. more fighting
   c. less cooperation
   d. more fighting and less cooperation

Multiple-Choice Justification

   a. This is/is not the correct answer because _____

   _____

   b. This is/is not the correct answer because _____

   _____

   c. This is/is not the correct answer because _____

   _____

   d. This is/is not the correct answer because _____

   _____

_____ **3.** We can infer that this study caught the media's attention because

   a. there had never been a study before on the effects of day care on children.

   b. every American is greatly concerned about how best to raise children.

   c. many Americans whose children are in day care settings would want to know about this study.

   d. this type of story often involves a Hollywood scandal.

Multiple-Choice Justification

a. This is/is not the correct answer because _____

_____

b. This is/is not the correct answer because _____

_____

c. This is/is not the correct answer because _____

_____

_____

d. This is/is not the correct answer because _____

_____

READING

Selection 3

Textbook excerpt

Marriage, Divorce and Gender

Pre-Reading Questions

Discuss the following questions with a classmate before reading the textbook excerpt on marriage and divorce.

1. Some people believe that being married or just living together is pretty much the same thing. Would you agree or do you think marriage holds a special status? Explain.

2. In your opinion, what are the secrets to a successful marriage?

3. What are the main causes of divorce?

Marriage, Divorce and Gender

By John J. Macionis

U.S. Families: Gender

1   The sociologist Jessier Bernard (1982) claimed that every marriage is actually two different relationships: the woman's marriage and the man's marriage. The reason is that few marriages have two equal partners.

Although **patriarchy** has weakened, most people still expect husbands to be older and taller than their wives and to have more important, better-paid jobs.

2   Why then do many people think that marriage benefits women more than men? The positive stereotype of the carefree bachelor contrasts sharply with the negative image of the lonely spinster, suggesting that women are fulfilled only through being wives and mothers.

3   However, Bernard claimed, married women actually have poorer mental health, less happiness and more passive attitudes toward life than single women. Married men, on the other hand, generally live longer, are mentally better off, and report being happier overall than single men (Fustos, 2010). These differences suggest why, after divorce, men are more eager than women to find a new partner.

4   Bernard concluded that there is no better assurance of long life, health and happiness for a man than a woman well-socialized to devote her life to taking care of him and providing the security of a well-ordered home. She is quick to add that marriage could be healthful for women if husbands did not **dominate** wives and expect them to do almost all of the housework. Survey responses confirm that couples rank "sharing household chores" as among the most important factors that contribute to a successful marriage (Pew Research Center, 2007).

Divorce

5   U.S. society strongly supports marriage, and 90 percent of people who have reached the age of forty have at some point "tied the knot." But many of today's marriages unravel. The U.S. divorce rate has more than tripled over the past century. Today, about 20 percent of marriages end in separation or divorce within five years, and about half eventually do so (for African-Americans, the share is above 60 percent). From another angle, of all people over the age of fifteen, 21 percent of men and 22 percent of women have been divorced at some point. Our divorce rate is the fourth highest in the world—almost twice as high as in Canada and Japan and more than four times higher than in Italy and Ireland. The high U.S. divorce rate has many causes:

1. **Individualism is on the rise:** Today's family members spend less time together. We have become more **individualistic** and more concerned about personal happiness and earning income than about the well-being of our partners and children.
2. **Romantic love fades:** Because our culture bases marriage on romantic love, relationships may fail as sexual passion fades. Many people end a marriage in favor of a new relationship that promises renewed excitement and romance.
3. **Women are less dependent on men:** Women's increasing participation in the labor force has reduced wives' financial dependence on husbands. Therefore, women find it easier to leave unhappy marriages.
4. **Many of today's marriages are stressful:** With both partners working outside the home in most cases, jobs leave less time and energy for family life. This makes raising children harder than ever. Children do stabilize some marriages, but divorce is most common during the early years of marriage, when many couples have young children.

5. **Divorce has become socially acceptable:** Divorce no longer carries the powerful stigma it did several generations ago. Family and friends are now less likely to discourage couples in conflict from divorcing.

6. **Legally, a divorce is easier to get:** In the past, courts required divorcing couples to show that one or both were guilty of behavior such as adultery or physical abuse. Today, all states allow divorce if a couple simply declares that the marriage has failed. Concern about easy divorces, shared by more than one-third of U.S. adults, has led a few states to consider rewriting their marriage laws.

—From *Sociology*, by John Macionis, 15th edition, Pearson, pp. 523–525

Thinking about the Reading

1. In the author's view, "most people still expect husbands to be older and taller than their wives and to have more important, better-paid jobs." Do you agree with the author's assessment? In this day and age, do these husband and wife stereotypes still hold?

2. According to survey responses, which factor ranked very high in contributing to a successful marriage?

3. Review the statistics on the rate of successful marriages in paragraph 5. Which statistic did you find the most surprising? Explain.

4. Examine the list of possible causes for the high divorce rate in the United States (paragraph 5). In your opinion, which of these causes has the largest influence on our high divorce rate?

Reading Comprehension Check

1. "The sociologist Jessier Bernard (1982) claimed that every marriage is actually two different relationships." What was Bernard's point in making this claim?

a. Marriage steals our individuality.

b. Each marriage partner has a different perspective on the relationship.

    c. Men are less understanding than women.

    d. Marriage partners should have equal romantic attachments to each other.

_____ **2.** The negative image of the "lonely spinster" is mentioned to illustrate

    a. the cultural divide between the United States and Europe.

    b. how negative male stereotypes play out in society.

    c. how men control most marriages.

    d. that single women are perceived as unfulfilled.

_____ **3.** We can infer from the information in the third paragraph that

    a. after divorce, many women are not in a rush to find a new husband.

    b. after divorce, most men have no interest in remarrying.

    c. divorce takes a heavy toll on young children.

    d. most women hold similar views as men on the issue of remarrying.

_____ **4.** "Children do **stabilize** some marriages, but divorce is most common during the early years of marriage." In this sentence, the word *stabilize* means _____.

    a. build   c. neutralize

    b. steady   d. dismantle

_____ **5.** Which of the causes listed below for the high divorce rate in the United States is not stated in the selection?

    a. Marriage is stressful.

    b. Romantic love fades.

    c. Men are less dependent on women.

    d. Individualism is on the rise.

_____ **6.** According to the reading, a belief in romantic love as the basis for marriage is likely to lead to divorce because

    a. marriage should be based on having common interests, education levels, and backgrounds, not on romance.

    b. people often end marriages to start new relationships that are more passionate than their relationships with their spouses.

    c. most husbands are not motivated to keep romantic love alive in a marriage.

    d. too much passion in a marriage means that the household chores will not get done, thus causing stress in the relationship.

_____ **7.** Marriage is healthful for most husbands because society expects women to

    a. take care of their husbands and provide them with an orderly home life.

    b. work outside the home in addition to doing all the household chores.

    c. ensure that their husbands get regular medical checkups.

    d. accept that their husbands will continue to behave like carefree bachelors.

_____ **8.** Which of the following statements about the reading is *false*?

    a. Divorce is much more socially acceptable in the eyes of society than it was in the past.

    b. One of the most important factors contributing to a successful marriage is sharing chores.

c. Married men report more overall happiness than single men.

d. Canada's divorce rate is more than double that of the United States.

_____ **9.** According to the author, in what way has the increase in the number of women who work outside the home affected the divorce rate?

a. Women who work outside the home are more individualistic and therefore more likely to stay in a marriage and try to make it work.

b. It has resulted in fewer divorces because married women who work are happier than those who stay home.

c. It has made it easier for women to decide to leave unhappy marriages because they are less financially dependent on their husbands.

d. It has had no effect on the divorce rate because financial issues have little bearing on a marriage's success or failure.

_____ **10.** According to Bernard, married women have poorer mental health, less happiness, and _____ than single women.

a. more passive attitudes to life

b. less financial security

c. spend less time socializing with friends

d. make less money

THEMATIC LINKS

If you want to read more on the topic of marriage, type the following words into your browser and explore the two sites that come up:

1. Unemployment Can Spell Divorce for Men Live Science

2. What Divorce Does to Women's Heart Health Time

Think to Write

Now that you have completed three readings in this chapter on psychology, think about which of the three is most interesting to you. Write a paragraph response about this reading and post it to The Wall.

It's SHOWTIME!

Watching a video clip related to the chapter content can be an enriching experience. Go online and find a video link whose topic ties into one of the chapter readings (maximum length = ten minutes). After viewing the video clip, write a half-page summary of the video's key points. Post your personal reaction to the ideas in the clip (between 150 and 400 words) on The Wall.

WRITING SKILL FOCUS

Keeping It Together: Revisiting Unity and Coherence

OBJECTIVE

5

Ensure your paragraphs are
unified and coherent

As your integrated journey through *Read Think Write* winds down, it is useful to revisit the critical area of essay unity and coherence. As a writer, you want to make it easy for your readers to follow the flow of your ideas as they read through your essay.

When you are composing a first draft it is natural that new ideas will come to you as you write. The key question then is what to do with these fresh ideas as they flash into your brain. Well, write them down, of course! It is very helpful to get your thoughts down on paper or on your computer screen. At the same time, once you have done that, it is important to take a step back and consider where this new information most logically fits in the flow of your paragraph and the whole of your essay.

The key to revising for unity and coherence is to invest the necessary time to carefully reread what you have written. A huge part of writing involves moving things around, shifting this sentence here and placing that example there in order to make your essay tighter. You can add some key transitional phrases, add one more sentence to an example to tie it more clearly back to the central point it is supporting, and/or add a paragraph link to help one paragraph flow more smoothly into the next.

To test if your paragraphs are internally unified, reread your work to make sure the details you include support the topic sentence. To check if your paragraphs are externally unified, read your whole essay and check to see if each of your topic sentences supports your thesis statement and that each paragraph connects logically to the paragraphs that precede and follow it.

Review these guidelines for writing in a more unified and cohesive manner.

Keys to Coherent Writing

1. **Outline:** Make an outline before you begin writing, so that you can plan out how each piece of your essay fits together. Remember that this outline is not written in stone: it is there to guide your writing, but it is very likely you will move paragraphs around as you reread and revise your essay.

2. **Transitions:** Use transitional words and phrases effectively to ensure that your ideas are connected smoothly.

3. **Paragraph links:** To guide the reader from one idea to the next, or from paragraph to paragraph, try integrating *paragraph links*.

4. **Read your draft carefully and look for issues in unity and coherence.** Ask yourself the following questions:

   1. Have I repeated the same point more than once?
   2. Is every piece of the essay in the right place?
   3. Are ideas and examples grouped together logically?
   4. Have I made use of appropriate transitional words and phrases to connect one idea to the next?
   5. Are the main ideas outlined in the introduction, stated in the body, and summarized in the conclusion?

EXERCISE 10.7 **Essay Coherence: Smoothing Your Sentences Out**

Directions: Examine the following short essay with a classmate and jot down suggestions to help make this piece of writing flow more smoothly using the revision checklist below. For each suggested revision, number the sentence, and use that number in the revision chart. The first revision has been made for you.

Revision Checklist

Cohesion and coherence issues to look out for include the following:

- Repetition of ideas
- Similar ideas not grouped together
- Dissimilar ideas grouped together
- Lack of a sentence transition where one would be useful
- Misuse of transitional words or phrases
- Supporting details do not support the argument presented

Issue	Suggested Revision
1. Misuse of the transitional phrase "on the other hand"	Use "more specifically" or another suitable transition instead.

Issue	Suggested Revision

Why We Do Not Always Pay Forward

In the article, "The Science of 'Paying It Forward'" by Michael Macy, the author discusses the effects of receiving generous acts from others. ① On the other hand, Macy explains the phenomenon known as "paying it forward" whereby someone picks up the bill for another person and the chain continues on with that person covering for someone else and so on. The author is exploring why this type of action has become so popular. The author believes this style of giving has gotten enormously popular. One theory is that being generous to strangers is somehow contagious. Macy points out that there have been many studies of this phenomenon in recent years and that one question has come up which puzzles social scientists. Macy has come to a conclusion based on his research. Is it the witnessing of an act of generosity that sets off one's desire to give, or if it is the receiving of a direct benefit from someone's kindness that pushes things forward? He found that if people observe a "high enough level of generosity," their desire to help goes down because they feel like their help is not needed.

One idea I found really interesting in the reading is when the author explains that when you observe a high level of generosity, you "become a bystander who feels that help is no longer needed." Living in a big city, we are always watching how others react to situations. If someone is hurt, we wonder if we should do something or if others will take care of the problem. If someone is begging for money on the train, why should we give if everyone else is already giving? Human beings are conformist by nature, so it is understandable that we feel most comfortable mimicking what we see around us. If many others have already rectified a problem, we feel that our assistance is no longer necessary. Social scientists were not sure exactly how people would react in different situations where giving or helping was a possibility. They conducted a series of studies to find out how people would react under a variety of circumstances.

In my own experience, I have seen this phenomenon at work in many situations in New York City. A friend of mine gave his younger sister all of the allowance money he received from his mother. His sister kept the money. In addition, once I was on the F train coming home and a woman came on the train holding a baby in her arms. She was screaming, "Help my family. Help my baby!" I felt bad for her. When the train rocked, I thought she might drop the kid. My first instinct was to give her a dollar to help her out. Clearly, as Macy's study suggests, our willingness to help decreases when there is a lot of giving already taking place. Furthermore, when I noticed that half the people around me were taking bills out of their wallets, I hesitated.

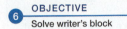

Writer's Block

"I can't think of anything else to say."

Have you ever said this to yourself when you felt stuck in the middle of composing an essay? If so, you are not alone. Many writers experience a "writer's block" moment and hit a wall when trying to develop their ideas further.

Here are four keys to solving writer's block:

- **Take a break and then step back into the process:** Sometimes you need some space away from your writing in order to see it more clearly. This is true for editing purposes, but it is also true for idea development. If you take a break and return to your essay two hours, or twenty-four hours, later, you will see it with fresh eyes and will have some new ideas and examples to add to what you have already composed.

- **Keep in mind that specificity is the key to development and interesting writing:** Which of the following descriptions is more interesting?

> **A.** I saw an interesting-looking woman on the bus today.
> **B.** On a crowded downtown bus today, there was a woman sitting next to me with a five-headed dragon tattoo running across her neck. She had black skull earrings and wore purple-studded cowboy boots.

Most readers would probably find B much more interesting than A. The key point here is that the more descriptive you are and the more you think like a reader—filling in the gaps to the types of questions a curious reader might ask ("What exactly made this woman interesting looking?")—the more effectively developed your essay will be.

- **Ensure you have enough time to write your essay:** What you might perceive as a "running out of steam" issue, might more resemble a "running out of time" issue. Many students write their essays under compromised circumstances. Maybe they have procrastinated for days and now it is midnight and the essay is due in the morning. Perhaps they have only an hour between their college class and the start of their shift at work and need to speed through the composition of an essay.

  Whatever the circumstance, rushed writing rarely produces well-developed, quality writing. Good writing takes time. There will be moments when ideas do not immediately jump out at you. Be patient. Read over what you have already written. Reflect on what it is you are trying to communicate. Try to spend sufficient time on each claim you are trying to explain and support. Jumping from point to point will not take your essay to a higher place. Stay where you are for a while!

- **Reread the essay assignment instructions:** Often an essay assignment outlines the types of content that should be included in your essay. So, for example, if your essay assignment is to "*Compose an essay based on our class readings that outlines at least three factors leading to divorce. Make sure to include specific examples and clear evidence to back up your claims*," these instructions point you in the direction of going back to the class readings to find more supporting evidence. The instructions also remind you to discuss at least three factors and to include specific examples.

EXERCISE **10.8** Adding Essay Expansion Notes in the Margins

Directions: Read the following essay, which was written in response to the second reading in this chapter, "The Boys Have Fallen Behind," by Nicholas Kristof (p. 407). As you read, pay attention to "description gap" moments where you feel the writer could have, or should have, said more. Share your essay expansion notes in the margins.

These notes can be in the form of questions you would like answered ("How do you know that boys are not paying attention?") or in the form of adding more specific detail to a point ("boys get frustrated because their interest is not held, and act out in a number of different ways").

When you have finished making expansion notes, rewrite the essay, fully incorporating your development ideas into the mix. This process of essay expansion will hopefully guide you when you are writing your own essay and feel like you are running out of steam.

Santiago Rodriguez   Rodriguez 1

Professor Warsi

ENG 100

8 March 2016

A Response to "The Boys Have Fallen Behind"

by Nicholas Kristof

In the essay "The Boys Have Fallen Behind" by Nicholas Kristof, the author discusses the recent phenomenon of boys in the United States lagging behind girls in academic achievement. He points to a recent report by the Center on Education Policy which states that girls are reading at a much higher level than boys at all school levels. Kristof shares a number of statistics from a new book and we learn that boys, on average, have lower grades, and are more likely to get suspended and drop out. A number of theories as to why boys are lagging in school are discussed, and a few possible solutions are mentioned.

One idea in the reading that I found to be significant is when Kristof writes, "poor reading skills snowball through the grades." This is really true. If you fall behind in reading, you don't magically catch up the next year.

In my own experience, I have seen this snowball effect with my best friend Roger. Roger learned to read late in 2nd grade, after most of our classmates were already reading. Later on he found himself always behind everyone else. Kristof mentions that boys should have the opportunity to read the kinds of books that will excite them. I have to agree because I'm pretty sure if our teachers had exposed us boys to more stimulating books, Roger would have been a better student.

THEN & NOW

Go online and do some research to gather information about two experts in the field of sociology: one from the past and another contemporary. For example, learn about a prominent feminist from the past such as Charlotte Perkins-Gilman and a contemporary feminist such as Camille Paglia. You might want to compare William Julius Wilson's ideas about black neighborhoods with W. E. B. DuBois's writings on race. Fill out the table provided below with pertinent information about the two sociologists.

Past Influential Sociologist	Present Influential Sociologist
Name	Name
Place of birth	Place of birth
Year of birth	Year of birth
Education	Education
What is s/he most famous for?	What is s/he most famous for?
Famous quote	Famous quote

After you fill out the table, discuss your findings with your classmates and learn from them about what they discovered on the Internet.

Working with a search engine, do the following search: "William Julius Wilson: Ending Poverty is Possible: NPR." Read this National Public Radio (NPR) interview with the famous sociologist on the topic of poverty in America. After doing a careful reading, write brief answers to the following questions about the article.

1. According to Wilson, how can the rising inequality in American society be explained?

   _____

   _____

2. How does Wilson explain the trend toward greater class polarization among African-Americans?

   _____

   _____

   _____

3. What is Wilson's view on our chances of eliminating poverty in the United States?

   _____

   _____

CHAPTER ESSAY ASSIGNMENT

Aside from physiological differences, are men and women truly different in any significant ways?

 OBJECTIVE 7

Read, think, plan, and write an essay in response to the chapter essay assignment.

Now that you have had the opportunity to read a number of articles and a textbook excerpt, you should have a deeper understanding of the topic area and be prepared to compose your chapter essay assignment.

Assignment: Write a two- to three-page essay on this topic, or your own topic. Support your claims with evidence or examples drawn from what you have read in the chapter and other relevant readings from other sources. You can also support your claims from what you have learned in school and/or personally experienced.

Be sure to include a clear thesis statement in your opening paragraph. After you have received constructive feedback from your instructor, be sure to incorporate some of his or her suggestions into your second draft and submit it for further feedback on form and meaning.

Chapter Essay Option: You are welcome to compose your own essay question based on the topics covered in the chapter readings.

| **FOCUS ON FORM** | # Putting It All Together |

Throughout this text, you have done editing focused around a number of key "typical error" areas in writing: subject–verb agreement, verb tense control, formal versus informal writing, transition words, fragments and run-ons, and punctuation. This final chapter of the text is the perfect opportunity to put it all together and focus on editing for *all* of these possible "error areas."

Read the following essay paragraph answering the question: Are there advantages to being shy? Do a careful edit of the paragraph. When you are done, compare your editing job with that of a classmate.

To many being shy are seen as a personality defect. The truth according to recent sociological research are that there are many advantages to having a shy demeanor. shy people are often more chill in their actions more dedicated to their jobs and more responsible for others. They were generally better listeners. are reliable friends. In addition, shyness have been correlated with a higher degree of empathy. Shy people is less likely to chatter on and on about themselves and are more likely to have the ability to give their full attention to others concerns. Finally many shy people pursues careers as writers painters inventors and engineers—all pursuits that required inner focus.

It's Your Turn!

Now that you have had a chance to practice general editing, review the essay you wrote for the chapter essay assignment, look for grammatical errors, and revise accordingly.

CHAPTER DEBATE

Aside from physiological differences, are men and women truly different in any significant ways?

This chapter's debate topic is the same as the essay assignment. Refer to Appendix 8, page 455, for detailed guidelines on how to set up and participate in a formal debate.

Pay Attention to Sentence Variety in Your Writing

As you compose your class essays, try to vary the length of your sentences. In the below example, all of the sentences are simple and the paragraph feels choppy.

> I need to work on time management. This skill is important. I want to succeed in college. Therefore, I will organize my schedule better. I will start right now. Tonight I will review my weekly responsibilities. I will organize my academic planner. Surely, this change will bear fruit.

If the writer varied her sentences, the same information could be conveyed more smoothly.

> I need to work on time management, as this skill is an important one. I want to succeed in college; therefore, I will better organize my schedule. I will start tonight by reviewing my weekly responsibilities and organizing my academic planner. Surely, this change will bear fruit.

The Four Basic Sentence Types

There are four basic kinds of sentences, and you will need to use a combination of them in your written work to achieve sentence variety. Too many short sentences can make your writing choppy and disjointed while too many long and complicated sentences can make it hard for a reader to follow your thoughts. Keep in mind that compound, complex, and compound-complex sentences are formed by combining dependent and independent clauses in different patterns.

1. **Simple Sentences**

   A simple sentence is an independent clause, containing a subject and a verb.

   The president vowed to punish the terrorists.

2. Compound Sentences

A compound sentence is two independent clauses connected as follows:

- **by a comma and a conjunction** (*for, and, nor, but, or, yet, so*)

  The game of cricket was invented by the British, but it is now popular in

  most parts of the world.

- **by a semicolon**

  The game of cricket was invented by the British; it is now popular in

  most parts of the world.

- **by a semicolon and a conjunctive adverb** (e.g., *also, as a result, consequently, however, nevertheless, therefore*, and so on)

  The game of cricket was invented by the British; however, it is now

  popular in most parts of the world.

3. Complex Sentences

A complex sentence is a combination of an independent clause and at least one dependent clause. Complex sentences can be formed in the following ways:

The instructor required students to answer multiple-choice questions

every day because she wanted them to prepare for the standardized

exam that they had to pass before registering for credit-bearing courses.

The first 30 questions were multiple-choice, which were part of a high

stakes reading exam.

4. **Compound-Complex Sentences**

   A compound-complex sentence contains at least two independent clauses and at least one dependent clause.

   The first 30 questions were multiple-choice, which were part of a high

   stakes reading exam, and the rest of the questions were open-ended.

You may make several copies of this worksheet and use them as you read the different selections in this book.

Before Reading

Before you read an article, read the title and subtitle (if any). Examine any photos, graphs, and charts the article may contain. Then make predictions about what the article is about.

Make two to three predictions about the reading.

I think this reading is about …

1. _____
2. _____
3. _____

During Reading

As you read, look for information that is interesting to you, and jot down any questions you may have about the reading. You may also include your reactions to the ideas in the reading.

Information I find interesting:

1. _____
2. _____
3. _____

Questions I have about the reading:

1. _____
2. _____
3. _____

My reactions to the reading:

1. _____
2. _____
3. _____

After Reading

After you finish reading, refer to the predictions you made about the reading and see if they were true or false. This is also a good time for you to reflect on the reading and summarize the key points the author makes.

Reflection

Now that I have read the article, I think …

1. _____

2. _____

3. _____

Summary

The key points that are important …

1. _____

2. _____

3. _____

4. _____

5. _____

APPENDIX 3
The Writing Process

As you write your essay, remember the five general stages in the writing process recommended by the Online Writing Lab (OWL) at Purdue University. Following these stages will help you write your best essays.

1. **Understand the requirements and expectations of an assignment:** When your instructor gives you a writing assignment, read it carefully to understand the purpose and the audience of the assignment. If you are confused about the assignment, it is always a good idea to speak to the instructor about what s/he expects from you as a writer.

2. **Generate ideas:** There are several ways you can generate ideas before you write the first draft of your essay. You can read source materials, take notes, make an outline or list bullet points, read more on the topic, and talk to friends about your ideas for the essay. Generating ideas will give you a sense of what you want to say about the topic. No matter what you do, it is important for you to keep taking notes and writing a little bit every day. This will give you much-needed fodder for thought before you begin to write the first draft.

3. **Draft:** Now that you have generated ideas for your essay, write the preliminary draft at least a week before the essay is due. Remember that nobody ever writes a perfect first draft, so it is important that you give yourself some time to revisit your first draft and do the necessary revisions.

4. **Revise:** If your first draft is shorter than the required length, you need to provide more information by adding new ideas and by clarifying any points your reader may find confusing. If you have written more than the required length, spend some time paring your essay down by reorganizing ideas and cutting redundant information.

   Take time to check that you have a clear thesis statement, your topic sentences support your main idea, and each paragraph contains sufficient evidence to support the topic sentence. You may need to add, cut, move, and rewrite content to create a final draft.

5. **Proofread:** Leave sufficient time for proofreading. Read your essay several times and focus on only one type of error each time you read it. For example, you may focus on spelling errors the first time and look for punctuation errors the second time and so on.

Rather than going through these stages sequentially, you can cycle through the process until you determine that your essay is ready for submission. In other words, you may write your first draft and generate more ideas, revise the first draft, proofread it, and revise it again if you deem it necessary. Engaging in the process to continually write, revise, and proofread your essay will lead to greater success.

APPENDIX 4
Linguistic Conventions of North American Academic Written Discourse

In your written work, adhere to the following linguistic conventions of academic writing.

1. **The introduction:** The introductory paragraph of an academic essay generally contains a thesis statement, a central idea, which gives the reader a clear sense of the primary focus of the essay. The thesis statement does not have to be the last sentence of the introduction, but it must appear somewhere in the first paragraph. The first paragraph should not be a one-sentence introduction, nor should it be an empty introduction without a thesis statement.

2. **The body paragraphs:** Each body paragraph usually begins with a topic sentence that states the controlling idea to be developed in the paragraph. The purpose of the topic sentence is to explain and support the thesis statement.

3. **Discuss only one idea in a body paragraph:** A body paragraph generally focuses on one idea, which is developed by using supporting details. Resist the tendency to discuss more than one idea in the same body paragraph. If you must discuss another idea, begin a new paragraph.

4. **The conclusion:** The concluding paragraph usually summarizes the main points of the essay, restates the thesis, and leaves a lasting impression on the reader by making a clear call to action or an emotional appeal, especially if it is a persuasive essay. Remember that the concluding paragraph should not provide new information to the reader.

5. **SAY WHAT YOU MEAN:** After you have written a preliminary draft of your academic essay, revise it carefully to make sure that there is no chasm between what you have written and your intended meaning. Revision can involve significant rewriting and reorganization. Ensure that your thesis clearly states your main idea; reread your topic sentences to check that each supports your thesis; read each paragraph to make sure you have provided adequate support for your topic sentences; evaluate your organization; include transitions to ensure unity and cohesion; review your word choices; and proofread for grammar, spelling, and mechanics.

6. **No contractions:** With the exception of the genitive case, also called the possessive case, do not use contractions in essay form. Instead of writing *don't*, *didn't*, and *can't*, write *do not*, *did not*, and *cannot*. *Jamie's height* is acceptable.

7. **Substantiate claims with evidence:** All claims must be substantiated with facts. Novice writers tend to make lofty claims without providing concrete evidence to support them. In academic writing, it is imperative that the writer support claims with empirical evidence.

8. **Define technical terms:** Rather than using jargon frequently and assuming your reader knows what the technical terms mean, provide a definition each time you introduce or refer to a new term. The tendency to simply use

a technical term and ignore the definition is called *the assumption of knowledge*. A better assumption is that the reader does not know anything about your topic. The burden of clarity is upon the writer, not the reader.

9. **Be specific:** Avoid being vague, and be specific about your references to researchers and scholarly work throughout your academic essays. Do not say, "Some researchers believe …" and "many theories have…" The reader might want to know who the researchers are and what the theories postulate. Refer to specific scholars (Johnson 1992) and theories (Chomsky's theory of Universal Grammar). The same goes for "many issues" or "several problems." If you are not specific, the reader might wonder what issues/problems you are referring to.

10. **Formal writing:** Avoid using spoken forms of language, slang, and idiomatic expressions in an academic essay. If your paper reads like you are speaking to someone in person, there is a good chance that there are instances of spoken forms of communication in the essay. Rather than saying, "come up with, figure out, or find out," use academic vocabulary and say, "findings of this study indicate that…"

APPENDIX 5
Transitions and Patterns of Organization

Patterns of organization	Transition words
To add or show sequence	again, also, and, and then, besides, equally important, finally, first, further, furthermore, in addition, in the first place, last, moreover, next, second, still, too
Comparison	also, in the same way, likewise, similarly, in comparison, as compared to
Contrast	although, and yet, but, but at the same time, despite (this/that), even so, even though, for all that, however, in contrast, in spite of, nevertheless, notwithstanding, instead, rather, conversely, in comparison, on the contrary, on the other hand, regardless, still, though, yet
Exemplification	after all, an illustration of, for example, for instance, indeed, in fact, it is true, of course, specifically, that is, to illustrate, truly, namely
Spatial order	above, adjacent to, below, elsewhere, farther on, here, near, nearby, on the other side, opposite to, there, to the east, to the left
Chronological order	after a while, afterward, as long as, as soon as, at last, at length, at that time, before, earlier, formerly, immediately, in the meantime, in the past, lately, later, meanwhile, now, presently, shortly, simultaneously, since, so far, soon, subsequently, then, thereafter, until, until now, when, currently
Summarize or conclude	all in all, altogether, as has been said, in brief, in conclusion, in other words, in particular, in short, in simpler terms, in summary, on the whole, that is, therefore, to put it differently, to summarize
Cause and effect	accordingly, as a result, because, consequently, for this purpose, hence, otherwise, since, then, therefore, thereupon, thus, to this end, with this object, so
Process	first, second, third, next, then, finally
Emphasis	even, indeed, in fact, as a matter of fact, of course, truly

Local and Global Errors in ESL Writing

Students whose first language is not English often make errors in their written work. These errors can sometimes make it very difficult for the reader to understand their ideas and thoughts. It is important to note that there are two types of errors: local and global. Local errors usually do not impede comprehension, but global errors cause confusion for the reader. What follows are examples of both types of errors.

Local Errors

A local error violates one of the following grammar rules, but an intelligent reader can still understand the writer's intended meaning:

1. **Subject–Verb Agreement:** The verb must agree with the subject.

    - "The college <u>have</u> addressed the issue of attrition."
      Corrected sentence: The college *has* addressed the issue of attrition.
    - "The student <u>like</u> to argue with the instructor."
      Corrected sentence: The student *likes* to argue with the instructor.

2. **Participles:** Appropriate participles need to be used to convey meaning.

    - "I am not <u>interesting</u> in this topic."
      Corrected sentence: I am not *interested* in this topic.
    - "I am <u>boring</u> in class."
      Corrected sentence: I am *bored* in class.

3. **Articles:** Indefinite articles such as "a" and "an" and the definite article "the" should be used appropriately.

    - "<u>The</u> life is interesting."
      Corrected sentence: Life is interesting. ("Life" is an uncountable noun.)
    - "I need <u>the</u> happiness in <u>the</u> life."
      Corrected sentence: I need happiness in life. ("Happiness" cannot be counted.)

4. **Countable/Uncountable Nouns:** Uncountable nouns do not take the plural suffix "-s".

    - "I need <u>informations</u> about the course."
      Corrected sentence: I need *information* about the course.
    - "I have to buy some <u>furnitures</u> and <u>equipments</u>."
      Corrected sentence: I have to buy some *furniture* and *equipment*.
      [These errors occur because in the student's first language, nouns such as "information," "furniture," and "equipment" are considered countable.]

5. **Spelling:** Words should be spelled correctly to avoid confusing the reader.

   - "We are going to a Greek <u>theatre</u> tonight."
     Corrected sentence: We are going to a Greek *theater* tonight.
   - "I am <u>definately</u> going to attend the event tomorrow."
     Corrected sentence: I am *definitely* going to attend the event tomorrow.

6. **Word Order:** Adverbs usually follow verbs, and adjectives precede nouns.

   - "I <u>very much</u> like you."
     Corrected sentence: I like you *very much*. (Place the adverb "very much" after the verb "like.")
   - "She liked the <u>man</u> handsome."
     Corrected sentence: She liked the *handsome man*. (Place the adjective "handsome" before the noun "man.")

7. **Prepositions:** Certain prepositions are used before certain nouns.

   - "I am learning many things <u>on</u> the course."
     Corrected sentence: I am learning many things *in* the course.
   - "Success depends <u>of</u> perseverance."
     Corrected sentence: Success depends *on* perseverance.

8. **Plurals:** Countable nouns take the plural suffix "-s".

   - "My sister has three <u>cat</u>."
     Corrected sentence: My sister has three *cats*.
   - "My father owns two <u>store</u>."
     Corrected sentence: My father owns two *stores*.

9. **Word Forms:** Word endings indicate certain parts of speech.

   - "I have been working <u>hardly</u>."
     Corrected sentence: I have been working *hard*.
   - "The test was incredibly <u>difficulty</u>."
     Corrected sentence: The test was incredibly *difficult*.

10. **Verbs Forms:** Verb forms should be used appropriately.

    - "I am strongly <u>disagree</u> with her."
      Corrected sentence: *I strongly disagree* with her (without "am").
    - "I enjoy <u>to read</u> novels."
      Corrected sentence: I enjoy *reading* novels.

Global Errors

Global errors have a negative impact on readers, making it extremely difficult for them to comprehend the writer's intended meaning. What follows are some examples of global errors:

1. **Fragments:** Fragments are incomplete thoughts, which confuse the reader. Refer to Chapter 6, page 244, for more information on how to avoid fragments.

- "Since the college embraces diversity."
  Corrected sentence: Since the college embraces diversity, *it recruits faculty members from various racial and ethnic groups.*
- "Many businesses and educational institutions in the area."
  Corrected sentence: Many business and educational institutions in the area *have offered scholarships to qualified students.*

2. **Run-on Sentences:** These are two or more sentences run together without using proper punctuation and/or conjunctions. For information on how to avoid run-on sentences, see Chapter 6, page 245.

   - "Maria came from Ecuador she studies at a junior college in Queens after she graduates she plans to move back to Ecuador and start her own practice."
     [The reader does not know where one idea ends and another begins. Run-on sentences can be extremely confusing for the reader.]
     Corrected sentence: Maria came from Ecuador. She studies at a junior college in Queens. After she graduates, she plans to move back to Ecuador and start her own practice.

3. **Comma Splices:** Comma splices are two main clauses joined with a comma without a coordinating conjunction.

   - "Students from Bangladesh have a poor educational background, they do not perform well on standardized tests in the United States."
     Corrected sentence: Students from Bangladesh have a poor educational background, *so* they do not perform well on standardized tests in the United States.

4. **Syntax:** Words have specific places in a sentence. Misplacing or dropping them completely can cause a great deal of confusion for the reader.

   - "If my friend had not warned me, my bag would have lost."
     Corrected sentence: If my friend had not warned me, my bag *would have been* lost."
   - "He is easy learning computer science."
     Corrected sentence: He is *learning* computer science *easily.*
   - "Because of the earthquake, many people would destroyed."
     Corrected sentence: Because of the earthquake, many people *were affected.*

As a college student, your goal is to minimize the occurrence of global errors so that your reader can easily understand what you mean. It is possible that some local errors will continue to appear in your written work. However, you should work to eliminate both types of errors to ensure your reader can follow your thoughts without difficulty.

Your instructor may use most of the following correction codes to draw your attention to the grammar errors you make in your written work. It is important for you to become familiar with each of the codes, so you can reformulate erroneous structures in your writing when your instructor or classmate points them out. You also may use the same codes while editing your classmate's essay.

Code	Meaning	Error	Correct sentence
cap	*capitalization*	The library is located at *cap* main and *cap* linden streets.	The library is located at Main and Linden Streets.
vt	*verb tense*	I had *vt* work at IBM for 5 years, so the experience *vt* matter.	I had worked at IBM for 5 years, so the experience mattered.
agr	*subject-verb agreement*	Some students *agr* takes their academic work seriously.	Some students take their academic work seriously.
ref	*pronoun reference*	The college's nursing program is popular. *ref* Their graduates find jobs easily.	The college's nursing program is popular. Its graduates find jobs easily.
⌣	*connect the letters*	One can not become a good writer without reading.	One cannot become a good writer without reading.
sp	*spelling*	This passage is taken *sp* form a novel.	This passage is taken from a novel.
p	*punctuation*	Incoming students have to pass tests in math *P* reading *P* and writing.	Incoming students have to pass tests in math, reading, and writing.
∧	*something is missing*	My older brother is ∧ teacher.	My older brother is a teacher.
⟳	*move word or phrase*	The professor in the morning teaches a history course.	The professor teaches a history course in the morning.
wd	*wrong word*	We must find a solution to this *wd* important problem.	We must find a solution to this serious problem.

451

Code	Meaning	Error	Correct sentence
wf	*word form*	I am not (interesting) *wf* in this topic.	I am not interested in this topic.
frag	*fragment*	Since the rate of attrition is increasing. *frag*	Since the rate of attrition is increasing, the college president has called a meeting to discuss why students are dropping out of college.
run-on	*run-on sentence*	Students entering college must pass standardized tests in math, reading, and writing they are not *run-on* allowed to take credit-bearing courses unless they pass these tests.	Students entering college must pass standardized tests in math, reading, and writing. They are not allowed to take credit-bearing courses unless they pass these tests.
cs	*comma splice*	Most students failed the math test, they are very *cs* upset.	Since most students failed the test, they are very upset.
X	*delete*	The professor ~~he~~ is notorious for failing his students.	The professor is notorious for failing his students.
trans	*transition*	Jacob did well on his math examination. He *trans* failed the writing course.	Jacob did well on his math examination. However, he failed the writing course.
w trans	*wrong transition*	Maria plays soccer. (On the other hand,) *w trans* she plays tennis.	Maria plays soccer. In addition, she plays tennis.
/	*separate*	Ahmed does/not understand grammar rules.	Ahmed does not understand grammar rules.
awk	*awkward*	Basic four flavors make Chinese food the special taste. *awk*	Four basic flavors give Chinese food its special taste.

Code	Meaning	Error	Correct sentence
nfs	*needs further support*	The Bengal tiger has been classified as an endangered species since 2010. There are not many Bengal Tigers left in India. *nfs*	The Bengal Tiger has been classified as an endangered species since 2010. Only about 1900 Bengal tigers live in India.
sing/pl	*singular or plural*	John treats his employees like slave. *sing/pl*	John treats his employees like slaves.

Overview

In a debate, two teams participate in a verbal contest, presenting their positions on a contentious issue such as whether marijuana should be legalized or criminals sentenced to death. The Pro team argues in support of the controversial proposition, providing arguments substantiated with evidence, and the Con team argues against it, presenting evidence to convince the opposing team and the audience members that their position is logically sound.

Unlike a panel discussion, where the primary purpose is to have an open dialogue with those who may have differing points of view on a topic, a debate is highly structured: the debaters present their arguments; a moderator keeps track of time; and audience members, who watch the debate closely, ask questions of the debaters and declare a winning team using evaluation criteria. Because the debaters have a limited amount of time to present their viewpoints, raise pertinent questions, and provide answers to the opposing team, they have to listen to their opponents attentively, think quickly, and use precise language to get their message across to the audience members clearly.

Why It Is Necessary to Participate in a Debate

It is common in colleges and universities in the United States to have a public speaking component built into content courses. Debates, therefore, are crucially important as they give you the opportunity to improve your presentation, argumentation, and critical-thinking skills. Participating in a debate presents you with a challenging task, as it requires taking a firm position on a controversial topic and convincing your audience that your position is both correct and logical.

It is worth noting that to prepare for a debate you need to do a fair amount of reading to determine your strongest points and find good supporting examples to buttress your main argument. Furthermore, effective debaters cite evidence from secondary sources to lend credibility to their claims. Use the chapter readings and Internet sources to substantiate your claims with facts, and be sure to acknowledge your sources as you defend your position.

How a Debate Is Structured

As mentioned previously, two opposing teams participate in a debate. The Pro team defends the controversial proposition, and the Con team challenges it. There are usually at least two members in each team, and they sit at a table facing each other. The moderator sits between the two teams and keeps time as the debaters present their points of view.

Each of the debaters has three (3) minutes to introduce his or her thesis statement, provide supporting examples to substantiate the position, and make a concluding statement restating the thesis. Usually, the Con team outlines their challenge to the controversial position first, so that the Pro team can defend its position accordingly. After the debaters have finished presenting their positions in the allotted three (3) minutes, the moderator gives them an opportunity to ask questions of each other. Each debater is allowed to ask only one question.

Finally, the moderator opens the debate up to audience members, who ask the debaters questions about their main arguments and supporting evidence.

The debate format is summarized below:

Debate Format

1. **Choosing a Topic and Pairing Up with a Partner**

   Brainstorm controversial topics for the debate with your peers and instructor. For each debate, you will need at least five participants, two debaters in the Pro team, two debaters in the Con team, and one moderator. Your instructor may choose to moderate the debate, or a student may be a moderator for one of the debates.

   Once four students express an interest in debating a particular topic, spend at least 30 minutes discussing your viewpoints. Depending on your stance on the contentious issue, you may be in the Pro team or the Con team. Use Form 1 (see p. 458) to list your main arguments, to anticipate your opponents' main arguments, to predict the questions they might ask you, and to formulate questions you will ask of your opponents.

   Allow yourselves at least one (1) week to do research on the topic and find secondary sources such as the reading selections in this chapter, a leading newspaper, a peer-reviewed journal, a Web site, or a book written by an expert. You may wish to write your speech and practice presenting your position with your partner several times, if possible, to feel prepared and confident.

2. **Moderator Introduction**

   The moderator usually sits at the head of the table, facing the audience members, with the Con team to his right and the Pro team to his left. The moderator begins the debate as follows:

   a. Greets and welcomes the audience members (Good morning, good afternoon, etc.)

   b. Introduces the controversial topic (Today, we are here to discuss a topic that has stirred …)

   c. Introduces the debaters in the Pro team and the Con team (to my right is Mr. Hernandez …)

   d. Invites a member of the Con team to present (I will now ask Ms. Berlinger to speak …)

3. **Debate Arguments**

   Courteous behavior is expected of the debaters and the audience members throughout the debate. It is the moderator's responsibility to enforce the time limits and to ensure that neither the debaters nor the audience members interrupt while the debate is being conducted. Each of the debaters has only three (3) minutes to speak.

First, the moderator invites a member of the Con team to speak. After the debater has spoken for three (3) minutes, introducing the position, giving supporting evidence to strengthen the claim, and concluding by restating the position, the moderator gives the floor to a member of the Pro team for three (3) minutes. After that, the second member of the Con team is given three (3) minutes to speak, followed by the second member of the Pro team. Throughout the debate and the cross-questioning session that follows, the audience members use Form 2 (see p. 460) to take notes.

4. Cross-Questioning

When all four debaters have given their presentations, the moderator asks a member of the Con team to ask one question of the Pro team. The question is supposed to expose weaknesses in the Pro team's argumentation. If the question is not directed toward a particular debater, either member of the Pro team can answer it. The moderator's responsibility is to ensure that the cross-questioning session does not turn into a discussion. The same procedure is repeated with the Pro team. A member of the Con team then asks one more difficult question, followed again by a member of the Pro team. Under no circumstance are the debaters allowed to ask more than four (4) questions. It is, therefore, essential that the debaters ask their toughest questions, since it is their only opportunity to attack their opponents' arguments.

5. Question and Answer Session

After the cross-questioning alternating between the Pro team and the Con team, the moderator opens the debate up to the audience members who ask both the Pro and Con team members pertinent questions. The question and answer session is guided by the moderator, who invites the audience members to ask questions of the two teams in a courteous manner.

6. Evaluation

The moderator announces the end of the debate. After that, the instructor asks the audience members to rate the debaters using the evaluation criteria listed in Form 3 (see p. 463). The audience members, either individually, in pairs, or small groups, vote for the Pro team and the Con team. The instructor counts the total votes and declares either the Pro team or the Con team the winner.

Form 1: Debate Worksheet

Before the Debate: Use the following worksheet to prepare for the debate with your teammate.

Topic of debate: _____

_____

Put a checkmark next to your position.
I am Pro (defending) _____ I am Con (challenging) _____

Your Thesis Statement

I am in favor of/against the topic because _____

_____

_____

Write your strongest arguments here. Cite at least three secondary sources that provide factual support for each of them.

	Argument	Source
1.		
2.		
3.		
4.		
5.		

Anticipating Your Opponents' Questions

Predicting the questions your opponents are likely to ask about your position will enable you to provide convincing answers. Write down the questions you think your opponents might ask about your main arguments. Then prepare your counterarguments to them.

Opponent Question 1:_____

_____

Your response:_____

_____

Opponent Question 2:_____

_____

Your response:_____

_____

Opponent Question 3:_____

_____

Your response:_____

_____

Opponent Question 4:_____

_____

Your response:_____

_____

Opponent Question 5:_____

_____

Your response:_____

_____

Your Opponents' Thesis Statement

I am in favor of/against the topic because _____

_____

Brainstorm with your teammate, and make a list of what you think will be your opponents' main arguments here:

1. _____

2. _____

3. _____

4. _____

5. _____

Questions You Will Ask Your Opponents

Based on your list of the possible arguments your opponents may present, formulate questions to challenge their position. Keep in mind that your questions should expose weaknesses in your opponents' main arguments.

Question 1: _____

Question 2: _____

Question 3: _____

Question 4: _____

Question 5: _____

Form 2: Being an Active Listener During the Debate

During the Debate: As the debaters argue back and forth, your role as an active audience member is to listen to their main arguments attentively and determine whether they are convincing and logical. This is important as you will decide individually and with your peers, using evaluation criteria, which team presented the strongest arguments and won the debate. Taking notes during the debate will also enable you to ask good, pertinent questions during the question and answer session that follows it.

Topic of Debate: _____

_____

CON TEAM

Member 1: Main Ideas and Arguments

1. _____

2. _____

3. _____

4. _____

5. _____

Flaws in the Arguments, if Any

1. _____

2. _____

3. _____

Member 2: Main Ideas and Arguments

1. _____

2. _____

3. _____

4. _____

5. _____

Flaws in the Arguments, if Any

1. _____

2. _____

3. _____

Questions Asked

1. _____

2. _____

Answers Given

1. _____

2. _____

Weaknesses in the Answers, if Any

_____

_____

_____

PRO TEAM

Member 1: Main Ideas and Arguments

1. _____

2. _____

3. _____

4. _____

5. _____

Flaws in the Arguments, if Any

1. _____

2. _____

3. _____

Member 2: Main Ideas and Arguments

1. _____

2. _____

3. _____

4. _____

5. _____

Flaws in the Arguments, if Any

1. _____

2. _____

3. _____

Questions Asked

1. _____

2. _____

Answers Given

1. _____

2. _____

Weaknesses in the Answers, if Any

1. _____

2. _____

3. _____

Form 3: Evaluation Criteria (For the Audience Members)

After the debate: Refer to the notes you took in Form 2 to evaluate the debaters. It is important that you remain objective and declare a winning team based on the merits of their arguments, even if the team challenged a position you support. Similarly, if a team supported a position you oppose but nevertheless presented strong, foolproof arguments and exposed serious flaws in the opponents' position, do not let your personal views influence your decision. After all, as an evaluator you are assessing the debaters' argumentation skills, not the controversial topic itself. It is, therefore, imperative that you adhere to the evaluation criteria below and complete the form objectively.

Topic for Debate:_____

_____

Evaluate the two teams on a scale of 1 to 5 using the following criteria:

Weak	Somewhat Good	Good	Somewhat Strong	Strong
1	2	3	4	5

	Pro	Con
1. **Main Arguments**: The team provided strong, foolproof arguments to support its position.	_____	_____
2. **Support:** The team presented relevant examples that strengthened its position.	_____	_____
3. **Organization:** The team stated its position clearly, provided good supporting examples, and made a concluding statement restating the thesis.	_____	_____
4. **Questions:** The team asked hard, difficult-to-answer questions that revealed weaknesses in the opponents' argumentation.	_____	_____
5. **Answers:** The team provided convincing answers that defeated the counterarguments.	_____	_____
6. **Physical Delivery:** Members of the team used effective body language to present their arguments, made direct eye contact with their opponents and the audience members, and showed confidence throughout the debate.	_____	_____
7. **Active Participation:** Members of the team actively participated in the debate by presenting arguments, asking pertinent questions, and answering the opponents' questions and those of the audience members.	_____	_____
Total Points:	_____	_____

Winning Team: Pro   Con   (circle one)

APPENDIX 9
Giving a Speech

Overview

Most college courses require that students give a speech on a specific topic either individually or in small groups. Sometimes your instructor will ask you to choose a topic that piques your interest and prepare a speech for your peers. Keep in mind that your topic must be appealing and your speech must be well organized. You will need to do research on your topic to obtain information, write a brief speech, and practice speaking several times beforehand so that you can speak before your audience with ease and confidence. Last but not least, since you will only have 15 minutes to give your speech, you will need to speak clearly and concisely and finish within the allotted time.

Organizing Your Speech

You will need to choose a topic that is appealing to a wider audience. Your classmates will most likely have different areas of interest, so it is useful to find a universal topic and organize the speech around interesting and significant facts that relate to it. Health and nutrition, business, and communication are some of the topics that appeal to most people, but you can choose other subjects that might be of interest to your audience. It is also a good idea to speak to your instructor about your topic and its relevance to the theme being discussed in class.

It is recommended that presentation topics follow the chapter themes in *Read Think Write*. Perhaps you can focus your first presentation on a topic related to the focus of the chapter you are currently studying or on one you will be reading when your presentation is due. To further assist you, we have provided a worksheet (see p. 468) so that you can prepare an outline of your speech that will serve as a point of departure.

Handouts

Prepare a handout for your audience members, outlining your speech, so that they can follow your thoughts as you speak. Be sure to provide your name and e-mail address on the handout in case anyone wants to ask you questions about your topic in the future.

In addition, your handout should include references, especially if you have done preliminary research and collected information from secondary sources such as books, magazines, periodicals, and the Internet. This is important because if your audience members are intrigued by your speech, they can then go to the sources you have cited and gather more information about the topic.

Remember that your handout should follow the logic of your speech and list the main points in the same order you will present them. In other words, the handout should give your audience members a clear sense of how you have organized your speech. Finally, leave enough space between points for the audience members to take notes while you are speaking.

Visual Aids

In addition to the handout, you also may want to use slides or transparencies. If you do use slides, be sure to keep the font large so that the audience can read your main points easily. Also, each slide should probably have no more than five to seven lines. A total of five to eight slides is ideal for a 15-minute presentation. PowerPoint is a program that you can use to make your presentation attractive and engaging.

When you draw your audience's attention to a slide, be careful not to read the content word for word. Reading everything on the slide verbatim could be annoying to your audience. Use the slides as a point of reference, give the audience sufficient time to read them, and then elaborate on the content using your own words.

Presentation

Here are some guidelines for making a successful presentation:

1. **Conduct research.** You will need to do a fair amount of reading to gather information relevant to your topic from secondary sources such as magazines, journals, newspapers, and the Internet. The more evidence you have to support your main idea, the more likely it is that the audience will find your speech factual and convincing.

2. **Create an outline of your speech, prepare a handout for your audience, and gather and organize your visual aids.** Organizing your thoughts (you can use the worksheet on p. 468), outlining your speech for your audience, and ensuring you have relevant visual aids will help you prepare for your speech, ensure your audience follows your presentation, and build your confidence.

3. **Practice giving your speech.** Practice several times, especially if you are not comfortable speaking in front of an audience. Practice your speech on your close friends and family members and ask them to point out if you are speaking too slowly or too fast because of nervousness.

4. **Speak loudly and clearly so that everyone in the audience can hear you.** After you finish talking about a point, pause a few seconds to collect your thoughts, and begin talking about your next important point. Most people in your audience will probably not be familiar with your topic, so pausing will also allow them the time they need to process the information you are presenting.

5. **Mention at the outset the specific purpose of your talk, the main points, and how you have organized the talk.** As you move from one point to another, remind the audience what you have covered and what you are about to discuss. This will provide benchmarks for your audience members, making it easier for them to follow your ideas. Also, use specific examples to support each of your main points. Your examples may consist of statistics, personal anecdotes, research findings, and so on. Appropriate and specific examples help your audience see how they strengthen your main points, which in turn substantiate your central idea.

6. **As you speak, be sure to use your hands to gesture.** Public speaking experts believe that a speaker's body language is as important as the content

of the speech. Avoid reading your speech word for word. If you do, your audience members may feel ignored and lose interest. It is important that you maintain good eye contact with your audience members to keep them engaged in your speech.

7. **Stay within the time limit.** Your instructor or one of your peers will show you cards reading "10 minutes left," "5 minutes left," "1 minute left," and "Stop." During your speech, remember to pay attention to this person so that you will know exactly how much time you have left to finish your speech. You may have to adjust your speech, skip over a few points, and/or only discuss the more important points depending on the time remaining.

8. **Tip the audience members off when you are about to finish.** You can do this by saying, "In conclusion," or "to conclude." This will give them an idea that you are wrapping up your speech.

9. **Finally, leave a lasting impression.** At the end of the talk, briefly tell the audience the main points you discussed and the significance of your topic. Then say, "Thank you!" Do not say, "I am done," or "This is the end of my speech."

Question and Answer Period

You will have approximately ten (10) minutes to take questions from the audience members and provide good, convincing answers. Be prepared to receive interesting and sometimes difficult questions from the audience. Here are some tips for answering questions:

1. **Ask your friends and family members to ask you difficult questions in advance.** Answering these questions beforehand will better prepare you to handle them with confidence in case they are asked by your audience.

2. **Acknowledge audience members, especially if they ask good, relevant, and interesting questions.** Before you answer an interesting question, praise the audience member by saying, "That's a good question!" or "That's a really interesting question!" Then repeat the question using your own words for the benefit of those audience members who are sitting in the back row and may not have heard the question clearly. They are likely not to follow your answer or explanation if they did not understand the question in the first place.

3. **If, for some reason, you do not understand a question, ask the audience member to repeat it.** It is better to ask the audience member for further clarification than to assume that you understand the question and give the wrong answer.

4. **Do not answer irrelevant questions.** If someone asks you a question that has absolutely nothing to do with your topic, politely decline to answer by saying, "I am afraid that is not the focus of my presentation," or "I think that it is not a relevant question."

5. **Defer answering very difficult questions.** Sometimes an audience member may ask you an extremely difficult question, and you may not be prepared to answer it. Instead of embarrassing yourself in front of your audience by misunderstanding the question or by giving a wrong answer, ask for an e-mail address and assure her or him that you will respond later.

Worksheet: Preparing Your Speech

Once you have chosen an appropriate topic for your speech, your next task is to prepare an outline showing content and organization. Use this worksheet to prepare the outline, which you also may use as a handout for your audience. As you read newspapers, books, and the Internet to obtain information on your topic, be sure to cite your sources. Finally, show the worksheet to your instructor and ask her or him to give you suggestions for further improvement.

Topic: _____

_____

Introduction

State your central idea: The purpose of my speech is to examine/explain/discuss/ describe/convince … *or* In this speech, I will explain: _____

_____

_____

Body

Write three or four relevant main points to support your central idea:

I. First Main Point: _____

_____

Supporting Details: Write specific examples to support your first main point.

Example 1: _____

_____

Example 2: _____

_____

II. Second Main Point: _____

_____

Supporting Details: Write specific examples to support your second main point.

Example 1: _____

_____

Example 2: _____

_____

III. Third Main Point: _____

_____

Supporting Details: Write specific examples to support your third main point.

Example 1: _____

_____

Example 2: _____

_____

IV. Fourth Main Point: _____

_____

Supporting Details: Write specific examples to support your fourth main point.

Example 1: _____

_____

Example 2: _____

_____

Conclusion
Summarize your main points:

I. _____

II. _____

III. _____

IV. _____

Restate your central idea: As I stated at the outset of the speech, I think/I believe that

_____

_____

_____

Leave a lasting impression: _____

_____

Speech Evaluation Form (For Audience Members)

Use this form to evaluate and rate the speaker. You may evaluate the speaker individually, with a partner, or in a small group. Remember to remain objective. At the bottom of the form, write the strengths and weaknesses of the speaker and offer suggestions for further improvement.

Topic: _____

_____

Presenter: _____

Evaluator(s): _____

Evaluate the speaker on a scale of 1 to 5 using the following criteria.

Poor	Somewhat Good	Good	Somewhat Excellent	Excellent
1	2	3	4	5

Points

Introduction:	The topic was appropriate and interesting. The speaker seemed knowledgeable, enthusiastic, and confident and stated the main idea clearly.	_____
Supporting Details:	The speaker used clear, specific examples to support the main idea.	_____
Conclusion:	The speaker summarized the main points, restated the main idea, and left a lasting impression on the audience.	_____
Visual Aids:	The visual aids such as slides and posters, were easy to follow, well organized, and informative.	_____
Gestures:	The speaker used gestures effectively, made good eye contact with the entire audience, and was relaxed, pleasant, and animated throughout the presentation.	_____
Clarity:	The speaker spoke loudly and clearly. The speed was easy to follow, and the message was intelligible.	_____
Q & A:	The speaker encouraged the audience to ask questions and provided good, convincing answers.	_____
	Total	_____

Strengths: _____

_____

_____

Weaknesses: _____

_____

_____

Suggestions for Improvement: _____

_____

_____

_____

_____

_____

CREDITS

Photo Credits

Cover: Zadorozhnyi Viktor/Shutterstock; **p. 1:** Rendeeplumia/Fotolia; **p. 2:** Milanmarkovic78/Fotolia; **p. 2:** Photographee.eu/Fotolia; **p. 2:** valentint/Fotolia; **p. 3:** Rolffimages/Fotolia; **p. 5:** Jasminko Ibrakovic/Fotolia; **p. 5:** AntonioDiaz/Fotolia; **p. 5:** DragonImages/Fotolia; **p. 5:** Nerthuz/Fotolia; **p. 7:** Jasminko Ibrakovic/Fotolia; **p. 7:** DragonImages/Fotolia; **p. 7:** AntonioDiaz/Fotolia; **p. 8:** Jasminko Ibrakovic/Fotolia; **p. 8:** AntonioDiaz/Fotolia; **p. 9:** DragonImages/Fotolia; **p. 10:** Massimo_g/Fotolia; **p. 14:** PathDoc/Shutterstock; **p. 17:** Photka/Fotolia; **p. 19:** Olly/Fotolia; **p. 27:** Andrews McMeel Universal; **p. 29:** Thinglass/Fotolia; **p. 32:** LaCozza/Fotolia; **p. 33:** Fabioberti.it/Fotolia; **p. 34:** Dmytro Sukharevskyy/Fotolia; **p. 40:** Photo © Elena Seibert; **p. 45:** Photo © Elena Seibert; **p. 45:** Carloscastilla/Fotolia; **p. 46:** Godfer/Fotolia; **p. 47:** Gudellaphoto/Fotolia; **p. 51:** Godfer/Fotolia; **p. 57:** WavebreakMediaMicro/Fotolia; **p. 62:** Nyul/Fotolia; **p. 64:** Slikar/Fotolia; **p. 70:** Malchev/Fotolia; **p. 73:** Monkey Business/Fotolia; **p. 74:** Ivanfff/Fotolia; **p. 75:** Aijohn784/Fotolia; **p. 76:** Erikdegraaf/Fotolia; **p. 86:** carloscastilla/Fotolia; **p. 87:** Glenn Paul/Equal Justice Initiative; **p. 87:** Reprinted by permission of Marc Mauer; **p. 89:** Gudellaphoto/Fotolia; **p. 89:** Reprinted by permission of Kent Scheidegger; **p. 112:** Malchev/Fotolia; **p. 113:** Aijohn784/Fotolia; **Multi:** Nyul/Fotolia; **p. 115:** Sergey Nivens/Fotolia; **p. 116:** Romolo Tavani/Fotolia; **p. 117:** Erikdegraaf/Fotolia; **p. 123:** Marco De Swart/Getty Images; **p. 127:** Carloscastilla/Fotolia; **p. 129:** Gudellaphoto/Fotolia; **p. 130:** Aaron_huang86/Fotolia; **p. 134:** CBS Photo Archive/Contributor/Getty Images; **p. 140:** semanita/Fotolia; **p. 144:** Irochcka/Fotolia; **p. 155:** Malchev/Fotolia; **p. 195:** Romolo Tavani/Fotolia; **p. 158:** Thinglass/Fotolia; **p. 159:** wizdata/Fotolia; **p. 160:** Erikdegraaf/Fotolia; **p. 160:** Maksym Yemelyanov/Fotolia; **p. 165:** Gaelj/Fotolia; **p. 168:** National Park Service, Statue of Liberty NM; **p. 174:** Carol Edelstein; **p. 174:** carloscastilla/Fotolia; **p. 175:** Creator: Davies, Diana (1938–) From the Diana Davies Papers, Sophia Smith Collection, Smith College (Northampton, Massachusetts.) Reprinted by permission of the Sophia Smith Collection, Smith College.; **p. 178:** Gudellaphoto/Fotolia; **p. 181:** Gajus/Fotolia; **p. 188:** Ron Galella/Contributor/Getty Images; **p. 198:** LuckyImages/Fotolia; **p. 203:** Malchev/fotolia; **p. 204:** Slikar/Fotolia; **p. 208:** wizdata/Fotolia; **p. 210:** Cherries/Fotolia; **p. 211:** Tyler Olson/Fotolia; **p. 212:** cristovao31/Fotolia; **p. 212:** Erikdegraaf/Fotolia; **p. 226:** carloscastilla/Fotolia; **p. 227:** Bloomberg/Contributor/Getty Images; **p. 229:** Gudellaphoto/Fotolia; **p. 252:** Malchev/Fotolia; **p. 253:** Tyler Olson/Fotolia; **p. 255:** Minerva Studio/Fotolia; **p. 256:** Beeboys/Fotolia; **p. 257:** Marilyn Barbone/Fotolia; **p. 257:** Erikdegraaf/Fotolia; **p. 260:** Vladislav Gajic/Fotolia; **p. 267:** ilolab/Fotolia; **p. 268:** carloscastilla/Fotolia; **p. 269:** Aleksandr Lazarev/Fotolia; **p. 270:** Gudellaphoto/Fotolia; **p. 273:** Pathdoc/Fotolia; **p. 280:** Graja/Fotolia; **p. 284:** Nyul/Fotolia; **p. 292:** Malchev/Fotolia; **p. 295:** Giorgiomtb/Fotolia; **p. 296:** George Wada/Fotolia; **p. 297:** Rob/Fotolia; **p. 297:** Erikdegraaf/Fotolia; **p. 300:** Oleksiy Mark/Fotolia; **p. 301:** Jamdesign/Fotolia; **p. 301:** Valkh/Fotolia; **p. 301:** Andrzej Solnica/Fotolia; **p. 301:** Sergey Nivens/Fotolia; **p. 301:** Alexskopje/Fotolia; **p. 301:** artivista/werbeatelier/Fotolia; **p. 301:** valentint/Fotolia; **p. 301:** Andrey Burmakin/Fotolia; **p. 302:** ki33/Fotolia; **p. 302:** Ljupco Smokovski/Fotolia; **p. 302:** klikk/Fotolia; **p. 302:** Maxsim/Fotolia; **p. 304:** Fotolia; **p. 304:** Monkey Business/Fotolia; **p. 309:** carloscastilla/Fotolia; **p. 310:** Sandor Kacso/Fotolia; **p. 312:** Gudellaphoto/Fotolia; **p. 337:** LuckyImages/Fotolia; **p. 342:** Malchev/Fotolia; **p. 342:** George Wada/Fotolia; **p. 344:** Peshkova/Fotolia; **p. 345:** WavebreakmediaMicro/Fotolia; **p. 346:** Erikdegraaf/Fotolia; **p. 350:** Fotolia; **p. 354:** carloscastilla/Fotolia; **p. 356:** Fotolia; **p. 357:** Gudellaphoto/Fotolia; **p. 360:** olly/Fotolia; **p. 362:** Fotogestoeber/Fotolia; **p. 368:** Filipefrazao/Fotolia; **p. 372:** Nyul/Fotolia; **p. 372:** Igor Mojzes/Fotolia; **p. 378:** Fotomatrix/Fotolia; **p. 388:** Malchev/Fotolia; **p. 389:** WavebreakmediaMicro/Fotolia; **p. 391:** Kurhan/Fotolia; **p. 392:** Paul Hakimata/Fotolia; **p. 393:** Monkey Business/Fotolia; **p. 393:** Dmytro Sukharevskyy/Fotolia; **p. 396:** Arfo/Fotolia; **p. 403:** Fotosmile777/Fotolia; **p. 406:** carloscastilla/Fotolia; **p. 408:** Gudellaphoto/Fotolia; **p. 411:** zimmytws/Fotolia; **p. 423:** Nyul/Fotolia; **p. 424:** Agsandrew/Fotolia; **p. 424:** Tomasz Zajda/Fotolia; **p. 431:** Malchev/Fotolia; **p. 432:** Paul Hakimata/Fotolia

Text Credits

Chapter 2

p. 40–42: Reprinted by permission from Joe Richman of Radio Diaries, Identical Strangers Explore Nature vs. Nurture. Copyright © 2007 by Joe Richman of Radio Diaries.

p. 45: Carl Jung and Aniela Jaffe, translated by Richard and Clara Winston, *Memories, Dreams, Reflections* (New York: Pantheon Books, 1963)

p. 46–49: Excerpted from March 2012 Harvard Women's Health Watch 2012. For more information visit: www.health.harvard.edu. Note: Harvard health Publications does not endorse any products or medical procedures.

p. 57–59: Carole Wade, *Tavris, Carol, Invitation to Psychology*, 5th Ed., © 2012, pp 49–50. Reprinted and electronically reproduced by permission of Pearson Education, Inc. New York, NY.

Chapter 3

p. 80: James Fagin, *Criminal Justice: A Brief Introduction*. p. 324, chapter 10. Copyright © 2014 by Pearson Education.

p. 81–83: Reprinted by permission from William A. Welch, "Some Say Cop Videos Misleading" from *USA Today*; 11/29/2006; Text; 1,096 total words out of

p. 86: Sir William Blackstone, *Commentaries on the Laws of England*, 1st Ed., © Sir William Blackstone (Oxford: Clarendon Press, 1765)

p. 87–89: Reprinted by permission from Mark Mauer, "Room for debate: Young offenders locked up for life."

p. 96: Frank Schmalleger, *Criminal Justice Today: An Introductory Text for the 21st Century*, 13th Ed., p. 135. Copyright © 2015 by Pearson Education.

p. 96: Frank J. Schmalleger, *Criminal Justice Today: An Introductory Text for the 21st Century*, 13th Ed., © 2015, pp 242, 243–244, 248. Reprinted and electronically reproduced by permission of Pearson Education, Inc., New York, NY.

p. 96: Frank Schmalleger, *Criminal Justice Today: An Introductory Text for the 21st Century*, 13th Ed., p. 187, chapter 6. Copyright © 2015 by Pearson Education.

p. 99: James Fagin, *Criminal Justice: A Brief Introduction*. p. 202, chapter 6. Copyright © 2014 by Pearson Education.

p. 99–100: Frank J. Schmalleger, *Criminal Justice Today: An Introductory Text for the 21st Century*, 13th Ed., © 2015, pp. 242, 243–244, 248. Reprinted and electronically reproduced by permission of Pearson Education, Inc., New York, NY.

p. 100: Frank Schmalleger, *Criminal Justice Today: An Introductory Text for the 21st Century*, 13th Ed., p. 470, chapter 13. Copyright © 2015 by Pearson Education.

p. 101: Frank Schmalleger, *Criminal Justice Today: An Introductory Text for the Twenty-First Century*, 13th Ed., p. 148. © 2015. Reproduced and Electronically reproduced by Pearson of Pearson Education, Inc., New York, NY.

p. 101–102: Frank J. Schmalleger, *Criminal Justice Today: An Introductory Text for the 21st Century*, 13th Ed., © 2015, pp. 242, 243–244, 248. Reprinted and electronically reproduced by permission of Pearson Education, Inc., New York, NY.

p. 111: Frank Schmalleger, *Criminal Justice Today: An Introductory Text for the 21st Century*, 13th Ed., p. 51. chapter 2. Copyright © 2015 by Pearson Education.

Chapter 4

p. 123: Carl Zimmer, "Ocean Life Faces Mass Extinction, Broad Study Says." *New York Times*, 1/16/15. Copyright © 2015 *The New York Times*. All rights reserved. Used by permission and protected by the Copyright Laws of the United States. The printing, copying, redistribution, or retransmission of this Content without express written permission is prohibited.

p. 127: Edward O. Wilson, Quoted in R.Z. Sheppard "Splendor in the Grass." *Time*, 3 October, 1990. p. 78.

p. 128–130: David Biello, "How Biodiversity Keeps Earth Alive. Reproduced with permission." Copyright © 2012 by Scientific American, Inc. All rights reserved.

p. 134–135: Richard T. Wright and Dorothy F. Boorse, *Environmental Science: Toward a Sustainable Future*, 12th Ed., © 2014, pp. 2–3, 20, 43. Reprinted and electronically reproduced by permission of Pearson Education, Inc., New York, NY

p. 145: Teresa Audesirk, Gerald Audesirk, and Bruce E. Byers, *Biology: Life on Earth*, 8th Ed., pp. 570–577, chapter 28. Copyright © 2008 by Pearson Education.

p. 145: Teresa Audesirk, Gerald Audesirk, and Bruce E. Byers. *Biology: Life on Earth*, 8th Ed., p. 291, chapter 14. Copyright © 2008 by Pearson Education.

p. 146: Teresa Audesirk, Gerald Audesirk, and Bruce E. Byers, *Biology: Life on Earth*, 8th Ed., p. 358, chapter 18. Copyright © 2008 by Pearson Education.

p. 146: Teresa Audesirk, Gerald Audesirk, and Bruce E. Byers, *Biology: Life on Earth*, 8th Ed., p. 114, chapter 6. Copyright © 2008 by Pearson Education.

p. 146: Teresa Audesirk, Gerald Audesirk, and Bruce E. Byers, *Biology: Life on Earth*, 8th Ed., p. 130, chapter 7. Copyright © 2008 by Pearson Education.

p. 146: Gerald Audesirk, Teresa Audesirk, and Brice E. Byers, *Biology: Life on Earth*, 8th Ed., © 2008, pp. 588, 589–590, 598. Reproduced and electronically reproduced by permission of Pearson Education, Inc., New York, NY.

p. 146: Gerald Audesirk, Teresa Audesirk, and Brice E. Byers, *Biology: Life on Earth*, 8th Ed., © 2008, pp. 588, 589–590, 598. Reproduced and electronically reproduced by permission of Pearson Education, Inc., New York, NY.

p. 148: Gerald Audesirk, Teresa Audesirk, and Brice E. Byers, *Biology: Life on Earth*, 8th Ed., © 2008, pp. 588, 589–590, 598. Reproduced and electronically reproduced by permission of Pearson Education, Inc., New York, NY.

p. 150: Richard T. Wright and Dorothy F. Boorse, *Environmental Science: Toward a Sustainable Future*, 12th Ed., © 2014, pp. 2–3, 20, 43. Reprinted and electronically reproduced by permission of Pearson Education, Inc., New York, NY

Chapter 5

p. 165–166: "One: Fall 1952", from *And the Mountains Echoed* by Khaled Hosseini, copyright © 2013 by Khaled Hosseini and Roya Hosseini as Trustees of the Khaled and Roya Hosseini Family Charitable Remainder Unitrust No. 2 dated February 29, 2012. Used by permission of Riverhead, an imprint of Penguin Publishing Group, a division of Random House LLC.

p. 165–166: Reprinted by permission from Khaled Hosseini, *And the Mountains Echoed*. Copyright © 2005 by Riverhead Trade.

p. 168: Emma Lazarus, "The New Colossus." *The Poems of Emma Lazarus*, Vol. 1. Boston: Houghton, Mifflin and Company, 1888.

p. 168–171: Carol Edelstein. *The Disappearing Letters*, Perugia Press, Florence, Massachusetts, © 2005 by Carol Edelstein, pp. 38–39.

p. 177: Grace Paley, "Samuel" from *The Collected Stories* by Grace Paley. Copyright © 1994 by Grace Paley. Reprinted by permission of Farrar, Straus, and Giroux, LLC.

p. 185: Judith Cook, *Kill the Witch*. (London: Headline Book Publishing, A division of Hodder headline PLC, 1999) © 1999, Judith Cook, p. 1.

p. 186: Billy Collins, "Schoolville" from *The Apple That Astonished Paris*. Copyright © 1988, 1996 by Billy Collins. Reprinted with permission of The Permissions Company Inc., on behalf of the University of Arkansas Press, www.uapress.com.

p. 186: Reprinted by permission from Jim Northrup, *Walking the Rez Road*. Copyright © 1983 by Voyageur Press.

p. 187: Edgar Allan Poe, *The Raven*. © Edagr Allan Poe 1845 (New York: New York Evening Mirror, January 29, 1845)

p. 189–194: From *The Piano Lesson* by August Wilson, Copyright © 1988, 1990 by August Wilson. Used by permission of New American Library, an imprint of Penguin Publishing Group, a division of Penguin Random House LLC.

p. 196: Edgar V. Roberts, *Writing about Literature*, 13th Ed., © 2012, pp. 1–2. Reprinted and electronically reproduced by permission of Pearson Education, Inc., New York, NY.

Chapter 6

p. 218: James A. Johnson, Diann L. Musial, Gene E. Hall, Donna M. Gollnick, and Victor L. Dupuis, *Foundations of American Education: Perspectives on Education in a Changing World*, 14th Ed., © 2008 pp. 4–15. Reprinted and electronically reproduced by permission of Pearson Education, Inc., New York, NY

p. 222–223: Michelle Lefort, "Learning and Teaching at a Two-Way Calle in Boston" from *USA Today*; 12/20/2005; Text; 656 total words out of 656

p. 226: Hesiod, Works and Days, 293-7, @700 BCE, translated by *The Spectator*, August 11, 1894, (London: John Baker, 1894)

p. 227–229: Reprinted by permission from Doug Lederman and Ry Riward, *A More Nuanced Bill Gates*. Copyright © 2014 by Inside Higher Ed.

p. 239: George S. Morrison, *Teaching in America*, 5th Ed., © 2009 p. 27 Reprinted and reproduced electronically by permission of Pearson Education, Inc., New York, NY.

p. 248: Forrest W. Parkay, *Becoming a Teacher*, 9th Ed., © 2013, pp. 19, 67, 55, 21–23, 46. Reprinted and electronically reproduced by permission of Pearson Education, New York, NY.

p. 248–249: Forrest W. Parkay, *Becoming a Teacher*, 9th Ed., © 2013, pp. 19, 67, 55, 21–23, 46. Reprinted and electronically reproduced by permission of Pearson Education, New York, NY.

p. 249: Forrest Parkay, *Becoming a Teacher*, 9th Ed., p. 146, chapter 5. Copyright © 2013 by Pearson Education.

p. 250: Forrest W. Parkay, *Becoming a Teacher*, 9th Ed., © 2013, pp. 19, 67, 55, 21–23, 46. Reprinted and electronically reproduced by permission of Pearson Education, New York, NY.

p. 250: Forrest W. Parkay, *Becoming a Teacher*, 9th Ed., © 2013, pp. 19, 67, 55, 21–23, 46. Reprinted and electronically reproduced by permission of Pearson Education, New York, NY.

p. 250–251: Forrest W. Parkay, *Becoming a Teacher*, 9th Ed., © 2013, pp. 19, 67, 55, 21–23, 46. Reprinted and electronically reproduced by permission of Pearson Education, New York, NY.

Chapter 7

p. 261: Joan Salge Blake, *Nutrition and You*, 3rd Ed., p. 126, chapter 4. Copyright © 2015 by Pearson Education.

p. 263: Joan Salge Blake, *Nutrition and You*, 3rd Ed., p. 126, chapter 4. Copyright © 2015 by Pearson Education.

p. 264–265: Reprinted by permission from Study: Ban on Fast Food TV Ads may cut obesity. Published by *USA TODAY*, Copyright © 2008 by The Associated Press.

p. 268: Ann Wigmore, *The Hippocrates Diet and Health Program*, © Ann Wigmore and the Hippocrates Health Institute (Wayne: Avery Pub. Groupr, 1984)

p. 269–270: Justin McCurry, "Japan's women toast their own health as life expectancy rises again." *The Guardian*, August 1, 2010. Copyright Guardian News & Media Ltd 2015. Reprinted with permission.

p. 280–282: Janice J. Thompson and Melinda Manore, *Nutrition: An Applied Approach*, 4th Ed., © 2015, p. 502 Reprinted and electronically reproduced by permission of Pearson Education, New York, NY.

Chapter 8

p. 303–306: Eva Tahmincioglu, "Men are Much in the Sights of Recruiters In Nursing" from *The New York Times*; 4/13/2003; Text; 1,314 total words out of 1,314

p. 309: A quote from a letter to a friend printed in Sir Edward Yas Cook, *The Life of Florence Nightingale*, Volume 1, (London: MacMillian and Co. Limited, 1914)

p. 310–311: Reshman Jirage, "Qualities of a Good Nurse." Buzzle.com: Intelligent Life on the Web by Buzzle.com. Reproduced with permission of Buzzle.com in the format Educational/Instructional Program via Copyright Clearance Center.

p. 316–317: Roberta Pavy Ramont and Dee Niedringhaus, *Fundamental Nursing Care*, 2nd Ed., © 2008 Reprinted and electronically reproduced by permission of Pearson Education, Inc., New York, NY.

p. 317–318: Roberta Pavy Ramont and Dee Niedringhaus, *Fundamental Nursing Care*, 2nd Ed., p. 9, chapter 9. Published by Prentice Hall. Copyright © 2007 by Pearson Education.

p. 318–319: Roberta Pavy Ramont and Dee Niedringhaus, *Fundamental Nursing Care*, 2nd Ed., p. 17, chapter 7. Published by Prentice Hall. Copyright © 2007 by Pearson Education.

p. 319: Roberta Pavy Ramont and Dee Niedringhaus, *Fundamental Nursing Care*, 2nd Ed., © 2008 Reprinted and electronically reproduced by permission of Pearson Education, Inc., New York, NY.

p. 320: Roberta Pavy Ramont and Dee Niedringhaus, *Fundamental Nursing Care*, 2nd Ed., © 2008 Reprinted and electronically reproduced by permission of Pearson Education, Inc., New York, NY.

p. 321: Roberta Pavy Ramont and Dee Niedringhaus, *Fundamental Nursing Care*, 2nd Ed., p. 76, chapter 5. Published by Prentice Hall. Copyright © 2007 by Pearson Education.

p. 322: Roberta Pavy Ramont and Dee Niedringhaus, *Fundamental Nursing Care*, 2nd Ed., © 2008 Reprinted and electronically reproduced by permission of Pearson Education, Inc., New York, NY.

p. 322: Roberta Pavy Ramont and Dee Niedringhaus, *Fundamental Nursing Care*, 2nd Ed., © 2008 Reprinted and electronically reproduced by permission of Pearson Education, Inc., New York, NY.

p. 323: Roberta Pavy Ramont and Dee Niedringhaus, *Fundamental Nursing Care*, 2nd Ed., © 2008 Reprinted and electronically reproduced by permission of Pearson Education, Inc., New York, NY.

p. 323: Roberta Pavy Ramont and Dee Niedringhaus, *Fundamental Nursing Care*, 2nd Ed., © 2008 Reprinted and electronically reproduced by permission of Pearson Education, Inc., New York, NY.

p. 324: Roberta Pavy Ramont and Dee Niedringhaus, *Fundamental Nursing Care*, 2nd Ed., © 2008 Reprinted and electronically reproduced by permission of Pearson Education, Inc., New York, NY.

p. 325: Roberta Pavy Ramont and Dee Niedringhaus, *Fundamental Nursing Care*, 2nd Ed., © 2008 Reprinted and electronically reproduced by permission of Pearson Education, Inc., New York, NY.

p. 327: Roberta Pavy Ramont and Dee Niedringhaus, *Fundamental Nursing Care*, 2nd Ed., © 2008 Reprinted and electronically reproduced by permission of Pearson Education, Inc., New York, NY.

p. 328: Roberta Pavy Ramont and Dee Niedringhaus, *Fundamental Nursing Care*, 2nd Ed., © 2008 Reprinted and electronically reproduced by permission of Pearson Education, Inc., New York, NY.

p. 328–329: Roberta Pavy Ramont and Dee Niedringhaus, *Fundamental Nursing Care*, 2nd Ed., © 2008 Reprinted and electronically reproduced by permission of Pearson Education, Inc., New York, NY.

p. 329: Roberta Pavy Ramont and Dee Niedringhaus, *Fundamental Nursing Care*, 2nd Ed., © 2008 Reprinted and electronically reproduced by permission of Pearson Education, Inc., New York, NY.

p. 330: Roberta Pavy Ramont and Dee Niedringhaus, *Fundamental Nursing Care*, 2nd Ed., © 2008 Reprinted and electronically reproduced by permission of Pearson Education, Inc., New York, NY.

p. 331: Roberta Pavy Ramont and Dee Niedringhaus, *Fundamental Nursing Care*, 2nd Ed., © 2008 Reprinted and electronically reproduced by permission of Pearson Education, Inc., New York, NY.

p. 332–335: Reprinted by permission from Judith Wilkinson, *Nursing process and critical thinking*, 5th Ed. Copyright © 2012 by Pearson Education.

Chapter 9

p. 350–351: Sebastian Bailey, "Business Leaders Beware: Ethical Drift Makes Standards Slip" from *Forbes*; 5/15/2013; Text; 762 total words out of 762

p. 354: Douglas Adams quoting Retail Clerks International Advocate. Published 1901–1946 Publisher Retail Clerks International Protective Association, 1932 Vol. 38, Page 32 Digitized by Cornell University, June 13, 2011

p. 355–357: Reprinted by permission from Robert Klitzman, *Why Facebook Should Follow Ethical Standards – Like Everybody Else*. Copyright © 2014 by Huffingtonpost.

p. 365: Courtland L. Bovee and John V. Thill, *Business in Action*, 7th Ed., © 2015. Bovee and Thill, LLC. Reprinted and electronically reproduced by permission of Pearson Education, New York, NY.

p. 366: Courtland L. Bovee and John V. Thill, *Business in Action*, 7th Ed., © 2015. Bovee and Thill, LLC. Reprinted and electronically reproduced by permission of Pearson Education, New York, NY.

p. 366: Courtland L. Bovee and John V. Thill, *Business in Action*, 7th Ed., © 2015. Bovee and Thill, LLC. Reprinted and electronically reproduced by permission of Pearson Education, New York, NY.

p. 366: Philip Wood, Passage 4: "Authored by Assemblywoman Lorena Gonzalez, D-San Diego, Assembly Bill 1522 gives all employees, full and part-time, 24 hours of paid sick time form their employer, which includes being able to take time off to care for an ill family member.", The Roseville and Granite Bay Press Tribune, 8/8/14. http://www.thepresstribune.com/article/8/08/14/california-could-enact-mandatory-sick-pay-employees, Press Tribune Roseville and Granite Bay

p. 367–369: Ronald J. Ebert and Ricky W. Griffin, *Business Essentials*, 10th Ed., pp. 37–38 © 2015. Reprinted and reproduced electronically by permission of Pearson Education, Inc. New York, NY.

Chapter 10

p. 397: John J. Macionis, *Sociology*, 15th Ed., Chapter 14, p. 430. Pearson Education. ISBN: 0205985602.

p. 403: Brief excerpts from pp. 15, 18, 151 from *You Just Dont Understand* by Deborah Tannen, Copyright © 1990 By Deborah Tannen. Reprinted by permission of HarperCollins Publishers.

p. 406: Michael Kimmel, *Guyland* © Michael Kimmel 2008 (New York: Harper Collins, 2008)

p. 407–408: Nicholas Kristof, "The Boys Have Fallen Behind" from *The New York Times*; 3/28/2010; Text; 804 total words out of 804

p. 415: James M. Henslin, *Mastering Sociology*, 1st Ed., pp. 256–257. 2014. © James Henslin. Reprinted and Electronically reproduced by permission of Pearson Education, Inc. New York, New York.

p. 417: James M. Henslin, *Mastering Sociology*, 1st Ed., p. 93. 2014. © James Henslin. Reprinted and Electronically reproduced by permission of Pearson Education, Inc. New York, New York.

p. 419–421: John J. Macionis, *Sociology*, 15th Ed., Chapter 14, p. 523. Pearson Education. ISBN: 0205985602.

Icons

Maksim Kabakou/Shutterstock; Stevecuk/Fotolia; Alex Staroseltsev/Shutterstock; A Aleksii/Shutterstock

INDEX